Los Zetas Inc.

Los Zetas Inc.

Criminal Corporations, Energy, and Civil War in Mexico

GUADALUPE CORREA-CABRERA

University of Texas Press ◆◆ *Austin*

Requests for permission to reproduce material from this work should be sent to:
    Permissions
    University of Texas Press
    P.O. Box 7819
    Austin, TX 78713–7819
    http://utpress.utexas.edu/rp-form

♾ The paper used in this book meets the minimum requirements of
ANSI/NISO Z39.48–1992 (R1997) (Permanence of Paper).

Library of Congress Cataloging-in-Publication Data
Names: Correa-Cabrera, Guadalupe, author.
Title: Los Zetas Inc. : criminal corporations, energy, and civil war in Mexico /
    Guadalupe Correa-Cabrera.
Description: First edition. | Austin : University of Texas Press, 2017. | Includes
    bibliographical references and index.
Identifiers: LCCN 2016038241| ISBN 978-1-4773-1274-2 (cloth : alk. paper) |
    ISBN 978-1-4773-1275-9 (pbk : alk. paper) | ISBN 978-1-4773-1276-6
    (library e-book) | ISBN 978-1-4773-1277-3 (non-library e-book)
Subjects: LCSH: Zetas (Drug cartel) | Organized crime—Mexico. | Drug
    control—Mexico. | Drug traffic—Mexico. | Narco-terrorism—Mexico. |
    Transnational crime—International cooperation. | Paramilitary forces—
    Mexico. | Political violence—Mexico. | Energy industries—Corrupt
    practices—Mexico.
Classification: LCC HV5840.M4 C68 2017 | DDC 364.1060972—dc23
LC record available at https://lccn.loc.gov/2016038241

doi:10.7560/312742

To my parents, María Guadalupe Cabrera and Alfonso Correa

Contents

Maps, Tables, and Figures

Maps

Tables

Figures

Abbreviations

AHMSA	Altos Hornos de México
AUC	United Self-Defense Forces of Colombia (Auto-defensas Unidas de Colombia)
CDG	Gulf Cartel (Cartel del Golfo)
CENAPI	National Center of Planning, Analysis, and Information for Combating Delinquency (Centro Nacional de Planeación, Análisis e Información para el Combate a la Delincuencia)
CFE	Federal Electricity Commission (Comisión Federal de Electricidad)
CIA	Central Intelligence Agency
CJNG	Jalisco New Generation Cartel (Cartel Jalisco Nueva Generación)
CONABIO	National Commission for Knowledge and Use of Biodiversity (Comisión Nacional para el Conocimiento y Uso de la Biodiversidad)
CONEVAL	National Council for the Evaluation of Social Development Policy (Consejo Nacional de Evaluación de la Política de Desarrollo Social)
CRE	Energy Regulatory Commission (Comisión Reguladora de Energía)
CRS	Congressional Research Service
CSM	Multiple Services Contracts (Contratos de Servicios Múltiples)

DEA	Drug Enforcement Administration
DTO	Drug-trafficking organization
EIA	US Energy Information Administration
ELN	National Liberation Army (Ejército de Liberación Nacional)
EPL	Popular Liberation Army (Ejército Popular de Liberación)
FARC	Revolutionary Armed Forces of Colombia (Fuerzas Armadas Revolucionarias de Colombia)
FBI	Federal Bureau of Investigation
GAFE	Special Forces Airmobile Group (Grupo Aeromóvil de Fuerzas Especiales)
GANFE	Special Forces Amphibious Group (Grupo Anfibio de Fuerzas Especiales)
GATE	Group of Arms and Special Tactics (Grupo de Armas y Tácticas Especiales)
GROM	Group of Metropolitan Operative Reaction (Grupo de Reacción Operativa Metropolitana)
IACHR	Inter-American Court of Human Rights
ICE	Immigration and Customs Enforcement
INEGI	National Institute of Statistics and Geography (Instituto Nacional de Estadística y Geografía)
LNG	Liquefied natural gas
NAFTA	North American Free Trade Agreement (Tratado de Libre Comercio con América del Norte)
NORAD	North American Aerospace Defense Command
OAS	Organization of American States
OPEC	Organization of the Petroleum Exporting Countries
PAN	National Action Party (Partido Acción Nacional)
Pemex	Mexican Petroleums (Petróleos Mexicanos)
PGR	Attorney General's Office (Procuraduría General de la República)
PRD	Party of Democratic Revolution (Partido de la Revolución Democrática)

PRI	Institutional Revolutionary Party (Partido Revolucionario Institucional)
RNPED	National Registry of Data of Missing or Disappeared Persons (Registro Nacional de Datos de Personas Extraviadas o Desaparecidas)
SCT	Secretariat of Communications and Transportation (Secretaría de Comunicaciones y Transporte)
SEDENA	Secretariat of National Defense (Secretaría de la Defensa Nacional)
SEGOB	Secretariat of the Interior (Secretaría de Gobernación)
SEMAR	Secretariat of the Navy (Secretaría de Marina)
SEMARNAT	Secretariat of Environment and Natural Resources (Secretaría de Medio Ambiente y Recursos Naturales)
SENER	Secretariat of Energy (Secretaría de Energía)
SESNSP	Executive Secretariat of the National System of Public Safety (Secretariado Ejecutivo del Sistema Nacional de Seguridad Pública)
SGM	Mexican Geological Service (Servicio Geológico Mexicano)
TCO	Transnational criminal organization
UANL	Autonomous University of Nuevo León (Universidad Autónoma de Nuevo León)
UEDO	Special Unit on Organized Crime (Unidad Especializada en Delincuencia Organizada)
UNDP	United Nations Development Program
UNODC	United Nations Office on Drugs and Crime
USNORTHCOM	United States Northern Command

Acknowledgments

I knew about Los Zetas in 2006 when my family was directly affected by them—or, to be more precise, by the model they advanced. I had heard about this criminal group, but I only paid attention to it after my father received a direct threat in "the Zetas' name" and lost his business. In late 2006 the Zetas approached my father on his farmland to demand a monthly fee in exchange for protection. They did the same with most business owners and landowners in this productive agricultural zone, except for the richest ones and the administrators of transnational corporations operating there. The Zetas proceeded to extort almost everybody who owned something of value near my father's valuable land.

People at first thought that the extortionists had come from Central or South America to spread fear in a land that was not theirs. They spoke a "foreign" Spanish. My father was not willing to pay the extortion fee, commonly known as *derecho de piso*, and conceded that he would have to forfeit everything to save his family's lives. He left his land, and my brother left with him. Their lifetime investments, their dreams, their livelihood—everything was lost. My father has always been a visionary, and he decided to do the "right thing." If he had committed to pay *derecho de piso* to the Zetas, he likely would be dead by now. It happened to some of his friends and acquaintances and to some of the hardworking people he had known since childhood.

This book is dedicated to my father, my brother, and the untold numbers of victims of the Zetas' war, a war that I later learned was not about drugs. It was about the land and what is above and below it. This war, as I understood later, was really an economic or "modern civil war." In the first part of the twenty-first century, Mexico endured a hyperviolent armed conflict that ultimately benefited corporate capital and exacerbated inequalities in an already unequal society.

In August 2009 I moved to Brownsville, located at the southernmost tip of Texas across the Río Bravo (or Rio Grande as US citizens refer to it) from Matamoros, Tamaulipas. Soon afterward a series of battles for dominance of Tamaulipas and all of northeastern Mexico erupted. What had been a convenient partnership between two violent criminal organizations, the Gulf Cartel and the Zetas, was terminated, igniting a brutal and prolonged war that left thousands dead. The open warfare between the Zetas and the Gulf Cartel, the former partnership known as La Compañía (the Company), transformed Mexico's northeast region, including Matamoros, into one of the most violent zones in the Western Hemisphere. At the time, I was a faculty member at the University of Texas at Brownsville and Texas Southmost College (UTB-TSC), located across from the Mexican border. A few weeks after I arrived in early September 2009, our university, now the University of Texas Rio Grande Valley (UTRGV), was shut down for the weekend after reports that bullets from a shoot-out in Mexico had hit a building and a car on campus.

The war for Tamaulipas escalated in early 2010, as this Mexican border state turned into a bloody battlefield. Local and federal law enforcement had not expected or planned for such a high-intensity conflict that showed characteristics of a modern civil war. Massive assassinations, shootings, beheadings, dismembered bodies, kidnappings, generalized extortions, and violent crimes were soon part of life just across the border from my home and my university in the United States. The armed forces arrived soon after to complete the picture of a devastating war. Some of my students, especially those who lived in Tamaulipas, suffered directly from the conflict. They related their experiences. Members of their communities began paying *derecho de piso*; some lost their friends or family members; some found themselves in the middle of shoot-outs; and some had to flee to "the other side." They suddenly lived in fear, just as my father had.

This fear and a sui generis war that spawned new paramilitary criminal groups and activated Mexico's armed forces influenced my subsequent research and academic career. The war and the new players had affected my own family as well as many other families living in strategic territories of Mexico. Los Zetas were key players in the national strife and in my own personal dramas. My academic career had located me so close to the Zetas' birthplace and the destruction and fear that they created that I decided to study them and analyze their criminal and corporate model. In fact, when I conducted this study, the Zetas behaved like an emerging multinational/transnational corporation that had multiple tentacles to other major legal multinational/transnational corporations. This is why I titled this book *Los Zetas Inc.* (for "Incorporated"). I thank my friend and colleague Paul Kavanaugh, who suggested this title after understanding the core idea of this book.

This project has developed over the past six years. It combines on-the-ground research and a new theoretical framework to understand organized crime and violence in Mexico and, plausibly, other parts of the hemisphere. I have conducted more than one hundred interviews with individuals on both sides of the US-Mexico border. My Mexican citizenship and US residency, and the fact that I am bilingual, gave me a unique ability to gain access to key players—including some members of these criminal groups. I am thankful to the many people who agreed to be interviewed for this project. Some were inhabitants of violent zones, and others were social media users informing people about situations of risk in their disrupted communities. Many of my sources are not quoted in this text for security reasons. Their opinions and experiences were fundamental for me to understand the new configuration of organized crime in Mexico and its implications for the country's security.

I have benefited enormously from the experience and support of a number of individuals to whom I am deeply in debt. I would like to offer my thanks to the many people who helped me during this process. First of all, I would like to thank my students at UTB/UTRGV who participated as research assistants in this project; without their help this work would have never been completed. More than research assistants, they were my guides and my instructors. All of them lived in Mexico and experienced violence at first hand. Special thanks to José Nava, a US Marine veteran, who explained me the militaristic nature of Mexico's conflict and the forms of operation by the Zetas. He also introduced me to the world of social media and reports of situations of risk through electronic platforms. María Machuca and Carlos Daniel Gutiérez-Mannix were an important part of this project. I acknowledge their diligence and loyalty; their help was invaluable. María helped with the research on the new paramilitarism in Mexico. Carlos designed many of the maps and figures included in this book. He also helped me to apply a business model to analyze transnational criminal organizations and compare them to legal businesses. We learned so much together.

My special thanks also go to @MrCruzStar, Omar Masso, Sergio Chapa, Dawn Paley, and Shannon Young. This text benefited from my interactions with them. I was inspired by their ideas and reflections on war and violence in northeastern Mexico, particularly those of Dawn and Shannon, who are, in my opinion, the smartest and most coherent journalists living in and writing about Mexico. These two women know this country better than any other Mexican journalist or foreign correspondent. I am also grateful to @MrCruzStar, a citizen journalist in Reynosa, and a very active participant in (hashtag) #Reynosafollow.

@MrCruzStar participated as a research assistant in this project and contributed to the investigation on social media and the war on cyberspace. From my multiple virtual conversations with him, I learned the tasks and commitments of citizen reporters in war zones. @MrCruzStar also explained to me how organized crime operates in the state of Tamaulipas, particularly in Reynosa and the so-called Tamaulipas Small Border (Frontera Chica). He once formed part of a vibrant community of social media users, primarily Twitter users (*tuiteros*) based in Tamaulipas, who took the place of the formal media and communicated the situations of risk occurring during the most violent moments of Mexico's war. I also benefited from virtual interviews and interactions in cyberspace with many of them. They were important sources of information and contributed enormously to my understanding of the war for Tamaulipas.

Omar Masso has been my main source and my instructor in themes related to security and organized crime. Most of what I know about Tamaulipas security and history was acquired through lengthy conversations with him in the course of the past six years. I will never forget the times when we drove through the Frontera Chica or La Ribereña region during the most violent times of the war. Another unforgettable trip is the one I made during spring break in 2014 with my "brother" Sergio Chapa, then a reporter and interactive manager for KGBT-TV in Harlingen, Texas, to what was once considered "Zetas' Land" (Tierra de Zetas). We visited Ciudad Victoria, Ciudad Mante, Tampico, Tula, and the El Cielo Biosphere in the municipality of Gómez Farías, Tamaulipas. In May of the previous year we had traveled along the entire Texas-Tamaulipas border and visited each of the eighteen international border crossings that connected the two states at the time.

I am also greatly in debt to important organizations that funded key parts of this research. My research along the Tamaulipas border was supported by a 2011 Drugs, Security and Democracy (DSD) Post-doctoral Fellowship funded by the Open Society Foundations (OSF) in partnership with the Social Science Research Council (SSRC), International Development Research Centre (IDRC), and Universidad de los Andes in Bogotá, Colombia. My overall research for the book was also supported by the National Autonomous University of Mexico (UNAM) and the Freie Universität (Free University) of Berlin. The last two institutions invited me as a visiting fellow in the summers of 2012 and 2013, respectively.

My special thanks to colleagues, administrators, and friends at the University of Texas at Brownsville, now the University of Texas Rio Grande Valley, who supported my work at every moment and gave me the required permissions to perform this highly risky research project. They always believed in my research and facilitated all available resources to help me succeed in this endeavor. I wish to express my respect and appreciation for the support I received from Javier Martínez, Ruth Ann Ragland, Terry Garrett, Charles Lackey, Laurie Howell, Alan Artibise, and Juliet V. García. I am extremely grateful for the paid leave of absence proposed and approved by Javier in fall 2014 that allowed me to work exclusively on this book for an entire semester.

Finally, I would like to thank my friends in Brownsville for their great confidence and encouragement. I will not mention them by name. I do not wish to miss anybody; all are special to me. I have been extremely fortunate to have the support of so many wonderful people who have made this difficult task much more pleasant. Some of them even helped me to edit and revise this text. Many thanks to Ruth Ann Ragland, Lidiette Batista, William Yaworsky, Carlos A. Flores-Pérez, and Delinda Karle for their help, encouragement, and useful edits. Dawid Wladyka, Xavier Oliveras, Wendy Macías, and Krystal Rodríguez provided their expertise as mapmakers.

In closing, I would like to mention the greatest friend of all, María Guadalupe Cabrera-Pimentel, my mother, who gave me life and encouraged me at every moment, even when she worried so much while I was traveling to Zeta Land. This book is also dedicated to her. The book is about violence, death, and war, but my mother represents the opposite. She represents for me the courage, generosity, and life that I wish for Mexico after this terrible war.

Introduction

Overview

Violence in Mexico has reached unprecedented levels in recent times, particularly since the launch of military operations against drug-trafficking organizations in late 2006 during the administration of President Felipe Calderón (2006–2012).[1] To date, Mexico's so-called war on drugs, or security strategy to combat organized crime frontally, has claimed over 150,000 lives.[2] During this period, nearly 30,000 people have been reported missing, with many of those disappearances officially linked to organized crime. Thousands of citizens have become internal refugees, displaced within Mexico, or been forced to move abroad, while the violence has also taken a toll on Central American and other noncitizen migrants moving throughout the country. This momentous increase in violence has been accompanied by the widespread use of barbaric, terror-inflicting methods, such as decapitation, dismemberment, car bombs, mass kidnappings, grenade attacks, blockades, and the widespread execution of public officials.

At the same time, drug-trafficking organizations—popularly known as "drug cartels" but also characterized as transnational criminal organizations (TCOs)—have diversified their operations and are now involved in new lucrative businesses such as kidnapping for ransom, extortion, migrant smuggling, trafficking in persons, weapons smuggling, video and music piracy, illegal mining and logging, iron ore exporting, and the smuggling of hydrocarbons and their derivatives (for example, crude oil, natural gas, coal, and gasoline stolen from Mexico's state petroleum company), among others. These activities are made possible by a relationship developed between organized crime and a new set of actors. Innovative corruption networks have been built between criminal organizations, local police and law enforcement agencies, politicians at all levels, federal authorities, and a number of foreign actors.[3] Formal businesses, including transnational companies (such as banks and other financial firms, US energy companies, private security firms, arms-producing companies, and gambling companies), have also established new connections with TCOs.

This new model of organized crime emerged at the same time as the appearance of Los Zetas (the Zetas) in the northeastern Mexican state of Tamaulipas, bordered by Texas to the north and the Gulf of Mexico to the east. The Zetas were once the armed wing of the Gulf Cartel (CDG or Cartel del Golfo), which had dominated drug trafficking and other forms of organized crime in the Gulf region for several decades. This criminal syndicate has expanded its activities and zones of influence, particularly in the past few years, and thus transformed the face of organized crime in Mexico and other parts of the Americas. The group has also deeply influenced similar illegal organizations, such as La Familia Michoacana (the Michoacán Family), Los Caballeros Templarios (the Knights Templar), and the Cartel Jalisco Nueva Generación (CJNG or Jalisco New Generation Cartel), which have dominated criminal dynamics, the security situation, and a number of illegal economic activities in key areas of the Western Hemisphere. These groups have been inspired by the Zetas' paramilitary tactics, modes of operation, and diversification of criminal activities. It can be claimed that the Zetas' criminal model has transformed relationships between state and society as well as between transnational organized crime and other formal transnational businesses.[4]

The Zetas revolutionized the enforcement methodologies of criminal organizations, fostering a generalized arms race, with more militaristic troops who now carry more sophisticated weaponry. This development, coupled with the implementation of a complex businesslike model and a rupture with past governmental relations in a "new democratic" era, allowed for the evolution of drug-trafficking organizations into truly transnational entities. As a result of the appearance of the Zetas—who utilize a corporate model and whose founding members came from a specialized military background—the violence and the economic power of TCOs have increased to levels that had never been seen before. At the same time, the Mexican government has reacted to this new power of paramilitary-style criminal organizations by militarizing the fight against organized crime—or declaring a "war on drugs."[5] These events have significantly elevated the levels of violence and terror, in particular in several regions of Mexico and Central America. The ensuing environment bears a resemblance at times to a civil war.

A key argument of this work is that recent violent conflict in Mexico has its origins in a new criminal model introduced by the Zetas. But who really are the Zetas? How did they grow to become a transnational organization? How did they extend their sphere of influence to control large parts of Mexico (at one time) and widely diversify their activities both nationally and internationally? Who contributed to their expansion? It is not reasonable to think that the Zetas are just a hyperviolent group of killers (*sicarios*) that use barbaric tactics to commit extortion, kidnap for ransom, and compete in the drug market with other Mexican drug-trafficking organizations. Actually, this is a sophisticated organization that transformed the nature of organized crime in Mexico and other parts of the Americas. The emergence of this group also ignited an extremely violent confrontation among the most powerful criminal syndicates that had dominated drug-trafficking activities and routes since the second half of the twentieth century. Moreover, the resulting situation provoked a change of tactics by the Mexican government in order to confront a problem that appeared to be, at some point, unmanageable by conventional means.

In this new context, more questions arise. How has the Mexican government responded to the violent confrontations among criminal syndicates and to the new tactics and dynamics that were apparently brought by the Zetas? How did the Zetas grow so extensively in such a short time? What are their links to Mexican politicians, law enforcement agencies, and foreign actors? What are their economic and business connections in Mexico and abroad? What is the main impact of the creation of this group on national security policy, migration, foreign affairs, and economic reform in Mexico—oil reform, for example? Who has benefited from the Zetas model? In order to answer these questions, new theoretical frameworks need to be utilized, because recent analyses on this subject have not been very helpful for thoroughly understanding the new complex reality of Mexico and its extreme levels of violence.

Recent books on the topic of the Zetas, Mexico's so-called war on drugs, and organized crime and violence in this country include, among many others: George W. Grayson (2014b), *The Evolution of Los Zetas in Mexico and Central America: Sadism as an Instrument of Cartel Warfare*; Ricardo Ravelo (2013), *Zetas: La franquicia criminal*; Guillermo Valdés (2013), *Historia del narcotráfico en México*; George W. Grayson and Samuel Logan (2012), *The Executioner's Men: Los Zetas, Rogue Soldiers, Criminal Entrepreneurs, and the Shadow State They Created*; Diego E. Osorno (2012), *La guerra de los Zetas: Viaje por la frontera de la necropolítica*; and Ioan Grillo (2011), *El Narco: Inside Mexico's Criminal Insurgency.*

These texts have provided useful details about the Zetas organization and its practices. However, most of these works—many of them written by journalists—are mainly descriptive and relatively limited in theoretical scope. Most existing literature on the topic fails to explain clearly and accurately what is really happening in Mexico with regard to organized crime and the Zetas in particular. Most of these volumes sensationalize violence and mystify some key events and actors involved. Moreover, the most popularly known accounts do not adequately analyze the role of the Mexican government, foreign governments, or the consequences of and effects on foreign policy and transnational economic interests. These sources do not identify the main political and economic actors and interest groups related to this new model of organized crime, both national and transnational; nor do they identify who really benefits from the extreme violence in Mexico.[6] What is more, it is not possible to find a complete academic work to date that provides a useful theoretical framework for adequate analysis of these key phenomena.[7]

An important effort needs to be made to overcome the deficiencies of existing accounts. When analyzing organized crime and recent patterns of extreme violence in Mexico, most writers, journalists and scholars alike, focus their attention on drugs. However, drug trafficking is only one of the many criminal activities that currently afflict the country. The violence and lawlessness that undermine security in Mexico can only be understood by using a more complex theoretical framework, including more than just a characterization in terms of killers, drugs, drug lords, and antinarcotics operations. Studying the Zetas as a business organization is a promising alternative.[8] Equally useful is an analysis of the current environment of violence in Mexico employing "civil wars" academic literature, because some key characteristics of the recent conflict in Mexico—including the number of deaths, intensity of conflict, and tactics employed by government forces and organized crime—resemble those of a "modern" civil war.[9] We should also recognize that the Mexican government has been a key player in this drama. But even more important is to determine who benefits from this massive conflict that has led to a new socioeconomic order in Mexico, featuring more leverage by transnational businesses (both legal and illegal).

Research Design

In sum, this book proposes a new theoretical framework to analyze the Zetas' organizational structure and forms of operation and the reactions to this model by the government and by other criminal, foreign, and corporate actors. One key aspect of the present work is that the new configuration of organized crime in Mexico and the unprecedented violence of responses to it had its genesis a few years ago with the creation of the Zetas criminal organization in the Mexican border state of Tamaulipas. The main hypothesis of this work is that this new criminal model and government reactions to it mostly benefit transnational corporate capital.

By using a business administration framework and academic literature to analyze organized crime as a transnational and corporate phenomenon, the book explores the causes and consequences of the new forms of organized crime pioneered by the Zetas. It also explains which groups in Mexican society benefit from extreme levels of violence and from the Zetas' transformation from a freewheeling criminal organization to a "business," albeit one that produces revenue for its stakeholders through illicit activities and the violence that it uses to intimidate both its competitors and adversaries.

At the same time, this text delves deeply into the following associated phenomena linked to the government's participation: (1) the appearance of the Zetas and the so-called paramilitarization of organized crime; (2) the militarization of Mexico's security strategy; (3) a resulting "new paramilitarism" in Mexico; and (4) the impact of these developments on strategic economic activities and reforms, particularly the hydrocarbons industry and energy reform. For this analysis, the study makes use of "civil wars" academic literature (Hultman 2012; Kalyvas 2001, 2006, 2007; Lu and Thies 2011; Mansfield and Snyder 2007; Rost 2011; Snyder 1984), an analytical tool that rarely has been utilized by scholars focusing on this topic. This study also recognizes the recent transformation of the socioeconomic order in Mexico derived from a new configuration of organized crime as well as from the militarization and paramilitarization of Mexico's security strategy.

This book combines vivid on-the-ground research with in-depth analysis and a new theoretical framework to understand the causes and consequences of extreme violence in Mexico initiated by the Zetas. The main causes include the emerging face and new structure of organized crime as well as the government's reactions to this phenomenon in an environment that bears a resemblance to a civil war. The consequences have to do with a redistribution of territory and revenues toward economic activities that would essentially benefit transnational corporate capital, particularly extractive industries and global security contractors. The epicenter of this account is the Mexican border state of Tamaulipas, where the Zetas originated, gained strength and influence, and then expanded their activities to other parts of Mexico and abroad. This is a state rich in hydrocarbons that will be, at the same time, one of the epicenters of future rapid development of the energy sector following the recent passage of Mexico's energy reform legislation.

Methodology

It is worthwhile noting the many limitations that researchers face when attempting to track and analyze transnational organized crime and related clandestine activities. As Scott Stewart and Tristan Reed (2013, 11) recognize, "In addition to disinformation and misinformation, there is simply much we do not and cannot know unless we have a source of information inside the organization. Even technical intelligence coverage of such organizations sometimes provides only a limited understanding of the exact structure of an organization and the members' intentions and motives." For these authors, it is also "important to recognize that even in cases where inside information is available, rumors, disinformation and misinformation often run rampant inside organizations" (12). According to this view, researchers most probably will not know for sure what happens in an organization of this type and "can usually only infer what is going on internally within [this] group" (14). Therefore it would be desirable to form hypotheses by taking "a holistic approach and correctly using available intelligence" (15).

Hypotheses can then be tested based upon a number of observable indicators and the usage of diverse sources of information and methodologies. Available information on the structure, financial operations, and ulterior motives of TCO leadership is extremely limited; a significant portion of it is also unreliable. In order to analyze and track the Zetas and related criminal groups, the present research utilizes a number of qualitative research methods (including semistructured interviews and participant observation) as well as information contained in a variety of mainstream media outlets and open-source press reports. As a result of fear and extreme violence in some territories controlled by the Zetas, news coverage of organized crime by formal sources of information can be limited and otherwise inadequate. Hence some of the data and information included here were compiled through the examination of informal media outlets, including blogs (such as "El Blog del Narco"), Facebook, Twitter, wikis, podcasts, and other Internet fora and social networks.

This work does not make use of classified information and keeps to a minimum the use of quotations from anonymous sources. The present book is part of an academic study, so the basis for inclusion of information is clearly identified. It is worthwhile acknowledging the various limitations of the available sources of information and the fact that the conclusions of this work are mainly hypotheses constructed through inferences that are subject to further investigation. This is essentially what happens in any research project that intends to understand the structure and operation of TCOs and related clandestine activities. The reference section of the book contains a significant number of journalistic sources. It is worth noting that most available information regarding Mexico's drug-trafficking organizations, TCOs in general, drug-related activities, and other forms of transnational organized crime has been released and analyzed by reporters.

Academic work on these subjects is still in a very preliminary stage due to the extremely high risks of doing field research in TCO-controlled areas. A further difficulty experienced by academics studying this phenomena is the limited access to government intelligence and classified information that would provide them with a more accurate picture of the security situation and the clandestine activities of these groups. The use of secondary sources and media articles is therefore justified. Thus the present research also represents an attempt to systematize the available information contained in a variety of places.[10]

I initially conducted forty-three semistructured interviews with individuals on both the US and Mexican sides of the Texas-Tamaulipas border regarding drug violence and the activities of transnational organized crime syndicates, particularly the Zetas and the Gulf Cartel. Participant observation and informal interviews were conducted in several cities of Tamaulipas (Nuevo Laredo, Mier, Miguel Alemán, Camargo, Díaz Ordaz, Reynosa, Río Bravo, Valle Hermoso, Matamoros, Ciudad Victoria, and Tampico).[11] Additional interviews were conducted in Mexico City; Monterrey, Nuevo Léon; Piedras Negras, Saltillo, and Torreón, Coahuila; Veracruz and Xalapa, Veracruz; and Morelia, Michoacán. To protect the anonymity and security of the people who participated in the study, only very few short quotations are used in the present text.[12]

I conducted a total of 103 semistructured interviews with regular citizens, government officials, academics, journalists, and activists (70 of them in person and 33 through a combination of Skype and Twitter conversations). The online interviews were with Twitter users or bloggers who report situations of risk in the aforementioned cities, particularly those located in Tamaulipas. Most of these social media users asked that their names not be revealed. To protect the identity of these individuals, very few of these conversations are quoted in this text. The information collected through these means was utilized as a complement to the design of some hypotheses and the crafting of the analysis and certain arguments contained in this volume. The present research was enriched by information obtained through a daily follow-up of conflicts related to organized crime in northeastern Mexico on Twitter since March 2010 and through direct interaction with a number of Twitter users who report events related to TCOs and the so-called drug war in Mexico.[13]

Additional Criteria

It is worth noting that the use of social media in academic research is valid only under certain circumstances and when taking into account some key issues. Reliable information and analyses obtained through these informal tools require direct and constant participation in specific social media platforms. This type of work also requires a deep knowledge of the dynamics of social networks, the behavior of different key actors and groups of users, and their evolution in time. Researchers should acknowledge that changes in the dynamics of social networks and relevant participants occur at a very rapid pace. Moreover, platforms that perform quantitative analyses of data in social media (such as Twitter Analytics, Hootsuite, Buffer, and Topsy) are still very limited tools for advancing social science research and cannot be a substitute for the active presence of the researcher in specific social networks.[14]

We should also remember that data from social media are a complement and not a substitute for more formal media sources and more specialized literature on the subject. The process of verification of information obtained through social media is not easy and not always reliable. It is thus necessary to assess the value of this material by comparing different sources and analyzing it at different moments in time. Hence the present research involved more than six years of field research in northeastern Mexico and other Zeta-controlled regions; an uninterrupted usage of social media related to the subjects of organized crime and violence in Mexico; and the design of a timeline of key events involving TCOs, the government, and other civil, political, and armed actors. This timeline was elaborated by using information obtained through formal and informal media sources.

It is also worthwhile mentioning that this book is not about drugs. The focus of the present analysis is not drug trafficking, drug traffickers (*narcos*), or drug policy. Therefore I try to limit the usage of the term "drug cartel" in the essential parts of the present text. Only some parts of section I (chapters 1–3) make explicit reference to these concepts and name key characters (drug lords) and drug-trafficking groups in order to give some context and explain the formation of the Zetas organization within the drug-trafficking world.

The word "cartel" is predominantly used in this work when referring to the actual names of some criminal groups. Otherwise the term is rarely used, notwithstanding its common usage in the media and literature when speaking of groups that are dedicated to the cultivation, manufacture, distribution, and sale of illegal drugs. The formation of a cartel requires an agreement between competing firms or corporations with the aim of controlling prices and production or excluding the entrance of new competitors in a specific industry.

Because cartel formation requires cooperation between different firms, the term "cartel" should not be used to refer to drug-trafficking organizations in contemporary Mexico. Such groups have entered into violent fights in the past few decades for the control of territories and markets in different parts of the hemisphere. Moreover, the present research does not simplistically refer to drug-trafficking organizations (DTOs). Due to their influence, impact, and connections in various countries, security experts refer to the Zetas and to Mexico's major drug-trafficking groups or similar criminal syndicates as "transnational criminal organizations" (TCOs). This analysis uses the term "TCOs" to refer to those groups that started as drug-trafficking organizations but most recently have expanded the breadth and nature of their activities and now operate in and dominate global markets.

Finally, the present text does not specifically analyze or track the actions or decisions of leaders of these organizations, who are sometimes referred to as *narcos* or drug lords. Some key narcotraffickers and their main achievements are mentioned only in some parts of section I (especially in chapter 1), with the aim of contextualizing the Zetas' role in the present account. A large number of the accounts on drug trafficking and organized crime in Mexico mainly focus on the top leaders of these organizations as well as on their alleged ulterior motives, personal anecdotes, arrests, and pacts with other criminal leaders or politicians. Most journalists and analysts who have written popular texts on this subject and the Zetas organization in particular (Grayson 2014b; Grayson and Logan 2012; Osorno 2012; Ravelo 2009, 2013) have employed this type of analysis.[15]

Several authors mention multiple names and nicknames of TCOs' members, use hyperbolic language,[16] and suggest that violence in Mexico is essentially a product of "*narco* wars" or "cartel wars." According to these accounts, the confrontation between criminal groups has been transformed into a brutal conflict between "good" and "bad" characters, after the Mexican government decided to confront groups like the Zetas directly by taking down its most visible leaders, using what has been called a "kingpin strategy."[17] Likewise, some analysts and journalists focus essentially on the Zetas' violent practices and tactics of fear.

George W. Grayson provided good examples of this type of analysis in one of his last texts. In his view, while the Zetas' key leaders were important, the success enjoyed by the organization "springs from their readiness to use the most heinous forms of violence against their foes" (Grayson 2014b, 5). Without knowing the origin of the organization's "unspeakable brutality," he mentioned some factors that allegedly "illuminate how fiendishness . . . [advanced] . . . the organization's objectives," such as a maximization of extortion and ransom payments; "successfully recruiting newcomers and lofting to leadership spots these young cadres—often unknown to authorities—who understand that the path to success lies in beheadings, castrations, and immersing foes in vats of boiling grease; . . . intimidating the weak to commit crimes in a cost-effective manner; and, unlike other cartels, using women known as *panteras* (panthers) to seduce or kill key politicians, police, and military personnel who can assist Los Zetas" (Grayson 2014b, 7–8).

This type of language and analysis is not uncommon in popular news stories, open-source press reports, and trade books on Los Zetas. Accounts like this seem to misrepresent reality and direct attention away from the real causes and consequences of the appearance of this paramilitary-style criminal organization. It does not seem reasonable to believe that the Zetas are (or were) just a hyperviolent group of *narcos* using barbaric tactics to compete with other criminal groups for the control of drug markets and routes. A thorough investigation and new methods of analysis show that Los Zetas is not a conventional drug-trafficking group. It was once a very complex criminal organization functioning like a transnational corporation that had greatly diversified its markets and areas of operation. The group's origins, market strategies, control tactics, and main outcomes seem to differ greatly from those of groups that dominated drug trafficking in the last century.

Main Findings

Probably the most important question that we should ask regarding the Zetas' emergence, its new model of organized crime, and interaction with other criminal groups and government forces would be: Who benefits from this new criminal model and government responses to it? The present analysis demonstrates that several groups, both national and foreign/transnational, have benefited directly or indirectly from Mexico's current conflict involving the Zetas, similar TCOs, and the Mexican government. Among these groups are arms-producing companies; the international banking system (due to the billions of dollars that are laundered daily in the major banks of the world); the US border economy; the US border security/military-industrial complex; and several forms of corporate capital, particularly international oil and gas companies.

Hence this book does not center on drug-related issues. This study is about businesses (legal and illegal) and militarization (of criminal syndicates and the government's security strategy). In sum, the main aim of this analysis is to show how a new model of organized crime (transnational in nature) and new forms of militarization (criminal and state-related, including paramilitarism) have greatly benefited legal businesses or corporate capital. In other words, the present work shows the economic effects of criminal paramilitarization, militarization, and paramilitarism in Mexico. This account also demonstrates how these processes have resulted in an unconventional armed conflict with characteristics similar to those of a civil war. This war seems to have mainly benefited extractive industries, the transnational financial sector, and global security contractors.

Contents

This book is divided into three sections. The first section explains the origins of the Zetas in the state of Tamaulipas and its main developments to date. This criminal group is analyzed here as a corporate actor. The second section presents an assessment of the new model of transnational organized crime that emerged with the Zetas, government responses to it, and the resulting extreme levels of violence. The causes and consequences of extreme violence in Mexico are explained. Using "civil wars" academic literature, I examine the so-called paramilitarization of organized crime, militarization of Mexico's security strategy, and the "new paramilitarism" in Mexico. This analysis suggests that Mexico is experiencing some kind of modern civil war that has also been reproduced in cyberspace. The final section of the book describes the process through which Mexico experiences major constitutional and economic changes through the medium of energy reform and an unconventional security policy.[18] It also mentions the groups that seem to have mainly benefited (directly or indirectly) from this novel criminal scheme and from the resulting extreme levels of violence in the country. The main winners appear to be corporate actors of the energy sector and the US border security/military-industrial complex. This argument is exemplified by analyzing the case of the oil- and gas-rich state of Tamaulipas, the "cradle" of the Zetas, which has been one of the most violent states in the country and will plausibly be one of the epicenters of the future development of Mexico's energy sector.

THE ZETAS: CRIMINAL PARAMILITARIES IN A TRANSNATIONAL BUSINESS

Understanding how organized crime flourished in the Mexican state of Tamaulipas and how the Zetas came into existence is key to understanding the new configuration of organized crime and the recent levels of extreme violence in Mexico. The first section of this book outlines the origins of the Zetas in this border state and the group's development and current organizational structure. This section also identifies new forms of organized crime devised by the Zetas that involve criminal paramilitarization and a corporate business model.

CHAPTER 1

The Zetas' Origins

This chapter explains how the Zetas first started—as the armed wing of the Gulf Cartel (CDG)—and describes the formation of "La Compañía" (the Company). It also examines the battle for Tamaulipas between this criminal partnership and "La Federación" (the Federation), an alliance formed by the Sinaloa Cartel and other criminal syndicates. Additionally, the chapter illustrates the Zetas' exceptionalism, initial victories against the Federation, and final independence from the Gulf Cartel. The Zetas' eventual autonomy signified the creation of a very successful and extremely violent transnational criminal organization (TCO) that has transformed the face of organized crime in Mexico and other parts of the hemisphere.

The Gulf Cartel

Tamaulipas-Texas: A Strategic Border

Sporting a long boundary with Texas and an extensive coastline, the Mexican state of Tamaulipas has one of the most dynamic borders in Latin America. Nuevo Laredo's customs alone handles approximately 40 percent of the trade between Mexico and the United States, and the three main maritime ports of Tamaulipas accommodate more than half of the ships destined for the European market (Alvarado 2012, par. 19). Given its location, the state is in a natural position to play a key role in drug trafficking and human smuggling going north into the United States and in arms trafficking going south into Mexico and Central America. Its main border cities (Nuevo Laredo, Miguel Alemán, Reynosa, Río Bravo, and Matamoros) are the closest points of

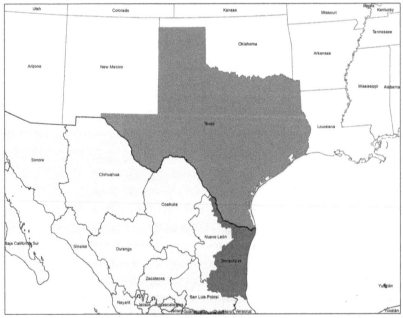

Map 1.1. Tamaulipas: A strategic Mexican border state.
Source: Texas Department of Transportation. Design by Krystal Rodríguez.

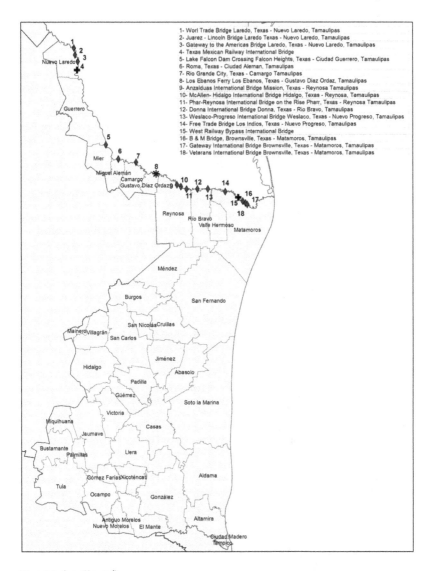

1- Worl Trade Bridge Laredo, Texas - Nuevo Laredo, Tamaulipas
2- Juarez - Lincoln Bridge Laredo Texas - Nuevo Laredo, Tamaulipas
3- Gateway to the Americas Bridge Laredo, Texas - Nuevo Laredo, Tamaulipas
4- Texas Mexican Railway International Bridge
5- Lake Falcon Dam Crossing Falcon Heights, Texas - Ciudad Guerrero, Tamaulipas
6- Roma, Texas - Ciudad Aleman, Tamaulipas
7- Rio Grande City, Texas - Camargo Tamaulipas
8- Los Ebanos Ferry Los Ebanos, Texas - Gustavo Diaz Ordaz, Tamaulipas
9- Anzalduas International Bridge Mission, Texas - Reynosa Tamaulipas
10- McAllen- Hidalgo International Bridge Hidalgo, Texas - Reynosa, Tamaulipas
11- Phar-Reynosa International Bridge on the Rise Pharr, Texas - Reynosa Tamaulipas
12- Donna International Bridge Donna, Texas - Rio Bravo, Tamaulipas
13- Weslaco-Progreso International Bridge Weslaco, Texas - Nuevo Progreso, Tamaulipas
14- Free Trade Bridge Los Indios, Texas - Nuevo Progreso, Tamaulipas
15- West Railway Bypass International Bridge
16- B & M Bridge, Brownsville, Texas - Matamoros, Tamaulipas
17- Gateway International Bridge Brownsville, Texas - Matamoros, Tamaulipas
18- Veterans International Bridge Brownsville, Texas - Matamoros, Tamaulipas

Map 1.1. (*continued*)

entry for traffickers who import illicit cargo through maritime ports in the states of Quintana Roo and Yucatán and along the Gulf of Mexico as well as the important ports in the Pacific between Puerto Madero and San Blas (Guerrero 2010, par. 1). Tamaulipas has more border crossings into the United States than any other Mexican state, eighteen in all (see map 1.1).

With such a strategic location, illegal trafficking activities inevitably developed and proliferated alongside legal business dealings in Tamaulipas. This not only generated violent land disputes but also rejuvenated "old and violent political confrontations for the control of everything . . . transported through this territory" (Alvarado 2012, par. 20).[1] As trade along the border grew, especially illegal trade, organized crime became well entrenched in the state. According to security consultant and former intelligence official Eduardo Guerrero (2014a, par. 42), "The shape and size of [the Tamaulipas] border encouraged smuggling activities, and thus there initially appeared a strong and cohesive organization with a strong leadership, the genesis of the Gulf Cartel." This criminal group "was not only a pioneer in drug smuggling on a large scale, but also a trailblazer in the development of an armed wing with military discipline and high firepower" (par. 42).

The Origins of the Gulf Cartel

Agriculture and manufacturing (*maquila*) have long been the primary sources of legitimate development in Tamaulipas, but during the last century drug trafficking began to be a key factor in the state's economy, with the Gulf Cartel acting as a major player. This criminal organization originated in the city of Matamoros and eventually dominated key illegal activities and organized crime in Tamaulipas for several decades (Correa-Cabrera 2014c). Its origins can be traced to the 1930s, when Juan N. (Nepomuceno) Guerra started smuggling whiskey into the United States during Prohibition. From whiskey, Guerra extended his operations to include a variety of other products, including alcohol, cigarettes, clothing, cars, machinery, and electronic devices. In the decades that followed he added gambling, prostitution, and car thefts to his portfolio. Guerra was not generally considered a drug lord (narcotrafficker), but rather a *contrabandista* (smuggler).[2] His organization, which would later become the CDG, started to grow and eventually became a "profitable criminal enterprise" (Tabor 2014, par. 7). In this process, Guerra began to build a complex network of relationships with politicians and officials at all levels of government and on both sides of the border (Flores 2013b).

Behind the contemporary history of Tamaulipas, according to Professor Israel Covarrubias, is a complex "history of political and entrepreneurial elites who encouraged criminal businesses for decades," making of this state a kind of "time capsule," in which the absence of democracy and transfer of power promoted the monopolization of economic resources. Under such conditions, a "system of feudal violence was fueled by not only members of organized crime, but by current and former public officials at very high levels" (quoted in Alvarado 2012, pars. 5 and 6). Guerra started this trend of mixing with elites and established a large network of political contacts in Mexico's northeast. He maintained a close friendship with influential union leaders of the region and with former Tamaulipas governors, including Práxedis Balboa (1963–1969), Enrique Cárdenas (1975–1981), and Emilio Martínez Manatou (1981–1987).[3] This network included not only local political figures but also influential leaders at the national level like union leader Joaquín Hernández Galicia (aka La Quina) and Raúl Salinas Lozano, former secretary of industry and trade and father of former president Carlos Salinas de Gortari (Guerrero 2014a, par. 3).

El Capo del Golfo (the Gulf's Drug Lord)

Guerra's organization grew considerably and became extremely influential in the illicit markets of Tamaulipas and the Gulf of Mexico. But in the mid-1980s—when the Tamaulipas border became a strategic drug-trafficking corridor that would eventually facilitate the arrival of narcotics into the US East Coast—the group's expansion accelerated dramatically. "Due to US interdiction successes in the Caribbean during the [late 1980s] and 1990s, Mexico [became] the single most important way-station for cocaine and heroin produced in the Andes, and [remained] a major producer of marijuana and methamphetamines" (Brands 2009a, par. 4). At the same time, the nature and permeability of the US-Mexico border allowed "for easy transit into the United States," and Mexico's share of the drug trade grew steadily.[4] This considerable growth of drug trafficking through Mexico's northern border was especially visible along the eastern part of the US-Mexico divide on the Tamaulipas-Texas border, an area that seemed to be neglected or forgotten by authorities. Very few analysts, public policy makers, and law enforcement agents paid attention to what was taking place there—particularly the illicit activities and trade flows.

During this time, Colombian drug traffickers began to establish important alliances with their Mexican counterparts as a response to an increasing demand of illicit substances. In this new context, Juan García Ábrego, Juan N. Guerra's nephew and successor, negotiated with the Rodríguez-Orijuela brothers of the Cali Cartel and agreed to transport drugs from Mexico's southern border to Texas in exchange for half of each load. As writer Damon Tabor (2014, 7) states: "It was a riskier but immensely more profitable arrangement, and it eventually birthed one of Mexico's first major narcotics organizations, the Gulf Cartel." These new operations would need logistic coordination on a large scale, the acquisition of airplanes and other sophisticated equipment, the construction of airstrips, clandestine warehouses, and arrangements to bribe law enforcement authorities along the southern border, in northeastern Mexico, and throughout the Gulf of Mexico region (Guerrero 2014a, 5).

Known by some as the "Gulf's Drug Lord," Juan García Ábrego made his uncle's business thrive by introducing drug trafficking on a large scale. The drug business became particularly profitable during the late 1980s and 1990s, a period during which the Gulf Cartel was introducing cocaine, marijuana, methamphetamines, and heroin to important US cities. In just one decade, from 1985 to 1995, police calculated that this organization introduced more than 5,000 tons of cocaine base paste. By the end of that period it was estimated that the annual income of the CDG for performing this activity was approximately $20 billion: ironically, the same amount of money that the United States lent to Mexico to overcome the 1995 financial crisis (Muñoz 1996, par. 4). By the mid-1990s the organization had grown considerably and consolidated its position in the Tamaulipas region thanks to the political relationships that Juan N. Guerra began to build and García Ábrego extended and strengthened. The CDG gradually created a complex corruption network involving organized crime and Tamaulipas government authorities (Alvarado 2012; Flores 2013b). This corruption network included government officials at all levels of state and local government. Close links were even forged between the CDG and the federal government, including the executive branch.[5]

In fact, the exponential growth of the Gulf Cartel was not just the result of García Ábrego's vision or leadership capabilities. The complicity of key politicians and the involvement of police at all levels in drug-trafficking operations were crucial and allowed the CDG's drug lord to control approximately 30 percent of the cocaine that crossed into the United States by land in the mid-1990s. Some calculated that those involved in the drug-trafficking business during that time spent nearly $500 million a year in bribes allocated to all levels of the Mexican government (Muñoz 1996, par. 3). The CDG, in alliance with parts of the Tamaulipas government, also succeeded in gaining almost total control of the media in order to force cooperation among dissidents (Correa-Cabrera and Nava 2013).

In sum, local authorities and other key social and political figures collaborated closely with this drug-trafficking group. With its intimidating practices, the organization became a predominant criminal actor that enjoyed close ties with corrupt officials at all levels of government, journalists, business owners, migrants, and gangs as well as with other groups linked to organized crime in the United States (Flores 2013b). In the coming years, the Gulf Cartel "would stop being a regional criminal organization acting as a subsidiary of the Colombian drug cartels to become a key player in the transnational drug trafficking business" (Guerrero 2014a, par. 5).

"La Compañía": History, Allies, and Enemies

Osiel Cárdenas and Los Zetas: The Origins of La Compañía

In 1996 García Ábrego was captured and deported to the United States.[6] His indirect successor was Osiel Cárdenas (aka El Mata-Amigos [the Friends-Killer]), a man who would transform the panorama of organized crime in Mexico.[7] Cárdenas's leadership and strategy helped strengthen the Gulf Cartel's local monopoly on illegal activities while continuing to diversify its sources of revenue. Cárdenas's leadership, however, was different from the style of his predecessor, partly because he did not have the same control mechanisms as García Ábrego, which favored the extensive use of government protection networks combined with low-profile surgical violence (Flores 2013b).

Once a mechanic in Matamoros, Cárdenas consolidated his power in the organization through the extensive use of violence and in particular through the introduction of the Zetas in the late 1990s as the armed enforcers of the Gulf Cartel.[8] Members of this enforcer group were "highly trained and brutally efficient"; the group was created to seize territory and dispatch rivals and reportedly took its name from the first commander's military radio call sign (Tabor 2014, par. 8). According to most accounts, the group initially consisted of Arturo Guzmán Decena (aka Z-1) and thirty members of the Mexican army, many of whom came from outside Tamaulipas. These were Mexican army deserters who belonged to elite forces.[9] They were trained in the use of highly specialized military equipment as well as in counterinsurgency operations.[10] According to some accounts, they received training from foreign governments in the United States, Israel, and other countries (Rodríguez 2006, par. 8).[11] Many consider the Zetas a paramilitary group (Correa-Cabrera 2014c; Paley 2014). They originally worked as hit men and bodyguards; Mexican journalist Ricardo Ravelo (2009) refers to them as a sort of "Praetorian Guard,"[12] which at first followed the orders of and protected Osiel Cárdenas.[13] Because of the precarious labor conditions and salaries of military personnel in Mexico, this group blossomed quickly. As Marco A. Rodríguez (2006, par. 10) recognizes, the most violent and dangerous group of killers in the history of drug trafficking in Mexico "moved from combating *narcos* on the border to working for them. It was much more profitable."

The introduction of the Zetas was destined to change the panorama of drug trafficking in Mexico as well as the ways in which organized crime operates in the country. By bringing this criminal group into the business, the Gulf Cartel secured its domination of illegal activities in Tamaulipas through "blood and fire" (Nava 2011, 16). Security expert Robert Bunker recognizes that "[b]efore the Zetas, it was basically low-quality foot soldiers and enforcer types. . . . What the Zetas brought to the table was that [military] operational capability. The other cartels didn't know anything about this. It revolutionized the whole landscape" (quoted in Tabor 2014, par. 8). Guerrero (2014a, par. 14) noted that "the appearance of the Zetas represented a paradigmatic change in the operation of drug-trafficking groups, since it inaugurated a special phase in the construction of professional criminal armies." In his view, it was easy for the other groups to observe the ways in which the Zetas helped Osiel Cárdenas and the CDG to consolidate their power in Tamaulipas and extended their influence over the rest of the Gulf of Mexico and parts of Mexico's southern border.

The Zetas' expansion in the state of Tamaulipas started with the incorporation of mercenaries from Matamoros, who then started operating along the border with Texas. Subsequently the group's influence expanded to other parts of the state and then to other neighboring states. The Zetas' practices and tactics, as well as their "politics of death," helped them eliminate enemies and incorporate all kinds of illegal businesses and smaller local groups of organized crime into their structure. The organization adopted business policies and strategies and turned into a kind of criminal monopoly that would eventually reproduce the model of a corporation with multiple subsidiaries, that is, with multiple criminal-related businesses (see chapter 3 and appendix 5).

According to military intelligence reports and investigations by what was once called the Special Unit on Organized Crime (UEDO),[14] the Zetas were able to stop the entrance of other powerful criminal organizations—such as the Juárez Cartel and the Sinaloa Cartel—into key cities along the Tamaulipas border through the use of paramilitary tactics (Pineda 2003, par. 5). One of the most contested plazas was the strategic city of Nuevo Laredo,[15] "the city that sits directly across the border from the terminus of IH-35, the chief north-south artery in the United States" (Brands 2009a). In fact, protecting this key plaza was one of the main reasons why Osiel Cárdenas first established contact with a small group of highly trained former members of Mexico's armed forces and asked for help.

Los Zetas' Capital City

Nuevo Laredo, Tamaulipas, can be called the "Zetas' Capital City." It "is the busiest cargo crossing from the United States to Mexico, and that heavy flow of traffic permits a large flow of contraband cargo to be hidden alongside legitimate goods" (Stewart and Reed 2013, par. 19). The city is considered the crown jewel in the drug-trafficking world, due to its strategic location and busy customs, which facilitate the smuggling of a number of substances and goods, including arms, people, and drugs. It is estimated that Nuevo Laredo handles approximately 40 percent of the total volume of trade between Mexico and the United States. Over eight thousand vehicles and more than three hundred thousand people cross on average each day through the international bridges that connect this city with Texas.[16] Thoroughly inspecting all the cars, trucks, and people that cross this segment of the border is almost impossible. According to journalist Alberto Nájar (2005), customs agents have approximately 10.6 seconds to check each of the vehicles that cross the border and only 3.4 seconds for pedestrians—all this in a 24-hour work day. The limitations in terms of time and resources for border management purposes allow considerable amounts of drugs, arms, and money to cross in both directions.

Being such a prime spot for smugglers, Nuevo Laredo was deeply contested, particularly after the arrest of Juan García Ábrego in 1996. At this time other drug-trafficking organizations (TCOs), like the Sinaloa Cartel, attempted to displace the Gulf Cartel to exercise control over this valuable border territory (Nájar 2005). From the late 1990s onward, with the creation of the Zetas, northeastern Mexico and the Tamaulipas border in particular experienced a dramatic increase in drug-related violence. It was said that the "bloodshed that followed was nowhere more intense than in Nuevo Laredo" (Brands 2009a, par. 6). Cárdenas used the Zetas to protect this valuable territory as well as to strengthen the Gulf Cartel's operations there and to intimidate or eliminate its main rivals. Professor Hal Brands (2009a, par. 8) explains this process as follows:

> Cárdenas initially employed the Zetas as hired guns and maintained a firm hold on the group and its activities. He charged the Zetas with protecting his territory in Nuevo Laredo, murdering or intimidating competitors, and accompanying drug shipments to the U.S. border. He also apparently relied on the Zetas as his personal protection detail, making the group an immensely valuable commodity at a time when drug lords such as Cárdenas were increasingly falling victim to the violence they themselves had spawned.

Journalist Manuel Pineda (2003) reported that the name "Zetas" was first mentioned in Nuevo Laredo on January 27, 2002—several months before their first public appearance in Matamoros. On that date, slightly before midnight, a convoy formed by at least twelve sports utility vehicles entered the city and waited in front of the Church of El Santo Niño (the Holy Child). Members of the convoy communicated through radio frequencies and identified themselves by using the letter Z and a number.

A Successful Company with "Official" Allies

As the Zetas grew in power, the group became more independent and formed an informal alliance with the Gulf Cartel. Together they began to be known as La Compañía (the Company). The process of economic transformation that allowed the Company to form and succeed coincided with a process of important political and economic transformation in Mexico. So-called neoliberal reforms were implemented in the second half of the 1990s. These reforms were accelerated after the signing of the North American Free Trade Agreement (NAFTA) and included privatization and free trade policies (or less government intervention in the economy). They had an impact on criminal syndicates, allowing them to diversify their activities and to operate more as modern transnational corporations with less centralized government control.

This transnational "company" formed by the Gulf Cartel and the Zetas grew considerably after its founding in this neoliberal atmosphere. Journalist Blanche Petrich (2011) reported that as of the first quarter of 2009, with the help of the Zetas, the Gulf Cartel had penetrated and economically participated in 34 percent of the productive activities in Tamaulipas, according to intelligence reports. Aside from extortion and prostitution, the Cartel "had absorbed at least 14 of the organizations which used to traffic migrants . . . and dominated the economic routes towards southeast Texas" (par. 20). While the original members of the Zetas started to be killed or arrested, the criminal syndicate recruited a significant number of "additional soldiers, policemen, and criminals" (Brands 2009a, par. 7). The Zetas at one point consisted of 1,000–3,000 members.[17] This core group was allegedly complemented by dozens of Kaibiles, elite Guatemalan special forces soldiers "who, like the original Zetas, deserted the army in search of higher pay," as well as by "a variety of middle-men, petty criminals, and other individuals who [assisted] the organization in various ways" (Brands 2009a, par. 7).[18]

The successful operations of the Gulf Cartel and the rapid growth of its ultraviolent armed-wing, the Zetas, were facilitated by the formation of corruption networks that became more sophisticated and extended their influence at all levels (Alvarado 2004; Flores 2013a; Reyes 2009a). Protected witnesses and other informal sources have revealed the corruption network that was built over almost a decade, when the Zetas became visible and extremely influential. The so-called Company prospered greatly, and the influence of the Zetas grew rapidly. Their business portfolio expanded to include drug trafficking as well as migrant smuggling, extortion and kidnapping, pirating DVDs, selling black-market oil, and other activities. This impressive growth was made possible by the help of political and police connections and was chronicled in documents released by Mexico's Attorney General's Office (PGR) that include key statements from FBI and DEA agents (Reyes 2009a, par. 1).[19] According to these documents, Osiel Cárdenas controlled Tamaulipas by making use of an "intricate network of accomplices," including Gilberto Lerma Plata, the nephew of state governor Manuel Cavazos Lerma, and the main federal, state, and local police chiefs (Reyes 2009a, par. 2).

Other people who ended up collaborating with La Compañía were Humberto García, then director of the Tamaulipas Ministry of Public Security; Juan Carlos González Sánchez, commissioner of the Matamoros Ministerial Police; Juan César Casillas Escobar, the Federal Highway Police commissioner; and many other government authorities at different levels. Some have even alleged that all the state's police forces had to ask the Gulf Cartel for permission to conduct most of their activities (Reyes 2009a, par. 3). It has been widely claimed that personnel of key law enforcement agencies used to collaborate directly with the Company: members of the Preventive Federal Police, the Federal Highway Police, and the Ministerial Police.

Since its inception, the Gulf Cartel has had a very close relationship with public officials at all levels. However, as Guerrero (2014a) explains, with the creation of the Zetas—who were initially recruited from the ranks of the Mexican army and from outside Tamaulipas—the criminal organization lost the strong links with the community that had existed in the times of Juan N. Guerra. In this new context, according to Guerrero (2014a), "the *narcos* were not appreciated in Tamaulipas anymore" (as they had once been appreciated by the community). Hence the deviation from the traditional leadership led to a spiral of conflicts and violence, which furthered the increase in predatory crimes, such as extortion and kidnappings, and hindered the economic activity of this Mexican state (par. 43).

La Federación (the Federation): The Company's Main Rival

The advancement of the Zetas in terms of territorial control and the group's growing power brought a new dynamic to the relations between criminal syndicates in Mexico. The conflict in (and fight for) Tamaulipas territory clearly exemplified these new relations. The first conflict between criminal organizations in this northern Mexican state took place in the region known as the Small Border (Frontera Chica) at the beginning of the twenty-first century. The Small Border is the portion of the Tamaulipas northern border formed by five small municipalities: Díaz Ordaz, Camargo, Miguel Alemán, Mier, and Guerrero—located between the important Tamaulipas cities of Reynosa and Nuevo Laredo (see map 1.1). But the epicenter of violence in the first few years of the new century was the key city of Nuevo Laredo.

The fight for the Tamaulipas border started with a failed alliance between a local smuggler (Edelio López Falcón, aka El Yeyo) and some drug-trafficking organizations operating on the Pacific coast that attempted to dominate the most profitable territory of the Gulf Cartel and its armed wing, the Zetas—in particular, the Sinaloa Cartel and the Juárez Cartel. Further attempts by rival groups to take control of some of the Gulf Cartel's main plazas were also ineffective during the first years of the twenty-first century. By this time the Zetas had become a very successful enforcer group. Due to the Company's rapid growth and success, the Sinaloa Cartel and the Juárez Cartel were forced to form additional alliances and expand their cooperation with other groups that were operating in different parts of the country.

According to some accounts, La Federación was formed at the very beginning of the present century. It initially included the Sinaloa Cartel, the Juárez Cartel, and some members of the Colima Cartel (also called the Amezcua-Contreras Brothers' Cartel) and the Michoacán organization known as the Milenio Cartel (the Cartel of Armando Valencia and his family) (De la O 2011, part 4, par. 2).[20] In the years that followed, the Gulf Cartel consolidated its power in the key plaza of Nuevo Laredo with the help of Los Zetas. As a response to the Company's actions, and in order to continue utilizing the Tamaulipas border as a smuggling route, the Federation attempted to enter Nuevo Laredo. This caused an extremely violent struggle for the control of this strategic city that lasted until 2006. The Company was victorious, and the Zetas started to protect this plaza, making Nuevo Laredo the center of its operations. This is where the Zetas started to gain some independence. They ceased to be just the enforcers and became a fundamental part of La Compañía.

Toward the Zetas' Independence

Cárdenas's Arrest and the Narco-Wars

Osiel Cárdenas was arrested on March 14, 2003, in Matamoros. After this event the Gulf Cartel started to lose some of its influence, and the dynamics of organized crime in northern Mexico and other parts of the country began to change. This was particularly the case in the states of Tamaulipas, Guerrero, and Michoacán, where the Zetas were heavily involved in the development of illicit activities—still as part of the Company. In Tamaulipas, Cárdenas's capture generated a slight rise in the level of violence. At the same time, the fight for the plaza of Nuevo Laredo between the Company and the Federation continued to escalate.

Even from prison Osiel Cárdenas maintained control of the Gulf Cartel and its armed wing. The Zetas had grown in strength and importance and continued defending Nuevo Laredo and the whole Tamaulipas border. At this moment the CDG and the Zetas formed an actual company. The Zetas ceased to be just employees and became entrepreneurs or partners in this company. Cárdenas made the key decisions for the organization from prison. In the maximum security prison of La Palma the drug lord met Benjamín Arellano Félix of the Tijuana Cartel. The Company then formed an alliance with this group to confront the Federation and stop its attempts to control the Tamaulipas border (De la O 2011, part 4, par. 5).[21]

The Federation's leaders thought that Cárdenas's arrest would eventually allow them to establish control over the Company's main territories in Tamaulipas. Hence, through Arturo Beltrán Leyva (aka El Barbas), they tried to enter Nuevo Laredo on repeated occasions, but the Gulf Cartel and the Zetas responded strongly against these attacks. They fought back in some key territories controlled by the Federation, and violence expanded throughout different states and regions of the country (Guerrero 2014a). According to a number of journalistic accounts, key alliances were formed within maximum-security prisons, and the different criminal syndicates increased their arms capacity. This marked the start of a large conflict among the main drug-trafficking organizations in the country (Ochoa 2005; Nájar 2006).

The existing accounts—including reports of the Attorney General's Office (PGR)—mention a period of preparation for the so-called cartel wars, when the main criminal federations increased their military capacity, even with the support of foreign killers. According to these accounts, the Tijuana Cartel enlisted the support of its old allies, the gang members of the Mexican Mafia (MM or La Eme) and Barrio Logan of San Diego, California. The Gulf Cartel involved the Zetas in this battle as well as Guatemala's Kaibiles, while the Sinaloa Cartel (part of the Federation) formed alliances with members of the Mara Salvatrucha in Chiapas and Tamaulipas and complemented these efforts with the support of a group formed by military-style personnel known as Los Pelones (Nájar 2006).

At some point after Cárdenas's arrest there were two major blocs. One bloc was formed by an alliance between the Tijuana Cartel of the Arellano Félix brothers, the Milenio Cartel, and the Gulf Cartel. The main objective of this bloc seemed to be controlling and defending the key territories of Tamaulipas and the border region of Baja California. The second alliance was formed by drug-trafficking organizations operating in the so-called Golden Triangle (Triángulo Dorado, which included Chihuahua, Sinaloa, and Durango) and was led by Ismael (aka El Mayo) Zambada, Joaquín (aka El Chapo) Guzmán Loera, Juan José Esparragoza Moreno (aka El Azul), and Arturo Beltrán Leyva (Ochoa 2005; Nájar 2006).[22] Arturo Beltrán Leyva hired Édgar Valdez Villarreal, known as "La Barbie," who formed an elite commando unit called Los Negros (the Black Ones) to fight the Zetas. Los Negros then became the new armed wing of the Federation (De la O 2011, part 4, par. 5).

An extremely violent conflict developed between these two groups, which by the end of 2005 had extended throughout the country. The most violent confrontations took place in the city of Nuevo Laredo as well as in some regions of Michoacán and Guerrero. In Nuevo Laredo, La Barbie coordinated the cell of killers working for the Sinaloa Cartel. La Barbie—born on August 11, 1973, in Laredo, Texas—knew the territory well, was extremely violent, and was able to work with other gangs, such as the Central American gang MS-13. He was responsible for more than 120 assassinations in just one year (Nájar 2006). Some months later Michoacán and Guerrero became epicenters of violence. In 2006 members of La Familia Michoacana separated from the Zetas and established a truce with the Federation, which allowed them to establish an independent criminal syndicate in this Mexican state.[23]

Communicating a Narco-War

A key aspect of the violent conflict between the two major blocs of Mexican criminal syndicates was the use of mass media, social media, and other publicity devices to send messages to or threaten their respective rivals. A war in the traditional mass media and social media, as well as new methods to communicate through novel visual media, arrived with the Zetas; but the Zetas were not the only players in this conflict. These threatening messages transmitted through a number of visual devices were initiated by this group or by its criminal rivals or by the Mexican government. It is worth noting that most of these other communications were allegedly a response to the Zetas' violence (real and virtual). The use of these tactics was generalized in the following years and extended to different areas of Mexico.

The confrontation with La Barbie was key at that time and contributed to further the image of the Zetas as the most violent criminal organization in the country. The visual messages and communiqués through the mass media and social media between him and the

Company's armed wing became quite frequent and spectacular in the last months of 2004. Probably the first event of this kind took place on October 10, 2004, when the major newspapers in Mexico, such as *La Jornada* and *El Universal*, published a story of the finding of five bodies—allegedly members of the Sinaloa Cartel—inside a house in Nuevo Laredo with a colorful message threatening La Barbie and his allies in the Federation, including El Chapo Guzmán and Arturo Beltrán Leyva (Reynowarrior 2010).[24]

The communication between criminal syndicates (and between the government and criminal groups) has since become public. Messages that included dead or dismembered bodies and other visual threats started to circulate massively in Mexican mainstream media and social media as well. The war in cyberspace also started with the Zetas and their enemies, particularly members of the Federation, such as Édgar Valdez Villarreal (aka La Barbie). This reflected and complemented the dynamics of war between TCOs (and between the Mexican government and TCOs) taking place in different parts of the country and particularly in Tamaulipas, Guerrero, Veracruz, and Michoacán (Correa-Cabrera 2015b).

La Barbie, for example, became skilled at using videos and was present in the mass and social media for some years. He was a pioneer in the use of war tactics through these devices. His actions greatly contributed to the perception of an unmanageable country, where the main enemy to defeat was the Zetas organization. Actually La Barbie may have been the pioneer in the use of videos for sending messages to other groups of organized crime and government agencies. He might be considered the father of the "narco-videos," when he distributed through the international media a short film produced in May 2005 showing the bloody assassination of four men who belonged to the Zetas and were captured in Acapulco by members of the Sinaloa Cartel (Reynowarrior 2010).[25] The event was then covered by the Mexican mainstream media, causing terror among the population in several parts of the country, particularly in those areas where the Federation was fighting against the Company and particularly against the Zetas.

With this video members of the Federation—with the help of La Barbie—escalated their levels of violence and desire to cause terror. They were among the first ones who utilized fragmentation grenades in public spaces.[26] The use of such devices to terrorize the population in several parts of the country became a frequent practice by the different criminal organizations. The war between criminal syndicates in Mexico through the mass media continued. In 2006, in the context of the war between the Company and the Federation for the plaza of Acapulco, La Barbie once again became a pioneer in terror practices against other criminal groups. According to some accounts, he allegedly initiated the public exposure of beheadings through the mass media. In April 2006 the major Mexican media outlets reported two human heads found in Acapulco that were left in front of the building of Guerrero's Ministry of Finance. This was allegedly the first time in which the beheadings were utilized to send messages to other criminal groups or to the government. As with the fragmentation grenades and narco-banners, this practice proliferated in the following years (Reynowarrior 2010).

An interesting aspect of this war in the traditional mass media and social media was the focus on the Zetas. The Zetas started to utilize these new means of communication extensively for their criminal purposes. At the same time, their enemies started to form a large bloc and targeted this group, allegedly for its brutality and the unprecedented violence that it had originated. For example, in May 2006—some weeks before Mexico's presidential elections—La Barbie signed a communiqué, using a whole page in an important newspaper (*Milenio*). It was directed toward the business community (represented by the Employers' Confederation of the Mexican Republic, COPARMEX); Natividad González Parás, the governor of Nuevo León; the presidential candidates; and Mexico's civil society. According to the message, "it was not [his] intention to clean [his] reputation"; he only wanted to alert the public about the "big cancer that Los Zetas represented, as every territory that they stepped in turned into a death zone" (quoted in Reynowarrior 2010, par. 41).

These new practices and visual devices that initiated a war in the traditional mass media and the social media were reproduced throughout the country. Numerous decapitated and dismembered bodies with messages started to appear in a number of public places and were widely covered by the Mexican—and frequently also by the international—media. Likewise, other groups like La Familia Michoacana started to utilize these tactics to generate fear and communicate with their enemies. In various cities of Michoacán, this group perpetrated decapitations and left heads with messages in public places, including government buildings, bars, and dancing clubs.

These phenomena coincided with the success of social media and the widespread use of the internet among the groups involved in the so-called narco-wars. In a new context of wide access to technology and interactive platforms, criminal groups started using tools such as YouTube, Facebook, Twitter, and blogs to send their messages of terror. The different groups forming the Federation, the Zetas, and other criminal syndicates began to publish numerous YouTube videos in which their rivals were interrogated and decapitated in front of a video camera. At the same time, criminal organizations started using fragmentation grenades and car bombs and assassinating politicians (even a gubernatorial candidate was killed in Tamaulipas). This new situation is clearly expressed in the following comment:

> From now on, executions would be more graphic, more convincing and more media savvy. It was not enough to leave a simple message to an enemy. [The message] needed to be communicated more clearly to those who protected [the enemy], and above all, to the whole society in order for everybody to be informed about the dangers faced by those who defied the ones in charge of the plaza.
>
> Including images of a simple *coup de grâce*, [criminal groups] started leaving [multiple] messages via narco-banners on the bodies of the murdered people; videotaping the executions; detonating fragmentation grenades in public places; decapitating people, and even buying space for their communiques in the most important newspapers in the country. (Reynowarrior 2010, pars. 8–9)

Cárdenas's Extradition: Toward the Zetas' Independence

In 2007 the Gulf Cartel leader was extradited to the United States, provoking a definitive but initially friendly break with the Zetas, which chose to become more independent from the tutelage of their former bosses (and later partners). After Cárdenas's extradition, the two organizations divided among themselves the control of the Tamaulipas border but continued to collaborate. In 2008, however, tensions within the Company increased significantly. The fights between the CDG and its powerful allies for some key plazas and the control of some illegal businesses and prisons became more and more frequent. At the same time, there were important divisions within the Federation.

One key division of La Federación involved the Beltrán Leyva family, which used to form part of the Sinaloa Cartel.[27] This event contributed to the elevation of tensions within the Company due to the possibility of an eventual alliance between the Sinaloa Cartel and the Gulf

Cartel. The Zetas finally started to collaborate with the Beltrán Leyva family, and the other member of the Company, the Gulf Cartel, began a mutually beneficial relationship with its rival, the Sinaloa Cartel. The relationship between the CDG and the Zetas deteriorated significantly. The Zetas disagreed with the recent negotiations between its then allies and the Sinaloa Cartel. Tensions continued growing until the end of 2009. It has been said that in that year Zeta leader Heriberto Lazcano called for a massive meeting inviting the highest-ranking Zetas to vote in regard to the possibility of signing a truce with the organization led then by El Chapo Guzmán. The voting does not seem to have favored the proposal; the Company disintegrated soon after (De la O 2011).

The Partnership Is Broken

The rivalry between criminal organizations does not seem to be the only or the main explanation of the Company's dissolution. Other economic reasons came into play. According to some accounts, the Zetas' leadership believed that the group deserved a higher status within the Company, particularly with regard to the big business of drug trafficking, in which the Zetas' role was marginal. After Cárdenas's extradition in January 2007, this group of killers apparently tried to renegotiate the distribution of plazas and drug-trafficking routes, resulting in elevated tensions between the Zetas and the Gulf Cartel as well as increasing the frequency of confrontations in cities like Matamoros, Reynosa, and Nuevo Laredo, key in the drug-trafficking business (Guerrero 2014a).

Eventually the Zetas declared their independence from their erstwhile overlords in the Gulf Cartel. The split between the two organizations occurred in the first months of 2010. According to most accounts, the most significant event that precipitated the disintegration of the Company took place in January 2010 in the city of Reynosa, Tamaulipas, when a Zeta chief of finance, Sergio Peña Mendoza (aka El Concord 3), was kidnapped and assassinated, allegedly by other members of the CDG led by Samuel Flores Borrego (aka El Metro 3). This event led to an extremely brutal battle for control of the Tamaulipas territory, which had an enormous impact on the state's economy and society.

After the split, the two groups showed some differences in their structures, business objectives, and ways of exercising violence. Initially the

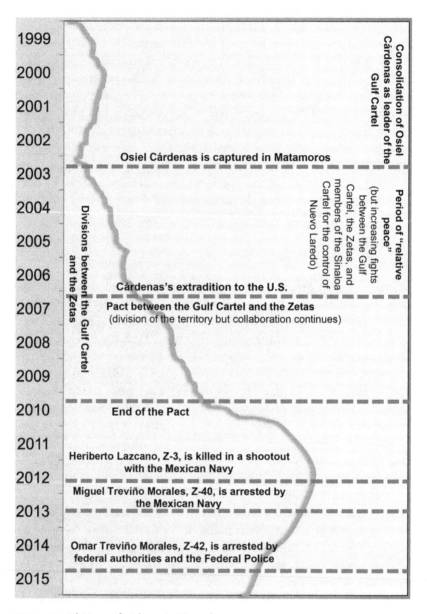

1999
2000
2001
2002

Consolidation of Osiel Cárdenas as leader of the Gulf Cartel

Osiel Cárdenas is captured in Matamoros

2003
2004
2005
2006

Divisions between the Gulf Cartel and the Zetas

Period of "relative peace"
(but increasing fights between the Gulf Cartel, the Zetas, and members of the Sinaloa Cartel for the control of Nuevo Laredo)

Cárdenas's extradition to the U.S.

2007

Pact between the Gulf Cartel and the Zetas
(division of the territory but collaboration continues)

2008
2009
2010

End of the Pact

2011

Heriberto Lazcano, Z-3, is killed in a shootout with the Mexican Navy

2012

Miguel Treviño Morales, Z-40, is arrested by the Mexican Navy

2013
2014

Omar Treviño Morales, Z-42, is arrested by federal authorities and the Federal Police

2015

Figure 1.1. A history of violence in Tamaulipas.

Gulf Cartel's main focus was drug trafficking. The Zetas, in contrast, introduced a model to inflict terror and violence with the aim of extending their control over larger territories and moving drugs through the so-called Small Border. But in reality both groups perpetrate kidnappings and extortion, collect informal taxes, and provide security in exchange for fees (Gómez and Torres 2011, par. 5; Correa-Cabrera 2014c).

The break within the Company laid the groundwork for the development of different forms of organized crime in the state. As a result, the levels of violence drastically increased as the two criminal syndicates began to compete (figure 1.1). Suddenly a new order appeared in the Tamaulipas border region, characterized by massive executions, extortions, kidnappings, and changes in the relationships among criminal groups and between criminals and public authorities. This was an era of terror linked to the Zetas' model. The bloodiest period of the history of Tamaulipas started at this time and included the assassination of critical politicians, paid protests against the military, massive escapes from (and assassinations in) prisons, almost total control of the municipal police and other local security institutions, growing rivalry among antagonistic criminal groups, and increased amounts of arms crossing though the very porous Tamaulipas border.

CHAPTER 2

The Zetas' War

This chapter explains the "Zetas' war," or the new independent organization's fight against its previous allies, other criminal groups, and the Mexican government. It also describes the Zetas' new tactics, forms of operation, areas of influence, and territorial control as well as the group's links to and impact on other criminal and political groups. The chapter shows how the Zetas' unique fight for territories led to an escalation of violence in Mexico and other parts of the continent—particularly Central America—in unprecedented ways. In Mexico this generated a condition of insecurity that seemed to require the application of extreme measures by the federal government. The final part of this chapter analyzes the rise and alleged decline of the Zetas organization, and discusses the speculation about its demise.

The Zetas Exceptionalism and a Fight for Territory

The Zetas and the Professionalization of the Killing Industry

In the years following their separation from the Gulf Cartel, the Zetas became an extremely successful transnational criminal corporation. According to Dwight Dyer and Daniel Sachs (2013, par. 1), this success can be explained by the group's "military background, as well as its access to state-of-the-art weaponry and communications technology." At one point even the US State Department described the Zetas as "the most technologically advanced, sophisticated, and dangerous cartel operating in Mexico" (quoted in Dyer and Sachs 2013, par. 1). Professor Hal Brands (2009a) notes that the Zetas established "themselves as the most violent, destructive, and lethal participant in that industry" by "drawing on a vast arsenal, military-style discipline and skills, and a sophisticated organizational apparatus." The Zetas eventually "outclassed their competition and defied government efforts to defeat the group." They also dominated large portions of northeastern Mexico at some point, established a presence in a number of cities and states throughout the country, and even became active in some regions of Central America and the United States (Brands 2009a, par. 2).

Beginning in 2010, the division between the Gulf Cartel and the Zetas—in other words, the disintegration of the Company—initiated an all-out turf war that fueled an exponential increase in violence in various parts of Mexico, particularly the northeastern region. As a result of the practices introduced by the Zetas, with their specialized military background, violence increased to levels that had never been seen before. The Zetas' tactics involved spectacular and sophisticated ways of killing, such as dismemberment, decapitation, and the dissolution of human remains in acid baths. The Zetas also introduced extreme criminal practices to the Mexican drug world. They extorted businesses for large sums of money, executed public officials, and used terror tactics against the public, such as car bombs, mass kidnappings, grenade attacks, and road blockades. The Zetas also were pioneers in utilizing traditional mass media and social media to publicize blood and gore, thus successfully defeating the government's strategy to provide a sense of security and control (Rodríguez 2014).

In other words, the Zetas created and professionalized a "killing industry." A side effect of this phenomenon was the creation, by imitation, of a host of enforcer wings that catered to the needs of most TCOs that operated in Mexican territory, such as Los Artistas Asesinos, Barrio Azteca, Gente Nueva, La Línea, MS-13, Los Negros, and Los Pelones, among others (Correa-Cabrera 2014c). The Zetas themselves helped create one spin-off group, La Familia Michoacana, a criminal organization whose formation and development had a very negative impact on security and the contemporary history of the Mexican state of Michoacán.

At the same time, as Brands (2009a, par. 34) claims, the Zetas exploited "the failures of the Mexican state, using violence and bribery to undermine government institutions and destroy them from within." It is worth noting the close links between these groups and government officials at all levels, including the armed forces, the federal police, former governors, mayors, and other local and state authorities. According to Ravelo (2013), the Zetas became a big industry, with political support. In his view, this criminal organization expanded considerably both within Mexico and in different regions of the world, including Central America, Europe, and the Rio Grande Valley of Texas. What is more, in less than a decade, the Zetas turned into the second most powerful criminal group in Mexico, surpassed only by the Sinaloa Cartel.

A War against the Zetas

When the Zetas and the Gulf Cartel disintegrated the Company and started their bloody war, Mexico was already under fire. The president had declared a "war on drugs," and various criminal syndicates were fighting to control different regions of the country. Some states experienced more violence than others; Tamaulipas, Chihuahua, Veracruz, Guerrero, Michoacán, Nuevo León, and Coahuila had extremely high levels of violence during this time. In this context, many of the criminal syndicates that were once rivals formed an alliance known as La Nueva Federación (the New Federation), with the aim of combating a new common enemy: the Zetas organization.[1] In this conflict extreme forms of violence such as assassinations of politicians, kidnappings, grenade attacks, car bombs, and urban war expanded throughout important parts of the country. Bodies were found hanging from bridges or dismembered, narco-groups blockaded roads, the media were silenced, and law enforcement agencies were attacked.

The Mexican government responded to these events with similar strong measures. With both sides having access to high-caliber weapons, the violence accelerated greatly. Each side in this war committed abuses, and Mexican society suffered immensely. When the armed forces arrived in some regions, human rights violations, forced disappearances, and other forms of state crime that are difficult to document and investigate occurred. During armed battles, civilians were often caught in the crossfire. Tourism suffered and businesses and homes were sometimes damaged or burned. Thousands of people disappeared. Overall this period in Mexico was characterized by impunity, the loss of social cohesion, and violation of basic civil liberties and human rights—including the absence of freedom of expression and the right to information.

In sum, the appearance of the Zetas brought new forms of exercising violence. At some point the group became the main target of other criminal organizations and of the Mexican state itself. La Nueva Fede-

ración and the federal government responded brutally to the vicious-
ness of this group that changed the face of organized crime in Mexico.
At this moment all armed actors in Mexico seemed to be involved in a
new type of war; the Zetas had set up the standards, and other criminal actors followed them. The violent conflict between these groups
was intensified by the participation of military personnel and the usage of new military tactics. In other words, a new militarized criminal organization brought with it the militarization of other criminal
groups and the militarization of the security strategy in Mexico.

The Zetas Areas of Influence: The Battle for Territory

When the Zetas separated from the Gulf Cartel, the two groups entered into an extremely violent fight for territory that started in Tamaulipas, the birth state of the Company, where the main smuggling plazas
were located. The CDG initially occupied the cities where it "held traditionally its operative bases," such as Matamoros and Reynosa (Guerrero 2014a, par. 25). The Zetas maintained control of Nuevo Laredo,
where they had become strong and apparently had their main sources
of income at that time. The rest of the Tamaulipas border, particularly
the municipalities of the Small Border (Díaz Ordaz, Camargo, Miguel
Alemán, Mier, and Guerrero) remained a zone of continuous conflict
(see map 2.1). As Guerrero (2014a, par. 25) recognizes: "The battle for
occupying [key] positions along these territories includes some of the
most violent chapters of the history of [organized crime] in Mexico."
     The most contested municipalities in Tamaulipas as a result of the
war between the Gulf Cartel and the Zetas were those located along
the border with Texas (from Nuevo Laredo to Matamoros), along the
Gulf Coast (San Fernando, Tampico, and Ciudad Madero, in particular), and in southeastern Tamaulipas (particularly El Mante), as well
as in the capital city of the state (Ciudad Victoria) and its surrounding
areas (see map 2.1). After Tamaulipas, the conflict expanded to important parts of Mexico's northeast, particularly to the states of Nuevo
León and Coahuila. These two states experienced a very high level of
violence, massive security problems, disappearances, and forced displacements, among many other tragic events resulting from a brutal confrontation between two very violent criminal organizations
and the involvement of Mexico's federal forces (the federal police, the
Mexican army, and the navy). The worst period for these three states
was concentrated in the years 2010–2012.

Map 2.1. The battle for the Tamaulipas territories. The municipalities with darker shading were the most contested. Source: Correa-Cabrera (2013b, 2014c). Design by Carlos D. Gutiérrez-Mannix and Wendy Macías.

Map 2.2. The Zetas' area of influence in Mexico (2010–2013).
Source: *El Universal.*

The Zetas organization grew enormously after its separation from the Gulf Cartel. In the first years of this conflict, the criminal group extended its presence to important portions of Mexico's territory, including vast areas of Coahuila, Nuevo León, Tamaulipas, Veracruz, Zacatecas, San Luis Potosí, Durango, Puebla, Tlaxcala, Tabasco, Campeche, and the Yucatán Peninsula (see map 2.2). The Zetas also established key connections with transnational criminal syndicates in Central America and the Caribbean. Reporter Felipe Moreno (2008, par. 20) recognized that this criminal organization possessed, at some point, "several thousand assets spread out in Latin America and in other regions of the world."

At the beginning of the current century, the Zetas were the Mexican TCO that experienced the greatest geographic growth. In just a few years, after 2010, they were able to control most of the Gulf corridor. According to a number of reports, their cells had a presence in twenty-one states of the Mexican Republic. In the United States this TCO allegedly has operated in Texas, Oklahoma, New Mexico, New Jersey, Michigan, Colorado, Illinois, Tennessee, Georgia, and California (*El Universal* 2013, par. 2). The Zeta presence in Central America is also important, particularly in Guatemala, Honduras, and El Salvador. According to some accounts, the organization's international expansion allowed it to establish close links with the Italian criminal group known as the 'Ndrangheta.

The Zetas' War (by Territory)

Tamaulipas

The expansion of the Zetas originated in Tamaulipas; the group first controlled Nuevo Laredo, the western part of the Small Border, San Fernando, Ciudad Mante, and Ciudad Victoria. The state saw violence rise sharply at the beginning of 2010 (January 25) with the definite rupture between the Zetas and the Gulf Cartel (figure 1.1). In an unprecedented wave of violence, more than a thousand people were killed in the state in events related to organized crime that same year (Correa-Cabrera 2013b). The violence also claimed the life of the Institutional Revolutionary Party (PRI) candidate for governor, Rodolfo Torre Cantú, who was gunned down along with his bodyguards a short distance from the airport at Ciudad Victoria.

The open warfare between the two criminal organizations led to a massive displacement of people from this northeastern Mexican state. For example, hundreds of people were forced to leave Ciudad Mier and moved temporarily to the neighboring city of Miguel Alemán in November of 2010 after extremely violent clashes between the Zetas and the Gulf Cartel in the city. Killings skyrocketed. In the municipality of San Fernando, 72 migrants were massacred in August 2010, and approximately 200 corpses buried in mass graves (so-called narcograves or *narcofosas*) were discovered in the same area in April 2011. These violent acts were accompanied by kidnappings of bus passengers, attacks on military bases, road blockades, car bombs, grenades thrown at government offices in various municipalities, and the mass breakout of hundreds of prison inmates from penitentiaries in different municipalities of the state. Political assassinations also took place during this time; the mayor of the municipality of Hidalgo was killed in August 2010, and the mayoral candidate for the city of Valle Hermoso was murdered in May 2010.

Nuevo León

The war between the two organizations that once formed the Company and the expansion of the Zetas also escalated violence in Nuevo León and particularly in its capital city, Monterrey, where the two organizations fought for control of the extortion business. Violence in the state reached its highest level in 2011 (Guerrero 2012a), including attacks and mass assassinations at public places, such as the Café Iguana (May 22), Sabino Gordo Bar (July 8: twenty-one dead), and the Casino Royale (August 25: fifty-two dead), and numerous killings of local police and municipal authorities. These events received widespread media coverage and allegedly involved members of the Zetas fighting against the Gulf Cartel. Another tragedy in the state took place on May 13, 2012, when the decapitated and mutilated bodies of forty-nine people were found alongside a road in Cadereyta Jiménez, Nuevo León (near Monterrey), less than 300 kilometers away from the border with the United States. This massive assassination was allegedly perpetrated by the Zetas.

Veracruz

Violence in Veracruz also reached its highest level in 2011. The metropolitan area of the state capital, which includes the municipalities of Boca del Río and Veracruz, was the epicenter of violence during this time. But here the main cause of violence was the confrontation between the Sinaloa Cartel and the Zetas. According to several versions, cells of the so-called Cartel Jalisco Nueva Generación (CJNG) started collaborating with the Sinaloa Cartel to fight the Zetas, which elevated tensions significantly. In September 2011 two trucks containing thirty-five dead bodies of alleged Zetas were found on a busy street in Boca del Río. This event, perpetrated by the so-called Mata-Zetas (Zeta-Killers), was again widely covered by the national and international media;[2] the Zetas were again the protagonists. As a response to these violent events, the federal government implemented the program "Veracruz Seguro" (Secure Veracruz), thus reinforcing its military operations in this Mexican state (Guerrero 2012a).

Coahuila

Coahuila is another Mexican state that experienced extremely high levels of violence involving the Zetas. Key territories of this state were allegedly in control of this criminal organization. Important cities of this state such as Torreón, Saltillo, Piedras Negras, and Ciudad Acuña registered, at some point, violent crimes, frequent shootings, and massive assassinations, all products of violent confrontations between the Zetas, state authorities, the federal government, and other criminal groups that were interested in controlling the Zetas' plazas in the state (for example, the Sinaloa Cartel, the Familia Michoacana, and the Gulf Cartel). The most violent years were 2011 and 2012. Approximately 1,835 people disappeared in Coahuila from December 2006 to April 2012, according to statistics cited in a Human Rights Watch report, but it is difficult to know the exact figures (García and Alvarado 2014, par. 14).[3] By the end of 2012 the main battles in the state seemed to be between the Zetas and the Mexican government (both state and federal government authorities).

This northern Mexican state was witness to one of the largest mass killings in the country in recent years. According to some unofficial accounts, this tragic event resulted in 300 victims and took place in the municipality of Allende, Coahuila, in March 2011. According to witnesses and court testimony, "entire families were yanked from homes and off the streets before vanishing into the brush, their homes later demolished. State officials attributed the violence to Los Zetas, . . . saying the group set out to exact revenge on the families of two traitors" (García and Alvarado 2014, par. 3).

At the time of the Allende massacre, according to García and Alvarado (2014, par. 13): "Coahuila and its neighbors to the east, Nuevo Leon and Tamaulipas, had become black zones, with news suppressed and killings unreported, much less investigated. The region is best described as a massive unmarked grave site, with the number of disappearances among the highest in the country."[4] The Allende massacre was preceded and followed by several other violent crimes related to organized crime. Recent operations to search for the disappeared have revealed an estimated 2,500 remains, the existence of numerous narco-graves, and the use of barrels with acid to dissolve bodies (García and Alvarado 2014).

A more recent wave of violence in Coahuila primarily involved the state government, which engaged in direct confrontation with the Zetas. In October 2012 a unit of the state police created under the administration of Rubén Moreira (2011–2017) killed a nephew of Miguel Ángel Treviño Morales (aka Z-40), then an important leader of the Zetas. The Zetas responded to this action: hours later José Eduardo Moreira—son of Humberto Moreira, former governor of Coahuila and former president of the PRI—was found dead in his vehicle in Ciudad Acuña. Four days later the military allegedly killed Heriberto Lazcano, founding member of the Zetas, but his body soon disappeared; it was stolen from the funeral home (García and Alvarado 2014).

The Zetas in Central America

The Zetas also had a strong presence in Central America. The United Nations Office on Drugs and Crime (UNODC) used to call it the "dominant" drug-trafficking group in the region (Grayson 2014a). According to a number of reports, the group operates in Honduras, El Salvador, and Guatemala. Their presence has been most notorious in Guatemala, and particularly in the El Petén region, "a sparsely populated department, contiguous to Mexico, which is endowed with Tikal and other . . . Mayan ruins." The Zetas allegedly entered Guatemala via El Petén in 2007 and established bases in Poptún and Sayaxché. According to Grayson (2014b, 15), Poptún is "a zone honeycombed with small roads and clandestine landing strips [that] borders Belize and is a haven for recruiting cadres." It is worthwhile mentioning the massacre that took place in the municipality of La Libertad,[5] in which the Zetas beheaded twenty-seven farmworkers (Dyer and Sachs 2013). According to Fernando Andrade-Díaz-Durán, a former ambassador from Guatemala to Mexico, the Zetas consolidated their presence in Guatemala in a period of approximately three or four years (Grayson 2014b, 17).

Several reports state that the Zetas operated with Maras (MS-13 and Barrio 18) and Kaibiles in Central America. For example, Grayson (2014b, 15) claims that Poptún is (or was) the location of a Kaibiles' training camp known as El Infierno (Hell). In his account, "Mexican authorities contend that alumni of this facility have aligned with Los Zetas and operate in Mexican territory." Similarly, some reports state that the organization has used members of MS-13 "to conduct kidnapping and extortion operations in Guatemala and Honduras" (Dyer and Sachs 2013, par. 8). In El Salvador, according to former public security and justice minister Ricardo Perdomo, the Zetas sold high-powered rifles to MS-13 and other gangs in Honduras and Guatemala and also trained these groups (Grayson 2014a).

Michoacán and the Reproduction of the Zeta Model: La Familia and Los Caballeros Templarios

As already mentioned, the Zetas were pioneers in the use of military tactics and the diversification of criminal activities beyond drug trafficking. They created a new model of organized crime that extended throughout the country and to other regions of the Americas. The Zetas initiated their activities in Tamaulipas and expanded their influence to other parts of Mexico. In their rapid conquest of territories, other criminal groups started imitating their tactics and forms of operation. The case of Michoacán is emblematic in this sense. It is worth noting that the Familia Michoacana (Michoacán Family) and Los Caballeros Templarios (Knights Templar) essentially followed the Zeta model and applied it—with some key modifications involving a specific ideology and local values and beliefs—to their forms of operation in a state that became extremely violent after the arrival of these criminal influences.

By the end of the 1980s illicit crops and drug production were controlled by a group of farming families with a long tradition in Michoacán: the Valencia family from Uruapan. In the 1990s, thanks to an alliance made with the Tijuana Cartel, they were able to expand and consolidate into the most important drug-trafficking organization in Michoacán (Guerrero 2014b). This group is also known as the Milenio Cartel. Michoacán became a very valuable plaza in terms of drug production and smuggling due to its strategic location and the state's important port of Lázaro Cárdenas, which connects Asia to Mexico's markets, both legal and illegal. It is worth noting that Michoacán has been a very contested state. It is considered the gateway to the Pacific Route ("puerta de entrada de la llamada 'ruta del Pacífico'") (Ravelo 2011, 36).

The rapid success and expansion of the Milenio Cartel was noticed by its competitors and particularly by the Company, which expanded to Michoacán with the aim of controlling the territory and opening a new route of drug smuggling that would link Tamaulipas and the Pacific. In order to achieve this goal, as explained by Guerrero (2014b), the Company created a key alliance with another criminal group that operated in the state, La Empresa (the Enterprise), in 2001.[6] This group allied with the Company—particularly with the Zetas—in order to end up with the monopoly of the Valencia family in drug production and smuggling in Michoacán. Finally, the alliance was successful: the newcomers rapidly gained control of the region, taking advantage of the resources and tactical experience of the Zetas (Guerrero 2014b).

The Company, through the Zetas, established a base in Apatzingán and created a network of extortion and provision of protection services (*cobro de derecho de piso*) that reached most of the productive activities in the region of Tierra Caliente (Hot Land). As Guerrero (2014b) explains, the organization created a local drug market, opened a trafficking route toward the northeastern border, and co-opted a significant number of state and municipal authorities. The alliance between the Enterprise and the Company started to deteriorate. The leadership of the Enterprise decided to start operating independently and founded a new organization in 2006 named La Familia Michoacana or La Familia (the Family). This criminal group only recruited people from Michoacán and allegedly protected the Michoacán population. However, La Familia imitated the Zeta practices and extended the network of extortion and kidnapping for ransom that was initiated by the most violent component of the Company. With a mission statement that combined elements of social vindication, evangelism, and regional identity, this new organization presented itself as the one that would "liberate [the Michoacán people] from the oppression of the Zetas" (Guerrero 2014b, par. 9).

In 2004 the Company held control of the main trafficking plazas of Michoacán. But since 2006 the main objective of La Familia had been to expel the Zetas from the state and particularly from the Tierra Caliente region,[7] its main area of operation. The Zetas by then controlled a very large portion of the state of Michoacán. After Tamaulipas, it seems that this group occupied the largest amount of territory in Michoacán. This is probably why its former local allies rebelled and broke the alliance (Aguilar Camín 2014, par. 16). Afterward, the war for Michoacán started and ended up in multiple confrontations and assassinations between the Company and La Familia. On September 15, 2008, during the Independence Day celebration, a gre-

nade attack took place in the central plaza of the capital city, Morelia; this was considered by some an act of "narcoterrorism" (Guerrero
2014b).[8]

Violence in Michoacán reached extremely high levels that lasted for
several years—taking place in different forms and incorporating different groups, including the Mexican federal government. Subsequently,
another criminal organization with origins in La Familia Michoacana
appeared in the state: Los Caballeros Templarios (the Knights Templar
or Los Templarios). Both La Familia and Los Templarios applied the
Zeta model and committed numerous crimes. Extortion, kidnappings,
and other practices introduced by the Zetas were perpetrated by these
two very violent groups throughout the state. Moreover, their network
of conspirators included municipal authorities and state law enforcement officials, the same as the Zeta model.

Due to the extreme violence generated by the fight between the
Company and La Familia, and the extreme brutality of the criminal
groups operating in Michoacán, the federal government reacted by
dispatching the military and federal police, thus increasing the levels
of violence and the number of assassinations and disappearances in
the state. As a response to the attack by the federal government and
the weakening of La Familia, the Knights Templar surged as the most
important crime group in the state. It grew by utilizing the structure
of the group that once dominated the state after the Zetas. According to some versions, Los Templarios introduced themselves in March
2011, declaring that they would continue with the "altruistic activities
that were previously performed by La Familia Michoacana" (Guerrero
2014b, par. 23).

In fact, the leadership of the "new" organization was able to incorporate most of the structure of La Familia and thus "was able to retake
the control of most of their criminal activities, reactivate their political
connections and reorganize their bases of social support" (Guerrero
2014b, par. 23). The Zeta model was evident in the future development of this group and its main practices. According to some sources,
a number of members of the Knights Templar had received military
training. Some have even alleged that, like the Zetas, Los Templarios
were "trained in special operations by the governments of the United
States, Israel and Egypt when they were part of the Armed Forces"
(Reyes 2014, par. 3). As in the case of the Zetas, "the formation of the
leaders, killers and operators of the Knights Templar was similar to

the one acquired by members of the Special Forces Airmobile Group (GAFE) of the Mexican army" (Reyes 2014, par. 4).

The Zetas Today

Rise and Decline of the Zetas

RISE: THE "NUMBER ONE" CRIMINAL ORGANIZATION?

The Zetas' growth was so rapid and extended to such a vast territory of the Mexican Republic that some thought of this group at some point as the number one cartel. Actually, according to one source, in 2012 "[t]he Zetas organization had turned into the criminal group with the highest presence in the nation, even above the Sinaloa Cartel" (*Vanguardia* 2012, par. 1). According to a document released by the Division of Intelligence and Research of the Federal Police, by 2013 seven TCOs were operating in Mexico and fighting for the control of the main smuggling plazas. Of these groups, the document says, the Zetas had the greatest presence in the country, operating in twenty-one states. In five states (Hidalgo, Campeche, Puebla, San Luis Potosí, and Yucatán) the Zetas operated without the presence of any other criminal organization (*Vanguardia* 2012).

The Zetas' expansion and the control that they exercised in large parts of Mexico were acknowledged by Strategic Forecasting Inc. (Stratfor), a Texas consulting firm specializing in security (*Vanguardia* 2012, par. 10). In 2013 this company mentioned that the growth of the criminal organization had been higher than expected, notwithstanding the attack by the federal forces (ADN Político 2013). Moreover, according to Stratfor, the Zetas operated in the largest portion of the Mexican territory compared to other criminal groups. According to this view, their presence was even higher than that of the Sinaloa Cartel (*Vanguardia* 2012). This so-called third-generation gang was also considered the most dangerous criminal syndicate in Mexico and Central America.[9]

Notwithstanding the significant power acquired by the Zetas during their first years of independence from the Gulf Cartel, the organization started to weaken considerably, allegedly because of the operations by the federal police and the armed forces, which killed or detained a significant number of its members. They also arrested the top leaders, which caused fragmentation of some key cells within this criminal syndicate. Moreover, the Zetas were persecuted and targeted by other rival TCOs.[10]

DECLINE

Some analysts point to the decline of the organization created by Osiel Cárdenas (Pérez 2014, par. 2). However, this criminal group had experienced important losses in previous years.[11] For example, in 2011, two top Zeta leaders, Jesús Enrique Rejón Aguilar (aka El Mamito) and Iván Velázquez Caballero (aka El Talibán), were arrested. A year later, on October 7, 2012, the alleged Zetas' top commander, Heriberto Lazcano (aka El Lazca, Z-3, or the Executioner), was purportedly killed by the Mexican navy.[12] In mid-July 2013, his successor, Miguel Ángel Treviño Morales (aka Z-40), was arrested in Tamaulipas, reportedly with the help of US intelligence.[13]

According to most sources, after the arrest of Z-40, his brother Omar Treviño Morales (aka Z-42) became the top leader of the organization.[14] In subsequent months the Mexican federal forces captured or killed a number of important Zeta leaders in Tamaulipas, Coahuila, and Veracruz, such as Román Ricardo Palomo Rincones (aka El Coyote), who was identified as the person in charge of the migrant massacre in San Fernando, Tamaulipas (Guerrero 2014a). Another example was the assassination by the Mexican armed forces of Galindo Mellado Cruz (aka Z-9), who was allegedly an original Zeta member. The death of Mellado Cruz is considered by some to be evidence of the erosion of the Zetas (Pérez 2014, par. 3).

All these high-level arrests and assassinations of Zeta leaders by Mexico's federal forces have apparently weakened this criminal organization considerably. Moreover, the confrontation that the Zetas have maintained with their former allies of the Gulf Cartel might also have contributed to their decline. According to the testimony of El Mamito (a historic leader of the Zetas) at a federal trial in Austin, Texas, the organization had an income of nearly $350 million a year from transporting 40 tons of cocaine to the United States. He explained that most of the money had been utilized to finance the war against its former allies of the CDG since 2010 (*Reforma/El Norte* 2013).

The decline of the Zetas organization might have to do with a number of failures in its model of organized crime. According to Guerrero (2014a, par. 19), one of them was "the lack of family links that would add certainty and trust to the relationships between the top members of the organization." Actually, this criminal organization resorted to violence as a way to spawn discipline and assure internal control. This generated tension among its members and instability in its leadership structures. In Guerrero's view, another problem was the "indiscriminate use of violence"; "this engendered fear and limited the construction of a social base" that would support the group's activities. Such elements seemed to be important for other traditional drug-trafficking organizations such as the Sinaloa Cartel or the Juárez Cartel. A further limitation of the Zeta model was their recruiting methodologies. As Guerrero (2014a) explains, the Zetas did not recruit their members from family or friends like other organizations did, which assured some control over the people they hired. The Zetas established some important controls initially, since they "recruited military personnel and applied a strict military discipline," but they started losing these controls when they started recruiting "any local criminals willing to work for them" (Guerrero 2014a, par. 19).

The End of the Zetas?

According to a number of versions, the Zetas have been significantly weakened and their decline is a result of the Zeta model itself and effective operations by Mexico's federal forces. According to Malcolm Beith (2013, 19), "Los Zetas will likely remain a ragtag operation, intent on violence and willing to engage in almost any illicit activity for profit, but increasingly disorganized and, as a result, less in control of drug trafficking and less capable of undermining the authorities and the state." Juan Pérez (2014, par. 19) adds that today drug trafficking is not the Zetas' main activity, so the membership now consists of inexpert and young plaza chiefs, who have worked for the organization for a very short time and who dedicate themselves to any criminal activity—such as kidnapping and extortion—in a disorganized way.

However, not everybody agrees with these ideas. For example, after the arrest of Omar Treviño Morales in March 2015, Arturo Fontes, a former FBI agent who worked in several investigations related to the Zetas, declared in a *Dallas Morning News* article: "The Zetas remain formidable and are revamping. The infrastructure remains intact, largely made up of family members waiting for their turn" (Corchado 2015, par. 14). This vision is shared by the global-security consulting firm Stratfor. In a report titled "Mexico's Zetas Are Not Finished Yet," Stratfor analysts Scott Stewart and Tristan Reed (2013, par. 1) suggest that the Zetas have not been dismantled and reject the idea that this group is now little more than a "ragtag operation." They recognize that both the current and past administrations have specifically listed the group as a priority target and that all this attention has indeed impacted the organization. Stewart and Reed (2013, par. 2) also highlight the arrest or killing of several key plaza bosses; despite the leadership losses, however, they believe that the Zetas "have maintained their operational capabilities in terms of drug smuggling and other criminal activities, and that they have retained the ability to defend their operations and to continue conducting offensive operations deep in their rivals' territory."

According to some accounts, the organization recently has been trying to change its extremely violent image and is trying to do business more silently, without attracting so much attention from the federal authorities. Stewart and Reed (2013, par. 18) support this idea and claim that the group "has adopted a lower profile, with far fewer high-profile acts of violence and public displays of bodies and *narcomantas*." For the Stratfor analysts, this does not mean that "the group is any less violent"; nor do they see "indicators suggesting the group has weakened." According to them, it appears that the Zetas "have made a conscious decision to attempt to lower their press and public profile in hopes of reducing government pressure on them" (par. 18).

The Stratfor analysis makes a further interesting point about what happens to the Zetas' main plaza of Nuevo Laredo and the key northern city of Monterrey—a major transportation hub in northeastern Mexico and allegedly a plaza that still has a strong Zeta presence. In this regard, Stewart and Reed (2013, par. 19) "hypothesized that if the organization had indeed been weakened, the other cartels would be aware of the weakness" and would make an effort to take the control of these extremely lucrative plazas. They observe that the death or arrest of the main Zeta leaders in recent years has not led to any major war or confrontation for the control of Nuevo Laredo. Based "on the lack of observable violence" in this city, Stewart and Reed (2013, par. 19) concluded that the "Zetas remain in control of that plaza and . . . contraband continues to flow through it." The same is true for Monterrey, which is a major industrial center and therefore also a "major hub for illicit trade" (par. 20).

In sum, although the main Zeta leaders have been executed or arrested, Stratfor has not found evidence of a true decline of this criminal organization that has been visibly successful since the beginning of this century. In their view, "law enforcement efforts, infighting, power struggles and plain old greed will eventually weaken, if not destroy, Los Zetas. But that has not yet happened, and Los Zetas remain a powerful organization engaged in a diverse range of criminal activities across a large portion of Mexico—and the globe" (Stewart and Reed 2013, par. 21). According to them, "a quiet plaza is a productive plaza." Therefore the less violence there is in a trafficking or smuggling corridor, "the better that is for the business of the organized crime group that controls it. A lack of violence in a plaza is also a sign that it is under the uncontested control of a particular organization" (par. 19).

Similarly, journalist Diego Osorno claims that "it is not possible to talk about a disintegration or 'balkanization' of the Zetas," because they were born fragmented—in cells. According to this view, the original Zetas created their own groups in various parts of the country and operated a number of different businesses. Subsequently they formed a coalition. That was the great novelty of the Zetas. "This is not like a family or a group of families like the Sinaloa Cartel" (quoted in Pérez 2014, par. 34). Journalist Ricardo Ravelo concurs, noting that "this group is totally different compared to the [drug-trafficking organizations] that we traditionally know" (quoted in Pérez 2014, par. 34). In his view, "the Zetas operate like cells, similar to the Revolutionary Armed Forces of Colombia (FARC)." These cells have a specific leadership, accounting bases, and a structure to kill and exercise violence. For Ravelo, these cells operate like "franchises" (quoted in Pérez 2014, par. 34). Ravelo also does not think that the criminal organization is in decline but thinks that it is actually experiencing realignment. "The fall of its main leaders would generate a sort of recycling within the organization." Actually, one of the main strengths of the Zetas, according to Ravelo, is their constant and successful "internal crisis management" (quoted in Pérez 2014, par. 35).

Likewise, the very active and well-known social media user "Valor por Tamaulipas" (Courage for Tamaulipas) does not believe that the Zetas are disintegrating and argues that this crime group "has always acted independently, [and that] each of its cells is like a minicartel."[15] According to this view, the arrest of a leader (who controls only a cell) does not affect the organization as a whole (quoted in Pérez 2014, par. 41). For this social media user who covers events related to organized crime in Tamaulipas, the Zetas "can be more affected by adverse regional events than by a disarticulated leadership. If one leader is detained, the group continues operating with normalcy. Its structure and hierarchies allow the group to realign without much problem" (quoted in Pérez 2014, par. 42).

Journalist Diego Osorno agrees with this view. He stated that since 2010 he has been told by Mexican authorities about a definite crisis of the Zetas organization. But Osorno believes that this is not clear and that the solution to the insecurity problem in Mexico is not related to arrests or deaths of criminals. Actually, according to Osorno, "the problem has political roots": if the political and economic networks generated by the Zetas continue to operate, this criminal organization will survive and will continue mutating (Pérez 2014, par. 46). With regard to the recent arrests of Zeta leaders, particularly the detention of Omar Treviño Morales in 2015, he says that "we are now at number 42, but we can reach an infinite number of Zeta leaders" (Pérez 2014, par. 45).

Probably the main problem when trying to make an accurate assessment of the present situation of the Zetas—and to anticipate their future with more certainty—is that the criminal group has been analyzed as if it were a traditional drug-trafficking organization. But the Zetas apparently function in a different way and can be better understood by utilizing different analytic frameworks. Recent journalistic stories and reports produced by law enforcement agencies—both in Mexico and the United States—have focused on the Zetas' leadership. For example, after the arrest of the alleged top leader of the organization, Omar Treviño, US law enforcement agencies started to speculate about his plausible successor. The information and speculation about who could become "the next top Zeta boss" extended to both sides of the border (Padilla 2015). In this specific case, the discussion focused on individual leaders, but this approach might not be helpful in understanding the present and future of this organization. According to Arron Daugherty and Steven Dudley (2015, pars. 9–10):

> The Zetas are not just violent because their leaders have a penchant for aggression—they follow an economic model that relies on controlling territory in a violent way. Within that territory, they extract rents from other criminal actors and move only a limited number of illegal goods via some of their own networks. . . . Without that territory, they have no rent (known in Mexico as "piso"). The Zetas are, in essence, parasites. Their model depends on their ability to be more powerful and violent than their counterparts, so they can extract this rent.

Guerrero (2014a, par. 18) agrees with this interpretation. In his view, Los Zetas "transformed the traditional way in which drug trafficking organizations had operated in Mexico." The Zetas brought with them a new criminal model that transformed "hierarchical enterprises, predominantly familiar, guarded by amateur killers, that restricted their moves to specific territorial spaces and activities" into "more horizontal organizations with a professional armed wing, aggressive expansionist aspirations," and an interest in a variety of criminal activities that go beyond drug smuggling. For Guerrero (2014a, par. 18), one of the main reasons for this transformation is that the Zetas incorporated "a strong territorial feature into the drug-trafficking business, and thus it was not enough to control only strategic points along the route utilized to transport drugs; it was necessary to control it all to minimize risks."[16]

CHAPTER 3

A Transnational Criminal Corporation

Z: . . . Nosotros también tenemos reglas. Somos como una empresa.
[Z: . . . *We also have rules. We are a business.*]
OSORNO (2013, RESPONSE TO JON LEE ANDERSON)

This chapter illustrates how the form of organized crime pioneered by the Zetas might be better understood by utilizing business administration academic literature. The assumption here—after a thorough analysis of this criminal organization—is that the Zetas and other similar groups have organized themselves like a multinational or transnational corporation (such as Wal-Mart, Berkshire Hathaway, Exxon-Mobil, General Electric, Apple, IBM, Procter & Gamble, or Royal Dutch Shell). This part analyzes the Zetas organization as a transnational and corporate phenomenon, describing its business structure, including its board of directors, different subsidiaries and holdings, and various divisions and departments (purchasing, sales, marketing, finance, human resources, and research and development). The Zetas' subsidiaries correspond to the diverse illegal activities that are now performed by different cells of the organization, such as drug trafficking, protection services, extortion and kidnapping, migrant smuggling and human trafficking, arms trafficking, illegal mining and logging, and the smuggling of hydrocarbons.

Los Zetas: A Transnational and Corporate Phenomenon

The "Official" Structure

Some "official" documents describe the structure, training, and operating methods of the Zetas. They consist of information provided by protected witnesses who allegedly belonged to the organization and who now collaborate with law enforcement agencies such as the Attorney General's Office (PGR). These sources have revealed some details of the Zetas, including a description of their alleged hierarchies (which are based on military discipline) and their basic practices. The PGR reports also provide information on how different functions of the group, such as counterintelligence, recruitment, and even attacks and executions, operate and serve as control mechanisms.[1]

The most popular of these documents mentions a hierarchy of Zetas formed by Old Zetas (Zetas Viejos), New Zetas (Zetas Nuevos), Cobras (also called Ls), *halcones* (informants), and other civilian members of the organization performing different activities. Based on these reports, the Congressional Research Service (CRS) described the Zetas as "a sophisticated, three-tiered organization with leaders and middlemen who coordinate contracts with petty criminals to carry out street work" (quoted in Brands 2009a, par. 13). The Old and New Zetas are at the top and "draw on the support of a range of groups that operate according to a division of labor" (Brands 2009a, par. 14). Below them are other members involved in a number of activities, including smuggling and distribution of illegal products, enforcement, arms trafficking, intelligence gathering, and money laundering. "At the bottom of the organization are common criminals who perform a variety of unglamorous but essential tasks" (Brands 2009a, par. 13). It is also worthwhile noting that each Zeta plaza has a number of informants as well as a number of accountants. The accountants, who are in charge of the economic resources of the organization, not only pay salaries to members but also pay the bribes to public officials with links to the organization (Gómez 2008).

The Zetas, according to this information, organize into cells or formations called *estacas* (stakes) that operate like military squadrons. The *estacas* perpetrate kidnappings and executions of enemies to assure the control of the different trafficking plazas (Otero 2007). These cells are key to daily operations and provide security to high and mid-level leaders. They are formed by civilians or former military personnel (Otero 2007, par. 1). It is worth noting that the *estacas*, according to these reports, maintained a rotation of tasks inspired by military practices (Padgett 2013b).

At the top of its hierarchy were the original Zetas (so-called Old Zetas). Initially they were the top leaders who controlled the major drug-trafficking routes in cities from Matamoros to Nuevo Laredo (Brands 2009a, par. 13). Most of the Old Zetas were once part of the

GAFE (founded in the 1990s) or members of the Mexican army's Special Forces. According to a number of sources, this group had thirty to forty members.[2] Today they are dead or have been arrested.

The next level of Zetas were allegedly those in charge of the points of distribution of illegal products. They were called "New Zetas," and among their main tasks was the protection of the "Old Zetas." They were also well trained and equipped with high-caliber weapons. Some of them were Kaibiles (former members of the Guatemalan army), who had received especial training and had access to specialized military equipment. According to law enforcement reports, the New Zetas were in charge of committing executions and performing key operations under the command of the Old Zetas. This group was also formed by members who had deserted from the elite corps of the Secretariat of National Defense (SEDENA) but had arrived later in the organization.

The Zeta hierarchy also includes members without military background who perform important tasks or have been in the organization for a long time. These are the so-called Ls or Cobras.[3] Another relevant part of the Zetas' structure are the *halcones* ("the eyes of the city" or watchers) (Gómez 2008), who represent the intelligence networks of the organization. They facilitate the work of the *estacas* by collecting information on the movements and operations of the police or rival groups. Their work is to eliminate plausible threats to the organization and its members (Otero 2007).

Misconceptions about Los Zetas

The preceding explanation is drawn from official accounts of how the Zetas operate regionally, mainly in Tamaulipas, but these versions are incomplete and not totally accurate. There are several misconceptions about the Zetas, starting with the fact that this group is not a conventional drug-trafficking organization; it is difficult to track this group and discover exact details on its complex structure. One of the problems that researchers encounter when trying to understand the structure of TCOs is that "there is very little useful information about how [these groups] operate and how they are organized." Even though "Mexico's security forces arrest hundreds of suspects every year, . . . these arrests do not produce much useful intelligence on the organization of these criminal groups" (Bailey 2011, par. 2). Therefore it is sometimes necessary to work just with hypotheses due to the lack of solid information.

Table 3.1. The Traditional TCO Model vs. the Zeta Model

	Traditional TCO	Los Zetas
Activity	drug trafficking	diversification of criminal activities
Hierarchy	strong, vertical	horizontal, decentralized
Leadership/organization, structure	family ties, cronyism, compadre system	networks
Enforcers	guarded by amateur killers	professional armed wing
Territorial control	moves restricted to specific territorial spaces	aggressive expansionist aspirations
Violence	controlled, disciplined	indiscriminate, brutal

Several existing hypotheses seem to be mistaken and offer limited explanations of this very complex and novel criminal organization. The majority of those who have written about the Zetas in depth are journalists, and most of them have focused on narrow aspects of the organization. For example, in 2012 journalist Diego Osorno published a book titled *La guerra de los Zetas: Viaje por la frontera de la necropolítica* (The Zetas' War: A Journey through the Border of Necropolitics [Mexico City: Grijalbo]). In Osorno's book it is difficult to identify the main national and international political figures and interest groups participating in what he denominates the "Zetas' war." Neither can the reader clearly identify who really benefits from the extreme violence caused by this criminal syndicate. Moreover, Osorno's account is limited, as it is centered on only two Mexican states and does not acknowledge or mention the strong presence and connections of this group in other parts of the world, like Central America (Correa-Cabrera 2014b).

Osorno's text is just one of many recent works in the same vein, sensationalizing violence and blowing some key events out of proportion.[4] But texts like these are nonetheless useful because they provide some context regarding the criminal group's activities and its leadership. Unfortunately, however, fundamental questions remain unanswered (Correa-Cabrera 2014b). Some basic considerations need to be taken into account when analyzing the Zetas and similar groups—such as La Familia Michoacana, the Knights Templar, or the CJNG (see table 3.1

and appendix 6). First of all, it seems important to recognize the Zetas' exceptionality. Analysts Dwight Dyer and Daniel Sachs (2013, par. 3) correctly point out that the "Zetas are not the archetypal drug-smuggling organization." They say there are some basic characteristics that distinguish this criminal group from traditional TCOs.

First, this group "has managed to diversify its sources of revenue. Rather than concentrating on trafficking drugs, the Zetas' portfolio includes everything from piracy, extortion, kidnapping, and migrant smuggling to theft from oil pipelines and levying taxes on other criminal organizations" (Dyer and Sachs 2013, par. 3). In their view, "some of these activities provide the group with greater profits than they receive from drugs. And the Zetas' drug trade is itself diversified" (Dyer and Sachs 2013, par. 3). Moreover, not only does the organization "smuggle drugs into the United States, where there is a considerable markup in prices; it also supplies local drug markets along the entire route to the United States from Central America" (Dyer and Sachs 2013, par. 3).

In fact, the type of violence utilized by the Zetas does not seem to have its origins solely in the drug trade. Analysts, politicians, and journalists often attribute the current situation of extreme violence in some parts of the country exclusively to drug trafficking. Most analysts use the terms "organized crime" and "drug trafficking" as if they are synonymous. However, this approach does not seem very useful when trying to understand the real reasons behind the security problem in Mexico. Mexico's problem is certainly related to groups—or "companies"—dedicated to selling drugs. However, we should not forget that drug trafficking is not the only activity performed by the Zetas and similar groups. For analysts Viridiana Ríos and Steven Dudley (2013), the Zetas changed the paradigm of what was a territory for criminal activities. This criminal group was a pioneer in searching for markets located in areas in which drug trafficking had no significant role.[5] Hence this allowed an important diversification of criminal activities (par. 10).

Another relevant feature of the Zetas that has not always been well understood by reporters, analysts, and certain government officials is its organizational structure. Dyer and Sachs (2013, par. 4) recognize that "instead of developing a strong, vertical hierarchy," the criminal group has "built a horizontal, decentralized one. The Zetas do have identifiable leaders, but its individual cells have always been empowered to exploit opportunities available in their respective [plazas].

They do not have to wait for a top commander to issue ordei sense, their structure is quite different from that of other t TCOs, such as the Sinaloa Cartel.

Most believe that the leadership and organizational structi .... Sinaloa Cartel have functioned through family ties, so relationships within this organization have been historically built through marriage, cronyism, or the *compadres* system. This feature, according to journalist Alberto Nájar (2006), has been key to the group's success. The leaders would come from Sinaloa and act like a family. This is why sometimes the group has been called "the Alliance of Blood" (la Alianza de Sangre) (Nájar 2006). The Zetas seem to operate in a very different way. In the view of Professor John Bailey (2011), the group functions more through networks than through hierarchies (see table 3.1). In this regard he states:

> The networks are composed of different kinds of organizations, some of which may be hierarchies or loose alliances between friends or business associates. One advantage of networks is that the member organizations, or nodes, can be replaced and new connections can be easily constructed to replace the previous ones. Governments constantly attack a network just to see how new nodes replace the previous ones. (par. 3)

Another distinctive characteristic of the Zetas and similar groups is "a penchant for indiscriminate, brutal violence" (Dyer and Sachs 2013, par. 4). Beheadings, dissolving corpses in acid, and other similar practices became widespread since the appearance of the Zetas. On the surface, it seems to make no sense for criminal groups to attract attention from the law enforcement community (national and international) by utilizing such practices. However, the Zetas appeared to have different objectives than most criminal organizations. To members of the Zetas, generating fear in this way would benefit them in other endeavors, such as when they asked for ransom after a kidnapping or when attempting extortion. In these situations, fear would be on the Zetas' side.

In sum, the Zetas have changed the face of organized crime in Mexico. The new model introduced by them is quite sophisticated and complex, involving several factors. Among these elements, Salvadoran analyst and former guerrilla leader Joaquín Villalobos (2011) recognizes the "financial power" generated from different forms of illicit trade (involving different products, not only drugs). Other factors identified by Villalobos are the "social force" involving a significant number of persons dedicated to illicit activities, territorial control, the "state's cooptation or substitution," armed power, global interconnection, and cultural empowerment (11) (see table 3.1).

The Zetas Go Corporate

Criminal groups like the Gulf Cartel and the Zetas have the same essential goal as any other corporation: to maximize profits. Their operating structures are also very similar to those of any legal business (Correa-Cabrera 2012). This was evident in the seven-day trial of Juan Roberto Rincón-Rincón, a high-ranking member of the CDG who was convicted of drug trafficking.[6] In that trial Rafael Cárdenas-Vela, Osiel Cárdenas's nephew, pleaded guilty and provided detailed testimony about the CDG, including its structure, operations, and internal power struggles (FBI 2012). "When prosecutors asked Cárdenas to walk jurors through a decade of moves in the [organization's] command and control structure, he turned to a giant organizational chart that would be recognizable to anyone in the corporate world" (Sherman 2012, par. 4). He talked about the business's managers and accountants and all the activities that pertain to any legal corporation.[7]

The Zetas, like its mother organization, the Gulf Cartel, operated as a corporation. But as time passed by, it became more sophisticated and started operating in more countries and regions and turned into a multinational or transnational criminal organization. When the Zetas and the CDG formed the "Company," they actually offered "what any other company would in benefits," except they were devoted to criminal activities, including drug trafficking (Paley 2011, 23). What is more, the two organizations, as well as other groups of the same kind in Mexico, adopted business practices and strategies similar to those characterizing any other multinational corporation. Hence we can affirm that organized crime in Mexico can be analyzed as a transnational and corporate phenomenon. And, as stated by US Marine veteran José Nava, "This phenomenon involves criminal entrepreneurs."[8]

Some onlookers have started to analyze organizations like the Zetas by scrutinizing their business model (for example, Wainwright 2016). Ríos and Dudley (2013, par. 6) also attribute the success of the Zetas to their adoption of a "unique business strategy in the criminal world." In their view, this criminal corporation "not only tried to conquer new markets but snatched existing ones" (par. 7). For these analysts, the Zetas' expansion can be better understood by considering its unique "business focus—strategic, diversified, pragmatic, risk taking, and searching for 'criminal talent'"—more than its terrorist tactics or military capacity (Rios and Dudley 2013, par. 16). This idea coincides with that of Ralph Reyes, the chief of the DEA office for Mexico and Central America in 2014, who claimed that the Zetas "evolved from a militaristic chain of command to a business structure, with quarterly meetings, business ledgers, even votes on key assassinations" (quoted in Grayson 2014b, 25).

Los Zetas: A Criminal Franchise?

According to Mexican journalist Ricardo Ravelo, the Zetas organization is the most violent "criminal franchise" that has operated in Mexico in the last few decades. Ravelo published a book titled *Zetas: La franquicia criminal* (Zetas: The Criminal Franchise, 2013), where he tried to explain the origins, structure, and particularly the causes of the very successful expansion of this criminal organization in the recent past. Ravelo claims that this criminal group turned into a large industry, with the support of political power. He also noted that the Zetas have multiplied by forming small cells throughout Mexico; he considers such cells "franchises" (Ravelo 2013).

In his book Ravelo picks up John Bailey's idea, as expressed in an opinion piece in Mexico's newspaper *El Universal*, called "Los Zetas and McDonald's" (2011). Bailey argues that using a "franchise business model" to analyze the Zetas organization could be useful. In particular, he refers to a "mechanism in which different businesses may join under a recognized quality brand name. The McDonald's corporation operates only about 15% of its restaurants, while the rest are handled by independent contractors who pay fees to the parent company" (Bailey 2011, par. 6). In a model of this kind, "the most entrepreneurial Zetas can apply to operate in a particular plaza and pay fees to the lead organization for the use of its commercial name. Or a gang can independently negotiate a franchise with the most relevant Zeta node. In addition, Los Zetas' franchisees typically diversify into activities such as extortion or kidnapping to earn additional profits" (par. 7).

Ravelo explains in his book how the Zetas have multiplied into small cells (*estacas*) that operate like franchises made up of a team of killers, informants, and accountants. He also shows the difference between this kind of franchise organization and the pyramid structure of more traditional drug-trafficking organizations. The Zetas' structure, according to Ravelo, allows more flexibility. But Ravelo's analysis seems to be essentially focusing on the killing industry (*sicariato*), which is just one part of a complex organization that includes many other business activities.

Notwithstanding his recognition of the existence of other areas that form part of this corporation, Ravelo does not analyze them separately or thoroughly and does not design a conceptual framework that can help the reader understand the organization's real structure and operating methods. The utilization of the "criminal franchise" concept seems to apply solely to the killing industry and demonstrates a limited understanding of the organization's complexity and its aggressive and extensive diversification of activities. The Zetas group seems to operate by cells. However, the majority of these cells do not seem to act like franchises. In a business administration model, some of these cells are apparently functioning like subcontractors that make use of headhunters, trusted employees, and regional managers. In the Zetas case, the franchise model that involves a standard payment for brand usage and training does not seem to apply. Citizen journalist @MrCruzStar agrees with this idea by noting the following:[9]

> The Zetas operate as a transnational corporation that uses an expansive, aggressive, and predatory model based on territorial control. Such a model involves lobbyists who recruit key personnel in each plaza where the group arrives. They start new businesses with trusted employees that operate as regional managers—after training them in the areas of managerial development, public relations, and the use of military tactics. The Zetas' recruiters first obtain the local map of criminal activities in each plaza and then locate key regions and delinquent actors; subsequently, they proceed to recruit. In this process, local criminals decide whether or not they join the Zetas business as subcontractors—doing what they used to do (that is, participating in criminal businesses or illegal activities, killing, etc.)—and have no possibilities of negotiating the terms of the contract. In fact, these subcontractors will be signing a contract "in blood" [*contrato de sangre*]

most of the time. The recruitment would start with an "express kidnapping" or the performance of a mass execution—possibly one in which the bodies are displayed in a public place with a message that functions like a business card.

A franchise sells goods or services that are provided by the brand owner or franchisor that meet specific quality standards. Under this structure, the franchisee pays a royalty to a franchisor for the trademark and for acquiring training and advisory services in order to provide standard goods or services. The Zetas do not seem to function this way. According to @MrCruzStar, "Here the model functions in a reverse way. You do not approach the Zetas' brand owner to use this specific criminal trademark. The newcomers search for potential employees who already participate in criminal activities or illegal businesses, with the purpose of monopolizing such markets." The managers of this corporation "are able to accomplish these goals—which include the expansion of their existing businesses and the diversification of their supply of criminal goods and services—by conducting thorough market research and maintaining great lobbying capacity thanks to their possession of high-caliber weapons."

To utilize a business administration model with the aim of analyzing criminal organizations like the Zetas is reasonable, but the franchise model proposed by Bailey and Ravelo does not seem to be the most appropriate one. Hence, to compare the Zetas with companies like McDonald's, Subway, 7-Eleven, or Pizza Hut does not seem to be very useful. A better comparison seems to be likening the Zetas to transnational corporations like Wal-Mart, Coca-Cola, HP, Nike, Berkshire Hathaway, ExxonMobil, and Royal Dutch Shell (see Wainwright 2016).[10]

The Zetas' Business Model

The Zeta Business Structure

When talking about the Zetas, most reporters and analysts mainly refer to killers and drug traffickers, utilizing the same analytical frameworks used to analyze more traditional drug-trafficking organizations. However, the Zetas are a different type of organization that has greatly transformed the face of organized crime in general. As already mentioned, the different components of the Zetas seem to operate more like networks than like hierarchies; these networks are transnational. Under this new model, "local networks" transform into "global structures" once they get interconnected (Villalobos 2011, 17). In fact, it is possible to consider Los Zetas a criminal transnational corporation that has greatly diversified and has transformed and reinvented itself in order to adapt to the new realities and reactions by the Mexican government—which has also adopted a military strategy allegedly to combat the new forms of organized crime.

Hence the Zetas organization should have a structure resembling that of any other transnational corporation, including a board of directors, probably made up of politicians and entrepreneurs. Underneath that board of directors we would expect to see a CEO and regional managers who would be in charge of trafficking different types of illegal goods and would perform certain illicit activities.[11] It might well be the case that these managers do not lead all the illegal businesses controlled by the Zetas in a particular region but only one or some of these businesses in key territories. This would be equivalent to having different directors of the different (tiered) subsidiaries in a transnational company (see appendix 5).

Professor Hal Brands (2009a, par. 15) states that "the Zetas have remained comparatively less hierarchical and less centralized" than many other Mexican drug trafficking organizations. In his view, as in the view of many analysts, "the group is divided into various cells, which take direction from . . . the central command but have little knowledge of the activities of other cells." Overall, this arrangement would be "beneficial from a security perspective, as it impedes police efforts to penetrate the organization and limits the damage that can be done by turncoats."

Below the regional managers and directors of the subsidiaries, the Zetas have regular employees who participate in different illegal activities—selling or moving drugs, stealing hydrocarbons, participating as killers, and so forth. In sum, the Zetas have developed a complex organizational structure that encompasses all of their criminal activities. The different subsidiaries of this transnational company seem to operate in a relatively independent way, and, at the same time, subcontract other companies to acquire some key services. The different subsidiaries of what can be called Los Zetas Inc. have a number of divisions or departments, including (1) marketing; (2) research, development, and technology; (3) human resources; and (4) finance. Moreover, the Zetas' business structure also contains a number of holding companies that allow the criminal corporation to diversify its risks and in particular to launder money.[12]

A Key Division: Marketing and the Zeta Brand

TCOs like the Zetas have some basic elements in common: (1) their transnational nature; (2) the diversification of their activities in an era of globalization; and (3) the strength of their brand. With regard to the "Zeta brand" (la marca Zeta), violence and fear are crucial elements. But it seems that the Zetas are not only an "assortment of sociopaths that terrify the cities they enter." According to Professor Rodrigo Canales (2013), the phenomenon that we observed over the past few years involving this group "is the result of a very careful branding and business strategy." In his view, the "carnage [was] not about faceless, ignorant goons mindlessly killing each other, but [was] rather the result of some seriously sophisticated brand management."

What could be considered the marketing division of Los Zetas Inc. is central to understanding the group's functioning and relative success. While not being formally established, "it would perform tasks similar to those carried out by marketing divisions of legal enterprises, including developing market strategies and doing market research, public relations, advertising, promotion, and creative services," says Mexican entrepreneur Eloy Garza.[13] The initial success of this criminal organization seemed to stem from its effective propaganda, which made use of social media and sophisticated communication technology.

At the same time, the organization used fear as a tactic for marketing purposes through its mass assassinations, decapitations, narco-blockades, and display of narco-messages, which generated its ruthless reputation. Hence a "perverse public relations campaign [helped to disseminate] the Zetas' exploits to a wide audience and [reinforced] the mystique that [surrounded] the organization" (Brands 2009a, par. 22). Professor Fernando Escalante (2009: 92) claims that the appearance of the Zetas for the first time brought "assassinations used to send messages to the public; decapitated and mutilated bodies with written messages; . . . massacres, mass assassinations of between 10 and 20 persons; and [generalized] attacks against police and military personnel." Most of these events, he believes, were covered by the mass media and contributed "to create a sensation of insecurity," which was in the end "echoed by international public opinion" (92).

Overall, these spectacular assassinations contributed to a climate of fear and a general sensation of insecurity that would benefit this criminal organization in its performance of predatory activities (93).

The Zetas introduced a generalized usage of the mass media to cover their violent actions. The organization was also a pioneer in using social media (blogs, Twitter, Facebook, and so forth) to fight other rivals and the government itself. By promoting their image and violent reputation through these marketing strategies, the Zetas presented themselves as a credible threat, which helped them move into new activities, such as kidnapping and extortion. To Ríos and Dudley (2013), the Zetas' model was created with the idea that it was not necessary to be involved in drug trafficking to be successful. The group would then dedicate itself to a number of new different activities and also subcontract other criminal actors to perform additional tasks. Some of these groups would be forced to participate in the Zetas' businesses through terror tactics. "The Zeta brand [was] a sign of terror, and this is why people [responded] to it" (par. 11).

In the opinion of a citizen journalist based in Reynosa, "Communication media (formal and informal) was the key tool utilized by the Zetas to elevate its prestige as an organization that could provide effective private protection as one of its main services."[14] As analyst Marco A. Rodríguez (2006, par. 44) recognizes, media have acted independently as vehicles to communicate "business propaganda," at no cost to the Zetas. Media coverage of different types has effectively promoted the Zeta brand and furthered its reputation as a keeper of the peace. After reading in the press or listening to radio horror stories about mass executions and extreme violence perpetrated by the Zetas, it is difficult to imagine that a potential client visited by members of this group would ignore them and abstain from paying the required fees. The same would happen with kidnappings for ransom.

Marketing strategies like this have also been used by other criminal groups. The Federation's battle against the Zetas, and the involvement of Édgar Valdez Villarreal (La Barbie) in this fight, greatly contributed to elevate the public exposure of two criminal alliances through the use of narco-messages, videos, and mass and social media (see the section on "Communicating a Narco-War" in chapter 1). Even some academics contributed to promoting the Zetas' image as the most violent criminal gang operating in Mexico. Professor George W. Grayson (2014a, par. 2), for example, states that Los Zetas "acquired training in butchering their prey—with an emphasis on lopping off heads, performing castrations, and skinning bodies of live victims." Grayson (2014a, par. 4) even considered them "agents of Satan":

> To attract broad print and electronic media coverage, these agents of Satan began slicing and dicing multiple enemies and arrayed their corpses in a pattern convenient for TV and newspaper photographers. In December 2008, Los Zetas captured and executed eight Army officers and enlisted men in Guerrero, a violence-torn, impoverished southern state that is home to Acapulco. Pictures of the headless cadavers lying side-by-side flashed around the world on television and YouTube. In addition, Los Zetas adeptly employed Google, Facebook, Twitter, and other social outlets to alert authorities and the populace to their ineffable viciousness.

Research, Development, and Technology

The Zetas also pioneered the use of new technologies and tactics, such as "coordinated infantry-style attacks, hyperviolent 'psy-ops' campaigns, sophisticated intelligence collection and communications." Through these alternative practices, it is believed by some that "the Zetas created a new road map for criminal enterprise." In this new context, "cartel-deployed aerial drones and sophisticated data-mining software that tracks law-enforcement patterns and predicts ideal smuggling schedules and routes may not be far off" (Tabor 2014, par. 32). In a transnational corporation, the development of these strategies would be part of a division of research, development, and technology. In the Zetas case, this division would include a complex covert communications and transportation network. In fact, each subsidiary of this criminal transnational corporation would need to acquire new communication technologies, military equipment, a sophisticated communication network, and effective transportation systems. Damon Tabor (2014, par. 29) describes these new developments as follows:

> At the height of its power, the group developed a Stasi-like army of spies and integrated technology and social media into their operations. The result, according to a report from the Mexican attorney general, was an intelligence network "without equal in the Americas." The Zetas monitored Twitter feeds, blogs, and Facebook accounts. They reportedly employed a team of computer hackers to track authorities with mapping software, and, according to one paper, 20 communications specialists

to intercept phone calls. On the street, the cartel's informants included taxi drivers, taco vendors, shoe shiners—and often the police. In Veracruz, an entire department was dissolved after a commander was recorded ordering subordinates to serve as what the Mexican public, increasingly wary of its law enforcement, has come to call "polizetas."

The Zetas were at some point considered to be the "most technologically advanced, sophisticated and violent" TCO in Mexico (Brands 2009a, par. 22). They built an "extensive, interconnected and very sophisticated" (Tabor 2014, par. 14) communications system on which they spent a significant amount of money. As part of this system, around 2006 the criminal organization began expanding a radio network, "first along the Texas border, then down the Gulf Coast to Guatemala, and eventually into Mexico's interior" (Tabor 2014, par. 14).[15] The system included handheld walkie-talkies, antennas, and signal repeaters to boost transmissions. This elaborate covert communications network enabled the criminal corporation to track everything related to its different illegal businesses, other criminal groups, and different law enforcement agencies. It also provided the Zetas with what is known as a command-and-control capacity, which connected the different members of this criminal group (Tabor 2014, par. 9).

Human Resources

At its peak, the Zetas were a very complex organization involving a large number of people. To perform their diversified illegal activities, the Zetas utilized a number of individuals, such as former military personnel, former police, gang members, street vendors, taxi drivers, homeless persons, and a number of people who served as couriers, spies, or lookouts. The Zetas made widespread use of a network of informants, so-called *halcones* (hawks), who perform their regular activities as taxi drivers or street vendors but also inform the organization about the movements of law enforcement agents and encroachment by other criminal groups. The *halcones* also guard or watch drug distribution areas. In other words, they seem to perform intelligence functions for departments or divisions in the corporation.

In order to recruit members who could fulfill all these duties, the Zetas needed some type of division that would focus specifically on human resources. This division would be in charge of assigning benefits and compensation, determining labor relations, developing human resources administration and information systems, and procuring professional and organizational development. The recruitment of personnel to further their brand strategy and to confront adversaries—such as other TCOs and the Mexican government—would be a key task for the Zetas' human resources division. In other words, this criminal group would be interested in hiring a significant number of people for the killing industry (*sicariato*). Actually, according to Professor Rodrigo Canales (2013):

> [The Zetas] focus most of their recruiting on the army, and they very openly advertise for better salaries, better benefits, better promotion paths, not to mention much better food, than what the army can deliver. The way they operate is that when they arrive in a locality, they let people know that they are there, and they go to the most powerful local gang and they say, "I offer you to be the local representative of the Zeta brand." If they agree—and you don't want to know what happens if they don't—they train them and they supervise them on how to run the most efficient criminal operation for that town, in exchange for royalties.

CONTRACT KILLINGS (*SICARIATO*)

The Zetas frequently subcontract other criminal groups to perform their killing activities. They usually approach local criminal groups or gangs that at one point operated independently.[16] According to Grayson (2014b, 40), in order to save resources, the Zetas subcontracted gangs like Barrio Azteca, the Texas Syndicate, MS-13, and the remnants of the Carrillo Fuentes and the Beltrán Leyva organizations.[17] He noticed that they have collaborated "with smaller drug trafficking groups in Guatemala, Colombia, and Venezuela." The Zetas have also recruited youngsters, minors, and illegal migrants trying to get to the United States to act as their assassins. It also appears that the group uses different groups of people for assassinations according to the available human resources in each region. For example, they have recruited gang members in Monterrey and Nuevo Laredo (where they are numerous and well organized),[18] and they recruit or force unauthorized migrants to participate with them in the *sicariato* in states like Tamaulipas or Coahuila, where the migration routes coincide with Zetas' drug trafficking or arms smuggling routes.

PARAMILITARY TRAINING CAMPS

According to some accounts, the Zetas organization "built remote narco-camps to train new recruits in military tactics, weapons, and communications" (Tabor 2014, par. 7). As previously mentioned, they also allegedly recruited former members of foreign armies' special forces, such as Guatemala's Kaibiles. In *Escuadrones de la muerte en México* (Death Squads in Mexico), former senator Ricardo Monreal (2013) describes how TCOs' groups of enforcers are formed, and alleges that some of them are supported by the Mexican government and others by private businesses. The Zetas would be an example of this. In Monreal's view, in order to belong to the Zetas organization, each key member received specialized training. Such training was acquired in ranches called *arroyos* (creeks), located in Tamaulipas, Nuevo León, and Coahuila. The training was allegedly military style and inspired by the training received by the special forces of the Mexican army (Padgett 2013b; Gómez 2008).

The Finance Department, Holdings, and Money Laundering

The finance department of such a complex organization like the Zetas would have a number of divisions, including accounting, purchasing, and administration and payroll. It would also operate with a number of treasurers, controllers, and accountants, probably organized by plaza or region. Tabor (2014, par. 8) claims that this criminal organization "instituted an accounting system" and at the same time "kept detailed ledgers and employed a dedicated team of number crunchers." In addition to the regular divisions that form part of the finance department of any corporation, a TCO like the Zetas would include a key area to transform illicit earnings and incorporate them into the legal economy.

MONEY LAUNDERING

There are several ways in which transnational criminal businesses like the Zetas move or invest the money that is illegally obtained. Organizations of this type launder money by acquiring properties, making bank deposits, and investing in a number of financial instruments within the "legal" financial system. Moreover, some of the Zetas' main money-laundering operations seem to have been performed through holding companies. A holding company or parent company is one that controls more than 50 percent of another company. It owns "enough voting stock in another company to control its policies and management. A holding company exists for the sole purpose of controlling another company, which might also be a corporation, limited partnership or limited liability company, rather than for the purpose of producing its own goods or services." The Zetas would launder money through companies of this kind that "also exist for the purpose of owning property such as real estate, patents, trademarks, stocks and other assets."[19]

In March 2015 Mexico's federal government captured Omar Treviño Morales (aka Z-42)—the alleged leader of the Zetas at the time. According to an investigation reported by *Milenio* newspaper, Treviño Morales was not the only one who led the organization's money-laundering operations. Behind the financial operations of this group were at least eight companies and at least four brokers. According to this report, the US Treasury identified the following companies that laundered money for the Zetas: Compañía Ganadera 5 Manantiales in Coahuila; ADT Petroservicios of Francisco, Colorado; a company located in Monterrey, Nuevo León, that distributed medical equipment, named Distribuidora e Importadora de Productos Médicos del Norte; Prodira Casa de Cambio and Trastreva in Zacatecas; and three US companies, Prodira Internacional and Nacional de Valores Services Inc. in Texas, and Prodira Inc. with branches in Arizona, Colorado, Iowa, and Texas (*Milenio* 2015).

One interesting way in which the Zetas laundered money was by buying and training racehorses in the United States. These operations were highlighted in a case heard by a Texas federal court in Austin in 2013. The trial has been touted as one of the biggest and most complex money-laundering cases ever prosecuted in central Texas. The case involved approximately twenty defendants, more than a dozen of whom pleaded guilty (Ulloa 2015, par. 7). The list of defendants included members of the family of the then leader of the organization, Miguel Ángel Treviño Morales (aka Z-40), "who allegedly ran a money laundering operation that stretched from Chicago to Venezuela" (Forsyth 2013, par. 3), through a shell company named Tremor Enterprises LLC. Reporter Jim Forsyth (2013, par. 11) explains how "prosecutors claim the defendants purchased a horse ranch in Oklahoma, bought several hundred horses, and managed to win several substantial races, including the All American Futurity, the major competition on the quarter horse circuit."

The transcripts of this case provide details of the activities and financial operations of this criminal organization. From this trial, the public learned that thanks to the protection of Mexican authorities—including the armed forces and Mexican police—the Zetas were able to transport to the United States approximately half a ton of cocaine per month, which represented for the organization income of nearly $15 million. Authorities said that the earnings were taken back to Mexico in cash and invested into several different front companies (Ulloa 2013). Testimony also provided information on the banks utilized by the Zetas to move or launder their illicit earnings. The organization allegedly utilized some of the largest US banks, including Bank of America and JPMorgan Chase and Co., to move the money.[20]

This is not the first time that a TCO has laundered money through the international banking system. The Sinaloa Cartel, for example, had used HSBC Bank to launder its illicit earnings. British journalist and writer Ed Vulliamy (2014) reports how HSBC acted as the organization's financial services wing and how the bank permitted TCOs and other criminal groups (even terrorist organizations) to launder hundreds of millions of dollars through its subsidiaries and facilitated their illicit transactions in a number of countries. Cases like these are only a few examples of the many money-laundering operations involving billions of dollars coming from illicit and criminal activities. For Melissa del Bosque, a *Texas Observer* reporter who covered the Zetas' money laundering case in Austin, "these operations do not recognize borders; they are all of transnational nature and involve government authorities at the highest levels as well as other multinational legal businesses."[21] What is more, it seems that money-laundering operations of transnational illicit businesses like the Zetas or the Sinaloa Cartel extend beyond the acquisition of properties (like houses or ranches) and deposits in Mexican banks. These organizations also seem to operate like holding companies—investing some portion of their illicit earnings in the acquisition and operation of "legal" businesses—and also make use of the transnational financial system and a variety of sophisticated financial instruments.

The Board of Directors

In order to understand how the Zetas' new entrepreneurial model of organized crime functions, it is necessary to identify the organization's main sources of support, beneficiaries, and key decision makers. In a business administration model, this would be equivalent to knowing more about the Zetas' finance department, shareholders, and board of directors. It does not seem very useful simply to know about regional managers or area directors—represented by popular leaders or plaza chiefs, whose actions are widely covered by the media. Organizations like the Zetas are illicit businesses that move billions of dollars and operate transnationally. As Center for Research and Advanced Studies in Social Anthropology (CIESAS) researcher Carlos Flores recognizes, "It is difficult to imagine that organizations of this type have been solely led by men with no business preparation like Miguel Ángel Treviño or Heriberto Lazcano or by other regional leaders that operate more like killers or drug smugglers, but might not have the entrepreneurial experience to lead such a sophisticated organization like the Zetas."[22]

Frequently, when talking about the Zetas, the focus has been on its leadership, particularly on key leaders who have the reputation of being extremely brutal and have had the capacity to order mass assassinations or have led massive battles against other criminal groups or the Mexican government. The Zetas seem to operate more like transnational corporations, so it is not possible to think of one single person—or even two or three—leading the operation of all the subsidiaries that the illegal company seems to have. In other words, because the Zetas controlled a vast portion of territory at some point and are dedicated to a variety of activities, it would make more sense to believe that their leadership is made up of a number of regional managers or directors of each subsidiary and maybe a CEO (see appendix 5). At the same time, as in any other transnational corporation, the Zetas could have a sort of board of directors that establishes "corporate management–related policies" and makes "decisions on major company issues."[23]

Thus the members of the Zetas' board of directors would be high-level politicians who have supported this criminal organization and contributed to its territorial expansion (such as governors, heads or regional directors of law enforcement agencies, and key figures in the federal government) as well as powerful entrepreneurs owning legal or illegal businesses (both national and foreign) that either launder money for the organization or greatly benefit from its criminal activities (energy companies, arms-producing firms, and companies that produce pirate videos and DVDs, among others: see appendix 5).

Some individuals mentioned in the 2013 Zetas money-laundering jury trial could form part of the "imagined" Zetas board of directors. It is worth noting that even if this board does not exist formally, the concept can help us to understand better the operation of this sophisticated criminal transnational corporation. As a matter of fact, the regional heads of the Zetas' killers (*sicarios*) and the local chiefs of plaza do not seem to be the real leaders of an organization of this kind; they seem to be just managers of an area, subsidiary, or region, for example. Some governors of states with an important Zeta presence such as Tamaulipas, Coahuila, and Veracruz have been key figures in this criminal organization, as have prominent entrepreneurs. People like Fidel Herrera, former governor of Veracruz, and oil businessman Francisco Colorado—two key figures in Los Zetas' 2013 money-laundering case—seem to have been actual decision makers who furthered the activities and businesses of this illegal transnational corporation.

In the 2013 Austin trial, a former accountant of La Compañía, José Carlos Hinojosa, testified that this organization (at that time including the Zetas and the Gulf Cartel) donated $12 million in 2004 to support the gubernatorial campaign of Fidel Herrera in Veracruz in exchange for political protection in the period 2004–2010. According to this testimony, Herrera accepted money from La Compañía via Francisco Colorado, owner of the company ADT Petroservicios (Pachico 2014). The US government claims that Colorado's company funded part of its activities through money coming from the Zetas' illegal activities. In these operations Francisco Colorado would utilize his "legal" business to launder money for the Zetas both in Mexico and in the United States.[24]

Allegedly, Colorado obtained contracts through Pemex (the Mexican oil company) and the Veracruz government, valued at more than 2,000 million pesos through its company ADT Petroservicios. At the same time, Colorado associated with Canadian energy companies, such as Xtreme Energy Group and West Rock Energy, and participated in Pemex's biddings processes of millions of dollars (MVS Research Unit 2014b). Actually, ADT Petroservicios participated in Pemex's public tenders until January 2014 and signed thirty contracts with the state-owned company during the period 2003–2011 that together represented around $170 million (MVS Research Unit 2014a, 2014b).

The case of the Zetas in Veracruz and the alleged involvement of the former governor and a prominent businessman is not the only one in Mexico. Other governors and ex-governors of states where the Zetas have had a strong presence also seem to have protected this criminal organization and contributed to its success in a number of illicit activities, including money laundering. The cases of two former governors of Tamaulipas, Tomás Yarrington and Eugenio Hernández, are emblematic.[25] We could think of these prominent politicians as members of the company's board of directors. Recent investigations on money laundering in the United States have shown the links of these two governors with the Zetas.

Eugenio Hernández, governor of Tamaulipas from 2005 to 2010, was charged with laundering bribes that were allegedly paid by the Zetas and with operating an unlicensed money transmitting business. US prosecutors have indicted a number of former Tamaulipas officials and business leaders and seized bank accounts and properties in Texas, particularly in San Antonio and the Rio Grande Valley, allegedly used to launder money (Contreras and Buch 2015). In a 2013 indictment,[26] Tomás Yarrington was charged with accepting millions of dollars to allow the Gulf Cartel and the Zetas to ship tons of cocaine through the state of Tamaulipas while he was governor between 1999 and 2005 (de Córdoba 2013). In November of the same year Jorge Juan Torres, who served as interim PRI governor of Coahuila (a Mexican border state with an important Zeta presence) from January 4, 2011, to December 1, 2011, was indicted on charges of money laundering and bank and wire fraud in Texas.

The Zetas' Subsidiaries

Under the present business model, the Zetas operate in several sectors and include a number of corporate divisions or "subsidiaries," plausibly managed by different people (see appendix 5). As already mentioned, the Zetas are involved in an array of activities, such as weapons smuggling, human trafficking, kidnappings, extortion, illegal mining, logging, and iron ore exporting as well as trafficking crude oil, natural gas, and gasoline stolen from Mexico's state petroleum company (Payán and Correa-Cabrera 2014a, 3). The Zetas seemed "willing to engage in any enterprise that would generate profit" (del Bosque and Ulloa 2014, par. 11). Other drug-trafficking organizations and criminal syndicates have also expanded their activities, inspired by this new model that assures alternative sources of income (for example, La Familia Michoacana, the Knights Templar, and CJNG). All of these activities are apparently relatively independent from each other and thus seem to operate as subsidiaries of the Zetas. A subsidiary is "a company that is partly or completely owned by another company that holds a controlling interest in the subsidiary company. . . . For the purposes of liability, taxation and regulation, subsidiaries are distinct legal entities."[27] The main subsidiaries of Los Zetas are discussed below.

Drug Trafficking

The Zetas organization is "a sophisticated, transnational enterprise trafficking in more than just illicit narcotics" (Ulloa 2013, par. 2), but drug trafficking is still a very extended and profitable business for this company. Some reports have identified a drug-trafficking network that "moved cocaine from Colombia and Venezuela to the northern Mexican border, where Zetas bosses directed the shipments as far north as Chicago" (Ulloa 2015, par. 8). Other investigations highlight the links between this transnational criminal organization and other sophisticated drug-trafficking networks in Europe and Africa. Apparently the Zetas learned well from the experience of their former partners in the Gulf Cartel and were able to extend this profitable business to various regions of the world in just a few years.

According to Libera (2012), an organization formed by a number of human rights associations from Europe and the Americas, the Zetas drug-trafficking business had extended to forty-three European countries by the end of 2012. In a report published in December of that year the organizations described the links between the Zetas and "the most powerful Italian mafia: the so-called 'Ndrangheta" (Proceso 2013c, par. 2). The report, entitled *Messico, la guerra invisibile* (Mexico, the Invisible War), identified the existence of a drug supply network operating from Central America to Mexico's northern border that expanded to Europe and was able to send to Italy approximately 40 percent of the cocaine production generated in Colombia, Bolivia, and Peru.[28] This study was elaborated with information collected by the Italian police (Proceso 2013c, par. 3).

Impunity and corruption in the countries involved in these operations contribute to the success of this criminal group worldwide. What is more, the alliance between the Zetas and the Italian mafia greatly benefits both groups.[29] Recent accounts explain that Los Zetas transport drugs from the Americas to Europe via African countries.[30] In these operations the 'Ndrangheta is responsible for guaranteeing the safe distribution of cocaine in European countries, particularly in Spain, Italy, the Netherlands, Germany, Portugal, and Russia. Apparently drug markets in Europe and Africa have become more significant for TCOs in the present era, particularly after the recent growing interdiction efforts along the US-Mexico border. In fact Mexican drug-trafficking organizations have been forced to look for alternative markets, particularly in Europe (Proceso 2013c; Libera 2012).

Protection Services

The Zetas found new markets and created subsidiaries that had never been part of traditional TCOs. The criminal group began to exercise some government functions that go beyond simply protecting its original business interests, related solely to drug trafficking. In its diversification of activities, this criminal syndicate began to exercise two additional functions that were once performed exclusively by the state: collecting taxes and policing or providing security. In fact the Zetas found new businesses closely associated with the extreme violence that they exercised and advertised through different means. The organization started to perform a variety of activities, including extortion and kidnapping, which were linked to the Zetas' capacity to exercise violence and provide protection because they had access to military training and high-caliber weapons. Of the categories of extortion prevalent in Mexico—including telephone extortion and cyber extortion—the so-called *cobro de derecho de piso* (forced protection payment) involved practices mainly introduced and extended by the Zetas. This mechanism operates as follows (Mexico Gulf Reporter 2011: par. 2):

> An extortionist drops by and has a friendly chat with a business owner, often a small proprietor. He explains that the two are now in business together. Once a week, or on some other regular basis, a collector arrives to pick up the designated rent from the owner. A failure or refusal to pay may be followed by disastrous consequences.

This mechanism illustrates new policing functions performed by the Zetas, who provide protection to those who pay the agreed fees. These payments represent more than a simple extortion; they are the fee, in essence, for the provision of a real service. The Zetas' clients avoid the harassment by other smaller criminal groups and local police forces, in a world in which property rights are rarely respected by public authorities (Rodríguez 2006). The Zetas actually started to compete directly with the municipal police for the provision of security services, which led to a large number of deaths among local police forces (Resa Nestares 2004, 3).

The Zetas started to offer protection services to clearly illegal businesses, such as those dedicated to the smuggling of narcotics or other illegal products, and continued to extort other businesses of unclear legal status, including bars that were subject to a number of official controls. Finally, forced protection payments were generalized and applied to legal businesses. The physical immobility of these types of businesses facilitated the extortion process and made them easy prey for the new criminal organization (Rodríguez 2006). It became easier for the Zeta *estacas* to extort a large number of local businesses once they acquired the "infrastructure and wherewithal to do it." In this particular activity, the Zetas were "not beholden to international revenue streams, but rather [lived] off of local criminal economies" (Daugherty and Dudley 2015, par. 13).

The Zetas were able to proceed this way thanks to the creation of their brand, which was founded on the extreme violence that they were able to exercise. Once they had acquired their prestige as an extremely violent group, it was relatively easy to extort a number of different persons and businesses. Thus the Zetas, according to Professor Carlos Resa Nestares (2004, 5), can be considered "a business card that intimidates on its own." With this idea in mind, security expert Eduardo Guerrero (2014a, par. 16) explains the Zetas' extortion process as follows:

> Their modus operandi consisted in grouping between 10 and 15 men in so-called "estacas," which operated in different cities—or plazas— in order to establish control over all the criminal activities that were developed there. The procedure to achieve this control was simple: they met the local criminal leaders to inform them that from [then] on everybody should pay a fee depending on their activity. If the owner of the business rejected the offer, he would be executed, and if he accepted, he would receive protection against government authorities or other criminal groups. Hence, through their association with criminals dedicated to different activities, the Zetas learned to operate a new business that allowed the group to diversify its sources of income. In particular, the provision of illegal protection services was in the end a very lucrative business. . . . [Overall, the Zetas] integrated a system-

atic and generalized form of exploitation of civil society to its criminal portfolio.

Migrant Smuggling and Human Trafficking

In order to diversify their revenue streams the Zetas also started to smuggle undocumented migrants, particularly along Mexico's eastern migration routes, from Central America to Mexico's northeastern border. As Sarah Stillman (2015, par. 22) recognizes, migrants are "easy prey." Thus the Zetas found a new business: they "took over northbound migration routes, charged fees to coyotes, and began snatching migrants from the tops of freight trains riding north; they [also] extorted victims' families," both in the migrants' countries of origin and in the United States. The vast majority of the migrants who have been extorted or trafficked by the Zetas—and then by other TCOs—come from the countries of Central America's Northern Triangle: El Salvador, Honduras, and Guatemala.

Scholars, journalists, and government authorities report that the Zetas have expanded their repertoire of illegal revenue-generating activities to include migrant smuggling and human trafficking for the purposes of labor, sexual exploitation, and body organ harvesting. Experts have documented that Mexico is a source, transit point, and destination country for trafficking in persons (Shirk and Webber 2004; Spener 2009; US Department of State, 2012, 2013). Events such as the brutal massacre of seventy-two migrants on August 25, 2010, in San Fernando, Tamaulipas, and the discovery of dozens of safe/stash houses along Mexico's northern border allegedly linked to the Zetas and other TCOs in the past couple of years demonstrate that drug trafficking, migrant smuggling, and trafficking in persons are becoming inextricably linked in unprecedented ways. "And the Zetas were the first ones who became involved in these three activities at the same time," says human-trafficking expert Jennifer Bryson Clark.[31]

The term "stash house" refers to a house where *coyotes* (migrant smugglers) keep the migrants—sometimes for several weeks and even months—while they await the next person who will guide them as they head north to the United States. Investigations show, for instance, that in 2008 police arrested members of a smuggling ring in San Marcos, Texas, "who had been holding immigrants at gunpoint in a safe house until they paid their transport fees to Los Zetas" (del Bosque and Ulloa 2014, par. 16). Many other migrant smuggling and trafficking operations—particularly along Mexico's eastern migration routes—have been linked to this criminal group. Official sources blamed the Zetas for executing the seventy-two undocumented migrants on a ranch in San Fernando, after the victims refused to work for the organization.

In the view of Marta Sánchez Soler of the civil society organization Movimiento Migrante Mesoamericano, the Zetas' strategy resembles "classic wholesale." According to Sánchez Soler, it is more profitable to kidnap and extort hundreds of undocumented migrants "whom nobody pays attention to," instead of targeting rich people. In her view, "when organized crime kidnaps somebody rich, the media and police mobilize," which would affect the criminals. This is not the case with poor migrants, who are crossing Mexico without authorization. Sánchez Soler estimates that "at least eighteen thousand migrants are seized in Mexico each year." Hence "if a third of their families pay a lowball ransom of four thousand dollars, that's twenty-four million dollars, with minimal risk or labor" (quoted in Stillman 2015, par. 27).

It seems that smugglers are "rational businessmen," and kidnapping and extortion of undocumented migrants is an exceptionally profitable business. According to Juan González, police chief of San Juan, Texas, in 2015, "you can make more money in the human-smuggling business than in the drug business" (quoted in Stillman 2015, par. 47). These operations have also involved Mexican authorities. Sánchez Soler also noted that local police officers have "also been known to take a cut of the ransom." She was referring to a document obtained by the National Security Archive, in Washington, DC, which revealed that "San Fernando police had helped turn migrants over to [the Zetas] in exchange for payoffs" (quoted in Stillman 2015, par. 28).

Stealing and Trafficking in Hydrocarbons

Another important division of Los Zetas is related to the hydrocarbon industry and Mexico's energy sector in general. The involvement of the criminal group in this sector has been extensive in recent times (Alvi 2014c). The Zetas actually have been infiltrating the state-run oil industry, Petróleos Mexicanos (Pemex), in order to diversify its sources of revenue. In fact the trafficking of large quantities of hydrocarbons has surged as one of the main sources of financing for Los Zetas. Some have even argued that earnings from this activity are higher than those obtained from kidnapping migrants and close to the amount made from selling drugs (Gurney 2014). For this type of criminal business, now "hydrocarbons are as lucrative as cocaine" (Pérez 2012, par. 4).

According to a number of investigations, the Zetas and other TCOs like the Gulf Cartel have "set up an extensive gasoline distribution system in north Mexico that rivals that of . . . Pemex, as oil-theft trade becomes an ever more sophisticated and lucrative criminal activity" (Gurney 2014, par. 1).[32] Grayson (2014a, par. 18), for example, describes how "the Zetas have tapped into oil and gas pipelines," allegedly "with the aid of Pemex personnel; hijacked gasoline tanker trucks; stolen TNT and other explosives acquired for well blasting; and robbed such solvents as toluene and xylene." Mexican professor Raúl Benítez also alleges the existence "of very close links between the Zetas criminal entrepreneurs and some members of the Mexican oil workers' union."[33] In just a few years this criminal group shifted "from selling stolen gasoline out of makeshift containers, to stealing and selling entire tankers" (Gurney 2014, par. 3). The sale of stolen gasoline today represents important earnings for groups like the Zetas. They not only sell fuel on the streets or on the side of highways but now also control certain gas stations.

Besides gas condensates, gasoline, and other oil by-products, the Zetas have found a new profitable business. For this group, according to Grayson (2014b, 24), "coal has become another attractive energy commodity."[34] In 2012 some sources pointed out that the Zetas produced or illegally bought around 10,000 tons of coal weekly to sell a ton for 600 pesos (approximately $30 today). They calculated that this illegal business generated at least between $22 million and $25 million a year. Most of these activities took place in the Mexican border state of Coahuila, once a Zetas' stronghold, where nearly 95 percent of the national coal is extracted each year (Grayson 2014b; AFP 2012).[35]

In fact former governor of Coahuila Humberto Moreira claimed that the Zetas extracted coal from five municipalities in the Sabinas region of Coahuila. He alleged that the group mined the coal and marketed it to intermediaries, who resold it to the government-owned Federal Electricity Commission (CFE) (Grayson 2014a). After Moreira's son was killed supposedly by Zeta members, he declared that this group participated in the coal business by exploiting mines directly or buying the resource from small producers and then selling it to the state company, in collaboration with corrupt business owners.[36] According to several sources in the state of Coahuila, Humberto Moreira himself was once connected to these criminal entrepreneurs.[37]

MEXICO'S DRUG WAR: A MODERN CIVIL WAR?

This section includes three chapters that utilize "civil war" academic literature to analyze three phenomena that have emerged as a reaction to the creation of the Zetas. This section explains paramilitarization of organized crime that coincided with the inception of the Zetas, which mimics the organization and culture of a professional military. It demonstrates how the security strategy of Mexico and other Central American countries became more militaristic, highlighting the paramilitarism that appears to be evolving as the preferred method for Latin American governments to fight drug trafficking and other forms of organized crime. Finally, it provides strong evidence that Mexico indeed has experienced a civil war with modern characteristics powered by economic opportunity.

CHAPTER 4

Paramilitarization of Organized Crime and a "War on Drugs"

The war started when members of the military left their barracks and started dressing as civilians.

"DON ARTEMIO," PERSONAL INTERVIEW, SEPTEMBER 1, 2013,
CAMARGO, TAMAULIPAS

The present chapter discusses the process of paramilitarization of transnational criminal organizations (TCOs) in Mexico, replicating the Zeta model in an era of democratization. It analyzes political reform that has contributed to the expansion of Zeta-like groups as well as to a significant increase in violence and loss of control over organized crime by the Mexican government. This chapter also reviews limitations of the Mexican state, which has had a clear impact on Mexico's security policy. Finally, it describes the government's response to criminal paramilitarization. This response evolved into a so-called war on drugs, i.e., the militarization of the nation's security strategy that has further elevated the levels of violence in Mexico.

Criminal Paramilitarization in a "New" Democratic Era

The creation of the Zetas and the emergence of a new corporate-military criminal model coincided with a period of economic reform and political liberalization at the beginning of the twenty-first century. At this time the coherence of the old Mexican political regime was lost. Professor Fernando Escalante (2009) explains how executive power became weaker as well as more surveilled and rigid during this period; at the same time it started to coexist with the more autonomous and opaque power of state and local governments. In this new context, the federal government began to lose the ability to command patronage networks and manipulate the informal sector in a self-serving way (see also Astorga 2015 and Valdés 2013). Limited budgetary resources further restricted the federal government's ability to act. In the view of Escalante (2009, 95–96), this process occurred in parallel with the decadence of the revolutionary regime and the adoption of neoliberal economic policies, which, together, contributed to limit the cohesion of the country's political system.

Democratization and Organized Crime in Mexico

An important political transformation in Mexico culminated with the victory of the National Action Party (PAN) in the 2000 presidential election, ending more than seventy years of hegemonic power by the Institutional Revolutionary Party (PRI). This change not only provided hope for a true democratic transition in the Mexican political landscape but also did away with previous power structures that gave the state sway in the country's affairs. For example, the state attempted decentralization during the era of democratic transition. This process challenged the dynamics of power that had existed until then and provided new opportunities for organized crime in Mexico.

The 2000 presidential election heralded an era in which the state increasingly found itself unable to control the nonstate illegal actors and groups that it had previously managed (Correa-Cabrera et al. 2015, 80). Under a new political context, the criminal scenario experienced an important transformation that created a clash of previous structures. The system that had grown for decades hand in hand with the state was now challenged by new players that were extremely violent and more committed to extortion and kidnapping than to trafficking narcotics. In this new context the previous institutional hierarchy broke down. Law-enforcement agencies at local, state, and federal levels (including the armed forces) lost coordination and began to fight with each other (Alvarado 2014). This process appears to have contributed to a visible increase in the level of violence in parts of the country, the loss of control of organized crime by the Mexican state, and the strengthening of TCOs. Some analysts have attributed the growing power of Mexican criminal syndicates to "the breakdown of the rules that once governed the narcotics industry." Professor Hal Brands (2009a, par. 5) explains:

For much of the twentieth century, Mexico's ruling . . . PRI, oversaw a system of "narcocorruption" that brought a measure of stability to the drug trade. The cartels provided bribes and kept violence to a minimum. In return, the PRI protected the kingpins and resolved conflicts between them, most notably by allocating access to the plazas, or drug corridors to the United States. The Mexican state . . . served as a "referee of disputes and an apparatus that had the capacity to control, contain and simultaneously protect these groups." As the PRI gradually lost power during the 1980s and 1990s, this system collapsed. The decline of one-party rule left the Mexican drug trade without a central, governing authority, and comparative stability soon gave way to a Hobbesian struggle for control of the plazas.

For the Zetas, change in Mexico's political power structure spawned evolution and expansion in areas of influence and diversification of revenue streams. The result was transformation into a formidable transnational criminal entity. Exploiting the inexperience of newly elected officials, this criminal group modified its relationship with the state. In this new political context the militarization of organized crime initiated by the Zetas ignited a spiral of violence that overwhelmed the government's capacity to respond effectively to criminal syndicates, which at the same time corrupted state, local, and federal law enforcement authorities. The resulting factionalism and the remaining patrimonial conception of political power created a political gridlock that hampered the further professionalization of Mexican law enforcement agencies. This became an increasingly serious problem, given the growing military power of organized crime (Correa-Cabrera et al. 2015, 80).

During this crucial period of democratic transition organized crime in Mexico began to augment its capability for warfare radically, dealing a crushing blow to any notion that the Mexican state held a comparative advantage in the use of force (Nava 2013, 13). The pioneers of this new criminal model were the Zetas.

Los Zetas' Criminal Paramilitarization: A New Corporate-Military Criminal Model

The militarization of cartel enforcement groups in Mexico can be traced to the inception of the Zetas. This group was the first in the country to adopt systematically militaristic techniques, tactics, and procedures while at the same time maintaining its primordial goal: a financial one. According to Brands (2009a), three factors undergirded the Zetas' successful criminal paramilitarization. The first and most important was their military expertise—their "advanced training and skills." Brands (2009a, par. 11) explains this trait:

> [The] initial group of Zetas came from an elite army unit created specifically for counter-narcotics and counter-insurgency purposes. [This group] received training from French and Israeli instructors, and possessed a wealth of specialized knowledge regarding advanced military tactics. When they defected, the original Zetas thus brought with them considerable expertise in "rapid deployment, aerial assaults, marksmanship, ambushes, intelligence collection, counter-surveillance techniques, prisoner rescues, sophisticated communications, and the art of intimidation," skills they subsequently put to good use in their new profession.

A second factor was the Zetas' sophisticated organizational apparatus, which facilitated a wide range of criminal activities. A third was their large arsenal, which included the full gamut of weapons, from assault rifles to helicopters (Brands 2009a, par. 16). The military proficiency and specialized training of the first members of the Zetas allowed the group to use weapons far more effectively than their competitors (Brands 2009a, par. 17). When the group attracted public visibility, it was described in this manner:

> [The Zetas] are capable of organizing deployments by earth, sea, and air and of making ambush operations and incursions, and of organizing patrols. They are specialized snipers. They can assault buildings, perform airborne and hostage search and release operations, they possess arms reserved for the exclusive use of the armed special forces that cannot be used by any other military unit, such as HKP-7 handguns and G3 rifles. . . . "The Zetas" are dressed in black, drive armored cars, and shoot using MP5s—German submachine guns that are more difficult to find on the black market than AK-47s (*cuernos de chivo*). "The Zetas" have rocket-propelled grenade launchers, 12.7 mm/50 caliber machine guns, land-air missiles, and have even utilized helicopters in some of their most successful operations. In the last [few] years they have killed more than a hundred people. The original members of the group have expanded their army. They re-

cruit young men between 15 and 18 years old, the "Zetitas," and train them in the use of military tactics. (Rodríguez 2006, pars. 9, 59)

Most of the Zeta former members of the Mexican army's special forces (ex-GAFEs) were quickly killed, slowing the growth of the organization's paramilitarization. But the Zetas were adept at adapting. They selectively recruited from Guatemalan special operation forces (Kaibiles), Mexican police, and military units. Interrogation techniques that included torture, psychological operations, and principles of military intelligence were taught to recruits along with more conventional military tactics (Brands 2009a, par. 12). The financial success of this complex transnational criminal corporation hinged on continued control of key territories and generating fear through military tactics, so top members initially concentrated on their military image. The Zetas were pioneers in the use of high-caliber weapons, military strategies, and a strong image to inflict violence and incite fear to achieve the goal of generating revenue (see Manwaring 2010, 2011). Their corporate-military criminal model by all accounts has proved to be a profitable one to follow.

Criminal Paramilitarization and the Loss of the Monopoly of Violence

Criminal Paramilitarization?

The concept of "paramilitarization of criminal organizations" refers to the new corporate-military criminal model introduced by the Zetas in Mexico. At first glance the term "paramilitarization" in this context does not seem to conform to the strictest meaning of the word. While paramilitaries can be considered repressive tools with links to the government, in Mexico's case "criminal paramilitarization" refers to the military influences reflected in the way in which TCOs changed their enforcement methodologies, ranging from their weaponry to the manner in which they executed their opponents (Correa-Cabrera et al. 2015, 83).

Using the term "paramilitarization" when referring to organized crime differs in some way from the definition of paramilitaries that is dominant in the collective conscience. The term "paramilitary" generally connotes images of the United Self-Defense Forces of Colombia (AUC) or Salvadoran death squads, which support regular state-sponsored armed forces in counterinsurgency efforts (Correa-Cabrera et al. 2015; Chernick 1998). Paramilitarization in relation to TCOs has a slightly different meaning than paramilitarization as it has been known in Colombia (Chernick 1998; Escalante 2009; Raphael 2009), Northern Ireland (Knox 2002; Monaghan and Shirlow 2011; Rolston 2005), or Africa (Mullins and Rothe 2008).

The concept of paramilitarization also can be associated with several other terms, such as "militias," "vigilantes," and "self-defense groups" (Kalyvas and Arjona 2005, 26). There is a consensus, however, regarding the concept of paramilitary: it involves participation of the state. As Professor Julie Mazzei (2009, 4–5) describes:

> [P]aramilitary groups are political, armed organizations that are by definition extramilitary, extra-State, noninstitutional entities, but which mobilize and operate with the assistance of important allies, including factions within the State. Thus while officially illegal, [paramilitary groups] enjoy some of the resources, access, and status generally exclusive to the State but which is funneled off by political and military allies. . . . Paramilitaries are offensive, not defensive in nature; their very purpose is to eliminate those who are perceived as threatening the socioeconomic basis of the political hierarchy . . . [paramilitary groups] may be conceptualized as a type of contentious politics that uses violence to protect the established order rather than overthrow it.

The degree of such state participation and specific government actions are still debated, both in the public discourse and in academia. But many would agree that "paramilitary groups tend to be linked to the state and their central activity is the production of violence" (Kalyvas and Arjona 2005, 29). Consequently, an adequate conventional definition of paramilitarism would refer to "armed groups that are directly or indirectly connected to the state and its local agents, supported by the state or tolerated by it, but that are located outside of its formal structure" (29). Social scientists describe different types of paramilitary groups, but most of them conclude that all of these types tend to be linked to the state and share the premise of violence as their central activity.

Yet these characteristics do not fully describe Mexican-origin TCOs as paramilitary groups. Despite branching out and influencing other activities, including political affairs, these criminal organizations are fundamentally money-driven. They appear to lack political/

societal values or interests such as those exhibited by traditional paramilitary groups. While criminal paramilitaries are in league with state elements, some argue, they are not primordially linked to the state. However, researchers Andrew Scobell and Brad Hammitt (1998, 220–221) make an important distinction that paramilitaries need not be linked to the state. In their words, a paramilitary group is a

> uniformed group, usually armed, neither purely military nor police-like in format or function but often possessing significant characteristics of both. It may serve as an agent or as an adversary of the state; it may or may not perform informal security functions; and it may or may not have a wartime role as an adjunct in the regular forces.

Based on this definition, the term "paramilitarization" does seem appropriate when referring to new forms of organized crime in Mexico inspired by the Zeta model. William Robinson, author of *A Theory of Global Capitalism* (2004), contends that the Zetas are a paramilitary force in the mode of Colombia. He sees in Mexico "the creation of paramilitarism alongside formal militarization, which is a Colombian model" (quoted in Paley 2014, 192). Critics of this perspective argue that Mexico cannot be compared with Colombia.[1] They claim that Mexico does not face a paramilitary problem because Mexican TCOs lack a political base. A further reason is the country's geography, which, according to some, allows the state security apparatus effectively to control Mexico's entire territory (Aguilar and Castañeda 2009, 104). As a response, Correa-Cabrera et al. (2015, 83) argue:

> While Mexican enforcer groups may lack a political base, their progressive specialization has allowed them to use violence not only as a "tool of the trade," but as a form of social control as well. In addition, the argument of the country's geography can be countered by the rampant corruption levels that have not only permeated local and state officials and agencies but the very same federal forces sent to specific regions to address the problem of organized crime and violence.

The widespread corruption in Mexico links TCOs and new forms of organized crime to certain parts of the state.[2] Government complicity appears to be a key component of the Zeta criminal model. In the words of journalists Michelle García and Ignacio Alvarado (2014, par. 9), a "network of corruption, collusion and impunity [was] concealed behind the letter Z." The Zeta model would only survive and develop through political protection. As Brands (2009a, par. 23) explains, the organization thrives "on the lack of professionalism among Mexico's local and state police agencies, offering sizable payouts to officers who [could] provide inside information or help the Zetas eliminate their enemies."

The local or municipal police in multiple areas of the country were particularly susceptible to corruption. In some municipalities, the majority of local police helped the Zetas. For example, in Nuevo Laredo, nearly 90 percent of the municipal police were allegedly on the Zetas' payroll at one point (Padgett 2013b). A citizen journalist based in Nuevo Laredo even affirmed in 2011 that "it [was] difficult to distinguish the municipal police from the *mañosos* [criminals] because they [belonged] to the same organization: Los Zetas."[3] Among the local police's illegal tasks were to identify drug shipments that were not the property of the organization, notify the killers (*sicarios*) when rival groups entered the city, guard safe houses, and serve as lookouts (*halcones*) to identify any suspicious activity by enemies or by other law enforcement authorities, such as the army or the navy (Padgett 2013b). The corruption network that protected the Zetas and other similar groups included not only the local police but also members of state police forces, the ministerial police or investigation units, and the federal forces, including police and armed forces.

In this milieu of extreme corruption and the use of paramilitary tactics by organized crime after the creation of the Zetas, some roles of the state and nonstate groups are blurred. This has been evident in the Zetas' birth state, Tamaulipas. According to Professor Carlos Flores, political control by organized crime is much stronger in Tamaulipas than in any other state of the Mexican Republic. Here it is difficult to establish the difference between legal and illegal actors and to identify "if what really operates is a criminal interest of illegal enterprise, or to which extent it is linked to an interest of a political nature" (quoted in Alvarado 2014, par. 50).

Other scholars recognize additional elements of criminal paramilitarization associated with the Zeta model that have had relevant policy implications. In the view of journalist Dawn Paley (2013, par. 30), for instance, "one example of how Zetas are more like a paramilitary group than an insurgent group is evidenced by events like the murder of 72 migrants in San Fernando, Tamaulipas, in the summer of 2010." According to Paley, this "kind of act directly serves the U.S. foreign policy goal of discouraging migration from Central America." What is more, "massacres and mass kidnappings and extortion are always political acts linked to the establishment of control over or elimination of a given community and, by extension, its territory."[4] Arguments like this suggest further links to the state and political agendas of the Zetas and other transnational criminal groups. Multiple accounts indicate that actions of TCOs like the Zetas have served as justification for the use of extreme measures by the government, such as militarization and the legitimization of an unconventional security strategy. In the specific case of Los Zetas, security analysts Scott Stewart and Tristan Reed (2013, par. 6) argue:

> Los Zetas' violent nature was clearly on display after they split from the Gulf cartel in early 2010 and became an independent cartel organization. The group's involvement in high-profile incidents, such as the September 2010 killing of U.S. citizen David Hartley on Falcon Lake and the February 2011 attack on two U.S. Immigration and Customs Enforcement agents that left one of the agents dead, also helped bring Los Zetas to the attention of the American government and public. This resulted in U.S. pressure on the Mexican government to act against Los Zetas. High-profile incidents such as the August 2010 San Fernando massacre, other large body dumps, attacks on media outlets and the killings of journalists also served to make Los Zetas public enemy No. 1 in Mexico's media and in the eyes of the Mexican government.

Losing the Monopoly on Violence

The paramilitarization of TCOs enabled them to take away the state's sole grasp on the means of violence. When confronted with a more professionalized criminal element, the government's initial response seemed slow, thus allowing for the widespread growth of criminal organizations. In his famous work *Politics as a Vocation*, Max Weber (1919, par. 4) affirms that only the state can claim "the monopoly of the legitimate use of physical force within a given territory" and that "the right to use physical force is ascribed to other institutions or to individuals only to the extent to which the state permits it." Therefore the state "is considered the sole source of the 'right' to use violence."

According to Weber (1919), three key elements characterize the state: (1) "the expropriation of the material means of power from formerly autonomous power-holders," (2) "the attainment of a monopoly of the legitimate use of the means of violence," and (3) "legitimacy according to advanced rational-legal principles of legitimation" (Redner 1990, 639). Weber's concept of legitimacy is construed as "an advanced form of authority that relies largely, though not exclusively, on rational-legal legitimation for its claim to be obeyed." This "form of legitimacy has its roots in ideas and practices which are far removed from militarism and violence, from representative and bureaucratic institutions, and from doctrines of sovereignty and consent" (Redner 1990, 640).

Weber's interpretation applies to legitimately established political entities, but what if the duties of those entities were usurped and ultimately shared by private actors? One could affirm that Mexican TCOs became, at some point, legitimate entities in the eyes of the population, not only by developing the means to compete or take over the state's monopoly on use of violence but also by assuring protection, through intimidation practices, and through close links to law enforcement authorities at all levels. "By challenging the institutions commissioned with the safekeeping and enforcement of justice and order, and imposing their presence and acting amongst the population at large," TCOs have been perceived by some as legitimate entities (Nava 2013, 17).

In summary, the paramilitarization of TCOs in Mexico was possible due to a loosening in the state-organized crime nexus in an era of democratization. In some parts of the country, the newly paramilitary-style criminal organizations have functioned as a parallel state. With money, not counterinsurgency, as their primary motivation, Mexico's TCOs cannot be viewed as traditional "loyalist paramilitaries." Instead TCOs have established complex relationships with the state, in some regions acting as the *patrones* (bosses) and in other regions as the clients. Decentralization of the Mexican government apparently went further than its authors intended (Correa-Cabrera et al. 2015, 83).

Recovering the Monopoly on Violence

Mexico's "War on Drugs": An Unconventional Security Strategy

One of the biggest challenges that paramilitarization of TCOs has posed to the Mexican state is fighting for control of the violence monopoly. The extreme violence that has afflicted Mexico in the past few years is indicative of this contest. Since violence is viewed as an important element for state formation, various actors have started to question the state's capacity in Mexico. The spiraling violence in Mexico caused by criminal paramilitarization and the government's inadequate response led some analysts to claim that Mexico was on the road to becoming a "failed state" (Friedman 2008; Grayson 2009; Hale 2010).

On the contrary, others do not believe that Mexico has "fallen completely to the control of private antagonistic groups" and allege that the term "failed state" does not apply (Nava 2013, 17).[5] According to this view, it is, rather, a "fragile state, one where a parallel government has risen and shares dominance of regional territories and can match the State's means of violence with their own brand of violence and terror" (17). Under these circumstances, Mexico experienced a security crisis that manifested itself in several ways: (1) a wave of violence derived from the confrontations between governmental forces and TCOs, (2) terror-inducing practices employed by such groups, and (3) the paramilitarization of crime with the aim of securing territories. Such a crisis has highlighted the ineffectiveness of law enforcement institutions to counter criminal organizations because of institutional inability and high levels of corruption (Nava 2013, 7).

The perceived risk of becoming a failed state, lack of an effective security policy, and sharing of the legitimate means of violence in the form of a forced duopoly between the state and criminal organizations led to the adoption of extreme measures by the government and an unconventional security policy. In this context, law enforcement agencies charged with maintaining order were pushed to respond to criminal paramilitaries with new tactics, new technology, and more violent practices. This increased the need for arms by both organized crime and law enforcement agencies. This situation had a lot to do with the rise of the Zetas, which had introduced an extremely militant element into criminal organizations and fostered a generalized arms race through the use of more militaristic groups carrying more sophisticated weaponry. The Zetas' model extended to various regions of the country and abroad. At the same time, the presence of the Zetas to some extent influenced government strategies to combat organized crime in Mexico and other countries in the Americas, particularly Central America. These strategies involved a high degree of militarization and the use of federal forces in tasks that were traditionally conducted by local and state authorities.

The expansion of the Zetas coincided with Vicente Fox's rise to power as Mexico's president and titular leader of the National Action Party (PAN) at the beginning of the twenty-first century. This first stage of organized crime reconfiguration occurred in regions not necessarily linked to drug trafficking. Criminals began populating these zones. In a second phase that coincided with the administration of Fox's PAN successor, Felipe Calderón, the same regions became militarized after Calderón declared a "war" against these criminal groups. Even before he was inaugurated as president, violence had been increasing as a result of reorganization of organized crime and Fox's revamped and reinforced security strategies aimed at federal involvement in both state and local security matters.

Fox initiated an operation in June 2005 called "Safe Mexico" (México Seguro), which was designed to target organized crime in several Mexican states and operated under "the coordination of local government agencies and with the intervention of civil and military authorities" (Federal Government of Mexico, Office of the Presidency 2005, par. 2). This program involved the participation of the Secretariat of the Interior (SEGOB), Executive Secretariat of the National System of Public Safety (SESNSP), the army, the navy, the Secretariat of Finance, and the Attorney General's Office (PGR), which coordinated with selected state administrations (Federal Government of Mexico, Office of the Presidency 2005, par. 3). Under "Safe Mexico," the government was able to placate a conflict that had erupted in Tamaulipas quickly. However, security in the state of Michoacán deteriorated rapidly, with the Zetas playing a key role (Guerrero 2014a).

Security in Mexico changed substantially after Calderón took office on December 1, 2006, and declared his "war on drugs."[6] Organized crime–related violence visibly intensified. This period, marked by the ongoing conflict between Mexican transnational criminal organizations and governmental forces, saw a momentous increase in violent crimes and assassinations as well as the widespread use of barbaric, terror-inflicting methods, such as dismemberment, decapitation, and even chemical dissolving of human remains. Other terror tactics during this time included car bombs, mass kidnappings, grenade attacks, road blockades, and the execution of public officials (Nava 2011, 1). "All these developments showed the militaristic nature of the war on drugs," one Mexican military veteran said.[7]

As part of the new and unconventional security strategy—and as a response to a request by Michoacán governor Lázaro Cárdenas Batel—President Calderón initiated "Joint Operation Michoacán" (Operativo

Conjunto Michoacán) on December 11, 2006, just ten days after he assumed the presidency. The federal government sent more than seven thousand members of the police and armed forces and promised approximately 250 million pesos for equipment, logistics, and intelligence. In the short term, these actions reduced the levels of violence in Michoacán (Guerrero 2014b).

Calderón's plans were welcomed by the United States, which complemented it by adopting the so-called Mérida Initiative (Iniciativa Mérida), a bilateral antinarcotics program designed to combat organized crime and violence.[8] President Calderón's strategy had three main objectives. The first was to confront, weaken, and neutralize criminal groups through the capture of their leaders as well as the dismantling of their structures and financial organisms. The second was the clearing and fortification of security and justice structures. The third objective was to reconstruct Mexico's society by creating economic opportunities (Carrasco 2014). Calderón's strategy initially deployed more than 45,000 members of the federal police and the armed forces to different regions of the country. By 2011 reports showed that approximately 96,000 military troops were engaged, alongside thousands of federal police.

Preliminary Outcomes of the New Strategy

Calderón's initial efforts focused primarily on targeting the leaders of the transnational criminal organizations to weaken them. The capture of kingpins led to the fragmentation of key criminal organizations into smaller groups that later began fighting with each other for the control of the plazas (Machuca 2014, 11). From 2008 to 2011 violence stemming from this visible fragmentation grew.[9] Deaths purportedly related to criminal rivalry totaled more than 2,500 in the first year of the Calderón presidency (Guerrero 2012b; see figure 4.1).[10] Some observers suggested that this fragmentation led to further diversification of organized crime into a larger number of criminal activities. Not all organizations had the capacity to smuggle drugs, so some would dedicate themselves to other activities that required less infrastructure, smaller criminal networks, and fewer political contacts (Machuca 2014, 12).

In the first few years of Calderón's "war on drugs," violence rapidly spread across the country. The northern border states of the Mexican Republic were particularly affected. According to an official database, released during Calderón's administration for a limited period, a to-

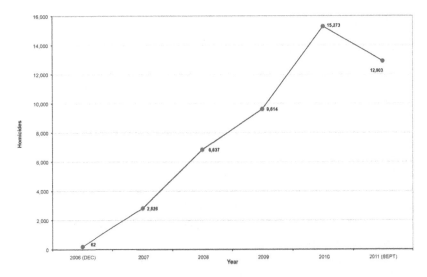

Figure 4.1. Homicides related to organized crime (2006–2010).
Source: Federal Government of Mexico, Office of the Presidency.

tal of 34,612 people were killed in incidents related to organized crime from December 1, 2006, through 2010 (see figure 4.1).[11] Assassinations linked to organized crime increased every year during Calderón's presidency, notably during the first five. Official reports produced at that time showed a total of 2,826 organized crime–related homicides in 2007 and 15,273 in 2010 (Federal Government of Mexico, Office of the Presidency 2010).[12]

The emergence of paramilitary criminal groups in certain regions and the new government strategy to fight organized crime changed long-established patterns of violence in Mexico as well as the geographical distribution of conflicts across the country. Violence linked to organized crime had tended to be concentrated in Mexico's northwestern border regions, especially Chihuahua, as well as in Pacific states such as Sinaloa, Michoacán, and Guerrero. The city of Ciudad Juárez registered the highest number of homicides during the first four years of Calderón's administration. "The violence here was out of control then, and we thought it would never stop," said Professor Tony Payán, who teaches at Universidad Autónoma de Ciudad Juárez.[13] In 2010 more than 3,000 people were killed in this border city across the Rio Grande from El Paso, Texas. In the second half of Calderón's administration, violence spread to other regions of Mexico and particularly increased in the states of Coahuila, Nuevo León, and Tamaulipas. In 2010 nearly half of Mexico's drug-related murders took place in Chihuahua, Sinaloa, and Tamaulipas (Federal Government of Mexico, Office of the Presidency 2010). In more recent years, after Calderón's presidency, organized crime–related violence has been particularly intense in the states of Guerrero, Jalisco, Michoacán, Tamaulipas, and Morelos.

The number of homicides connected to organized crime and statistics on overall organized crime violence vary from one source to another in a political environment that allows deaths to go unreported. The Trans-Border Institute of the University of San Diego, employing multiple sources, reported significant increases in organized crime violence during Calderón's administration: the number of murders related to organized crime grew by 141.9 percent in 2008; 40.6 percent in 2009; 58.8 percent in 2010; and 10–11 percent in 2011 (Molzahn et al. 2012). Organized crime violence appeared to have reached a plateau in 2011. It is worth noting that states with a strong Zeta presence were particularly affected by this violence and registered extremely high levels of murders during the Calderón years. In 2011 alone violence rose most noticeably in Nuevo León, which registered an increase of approximately 850 organized-crime homicides; Veracruz, with an increase of 709 homicides; and Coahuila, with an increase of approximately 470. From 2010 to 2011 Veracruz, with its multiple Zeta plazas, moved from the sixteenth most violent state in Mexico to the sixth (Molzahn et al. 2012, 16).

According to Human Rights Watch, the "war on drugs" in Mexico left more than 60,000 persons dead and more than 26,000 who had disappeared during Felipe Calderón's administration (late 2006–2012). These numbers approximately mirror official reports. However, some say that Mexico's conflict has claimed many more lives than official sources report. For example, Molly Molloy, a researcher at New Mexico State University who maintains the discussion site Frontera List, posits that the actual number of organized crime–related murders in the past few years is much higher, almost double what the government has claimed (Molloy 2013).[14]

Mexico's War on Drugs and the United States

Mexico's drug war coincided with a period of closer collaboration between the United States and Mexico in security and anti-drug-trafficking policies.[15] This trend had been visibly growing since the beginning of the twenty-first century, plausibly as a result of the terrorist attacks of September 11, 2001. In 2002 Mexico joined the United States Northern Command (USNORTHCOM) and aligned its security policies to the needs of its northern neighbor, which pursued a hemispheric project with the main objective of protecting its territory.[16]

According to security analyst Nydia Egremy (2007), Mexico's involvement in the USNORTHCOM suggests the country's submission to US national security goals and principles through a renewed border security policy and the involvement of its police and armed forces in regional security efforts. This applied not only to Mexico but also to several other Latin American countries and was part of a wider hemispheric effort that would support militarization of security in various regions of the continent. In this context, US military aid to some of its neighbors was justified. Because of its geographic location and potential for violence spillover, Mexico represented a key concern for the United States. For some US policy makers, this apparently justified much closer links with its southern neighbor and possible intervention, if needed, in case of extreme insecurity conditions.

Some contend that the United States and Mexico started collaborating closely on security strategies several years before USNORTHCOM, in particular, during the negotiations of the North American Free Trade Agreement (NAFTA). A document in which drug trafficking was identified as a "common threat" for the first time was produced in 1997 and an "alliance" was created to eradicate it (Egremy 2010, par. 27). Mexico then joined USNORTHCOM, and the collaboration instruments created under this new framework were amplified through the Mérida Initiative of 2008, which is essentially a mechanism that links the US and Mexican defense systems. For the United States this would be "a 'historic opportunity,'" since the Mérida Initiative opens the path for collaboration and dialogue." Similarly, the Initiative would allow Mexico to "intensify its training programs in USNORTHCOM and Washington through the National Defense University and other centers of higher education for Mexican officials, such as the US Naval War College" (Egremy 2010, par. 53; see also *El Universal* 2012).

From the US perspective, Mexico seems to be applying the correct strategy. The United States has constantly praised its southern neighbor's actions designed to eradicate drug trafficking. US support of Mexico's security strategy was expressed repeatedly during Calderón's administration. In March 2012 the head of USNORTHCOM, Charles H.

Jacoby Jr.,[17] affirmed that the Mexican armed forces were performing the appropriate actions to provide security and reduce violence in Mexico. Before the US Senate Armed Services Committee (2012, 18), Jacoby declared:

> As requested by Mexico, USNORTHCOM cooperates with the Mexican military in support of their efforts to build capabilities and capacities to employ against TCOs. Above all, we will continue to respect Mexico's sovereignty and we stand ready to increase coordination and collaboration to the extent that Mexico desires and in accordance with U.S. Government policies. Under the courageous leadership of Mexican civil authorities, the Mexican military is making progress against TCO activity. At the invitation of our Mexican partner, USNORTHCOM provided assistance in several key areas.

In November 2012 Jacoby also praised the work of Mexican admiral Mariano Francisco Saynez Mendoza at the end of his tenure as secretary of the navy, stating that his support of USNORTHCOM had been instrumental in the fight against transnational criminal organizations. This recognition was conferred during a ceremony organized at the North American Aerospace Defense Command (NORAD) and USNORTHCOM headquarters near Colorado Springs, where Jacoby presented Saynez with an engraved artillery casing. The Secretariat of the Navy perceived this act as an acknowledgment by US military authorities of the results obtained in the "fight to improve public safety in Mexico" (Mexico, Secretariat of the Navy 2012). In the same vein, William Brownfield, assistant secretary for international narcotics and law enforcement affairs of the US State Department, acknowledged a greater cooperation with Mexico in antinarcotics operations and praised the partnership forged between the two nations over the past years under the Mérida Initiative. In his view, this contributed to strengthen "citizen security" and promoted "trade, investment, energy development, and education" in the region (quoted in Paley 2014, 116).

The Real Effects of the War

One of the most visible results of the war on drugs in Mexico is the increasing level of violence and higher number of homicides following an unconventional security strategy by the Mexican government to combat organized crime. Héctor Aguilar Camín (2014, par. 17), for example, recognizes a "blood feud" after the incursion of federal forces (armed forces and federal police) in Michoacán in 2007. He said that instead of reducing violence these actions contributed to an increased number of killings. The government "obstructs routes, pressures criminal groups, and captures the leaders. The beheading of these organizations causes internal wars for power, fragments the groups, and spreads out the violence." Violence in Mexico is thus worsened by the direct involvement of the federal forces.

As part of the strategy, the federal police and armed forces were sent to the local communities to perform public safety duties traditionally handled by local and state police. These tasks were different from what the armed forces were originally trained to do. "Professional policemen are taught to separate adversaries, listen to complaints, negotiate, bargain, and compromise before using force against troublemakers" (Grayson, 2013, 34). Military training is designed to "annihilate the enemy" (Carlsen, 2012, 147). Consequently, when the Mexican military was sent into the communities, civilians ran the risk of being targeted as the enemy. "Soldiers and officers responded too often with arbitrary arrests, personal agendas, corruption, extra judiciary executions, the use of torture, and excessive use of force" (Carlsen, 2012, 147). It has been said that "the use of the military puts civil liberties and human rights at risk, as well as the rule of law" (Machuca 2014, 12).

Worth noting is a sharp increase in Mexico's homicide rate that coincided with Calderón's war on drugs (see figure 4.2).[18] The homicide rate surged after the "war" was initiated. The total number of homicides in Mexico "had been decreasing from 19 homicides per 100,000 inhabitants [by the beginning of the twenty-first century] to only 8 per 100,000 in 2007. In 2012, the figure would be 24 per 100,000 inhabitants." According to estimates, "this bloody spiral leaves a number of 60,000 people dead" (Aguilar Camín 2014, par. 17). However, this number is probably not accurate. Some place the real figures at 80,000 to 100,000. Regardless of which estimate is most accurate, it represents "the brutal costs for the country of a war against drugs" (Aguilar Camín 2014, par. 17), an initiative strongly supported by the United States.

Many have argued that Calderón's security strategy—which extended, in some forms, to the present administration—did not yield a positive result (Guerrero 2012b; Aguilar Camín 2014). Despite the number of casualties inflicted to decimate TCOs and the capture of

Table 4.1. Total Number of Homicides in Mexico (2000–2015)

Year	Homicides	Year	Homicides
2000	13,849	2008	13,155
2001	13,855	2009	16,118
2002	13,148	2010	20,680
2003	12,676	2011	22,852
2004	11,658	2012	21,736
2005	11,246	2013	18,332
2006	11,806	2014	15,653
2007	10,253	2015	18,650

Source: INEGI, with data from SESNSP of SEGOB.

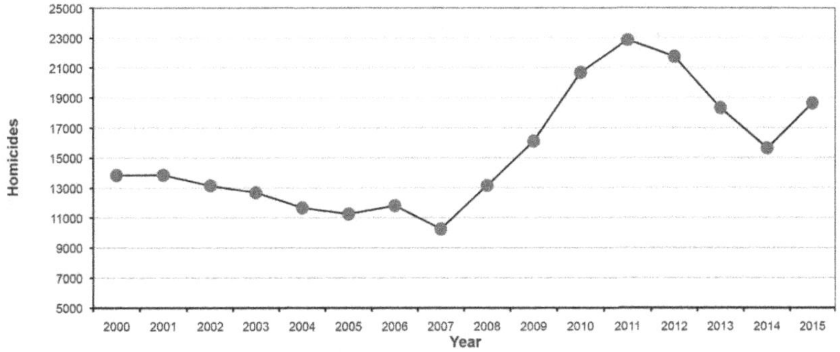

Figure 4.2. Homicides in Mexico (2000–2015).
Source: INEGI, with data from SESNSP of SEGOB.

top echelon members, the militarization and use of an unconventional security strategy did not immediately solve the security problem. It swept the nation into an ongoing violent cycle that also allowed for the "diversification of ventures owned and explored by organized crime" as well as for the "fragmentation of larger organizations into more localized groups." These actions augmented the number of warring groups and spread the wave of violence to "previously untouched territories" (Nava 2013, 14–15).

It has frequently been said that the number of homicides reported in recent years has overshadowed the achievements of arresting kingpins or seizing of drug loads. Because respect for the rule of law and the strengthening of institutions were never fully achieved, the aggressive tactics of the military do not seem to have yielded the desired results. In addition, the actions of Mexico's armed forces and federal police have essentially contributed to an increase in the levels of violence and number of deaths. "The massive violation of human rights by members of these federal agencies is particularly troublesome," affirms Mexican professor Sergio Aguayo.[19]

Militarization of Mexico's security strategy appears to have opened a pathway for use of paramilitary groups in a subsequent stage. An unconventional security policy apparently has transitioned into the use of paramilitary groups in some regions of the country, signaling that criminal paramilitarization inspired by the Zeta model may be giving status to new forms of paramilitarism in Mexico (Correa-Cabrera et al. 2015; Machuca 2014). Could this new stage support an objective of decreasing direct involvement of federal forces and reducing the high costs that the government has been paying in image and loss of legitimacy attributed to human rights violations?

CHAPTER 5

The New Paramilitarism in Mexico

This chapter considers paramilitarism as an additional strategy for fighting organized crime in some regions of the Mexican Republic. The so-called paramilitarization of drug-trafficking organizations inspired by the Zeta model and the resulting massive use of violence led to the implementation of an unconventional security policy by the Mexican government, in which the military and federal police were sent to perform the duties of state and local police. This exceptional approach seems to have turned into a noninstitutional policy whereby new paramilitary groups of different kinds acted as police without uniforms to combat TCOs and their armed groups.

The chapter sheds light on the effects that this unconventional security policy has had beyond the creation of more violence and determines the ways in which it has transitioned into a noninstitutional policy. It seems that the militarization approach to security policy utilized by ex-president Calderón also involved the creation of paramilitary groups that were later adopted by the current Partido Revolucionario Institucional (PRI) administration. This section analyzes three new forms of paramilitarism observed in Mexico (criminal paramilitaries, the elite-financed model of paramilitarism, and the self-defense model), compares them to groups in Colombia in previous decades, and assesses their general effects and risks in combating organized crime. It is worth noting that some analysts have strong reservations about the usefulness of comparing the security situation of Mexico with Colombia's (see Arnson and Olson 2014). Notwithstanding related critiques, such comparisons might be useful and quite appropriate.

Paramilitarism: A Noninstitutional Security Policy

From an Unconventional to a Noninstitutional Security Policy

Paramilitarization of TCOs and the government's response to it shook up the social structure of Mexico. In the view of security analyst José Nava (2013, 17), this process blurred "social divides and previous moral and ethical conceptions, effectively victimizing all social strata and opening the door to the introduction of obscure palliative methods as a desperate response [referring to paramilitaries] to the power of TCOs." Enrique Peña Nieto of the Institutional Revolutionary Party (PRI) took over as Mexican president on December 1, 2012. He maintained the basic aspects of Calderón's strategy, in particular militarization, but made some important changes, mainly in the government's communication strategy and a more general use of extrainstitutional forms of combating organized crime. This has set the tone for the possibility of government-linked or independent paramilitary forces becoming operational in the country (Correa-Cabrera et al. 2015; Nava 2013).

The presence of paramilitary groups (linked to, created by, or allowed to operate by the legitimate government) in Mexico is not a new occurrence; nor has their existence ever been acknowledged. "In times of social and political unrest, special groups and outfits with governmental ties have been introduced into conflictive environments in order to gain objectives that would otherwise be hampered by legal and/ or organizational measures" (Nava 2013, 18). Examples can be traced back to the tumultuous civil upheaval represented by the student movement of the 1960s and the creation of special shock units such as the "Batallón Olimpia" (Olympia Batallion) and the "Halcones" (Falcons), composed of military and law enforcement personnel in undercover roles, who engaged in extrajudicial activities against students' mobilizations. Further instances of paramilitarism in Mexico were the groups created and deployed during the 1970s and mid-1980s to pacify insurrections in central and southern Mexico and urban guerrilla movements. The formation of these groups initiated the period known as the *guerra sucia* (dirty war). More recent examples include politically affiliated groups seeking regional control in Chiapas after the Zapatista insurrection (Correa-Cabrera et al. 2015; Nava 2013).

In today's Mexico the radical response from the former federal government to the paramilitarization of criminal organizations seems to have evolved into the creation of independent paramilitary groups in some extremely violent regions of the country. The emergence of these groups appears to be a response to the state's inability to fulfill its security obligations to its citizenry. In this new context private individuals responded to the threat presented by TCOs in a variety of noninstitutional forms, sometimes in collaboration with government authorities (Nava 2013, 9). At the same time, as the violence escalated, the Mexican government began to rely on paramilitary tactics as mechanisms of counterinsurgency to avoid a direct involvement in a conflict perceived as extremely violent and costly in terms of image and legitimacy.

According to the *Counterinsurgency Field Manual* (US Army and Marine Corps 2007, 2), the word "paramilitary" is part of the counterinsurgency spectrum: "counterinsurgency is military, paramilitary, political, economic, psychological, and [includes] civic actions taken by a government to defeat insurgency." It is worth noting that paramilitaries "are not insurgents or rebels, because they do not fight government forces (though they may attack a particular government official or public agency). They function as militias allied with elements of the armed forces and some economic elites (licit and illicit)" (Gray 2008, 68). According to Cornelius Friesendorf (2011, 81), paramilitary forces "have both military characteristics and, de facto or de jure, policing powers. . . . Their tasks range from maintaining public order to operations against terrorists and organized crime groups." Friesendorf's definition "leaves room for the paramilitarization of other actors, such as regular police forces, military and intelligence agencies increasingly encroaching on policing terrain, and non-state or para-state paramilitary forces, such as citizen militias."

Paramilitarism in Comparative Perspective: The Colombian Case

To understand today's paramilitarism in Mexico, a comparison with the Colombian case can be useful. It has been said that "paramilitary groups come about as a response to the deficiencies exhibited by the State in terms of effective national security policies" (Nieto and Garcia 2008, 44). In other words, the paramilitary phenomenon is "a grave indicator of state weakness" (Gray 2008, 72). Colombia and Mexico are developed albeit fragile states and both have shown the government's inability to maintain public order and prevent social conflict. In the case of Colombia, as researchers Oeindrila Dube and Suresh Naidu recognize, military and counter-narcotics aid, "rather than enhancing the state's monopoly on the legitimate use of violence, [was] diverted to empower non-state armed actors, increasing extra-legal violence with no apparent effect on its stated goal of curbing drug production" (quoted in Paley 2014, 183). The same thing has happened in Mexico, where the war on drugs did not result in more stability or a visible reduction of drug trafficking.

Antinarcotic operations performed in collaboration with the United States, militarization, and the subsequent use of extraofficial armed groups with alleged links to the army clearly elevated the levels of violence in both nations. Colombia, for example, reported over 57,000 politically motivated assassinations (23.4 per day) between 1988 and 1994. These events occurred after a period of repressive social control administered by the Colombian armed forces, which ended up using extraofficial armed groups that would "do the army's job, though they seemingly have no organic links to the army" (Paley 2014, 82). Such a process involved a variety of armed groups, which fought among themselves, initially causing a widespread low-intensity conflict.

Professor Vanessa J. Gray (2008, 71) explains how "the state's failure to fulfill a range of functions" in Colombia resulted initially in "the rise of three different types of armed groups: guerrillas, criminal organizations, and paramilitary forces." In such a process, large businesses and landowners also hired armed groups to protect their property and interests.[1] According to Gray, "these manifestations of privatized security occur because the state cannot or will not prevent them, or has not managed to effectively reduce the demand for such services" (72). In her view, "the state has acquiesced when private elites have employed their own armies, and has succumbed to using private groups to battle state enemies. In both instances, the effect is to empower actors over whom state control is limited" (73). In the end almost a dozen distinct types of actors were employing illegal violence in Colombia. At some point it was not clear who was who in what became a high-intensity conflict. This is especially the case of paramilitaries. Gray (2008, 73) describes this phenomenon as follows:

> In some regions, paramilitary groups have functioned like collaborationist militias, even conducting joint operations with government forces. But other units of the same government have engaged in combat with paramilitaries, especially in recent years. Given that paramilitaries have carried out civilian massacres and high-profile assassinations with impunity—while some government agencies have

endeavored to prevent and prosecute such crimes—one can observe the weakness of such agencies relative to the military and civilian elites that support paramilitary actions.

Legally constituted armed groups—the Colombian armed forces, private security contractors, the US military, and the US Drug Enforcement Administration (DEA)—fought fiercely against illegal and extraofficial armed groups, whose motivations were difficult to identify and were not easily distinguished from purely criminal ones. In fact criminal organizations built in Colombia "private armies equipped with sophisticated weapons and trained by foreign mercenaries." At the same time, autonomous paramilitary groups emerged allegedly to fight these groups, with "the twin objectives" of controlling "regions where they could extract large rents" and denying "their guerrilla adversaries access to same" (Gray 2008, 65).

Thus government forces, right-wing paramilitaries, FARC, the Popular Liberation Army (EPL), the National Liberation Army (ELN), M19, groups of emerald smugglers, drug-trafficking organizations, urban gangs, and other unidentified illegal armed groups were all part of an extremely violent conflict that resembles to some extent—but without the guerrilla groups—what has happened in some regions of Mexico in recent years. The fact that Colombian paramilitaries fought mainly guerrillas and not only drug-trafficking organizations, as in the case of Mexico, does not negate the similarities between the effects of a war on drugs and the implementation of unconventional security strategies in both countries. Researchers Bilal Y. Saab and Alexandra W. Taylor (2009) establish some similarities between the United Self-Defense Forces of Colombia (AUC) and Mexican paramilitaries today based on the origins of their members. They identify similar actors in both cases: members of drug trafficking groups, regional landowning elites, and self-defense groups of local peasants and smallholders.

According to Dawn Paley (2014, 54), Colombia became "the sandbox for how nonstate armed actors can serve to control dissent and conquer territory." For example, she recognizes how organized rural and urban groups that "were rising up for land re-distribution" were attacked and repressed by paramilitary forces, "whose activities the state tolerated" (81–82). This toleration for repression also seemed to be present in Mexico. Paley explains how "paramilitarization took place in two waves in Colombia, the first as state-created and elite-supported groups formed in the 1960s and 70s, later as elite-created, state-supported groups through the 1980s and 90s." In those two waves she identifies the key role of self-defense groups (first wave) and criminal paramilitaries (second wave). From these experiences, we can identify three types of paramilitaries: self-defense, elite-financed, and criminal. These three types also seem to exist in Mexico today.

Three Models of Mexican Paramilitaries

The Mexican security strategy implemented in 2006 that managed to capture or kill several drug kingpins resulted in fragmented criminal groups that led to record levels of violence and the creation of new armed groups, some purely criminal and some paramilitary, sometimes with criminal components. Overall, new paramilitary groups in Mexico operate with two main aims: (1) to combat criminal organizations by working hand in hand with the government or elite/business groups and (2) to eradicate rival criminal groups in order to maintain the control of a certain portion of territory for criminal activity—also in conjunction with the government or elite groups. Hence, the "new paramilitarism in Mexico resembles what happened in Colombia in recent decades," says US Marine veteran José Nava.[2] With their particularities, we can also identify in Mexico three models of paramilitary groups—in addition to those that operate directly with government forces but whose agendas and links to the state are difficult to document. In contemporary Mexico there are some signs of the existence of criminal, elite-financed, and self-defense paramilitary groups (Machuca 2014).

This observation coincides with the findings of a 2013 study authored by Mexican congressman Ricardo Monreal, titled *Escuadrones de la muerte en México* (Death Squads in Mexico). Monreal claims that "up to 200,000 people in Mexico could be involved in death squads, whether at the service of organized crime, private interests, or even state actors" and highlights "the alarming proliferation of armed groups in Mexico" (McCleskey 2013, par 1). Monreal's study divides the death squads into four categories, depending on "who funds and supports them." The first category is "official groups" funded by state actors; it includes "paramilitary groups and clandestine armed forces units dedicated to exterminating criminals." A second category is "private groups" made up of mercenaries, contracted by elites or businesses for personal security. The third category is what Monreal calls "parallel groups," composed of members of criminal organizations; this model resembles Colombian criminal paramilitaries. Finally, there are "insurgent groups," which include Mexico's growing number of self-defense organizations (McCleskey 2013, par. 1).

Evidence has shown that Mexico's war on drugs—or direct confrontation of federal forces and TCOs—led to the creation of paramilitary groups with hints of support by Mexican government officials and wealthy civil groups. This section examines the paramilitarism experienced in some Mexican states that occurs when the government incorporates paramilitary groups as part of its security strategy. The spawn of paramilitary groups as means of defense against professional criminal organizations became noticeable in three states in particular: Veracruz, Nuevo León, and Michoacán. In these states the Zetas have maintained a strong presence and have caused terror or levels of violence that had never been expected before. Each of these cases features one model of paramilitarism identified above: criminal, elite-funded, or self-defense.

The criminal model was well represented by the "Mata-Zetas" in Veracruz. The group introduced itself through a YouTube video in September 2010, communicating its intention of killing all the Zetas. In Nuevo León a group called "Los Rudos" was introduced by the mayor of the rich municipality of San Pedro Garza García in 2009; this group was allegedly supported financially by local business owners (the elite-financed model). The self-defense paramilitary model seems to have had its best representation in Michoacán, where exasperated land workers united as a self-defense group to stop the extortions by the local criminal group, the Knights Templar (Machuca 2014).

The Criminal Model of Paramilitarism in Mexico: Los Mata-Zetas

The main purpose of the so-called criminal paramilitary groups is to kill or exterminate a rival group in order to maintain control of a territory for the establishment or continuation of criminal or illegal activities. As journalist Tracy Wilkinson (2011, par. 16) recognizes, "vigilante gangs purporting to be defending society and working with some level of official complicity have frequently acted in Mexico in recent years." She mentions in particular La Familia Michoacána, which "claimed that it was protecting residents from the Zetas." Another good example of this model of paramilitarism in Mexico is the appearance of Los Mata-Zetas (the Zeta-Killers) in September 2010 in Veracruz.

This group appeared in a YouTube video that showed five men wearing masks and black clothing, identifying themselves as the group who would "kill the Zetas." In approximately two weeks around 100 alleged members of the Zetas were killed in Veracruz. On these events Wilkinson (2011, pars. 6–7; see also *Animal Político* 2011) reports:

> On Sept. 20, nearly three dozen half-naked bodies were dumped in broad daylight on a busy highway underpass in a well-to-do tourist area of the city of Veracruz. Fourteen more turned up a few days later—during a convention of the nation's top state and federal prosecutors. Then, on Oct. 6, barely 48 hours after announcing a major security offensive, military and police found an additional 36 bodies, and 10 more turned up the following day. . . . Many of the bodies had a "Z" for Zeta written on the back with ink marker.

Masked men with military bearing claimed responsibility for these assassinations and in the video announced that they would eradicate the Zetas with the same violent tactics used by this criminal group. The Mata-Zetas also asked government authorities to stop collaborating with their rivals. They assured the public that they would not perform extortions or kidnappings and that they respect the authorities. They also portrayed their killings as "a cleansing operation." The success of the Mata-Zetas "points to highly qualified military trained personal [*sic*: personnel] with . . . very good access to information about the gangs" (Moon of Alabama 2011, par. 6).

The Mata-Zetas supposedly had their origins in the CJNG, when this group acted in collaboration with the Sinaloa Cartel. During this time there was allegedly an alliance that included the Mata-Zetas, La Resistencia, the Gulf Cartel, and the Sinaloa Cartel to exterminate their biggest rival, the Zetas (Gil Olmos 2011).[3] But according to some versions, it was the Sinaloa Cartel that had more incentive to seize key territory of Veracruz from the Zetas, because of its natural resources and "valuable routes for smuggling drugs, migrants and contraband" (Wilkinson 2011, par. 9). Notwithstanding the rivalry between the Zetas and other criminal organizations in this region of Mexico, the Mata-Zetas did not seem to operate independently. Many claimed that this group collaborated with the Mexican federal government. Wilkinson (2011, par. 4), for example, asked: "Just who is behind the killings of Zetas—another drug gang? Agents acting on behalf of the government or military? An ad hoc group whose presence is being tolerated by authorities as well as the public?" In her view,

> [The Mata-Zetas'] sudden rise and the surgical precision with which the killers systematically picked off nearly 100 people in 17 days has led to conjecture among some people that they may be operating with implicit or direct support of the government or military. Some suggest that the June kidnapping, torture and killing of three marine cadets in Veracruz might have propelled the marine corps to begin acting outside the law. Officials dismiss such speculation, and others wonder why a group aspiring to be a clandestine death squad would post videos on YouTube (par. 12).

Elite-Financed Paramilitaries: Los Rudos of San Pedro Garza García, Nuevo León

The "legitimacy" of the Mata-Zetas was allegedly founded on a vigilante-type construction based on a social cleansing policy. As for the rest of the cases in this section, economic or political actors have excused and to some extent supported the existence and mobilization of paramilitary groups (Machuca 2014). The second type of paramilitarism that has been observed recently in Mexico is the elite-funded model. An interesting example can be found in the state of Nuevo León. As violence increased in the Monterrey Metropolitan Area (see Steinberg 2011), on November 3, 2009, the mayor of the affluent municipality of San Pedro Garza Garcia,[4] Mauricio Fernández, announced the creation of a team of "intelligence squads" that would rid the municipality of organized criminals (Carrizales 2009). "It was actually a paramilitary group created by the mayor of the richest municipality of Mexico," says Monterrey-based journalist Obed Campos.[5]

This group was known as Los Rudos (the Rude Ones) and was sponsored by rich elites or business owners who lived in this wealthy municipality. San Pedro Garza García is home to some of the executives of the most important industries in the country.[6] According to some reports, this paramilitary group received nearly 2,000 million pesos from these wealthy executives. On February 26, 2010, the newspaper El Economista published a story in which Mayor Fernández revealed that the cash contributions per business owner ranged from 5,000 to 100,000 pesos a month.[7] Some of these resources were utilized for buying equipment and cameras to cover all the municipality (*El Economista* 2010).

On April 21, 2010, *El Universal* reported that Mayor Fernández announced the dissolution of his Rude Ones. He said the decision was the result of a visible decrease in the number of extortions and kidnappings and other organized crime activities in the municipality. The business owners who were providing financial support to the group also agreed that the services of Los Rudos were not needed anymore (*El Universal* 2010). Although the paramilitary group was allegedly created to fight organized crime, it is worth noting that reports on Los Rudos showed that its top members were either part of the Beltrán Leyva Cartel or high-ranking officials of the local public security agency. The mayor admitted that he paid the top leader of the Beltrán Leyva Cartel in the municipality (Alberto Mendoza Contreras aka El Chico Malo) in exchange for information that would aid the Rude Ones (Cepeda 2014).

A Self-Defense Model: Michoacán and a New Phase of Mexico's Security Strategy

The rise of self-defense forces in the Mexican states of Guerrero, Oaxaca, Mexico, and Michoacán is the latest glimpse of the rise of paramilitarism in Mexico. These groups seem to have followed the evolutionary course that paramilitary forces in Colombia took at their inception: they came from rural, traditional societies and were granted a certain degree of legitimacy by political actors (Nava 2013). According to 2013 statistics, thirty self-defense groups in Mexico were located in eight Mexican states. Some of these groups belong to what is known as "communitarian police" (*policía comunitaria*) and have a legal precedent that has set the ground for their existence. The creation of the "rural police" (*policía rural*) in 1861 is the oldest precedent of a self-defense force with direct ties to the government.[8] Under Mexican law such groups are regulated by chapter 3 of the Mexican Army and Air Force Organic Law, which allowed for the creation of twenty-six corps of rural police in twenty-two states. These corps were tasked with patrolling specific territory, collecting information on illegal activities, and guiding military personnel in rural areas as well as assisting them in a number of activities (Nava 2013; Gil Olmos 2013).

The communitarian police groups seem to form part of the self-defense model of paramilitarism in Mexico. Today this model has become much more complex, however, and involves a variety of groups with different origins and types of members that seem to be linked to the state in specific ways. Michoacán became the laboratory for this self-defense model, turning into a prime example of how the failed policies (Grant 2014) of the previous administration gave way to the formation of paramilitary groups in order to ensure the security of the residents in critical regions. In the past few years this state has seen the rise of self-defense groups—of different kinds—formed by rural communities to fight the Knights Templar organization. These groups gained the attention and support of the media, civil society, and government. The end result seems to be the government's embrace of this self-defense model (Machuca 2014).

The security strategy in Mexico seemed to take new directions once Enrique Peña Nieto arrived in power at the end of 2012. Organized crime had not been visibly weakened in Michoacán after the war on drugs was announced. On the contrary, the criminal model that had prevailed for the last eight years seemed to have gained strength and consolidated in this state. The Zeta model that influenced the Familia Michoacana gave place to the Knights Templar, which expanded considerably, diversified aggressively, and "dominated the most lucrative criminal activities in this Mexican state," says security expert Salvador Maldonado.[9] The extreme violence and atrocious abuses perpetrated by this group, as well as the government's incapacity to face this menace to public safety, finally led to the formation of self-defense groups in those territories where the Knights Templar dominated.

The self-defense groups that appeared in the state in the second decade of the twenty-first century—some of them linked to communitarian police corps—were aimed at protecting their own members and their allies from the Knights Templar and extreme forms of terror and violence. When this criminal group became the leading TCO in Michoacán, it continued trafficking narcotics but expanded its influence and activities widely to attain new sources of revenue. It started to terrorize key regions of Michoacán, targeting agricultural workers, landowners, and miners. Extortion and kidnappings became a major concern in a state that had not been able to deal with the problems caused by the arrival of Los Zetas and the creation of La Familia (Padgett 2013a). With the Knights Templar the situation worsened. Aside from dominating the key city of Apatzingán, this extraviolent criminal organization controlled a strategic location in the southwestern part of the state: the port of Lázaro Cárdenas (Machuca 2014).

As a result of the violence and extortion experienced in the rural sector of Michoacán, in February 2013—just a few months after Peña Nieto arrived in power—a Mexican vigilante leader named Hipólito Mora organized a movement of self-defense groups in the community of La Ruana, located in a region known as Tierra Caliente. Mora became one of the leaders of land workers and landowners who were tired of the extortion, murder, fear, and insecurity linked to the Knights Templar (Associated Press 2014; Machuca 2014). Other self-defense groups appeared in a number of communities of Tierra Caliente (like Buenavista Tomatlán and Tepalcatepec) and were able to oust the Knights Templar from their territories. Dr. José Manuel Mireles, leader of the self-defense groups in Tepalcatepec, also became a very visible figure in this new episode of Michoacán's security crisis (Guerrero 2014b).

In May 2013 the federal government reinforced its security operations in Tierra Caliente and sent hundreds of members of the armed forces and federal police to that region, allegedly to protect civilians from the confrontations between the self-defense groups and the Knights Templar. It is worth noting that the federal forces were only meant to operate at checkpoints and had no order to pursue the criminal syndicates (McCrummen 2013). From that moment on, self-defense groups gradually strengthened. In subsequent months vigilante groups registered important victories in the municipalities of Aguililla, Aquila, Coalcomán, Coahuayana, and Chinicuila (Guerrero 2014b, par. 32). Even with the involvement of the federal forces, the self-defense groups continued to participate in the fight against the Knights Templar. Moreover, they decided not to surrender their arms, arguing that once federal forces departed they would be left unprepared to fight the Knights Templar. Some groups became so powerful and sophisticated that their origins were at times questioned and linked to TCOs or government forces (Machuca 2014; Miroff 2013). Hence this process featured higher degrees of militarization, greater utilization of high-caliber arms, and control of the territory by military and paramilitary forces. This new model has been replicated in other areas of the country and has been adapted to specific local conditions.

At the end of 2013 vigilante groups in Michoacán started a more aggressive and seemingly organized strategy. The self-defense groups that had been successful in their own communities went to other communities to help oust the Knights Templar, generally with the support of the local population. This was the case of Churumuco, La Huacana, Múgica, Parácuaro, and Tancítaro (Guerrero 2014b). As of February 24, 2014, the one-year anniversary of the rise of self-defense groups in La Ruana and Buenavista Tomatlán, Dr. Mireles noted that Michoacán's self-defense groups had managed to free more than thirty municipalities in the state (Navarro 2014).

In mid-January 2014 self-defense groups entered the key municipality of Apatzingán with the aim of liberating it from the Knights Templar. As security analyst Eduardo Guerrero (2014b) recognizes, this municipality had approximately 150,000 inhabitants, a much bigger (and less dispersed) population than in the localities that the vigilante groups had previously liberated. At the same time the federal government once again reinforced its presence in Tierra Caliente to prevent a massive outburst of violence. By January 23 federal forces had assumed control of public security in Tierra Caliente (Guerrero 2014b). This probably means that the "citizen militias" and the federal government had been working together formally—and maybe also informally—to achieve the same goal.

Formal recognition or institutionalization of self-defense groups eventually occurred, but it was not immediate or spontaneous. It required the introduction of a number of policies to reconstruct the social environment and its adequate connection to law enforcement. In this new framework, on January 15, 2014, secretary of the interior Miguel Ángel Osorio Chong introduced the newly appointed Michoacán security commissioner, Alfredo Castillo, whose main task was to restore the links between state government authorities and the citizens of Michoacán (Machuca 2014). On January 27, 2014, a faction of the self-defense groups agreed to become part of the so-called Rural Defense Corps, as part of President Peña Nieto's strategy to institutionalize their existence and participation (de Córdoba 2014). But the former vigilantes should first agree to register their group members and all their weapons with SEDENA.

According to journalist José Gil Olmos (2014, par. 3), the military-police strategy implemented by the Peña Nieto administration in Tierra Caliente and efforts to institutionalize the participation of its informal collaborators were designed with the aim of appeasing the citizen militia groups that had been advancing in a considerable number of municipalities, attempting to "take and liberate the City of Apatzingán." According to this view, if the self-defense groups had not liberated the municipalities of Churumuco, La Huacana, Múgica, Nueva Italia, Tancítaro, and Parácuaro—threatening to take Apatzingán—

the federal government would not have changed its strategy. Others think that the strategy had been purposely designed that way since the beginning (Correa-Cabrera et al. 2015). But in the end "the federal government seemed to have been playing a role of referee in a fight among Michoacanos [citizens of Michoacán]." It can be said that the Mexican state experienced "an unconventional war that was observed by thousands of police and soldiers, who continue patrolling the communities of Tierra Caliente performing tasks of surveillance and security and not combat against organized crime, as was the original intention" (Gil Olmos 2014, par. 9).

To summarize, it was in the form of self-defense groups that paramilitarism seemed to be part of the security strategy of the southwestern Mexican state of Michoacán. Although not officially linked to the state, these groups helped deflect the accountability of the state for human losses and civil rights violations. The success of the self-defense groups in Michoacán did not go unnoticed by the federal government. Still, with an unconventional security strategy in place, the administration of Enrique Peña Nieto apparently worked with state authorities of Michoacán to provide indirect support to the self-defense groups. In the end, as a retired army officer said, "There were attempts to institutionalize these alleged paramilitaries by turning them into a rural police."[10] It is then plausible to claim "the use of paramilitary groups as part of a non-institutional security policy once the initial militarization strategy had failed" (Machuca 2014, 3).

The Effects of the New Paramilitarism in Mexico

The Role of the State

According to Nava (2013, 24), "the weakening of the State that led to the empowerment of TCOs opened the door to another dimension of illegality in a desperate bid to recover a semblance of governance in key territories that have been overtaken by criminal organizations." But probably the main question that follows is whether this phenomenon was just "the next evolutionary step in the development of new forms of organized crime—operating within a fragile justice system"—or was it "an intended consequence of the incoming national security policy" (24)? In other words, what was the role of the state in the evolution of vigilante gangs, elite-funded armed groups, and citizen militias that act as self-defense forces?

These examples suggest relatively strong ties between government forces and these groups and thus new forms of paramilitarism in Mexico. The appearance of paramilitary groups under the ideological banner of social cleansing aimed at organized crime—essentially the Zetas or groups following the Zeta model—might project, as Nava (2013, 35) recognizes, "basic weaknesses of the state." In such a scenario private individuals would take over security practices from governmental forces and the state would be "addressing highly controversial and costly affairs . . . through extrajudicial channels."

The government's support of the armed groups—of allegedly civilian nature—examined here has been tacit and sporadic, a "trademark of paramilitary phenomena, in response to excesses committed by TCOs" (Nava 2013, 24). These examples would be considered, according to Joshua Lund (2011, 64), "blunt variants of paramilitarism," characterized by "tacit or explicit" government support "of organized yet 'informal' vigilante or security forces" (p. 64). Such a phenomenon has to do with "ill-conceived policies that have not only exacerbated the violence presented by the warring factions of the drug trade industry but have also influenced the decision to allow third party elements to involve themselves in the conflict in order to protect self-serving agendas under the guise of justice and law preservation" (Nava 2013, 17).

There seems to be a fine line between the self-defense forces and paramilitary groups in some regions of Mexico. According to Mercedes Llamas (2014), the similarities lie in the types of arms possessed by these groups and in their relationship with the state. Paramilitary forces have an effective link to the state, whether "support in terms of resources (arms, personnel, and so forth) or being tolerated without belonging to the state's formal structures" (par. 5). In the cases analyzed here, particularly in the state of Michoacán, self-defense groups featured several elements of paramilitarism. Here the Mexican government played a fundamental role supporting vigilante groups but remained "behind the scenes" (par. 6).

Llamas (2014, par. 7) considers that in this context citizens are a representation of "the privatization or outsourcing of state violence." In her view, these vigilante groups—formed mostly by citizens—are "used by the government," which wishes them to be the ones who face transnational criminal syndicates in order to avoid accusations of human rights violations in international courts. It is not easy to know the level of the government's infiltration. According to Llamas (2014), it could be "a total implication (arms, resources, strategies, personnel, and so forth)" or a "simple toleration" of these vigilantes in order for them to do "the dirty job." This would greatly benefit the government, which would not be judged by the Inter-American Court of Human Rights (IACHR) or by any other international body. At the same time, as she recognizes, the deaths would not be attributed to the authorities; there would be no formal violation of human rights or direct accusations for crimes or atrocities committed by government forces (Llamas 2014, par. 9).

The Dangers of Paramilitarizing Security in Mexico

There are important risks in the use of paramilitary groups as a non-institutional security policy. One of them has to do with possible links between such groups and organized crime. In the case of the Mata-Zetas, for example, the government apparently joined with criminal groups to combat other organized crime groups that were thought to be much more dangerous—in particular, the much-feared Zetas. Michoacán's self-defense groups might also have connections to organized crime groups. The common enemy in this case would be the Knights Templar, another group that also followed the Zeta model. In such a context, security expert and researcher Carlos Flores warns that "the slightest connection between the government and organized crime in any form of paramilitarism could delegitimize actions aimed at fighting organized crime and assuring security."[11]

On February 5, 2014, Michoacán's security commissioner, Alfredo Castillo, held a private meeting in a warehouse in the municipality of Tepalcatepec with Juan José Farías (aka El Abuelo [the Grandfather]),[12] a self-defense leader and alleged member of Los Valencia Cartel, to discuss a course of action for the self-defense groups' incursion into the city of Apatzingán. The topics allegedly discussed included the strategy to be implemented in the city; the support that would be given by the federal forces; and the vigilantes' uniforms, among other things (*Reforma/El Norte* 2014). In recent years federal and state authorities have also claimed that some self-defense groups have been infiltrated by the CJNG, which is mainly based in the neighboring state of Jalisco and also combats the Knights Templar (*SDP Noticias* 2014). Most recently, at the beginning of 2015, a new armed group, Los Viagras (also called the Sierra Santa Brothers), appeared in Michoacán. Its members were commanders of G250, a rural police group in Michoacán, which claimed to be fighting for "social causes" within the tradition of the self-defense groups. However, Los Viagras were once part of the Knights Templar.[13] Therefore their real motivations and agenda are uncertain, but their criminal component is evident. It is plausible that they have used their connections with genuine self-defense groups and infiltrated some of these groups (Ortega 2015).

Although the self-defense groups were eventually legitimized by an executive mandate, not all the members of the paramilitary groups in Michoacán decided to join the Rural Defense Corps. In early April 2014, Dr. Mireles said that the vigilante groups he led would not disarm until all the leaders of the Knights Templar were arrested and the government demonstrated that it could protect the state of Michoacán from the entrance of other criminal organizations, such as the Zetas, La Familia, the Templarios, or the CJNG.[14] The federal government had set May 10, 2014, as the deadline for the self-defense groups to surrender their high-caliber arms and register any other weapons that the government had approved; those who did not comply would be arrested. This action came from the idea that the resistance to abandon a noninstitutional form of security was dangerous because the government would eventually be unable to manage groups operating outside the law (Machuca 2014).

Colombia experiences these problems today. In 2006 the Organization of American States (OAS) estimated that twenty-two paramilitary groups (totaling around three thousand people) were still active in this country (Saab and Taylor 2009, 463). Notwithstanding the official mandate to disarm established paramilitary groups—thus turning them into legal entities—they continue operating in key regions. It is worth noting that many of the Colombian paramilitaries "continue to have close ties with criminal groups" (Machuca 2014, 17). Saab and Taylor (2009, 462) recognize that autonomous self-defense groups or citizen militias unconnected to landlord and drug paramilitary organizations have remained rare in modern Colombia.

Although the use of paramilitary groups to fight organized crime initially brought positive results to several communities in Michoacán, there are still important risks stemming from the existence of armed groups that do not operate within Mexico's institutional framework. Notwithstanding the efforts by Mexican authorities to institutionalize the participation of the self-defense groups, this has not been an easy task and has encountered resistance among certain groups. Some leaders of citizen militias have expressed their reluctance to participate in these initiatives or to take political positions, arguing that they could lose the support "of loyal followers who are genuinely fighting organized crime" (Machuca 2014, 18). At the same time several members of self-defense groups have refrained from registering their guns or giving up those arms that are not approved by the federal government (Correa-Cabrera et al. 2015; Machuca 2014).

"Another problem that arises from the use of paramilitaries of different kinds in Mexico as part of the security strategy has to do with the fact that the government, indirectly, can push for harder strikes against criminal organizations without having to deal with the consequences of violating human rights," says policy analyst María Machuca.[15] Mexican armed forces face some key limitations when participating in conflicts like the one in Michoacán. They cannot just attack whoever they believe is linked to the Knights Templar or any other criminal organization, because in some cases they could be violating human rights. Vigilantes can participate more directly without paying the enormous cost in terms of image and legitimacy that the government would have to pay in case of a failed operation or a mistake.

The arms that are used by paramilitary groups in Mexico also raise another question. In the case of Michoacán, it has not been possible to identify who provided the arms to the self-defense groups in the state. The leaders of these groups have refused to mention the exact origin of their resources and the provider of the arms. Some of this support might have been granted by the government, but "there are also claims that organized crime has infiltrated some self-defense groups and provided them with weapons," alleged security expert Salvador Maldonado.[16] For example, some claim that the CJNG was taking advantage of the situation in Michoacán and began supplying the communities with arms to conquer territories then controlled by the Knights Templar (Correa-Cabrera et al. 2015).[17]

Although self-defense groups like the ones operating in Michoacán proved an initial benefit by helping with security, there are still dangers in using paramilitary groups as a noninstitutional security strategy. First, paramilitary groups are not official law enforcement actors; therefore the government does not have complete control over their activities and they cannot be held accountable for their actions. Second, because the state's involvement with paramilitary groups is not clear, the state acts as "an invisible hand" and cannot be held accountable for crimes or human rights violations committed by self-defense groups. Third, some of the paramilitary groups are involved with organized crime (such as Los Viagras in Michoacán and Los Rudos in San Pedro Garza García), so the government becomes directly or indirectly involved with organized crime as well. Also, because the source of high-caliber weapons used by paramilitary groups is unknown and their connections with other criminal syndicates cannot be distinguished, the alliances and loyalty of paramilitaries can shift easily, depending on the financial support that they receive.

As public policy analyst María Machuca (2014, 16) recognizes, "it may be hard to quit the power that paramilitary groups accrue over time." A refusal to disarm, and the negative consequences, have been experienced in Michoacán, as they have been felt in Colombia for decades. Finally, this noninstitutional security policy might be beneficial for government authorities because it keeps the military and law enforcement out of conflict, thus protecting the image of the Mexican state. Nevertheless, the involvement of paramilitaries as part of Mexico's security policy maintains extremely high levels of violence at the expense of civilians.

The paramilitarization of Mexico's security strategy has been the latest stage of a process that combined criminal paramilitarization inspired by the Zeta model with participation of the armed forces and federal police to combat organized crime. These collective phenomena have resulted in a conflict with multiple characteristics of such magnitude that we could think of it as a civil war.

CHAPTER 6

Mexico's Modern Civil War

The paramilitarization of organized crime (with the creation and expansion of the Zetas and its model), a more violent confrontation between criminal syndicates, and the militarization (and paramilitarization) of Mexico's government strategy to fight illegal actors have produced a situation in the country that can be analyzed by utilizing "civil wars" academic literature. This type of analytical tool has rarely been used by scholars focusing on this topic; but due to the dynamics, magnitude, and type of actors involved in Mexico's current conflict, a framework of this type might be of help to advance the understanding of the security crisis in the country.

The present analysis concludes that Mexico's armed conflict has the characteristics of a civil war, more specifically a "new" or "modern" civil war: "characteristically criminal, depoliticized, private, and predatory" (Kalyvas 2001, 100). It seems that economic agendas—and not ideologies—are driving the conflict in Mexico's new civil war. In other words, it is likely that conflict in Mexico has been mainly driven by economic opportunities more than by grievances. This view departs from classical theories on wars and armed conflicts.[1] This chapter analyzes the effects of the hostilities as well as the distinct forms of warfare and the dual function of violence in this massive armed conflict in some parts of Mexico.

The final section of this chapter analyzes the related war taking place in cyberspace, which is a new battlefield that reinforces the main objectives of the real-world armed conflict in Mexico. This phenomenon can be considered part of what experts refer to as a fourth-generation war, an asymmetric war in which military operations are complemented by using the media and particularly social media to support a cause. This section explains the dynamics of Mexico's security crisis in cyberspace as well as the virtual tools utilized to legitimize the "official" security strategy. The chapter describes and explains the social media dynamics of the so-called drug war in Mexico, highlighting the dominant role of the Zetas in online platforms. The analysis considers cyberspace as a new battlefield where organized crime, armed forces, paramilitaries, and civil society participate, combat, interact, and even collaborate in a virtual war that seems to reinforce the goals of each side.

On Modern Civil Wars

Mexico's War

In a *Milenio* article entitled "Mexico's Lost War," Mexican historian and writer Héctor Aguilar Camín (2015, par. 7) states that after analyzing what has happened over the past few years "it is difficult to claim that Mexico has not lived a sui generis civil war." He asks "whether this war has been worth the fight" and questions "whether the conflict's positive outcomes can be compared to the destruction of lives and criminal expansion produced in the past few years." For Aguilar Camín, the answer is no. In his view, Mexico has experienced a "pyrrhic war in which the damages have been evident and the benefits are impossible to describe" (par. 8). The Mexican situation can be compared to the one recently observed in Colombia, where political violence claims thousands of lives each year and conflict has displaced millions of people since the late 1980s. "High levels of organized violence have afflicted Colombia historically, and in the 1990s, a low-intensity conflict worsened to the point where some observers began using the term civil war" (Gray 2008, 63).[2]

There is no clear consensus regarding the usage of the term "civil war" when referring to what has been happening in Mexico. When considering its dimension, Salvadoran analyst Joaquín Villalobos (2011, 14) sees the security crisis in Mexico as a "military issue." But when considering its activity, he sees it as a "police issue." The involvement of the armed forces as one of the tools to solve this security crisis is the main reason why some think that a civil war started at some point. The situation in Mexico initially was posed as a matter of national security. In such a context the government strategy consisted of confronting directly the big drug-trafficking organizations with the aim of beheading and fragmenting them, thus making them smaller and easier to control. The idea was to turn an issue of national security into a problem of public safety (Aguilar Camín 2015, par 3).[3] In other words, the armed forces and federal police would eventually be replaced by competent and incorruptible local and state police who would finally do what they are supposed to be doing.

But Aguilar Camín (2015, par. 5) contends that the reality is that this "strategy has cost much more blood than originally anticipated." According to him, "this does not mean that the strategy has not worked, but perhaps we are now experiencing the final convulsions of the expected violence: gangs that can be dangerous in the communities where they operate but not as threatening to national security." In his view, "what we see in Tierra Caliente, Iguala, or Tamaulipas in terms of criminal savagery could be the last death rattles produced by the war initiated [a few years ago]. The landscape after the battle would be a long period of criminal dominance in isolated municipalities, minor cities, and marginal urban spaces" (par. 6).

When explaining the goals and the effects of Mexico's security strategy, Aguilar Camín is referring to a "lost war," but "a war" after all. Others—perhaps even former President Calderón, who declared a "war on drugs" at the beginning of his administration—also think that Mexico has lived through a war in recent years. In the view of Mexican poet and peace activist Javier Sicilia, for example, Mexico's war against drugs declared by the Mexican government in late 2006 was "a war between the state and parallel states" (quoted in Paley 2014, 25). In the same vein Villalobos (2011, 13) contends that there are indeed "technical reasons that confirm the existence of a war in Mexico." In his view, quantitative aspects are enough to identify a war; specifically, he refers to the number of participants, the geographic dimension of the affected zones, the considerable amount (and recurrence) of violent encounters, the number of victims, and the number and type of arms and technology used by the rivals.

According to Villalobos (2011, 13), the actual debate centers on whether or not Mexico has been through a "civil" war. This debate continues, because the kind of violence related to organized crime in Mexico cannot be typified, as was done in Colombia through the use of the term "narcoterrorism," which has political connotations. However, Villalobos recognizes that in Mexico there have been attempts to ascribe a political character to the conflict through the use of the concept "narcoinsurgency." He also notes that the use of the term "civil war" when referring to Mexico's conflict has been essentially avoided, particularly among the political class, due to the implications that this might have in foreign relations and in order "to prevent complications when forming internal consensuses."

For Villalobos, the main issue when trying to characterize the recent security crisis in Mexico as a civil war arises when defining drug-trafficking organizations and other TCOs. In particular, the problem arises when "determining their goals, due to the fact that they are clearly criminal groups with no political agenda, no demands on the state, and no historical grievances that motivate them to act against the state" (13). Because of this, Villalobos and others say that it is not possible to talk about a civil war or insurgency in Mexico even though the existence of organized crime can be linked to a fundamental weakness of the state or to extreme poverty in some regions of the country. Professor Raúl Benítez agrees with this idea, stating that "TCOs in Mexico are criminal businessmen but not political actors trying to overthrow the sitting government."[4] According to this view, the key and main motivations of TCOs are "greed and illicit enrichment." Therefore Mexico would just be facing what scholars like Paul Collier, David Keen, and others define as "wars based on economic agendas, in which criminal groups have no intention of changing the law, but making sure that the law does not work" (Villalobos 2011, 13).

Notwithstanding this view, there are key aspects of Mexico's recent security crisis, and the government's responses to it, that can lead us to characterize the resulting conflict as a civil war. In order to verify the veracity of this claim, it is important to define the concept of civil war properly and to determine whether Mexico's conflict fits into this category. It is therefore worthwhile to use civil wars academic literature to analyze the drug war, the functions of violence, and the human, social, economic, and political effects of the recent armed conflict in Mexico. The first step is to provide "a precise definition of an imprecise and poorly observed phenomenon, a process that provides considerable room for legitimate disagreement" (Collier and Hoeffler 2007, 712).

Defining Civil War

Civil war is a domestic high-intensity "political conflict [that] takes the form of military confrontation or armed combat" (Kalyvas 2007, 416). It is sustained, organized, and large-scale, resulting in large numbers of casualties and consuming an enormous amount of resources. Some scholars establish a threshold of a thousand dead people a year when talking about a civil war—and of these casualties, at least 5 percent must be combatants (Villalobos 2011, 13). Its average duration in the contemporary era has been about ten years. Such a long duration "seems to result from the way in which most of these conflicts have been fought: namely, by rebel groups using guerrilla tactics, usually operating in rural regions of postcolonial countries with weak administrative, police, and military capabilities" (Fearon 2007, par. 8). There are various definitions of civil war, but they seem to converge around the same key dimensions. With reference to the definitions of this phenomenon, Kalyvas (2007, 417) states:

> Civil war can be defined as armed combat taking place within the boundaries of a recognized sovereign entity between parties subject to a common authority at the outset of the hostilities. . . . This definition stresses two key features: the militarization of conflict, requiring at least two competing sides (including a relatively large rebel organization with military equipment and full-time recruits) and differentiating civil war from communal riots, terrorism, crime, and genocide; and a domestic challenge directed against the authority of the current holder of sovereign authority, which distinguishes it from interstate war.

A key aspect of the definition of civil war possibly has to do with its political nature. According to Nicholas Sambanis (2002, 217), civil war "represents the most poorly understood system failure in the domestic political process" (quoted in Kalyvas 2007, 430). James Fearon (2007, par. 7) sees it as "a violent conflict within a country fought by organized groups that aim to take power at the center or in a region, or to change government policies." Paul Collier and Anke Hoeffler (2007, 736) recognize that "[t]o date the study of civil wars has been dominated by political scientists" and that "this prejudges the phenomenon as being essentially political." But this phenomenon is much more complex and has further dimensions. In fact, civil wars "are intricate social, political and psychological phenomena" (Collier and Hoeffler 2007, 712). They also involve crucial economic aspects and dynamics. Hence economics can offer useful analytical tools to explain civil warfare.

New versus Old Civil Wars

There are a number of arguments attempting to explain the onset of civil war. Kalyvas (2007, 430), for example, identifies three key causal factors that have a measure of empirical backing. In his view, "ethnic antagonism, the presence of natural resources, and weak states may all increase the risk of a civil war, especially in poor states." Kalyvas's argument incorporates political, social, psychological, and economic elements. Collier and Hoeffler (2007, 712) acknowledge that "ideological, religious or ethnic differences are conventionally regarded as the causes of civil war" but also highlight the economic dimensions of this type of massive internal conflict:

> Economic theory explains civil war in the framework of incentives and constraints rather than ideologies or identities. This framework enables economists to analyze the distinctive feature of civil war: the emergence and persistence of a rebel army; some conditions make rebellion both more attractive and more feasible than others. Consistent with this emphasis on incentives and constraints, statistical studies suggest that economic characteristics, notably the level, growth and structure of income, are important influences on the risk of war. In addition to the explanation of the initiation and duration of civil wars, economic methods can also generate estimates of their costs and consequences. This is an essential step towards the cost-benefit analysis of policy interventions (712).

In fact, "Collier, [Hoeffler,] and like-minded researchers attacked the longstanding view that [only] ideologies and identities, which they refer to as grievances, cause civil violence." They form part of a "greed school," which considers "grievances to be rhetoric that insurgents invoke to try to legitimate preying on others and appropriating resources" (Gray 2008, 64).[5] For Collier (1999, 1), conflicts, including civil wars, "are far more likely to be caused by economic opportunities than by grievance." In his view, "if economic agendas are driving conflict, then it is likely that some groups are benefiting from conflict and that these groups therefore have some interest in initiating and sustaining it" (1).

According to Paley (2014, 116), Collier's point about economic opportunities applies to Mexico even if the drug war there "can hardly be called a civil war, due to the extent of international involvement in the conflict." Similarly, for Villalobos (2011, 10), "Mexico forms part of a group of countries which are experiencing what are known as 'new wars' and are moved by economic agendas."[6] Kalyvas (2001, 100) explains the difference between old and new civil wars, adding that the dividing line between the two coincides with the end of the

Table 6.1. "Old" vs. "New" Civil Wars

	Old civil wars	New civil wars
Causes	justice-seeking	loot-seeking
Support	have popular support	lack popular support
Violence	controlled and disciplined	gratuitous and senseless

Source: Kalyvas (2001, 102).

Cold War: "Old civil wars are considered ideological, political, collective, and even noble," while "new civil wars are characteristically criminal, depoliticized, private, and predatory." Thus he sees an analytical distinction between "justice-seeking" and "loot-seeking" civil wars and accepts "the assumption of rebellion as a criminal enterprise" (101). Kalyvas (2001, 102) explains how old and new civil wars vary along three related dimensions (see also table 6.1):

1. Old civil wars were political and fought over collectively articulated, broad, even noble causes, such as social change—often referred to as "justice." By contrast, new civil wars are criminal and are motivated by simple private gain—greed and loot.
2. At least one side in old civil wars enjoyed popular support; political actors in new civil wars lack any popular basis.
3. In old civil wars acts of violence were controlled and disciplined, especially when committed by rebels; in new civil wars gratuitous and senseless violence is meted out by undisciplined militias, private armies, and independent warlords for whom winning may not even be an objective.

Notwithstanding this widely accepted distinction, Kalyvas (2001, 113) observes that "old civil wars are not as different from new civil wars as they appear to be." He adds that "the distinction between them should be strongly qualified," because "the available evidence suggests that differences tend to be less pronounced than usually argued" (117). Both "the perception that violence in old civil wars is limited, disciplined, or understandable and the view that violence in new civil wars is senseless, gratuitous, and uncontrolled fails to find support in the available evidence" (116).

The same seems to be true with regard to the grievance/looting dichotomy. Kalyvas (2001, 105) recognizes that rebel motivations in new civil wars are diverse and include activities that go beyond mere banditry. For example, he points to rebel organizations in Africa that are "often dismissed as mere criminal gangs" but "develop a complex apparatus of rule in the areas they control—which is less visible but not very different from the order implemented by 'justice oriented' rebels." At the same time, these groups "engage in organized, systematic, and sophisticated economic interactions with foreign firms, which buy raw materials and sell weapons, an activity at odds with the extreme fragmentation implied by many views."

This is not exclusive to Africa. Criminal organizations in Mexico and a number of Central American countries—particularly the countries of the Northern Triangle—have some similar features and patterns. Mexican TCOs, Central American gangs, and African and Colombian rebel groups have elements in common. Taking all this into account, we could claim that Mexico has lived through a "new civil war." Considering Kalyvas's interpretation, looting by Mexican criminal syndicates should not prevent us from considering Mexico's drug war a civil war. In fact, for Kalyvas (2001, 106) "looting is a recurring element of civil wars, including the most ideological ones."

It is important to analyze the role of looting in Mexico's recent conflict, since it seems to be the main objective of the combatants (TCOs)—whose role might be equivalent to Colombian or African rebel groups—in a war on drugs declared by the Mexican government. Kalyvas (2001, 103) notes that "the concept of looting is analytically problematic because it is unclear whether it refers to the causes of war or the motivations of the combatants (or both)." He identifies three main problems regarding this concept:

The first problem is the direction of causality—do people wage war in order to loot or do they loot to be able to wage war? If the latter is the case, then looting may be no different from the widely accepted practice of "revolutionary taxation." Second, it is not always clear who is doing the looting—elites, autonomous militias, armed peasants? Third, the linkages between looting and grievances are complex and fluid. (102–103)

In the case of Mexico's new civil war, the analysis of looting by criminal groups, elites, paramilitary groups, and other external actors (such as transnational businesses) becomes extremely complex. From the time when Mexico's war on drugs was declared, several groups have benefited from this conflict. Criminal groups looted to be able to wage war. This increased the number of kidnappings and extended extortion practices throughout the country. However, the looting started even before the Mexican government became involved. Other key actors have also benefited from this "modern" civil war. The main winners appear to be certain political elites, arms-producing firms, transnational financial companies, security contractors, and the US border security/military-industrial complex, among other key national and transnational players.[7] These are the actors that usually benefit from any major armed conflict in the world.

Forms of Warfare in Mexico's Modern Civil War

Fearon (2007, par. 8) notes that civil wars "featuring conventional armies facing off along well-defined fronts" are highly unusual in the present era. It is much more common to see conflicts such as those in Algeria, Colombia, Sri Lanka, South Sudan, and Syria. Guerrilla warfare has been present in many of these conflicts and has allowed "relatively small numbers of rebels to gain partial control of large amounts of territory for years." This is what we know as "irregular" warfare. Mexico's modern civil war seems to have been fought by means of irregular warfare at the same time. Regarding this subject, Kalyvas (2007, 428) states that in irregular warfare the strategically weaker side refuses "to match the stronger side's expectations in terms of the conventionally accepted basic rules of warfare." He continues:

> A stylized description of irregular war goes as follows: the state (or incumbents) fields regular troops and is able to control urban and accessible terrain, while seeking to militarily engage its opponents in peripheral and rugged terrain; challengers (rebels or insurgents) hide and rely on harassment and surprise. Such wars often turn into wars of attrition, with insurgents seeking to win by not losing while imposing unbearable costs on their opponent. . . . The main empirical indicator of irregular war is the dearth of large-scale direct military confrontations or "set battles" and the absence of frontlines. Irregular war is not wedded to a specific cause (revolutionary, communist, or nationalist) but can be deployed to serve a very diverse range of goals. (428)

According to this description, the first form of warfare in Mexico's modern civil conflict might have been irregular. However, the rebels were not guerrilla members but criminal groups trained in counter-insurgency tactics and with access to high-caliber weapons—in other words, they were groups following the Zeta model. Irregular warfare began in the last month of 2006, when Calderón took power and declared a war on drugs. Mexico's war gradually transformed and incorporated new actors and strategies. In early 2013, at the beginning of a new administration, this transformation gave place to a different form of warfare in some regions of the country, particularly in the state of Michoacán. Hence, symmetric nonconventional warfare began to be visible in places where the Mexican federal forces had not been able to control the territory and recover it from criminal syndicates. In regard to symmetric nonconventional warfare, Kalyvas (2007, 428) explains:

> This type of warfare is often described as "primitive" or "criminal" war and entails irregular armies on both sides in a pattern resembling pre-modern war. . . . "[S]ymmetric non-conventional warfare" takes place in civil wars that accompany processes of state implosion. State implosion can be sudden or gradual; a way to identify this process is by examining the state of the government army and whether it has become indistinguishable from rival militias in terms of loose organization and fractured chain of command. . . . This [process] entails the disintegration of the state army and its replacement by rival militias which typically equip themselves by plundering the arsenal of the disbanded army.

Certain features of symmetric nonconventional wars were present in Mexico's conflict only at some points in time and in some regions of the country. Irregular armies appeared on both sides; the government began to utilize paramilitary strategies to fight its criminal rivals. Different forms of paramilitarism, applied selectively in certain areas, transformed an irregular war into a symmetric nonconventional one in some regions of Mexico. These zones first experienced a combination of criminal paramilitarization, formal militarization, and extreme violence. In a second stage the government participated by supporting irregular armies to fight criminal combatants.

Hence the new war in Mexico involved a number of irregular armed groups, some of them allegedly supported by the government. Among these groups are the self-defense groups in Michoacán and Guerrero; the Mata-Zetas in Veracruz; narco-paramilitary groups in Tamaulipas; Los Rudos in San Pedro Garza García, Nuevo León; and other state or local armed groups whose role was not formally or constitutionally regulated: their participation in the conflict often has been considered illegal. A new security strategy in certain Mexican states—particularly those located in the northeast—incorporated semimilitarized state or local police forces or "special forces" with the aim of reinforcing the actions of the military and federal police.

These groups included the Group of Arms and Special Tactics (GATE) and the Group of Metropolitan Operative Reaction (GROM) in Coahuila, Grupo Hércules (Hercules Group) in Matamoros, Tamaulipas, and the Fuerza Civil (Civil Force) in Nuevo León and Veracruz. The participation of some of these actors has been highly criticized, and allegations of extrajudicial disappearances and assassinations by members of these groups are not infrequent. Consider, for example, the case of the local Hercules Group of Matamoros, which was allegedly implicated in the kidnapping and deaths of three US citizens. Coahuila's GATE is another controversial elite corps that was created by the state's governor and a coalition of local business leaders with the aim of fighting organized crime. GATE started as a "group of anonymous, masked agents" who, according to some, had "the privilege of acting in the same callous fashion as the illegal groups they [were] fighting" (Osorno 2014, par. 26). Such experiences include some common elements also found in symmetric nonconventional wars.

Mexico's War

A Modern Civil War in Mexico?

There has been a big debate over whether Mexico has been through a civil war or not. Advocates of the classical school of thought about civil wars and armed conflicts would not include the Mexican conflict in the civil war category. For example, expert in armed forces and Universidad Nacional Autónoma de México (UNAM) Professor Raúl Benítez categorically rejects the usage of the term "civil war" when referring to Mexico. In his view, "Mexico has experienced a security crisis, but not a war of any kind." What is more, "if one understands the classics—for example, the work of Carl von Clausewitz—and the nonpolitical nature of Mexico's conflict, one would never use the word civil war."[8] However, more recent literature on wars would not necessarily agree with this view (Kalyvas 2001, 2006, 2007).

After a thorough analysis of more recent commonly accepted definitions of this term, we can conclude that Mexico's so-called drug war was indeed a new or modern civil war, essentially moved by economic agendas. The main actors in Mexico's war were citizens organized within criminal syndicates who rebelled and fought against government forces or law enforcement agencies at the three levels of government (local, state, and federal). Criminal organizations gathered big arsenals of high-caliber weapons and trained their members on war tactics in special camps. They had originated within the state and then achieved a certain independence but later received government support through corruption networks. These paramilitary-style criminal groups started fighting among themselves for the control of key territories in Mexico, with the biggest confrontation taking place in the northern part of the country. These zones subsequently became militarized after the declaration of war by the Mexican government—with the alleged intention of eradicating drug trafficking. Eventually the presence of the armed forces became a common part of the landscape in key cities and on highways.

Most confrontations between armed forces and paramilitary-style criminal groups took place first in urban zones and subsequently spread to rural areas in operations that sometimes involved irregular armies on both sides. Hence the assassination of local police and the massive executions among members of criminal organizations was a first phase of this war. The second phase saw the confrontation between federal forces and organized crime. The third phase of the war was the extrajudicial execution of criminal combatants by paramilitary groups. In Mexico's armed conflict, according to journalist Dawn Paley (2013, par. 18), "violence deployed against civilians . . . [came] from official, uniformed troops, as well as from irregular forces including 'drug cartels' or paramilitary groups."

It is worth noting that a large segment of the Mexican armed forces was made up of individuals born in southern states (which have comparatively higher levels of poverty), while the base of key drug-trafficking organizations and other TCOs was in the northern part of the country—mainly in the border region, near the main clientele. Hence "there seems to be a war in the Mexican territory between citizens of the north and citizens of the south. It was a war between the north (home and origin of an important percentage of drug traffickers and criminal organizations) and the south (where a large number of military personnel were born and raised)."[9]

But in this case it is the government that declared war, not the criminal groups who rebelled against the government with the aim of achieving a political or economic goal. The government justified its actions, however, by painting these groups as a major threat to national security, domestic security, and public safety. Drug-trafficking organizations had not represented such a threat in the past, but new forms of organized crime and violence, brought about and expanded by the Zetas, transformed the relationship between the state and these illicit actors—to the extent that at some point the state seemed to be losing the monopoly on violence. TCOs in Mexico started to exercise real "intimidating power"—the power needed to control territories and "assure economic benefits." This was considered a big problem, because the conflicts generated by such a situation "[threatened] the existence of the state itself" (Villalobos 2011, 14).

Mexico's modern civil war so far has not been exclusively motivated by economic agendas. According to Paley (2013, par. 37), "One of the most glaring misconceptions about the war in Mexico, and the drug war more generally, is that it is somehow post-political or non-political." She dismisses the idea of only ascribing "'political' status to a war when there is a national liberation movement or a guerrilla struggle." For Paley, "The war in Mexico is political." And this claim includes more dimensions than those already discussed. International considerations and aspects related to insurgency and counterinsurgency must also be taken into account in order to characterize Mexico's modern war.

In 2010 US secretary of state Hillary Clinton compared the situation in Mexico to an insurgency. At that time she asserted that Mexico was looking "more and more like Colombia looked 20 years ago" (quoted in Paley 2014, 113). Likewise, the "White House labeled the Zetas 'a unique and extraordinary threat to the stability of international economies and political systems,' comparable to the Camorra secret network in southern Italy, the Yakuza mob in Japan, and the Brothers' Circle of Eastern Europe" (Grayson 2014b, 9). Alleging insurgency in Mexico by "drug cartels," some actors proposed the utilization of counterinsurgency as an effective way to combat them.[10] For example, in 2009 the head of the US Joint Chiefs of Staff stated that he supported the use of counterinsurgency in Mexico: "the law enforcement segment of the Merida Initiative can be understood as the application of counterinsurgency war" (Paley 2014, 113).

In Paley's view (2014, 113), "counterinsurgency can be understood not only as a form of warfare but also as a kind of war with outcomes that may differ from those of traditional combat." The drug war in Mexico started as an irregular war and then transformed into a symmetric nonconventional war that involved insurgent and counter-insurgent actors. When labeling TCOs as insurgents and reacting with counterinsurgency, the problem in the country acquires a political dimension and TCOs become political actors. This reinforces even more the idea that Mexico has been through a civil war that started at the beginning of Felipe Calderón's administration. But this is not all: the so-called insurgents incorporated into the Mexican conflict key elements of the Central American civil wars. As Paley (2013, pars. 17–18) recognizes:

> There are certain lines of continuity among the wars (including genocide) in Central America in the 1970s, '80s, and '90s that are clearly traceable to Mexico today. For example, grenades used by the Zetas in attacks in Mexico have been traced back to the 1980s, when they were sold by the US to the military of El Salvador. Another thread connecting the 36-year war in Guatemala to today is the Kaibiles, the country's elite special forces, whose members were responsible for horrific massacres then, and who today are active both as an elite government force and as members of criminal groups. . . . In addition to these concrete examples, many of the practices of terror used by armies such as Guatemala's have resurfaced in Mexico and Central America at the hands of criminal groups.

Mexican TCOs, inspired by the Zeta model, incorporated into their regular practices and combat strategy some key features that characterize Central American gangs and other paramilitary groups, particularly the Maras and Kaibiles. The Maras can be considered "a new form of insurgency" (Etcharren 2006, par. 46). The Zetas and Kaibiles were trained in counterinsurgency operations; these groups demonstrate a type of power that transcends the use of weapons due to their capacity to define tactics and strategies through reasoning, intelligence, and logistics. Criminal insurgency and counterinsurgency generate high levels of violence, which greatly intensify with government intervention and its support of irregular counterinsurgent forces. The intensity of this violence is an effect of the war.

The Dual Function of Violence in Mexico's War

Civil wars show economic and military dimensions that are interrelated in complex ways. The main implication of simultaneously considering these two dimensions of civil wars "is that the violence

of belligerents has the dual instrumental function of extracting resources and increasing control" (Dufort 2014, 214). The case of Colombia is appropriate to illustrate this process and to understand what
has been going on in Mexico, because it also involves irregular actors
on both sides of the war. Moreover, this case is "especially interesting for the study of belligerents' modes of operation since both insurgents and counter-insurgents use irregular forms of warfare involving economic extraction from the civilian population" (Dufort 2014,
217). Something similar seems to have happened in Mexico, but without guerrillas.

In Colombia, as Dufort (2014, 217) notes, "paramilitaries were
created as natural competitors to the guerrillas as they aimed to take
control of the economic niches that allow insurgents to thrive." Here
paramilitaries established some opportunistic relationships with drug
traffickers and emerging landowners. Their appearance "radically
changed the financial condition of military competition: irregular
counterinsurgent forces started to compete with the guerrillas for [land
and] extractive opportunities" (224). Dufort (2014, 220–221) explains
how violence in Colombia had a dual function in civil war:

> The violence used by paramilitaries not only provoked the guerrillas
> to retreat, it simultaneously transformed the economic context. . . .
> Colombia's rural integration into the global economy [was] mediated
> through the expansion of the paramilitaries' mode of operation. At the
> national level, the dual function of this pattern of violence resulted in
> land concentration and counterinsurgent control consolidation. With-
> out a doubt, globalization and warfare have been closely interacting
> through this process.

In this case, "paramilitary violence seems to have the dual impact
of increasing counterinsurgent control and enhancing an agrarian
counter-reform" (Dufort 2014, 232). Such a process and the implications of the dual function of violence in the context of irregular warfare have not been exclusive to Colombia. In Malaysia, for example,
"under the command of the British High Commissioner Sir Gerald
Temple (1952–1954), counterinsurgent violence was used to promote
economic sectors particularly hostile to insurgents (e.g., extensive production of palm oil and rubber)" (232). The dual function of violence
has also been evident in Mexico's drug war and recent conflicts in
some Central American countries (such as Honduras and Guatemala).

As Dufort (2014, 216) recognizes, "Most studies on the relationship between armed actors and economic niches in irregular wars have concentrated their attention on guerrillas." However, the dual function of violence in the context of irregular warfare does not exclusively involve the participation of guerrilla groups. In fact any violent act in this type of conflict has "simultaneous impacts on resource extraction and control attempts" (214). Paramilitary-style crime groups can take the place of guerrilla movements in new civil wars and bring about similar end results. This is the case of Mexico (analyzed in detail in chapters 7 to 9 in section III). According to Paley (2013, 2014), the militarization of criminal syndicates creates forms of paramilitarism that can be extremely favorable to the expansion of capitalism. Paley (2014) sees resource extraction as a driving force behind drug-war conflicts in the Americas.

Casualties of Mexico's War

With regard to its duration and severity, the conflict in Mexico fits into most definitions of civil war. Mexico's drug war has resulted in more than 150,000 deaths. "To put these numbers in perspective, this is eight times larger than the number of casualties in the Iraq and Afghanistan wars combined" (Canales 2013, par. 4). Apart from the deaths of members of criminal groups and law enforcement agencies at all levels, much of the violence in this conflict was inflicted on civilians, including small entrepreneurs, farmers, indigenous groups, and regular citizens of all ages and professions. The Zetas model (involving such practices as extortion and kidnapping and followed by a number of criminal organizations) expanded rapidly during times of war, when more financial resources were needed to face the government's attacks. These actions affected civilians to a very large extent.

Mexico's drug war had extremely high human costs. Assassinations and disappearances—of criminals, government authorities, and regular citizens—extended throughout the country. The casualties were massive, as in any other civil war. In an interview given to journalist Diego Osorno at the end of 2011, Mauricio Fernández—a successful businessman who has served three times as mayor of San Pedro Garza García, Nuevo León, and who allegedly created the paramilitary group Los Rudos—explained the actions of irregular armed groups and the casualties of Mexico's war (quoted in Osorno 2014, pars. 21–23):

I hear about events occurring—through mayors, through friends of mine with cattle ranches, through people who say: "Well, they came, and landed in helicopters, and killed everyone." And none of this ever comes out in the press. According to many stories I have heard, they have also killed a tremendous amount of people savagely . . . one mayor said to me: "Hey, they ordered a bulldozer, from who knows where—to bury the bodies left from one of the federal government's special operations." . . . [O]n my friend's ranch . . . helicopters came in and basically massacred everyone. Additionally, there are many murders within the criminal organizations—victims of internal arguments—who get dissolved in vats of acid, or buried, or disappeared by some other method. You don't hear about those either. So, if you were to say to me, "There are 50,000 official deaths," I would believe that we are actually talking about, easily, a quarter of a million deaths. I believe that for every murder—whether committed by criminal organizations or by the government—that does get reported, there are five that do not. So, whether we are talking about 50 deaths or a quarter of a million—which is more my estimate—it doesn't really matter. It takes more than a death count to change a country.

In his comment Fernández highlighted that these massacres were not covered by the media. This frequently happens during civil wars. Due to the extreme violence in Mexico generated by armed groups, including government forces and paramilitary-style criminal organizations, the information usually released by the traditional media stopped flowing in some regions of the country. This happened particularly in locations where the Zetas had a strong presence (such as Tamaulipas, Veracruz, Guerrero, Coahuila, and Zacatecas). Tamaulipas was the most representative case (Correa-Cabrera and Nava 2013). The silencing of the media in particular zones of the country during Mexico's civil war was achieved through practices known as *plata o plomo* (silver or lead): intimidating journalists and communicators or bribing journalists and media entrepreneurs with the intention of limiting the coverage on events related to organized crime, thus making criminal actions practically invisible to public scrutiny (Dal Bó et al. 2006).

The silencing of the media and the control of transportation routes is a central feature of civil wars. Mexico experienced these phenomena in various parts of the territory, while criminal syndicates, official armed forces, and other irregular armed groups were vying for control. Another characteristic of civil wars are disappearances, by criminal groups or government forces. According to Itzel Reyes and Mónica Villanueva (2014, par. 1), approximately 75 percent of the Mexican territory has been used to build clandestine graves to bury abandoned bodies of rivals. In most of these cases, the names of the victims and the reason why they were assassinated remain unknown.

Reyes and Villanueva (2014, pars. 2–4) also mention that in 2014 the army, the navy, and local authorities found bodies of men, women, and children of all ages in twenty-four Mexican states. Tamaulipas, Veracruz, Coahuila, Guerrero, Jalisco, Michoacán, and Morelos all registered a large number of these discoveries. Mexican authorities have not been able to identify the bodies; they have no reliable official records, including fingerprints, DNA information, and photographs of the bodies found in these mass graves.

One of the most emblematic cases of mass graves in Mexico in the past few years was in San Fernando, Tamaulipas, where almost two hundred bodies were found. The mass assassination was allegedly perpetrated by the Zetas, and most of the victims were supposedly migrants. Most of the bodies have not been identified, however, and the people who were responsible for this massacre have not been detained yet.[11] Guerrero and Coahuila are two other states where several mass graves have been found recently. In January 2014 five hundred human remains were found in several clandestine graves in northern Coahuila; the Zetas were allegedly responsible for these assassinations (Reyes and Villanueva 2014, pars. 10–12).

Mexico's Cyberwar: Fourth-Generation Warfare

Mexico's modern civil war was not only fought on physical territory: it was also fought in cyberspace. This section discusses how cyberspace turned into a new battlefield in the so-called war on drugs in Mexico. Cyberspace seems to have functioned as a testing platform or a laboratory for new forms of war in Mexico, where all participants— including organized crime and Mexico's government—communicate their messages and justify their actions in the real-world armed conflict. Militarization and paramilitarization have arrived in cyberspace, where the passage from irregular to symmetric nonconventional warfare becomes evident. In recent times irregular armed groups have used these new platforms with the aim of influencing national and international perception of the situation in Mexico and maybe to justify the government's actions, especially the militarization of Mexico's security strategy.

The Zetas and the War in Cyberspace: A New Battlefield

In the context of extreme violence, paramilitarization of organized crime, militarization, paramilitarism, and the control of highways and the media in important areas by criminal and other irregular armed actors, social media became a key weapon. Cyberspace began to operate as a forum to post complaints and reports about violent events or situations of risk (SDRs: *situaciones de riesgo*) and then became a place where every actor involved in the so-called war against drugs could participate. This alternative space turned into the new battlefield where diverse groups—armed forces included—confronted each other, reinforced their tactics, and communicated with other actors, thus reproducing a "real war" that has resulted in the death of more than a hundred thousand people in the past few years.

As in the actual war, TCOs and citizens initiated a battle in cyberspace. "We, the *tuiteros* [Twitter users] and *blogueros* [bloggers], also became part of this war, but our war was virtual," says a citizen journalist in the city of Reynosa.[12] The use of social media in the context of extreme violence and constant SDRs sparked collective action. Civil society started to report events related to organized crime anonymously through a series of social media platforms, utilizing a variety of electronic tools that have been modified in the last few years.[13] In this violent framework, where terror dominated key territories and traditional media stopped reporting events related to organized crime, citizens began reporting SDRs through social media (Facebook, Twitter, WhatsApp, and so forth). They became what has been called "citizen journalists" or "citizen correspondents."[14] Numerous digital news websites containing timely information of violent events appeared quite quickly as well as different blogs and other forums focusing on organized crime and related themes (among them, Frontera al Rojo Vivo, Blog del Narco, Borderland Beat, and other local electronic platforms).

Twitter became the preferred platform that citizens used to transmit alerts and warn other members of their communities about shootings, road blockades, grenade attacks, and other violent events. Information on SDRs on Twitter made use of hashtags (#s) related to specific violent cities or acts related to organized crime. The most popular hashtags included #Balacera (shooting), #SDR (situation of risk), #CO (organized crime), #GA (armed group), #CA (armed citizens), #FA (armed forces), #Reynosafollow, #Laredofollow, #CdVictoria, #Matamoros,

#Tampico, #Mante, #Mantefollow, #Torreon, #Saltillo, #Monclova, #PiedrasNegras, #Acuna, #MTYfollow, #RiesgoMTY, #Verfollow, #Veralert, and #Xalfollow. It is worth mentioning that the most popular city hashtags used in this context belonged to cities where the Zetas had a significant presence and exercised significant control over the means of communication and transportation.

The success of these types of citizen platforms did not go unnoticed by criminal organizations and the government, which started to use them extensively. They even infiltrated some social media networks that had been extremely popular and were initially utilized exclusively by civil society (Correa-Cabrera 2015b). As a result, everyone was aware of the uncontrolled violence, with the Zetas and similar groups making sure that society was terrorized by images of beheadings, dismembered bodies, mass assassinations, and other horrors. "It seemed like a premeditated strategy," another citizen journalist claimed.[15] The images presented through the media in Mexico, and particularly those in social media, showed a country at war where the state was losing the monopoly on violence. It is worth noting that members of the Zetas were key players in this war—including the war in cyberspace. The organization at some point was considered "public enemy number one" of Mexico's government and society. This reputation extended beyond Mexico's borders and also reached cyberspace.

Irregular Warfare in Cyberspace

Mexico's cyberwar accurately represented the different stages of Mexico's armed conflict. At first it mirrored irregular warfare, where clearly defined criminal groups attacked society and responded to the government's actions. TCOs utilized social media to communicate their achievements, send messages to the government, and terrorize society by displaying blood and death in a series of photos and videos. "The intention of those messages was to generate fear and limit our ability to act as a group; they seemed like weapons of social control," said one Twitter user based in Reynosa.[16] These actions in cyberspace complemented real-world murder scenes and messages. In September 2011 four people were murdered in Nuevo Laredo for utilizing social media to denounce the activities of organized crime. Two of the victims were a man and a woman, who were found hanging from a footbridge located on the west side of the city. Billboards were placed near the bodies warning people that they would face the same fate if they continued posting complaints online. These scenes went viral on social media and appeared widely in the Mexican national press and TV.

Another emblematic case was that of María Elizabeth Macías, a 39-year-old woman known as "La Nena de Laredo" (the Girl of Laredo) who was the editor-in-chief of the daily newspaper *Primera Hora* and collaborator of the Nuevo Laredo en Vivo website. She constantly sent tweets against criminal groups and uploaded information on a blog denouncing the activities of organized crime. Her body was found decapitated, with her head on top of a well-known stone monument in Nuevo Laredo—a Christopher Columbus monument known as La Glorieta de Colón—in September 2011. This was the first documented murder of a journalist and blogger by organized crime in retaliation for information posted on a social media site. The message found then, signed by the Zetas, read (Vargas 2012, par. 6):

> OK Nuevo Laredo en Vivo and social media sites. I am Nena de Laredo and I'm here because of my [online] reports and yours. . . . For those who don't believe, this happened to me because of my actions, for trusting the army and the navy. . . .
> Thank you for your attention,
> La Nena de Laredo
> ZZZ

On November 9, 2011, in the same place in Nuevo Laredo, the decapitated body of an individual of approximately thirty-five years old was found with a message saying that his death occurred because of his social media reports denouncing organized crime activities: "Hello (XD) I am the 'Rascatripas' [Gut-scraper] and this happened to me for not understanding that I should not have reported on social media. I am . . . like La Nena de Laredo and with this report I say goodbye to Nuevo Laredo en Vivo." These violent actions were part of an irregular war that took place in a real space as well as in cyberspace and served to silence social media users and establish further control over the communications media, both traditional and social. The perpetrators of these actions were not fully identified. They could have been criminal groups or even government forces.

One of the latest attempts to silence social media users reporting activities of organized crime occurred on October 16, 2014, in the city of Reynosa, when a very popular Twitter user, María del Rosario Fuentes Rubio (who used the Twitter account @Miut3 and was also known as "Felina") was murdered after sending a message to the virtual community reporting SDRs in which she warned them not to continue performing such activity (Nelsen 2014). "No matter who was behind those actions and messages, they really affected our activity as citizen reporters. We suddenly became fearful, paranoid . . . and started to think twice before sending a report about a situation of risk in our community," a once very active citizen reporter in Tamaulipas said.[17]

Another example of media censorship in drug war times involved another highly popular social media user known as "Valor por Tamaulipas" (Courage for Tamaulipas), who mainly reported SDRs through Facebook and Twitter. According to this widely covered story—based on rumors and not on actual evidence or verifiable information—in February 2013 hundreds of flyers circulated in different locations in Ciudad Victoria, the capital city of Tamaulipas, through which organized crime supposedly offered a reward in exchange for information about the identity and whereabouts of Valor por Tamaulipas (VxT) (*Proceso* 2013a, 2013b). The flyers offered 600,000 pesos to the person who provided exact details of the administrator of the VxT website and Twitter account or for any information about direct family members, such as parents, siblings, children, or wife (Hernández 2014, 27).

Two days later a video circulated in which an alleged collaborator of VxT was murdered and left a message just before he died, saying: "This message goes to all the community dedicated to post information on Facebook and Twitter on the server of VxT. These people [the captors] are now using sophisticated means and special equipment to find the exact location of social media users through their IP addresses. I am not the first nor the last one to be located. For your own safety, refrain from publishing any information or else this is the price you will pay" (Hernandez 2014, 27–28).

A Symmetric Nonconventional War on the Web: Cyberparamilitarism

It is worth noting that during this cyberwar against drugs in Mexico censorship of social media has taken place for the most part in states where traditional media outlets were also silenced. This censorship essentially occurred in regions where the Zetas or similar groups had a strong presence (Correa-Cabrera 2015b). Moreover, in the most critical period of this conflict (2010–2012), these actions took place in plazas or cities that were clearly under the control of the Zetas (such as Nuevo Laredo, Veracruz, Reynosa, and Ciudad Victoria). This is part of an irregular war in cyberspace that eventually turned into a virtual symmetric nonconventional war in some zones of the country.

With Mexico's modern civil war being reproduced in social media, it is possible that the existing cases of paramilitarism in the real conflict moved over to cyberspace as well. By analyzing the development of the Mexican war in social media, "it is possible to observe actors with specific agendas who appear with citizen profiles, but who seem to have close connections with government agencies," said citizen reporter @MrCruzStar.[18] Also worth noting is the presence of cyberparamilitary practices and users with military profiles not directly associated with the armed forces but whose activity may hint that they kept a direct link with the government. In sum, cyberspace acted as a new stage for this war and seemed to provide a testing laboratory for national security agencies, perhaps even for foreign governments. It is possible to see the influence of Mexican government agencies on social media platforms, complementing strategies that were implemented in real life (Correa-Cabrera 2015b).

In addition to cases like Valor por Michoacán (VxM), which represented the self-defense movement in the southwestern Mexican state of Michoacán, other interesting storylines played out in this cyberwar, such as "#OpCartel," which involved the group of hacktivists "Anonymous" and the above-mentioned case of Valor por Tamaulipas (VxT).[19] It is worth mentioning that these cases occurred in regions where the Zetas or other groups following the same model (the Knights Templar, for example) had a significant presence (such as Veracruz, Tamaulipas, and Michoacán). The agendas of the groups participating in the cyberwar are unclear, but it is evident that these occurrences have contributed to spreading fear among Mexican society, thus validating to some extent the militarization of Mexico's security strategy in some parts of the country and justifying the implementation of drastic actions by the Mexican federal forces (Correa-Cabrera 2015b).

#OPCARTEL: A LABORATORY
FOR CYBERPARAMILITARISM

Possibly the first experiment of cyberparamilitarism in Mexico was the campaign started by the group of hacktivists Anonymous on Twitter, known as "Operación Cartel" or "#OpCartel."[20] The members of Anonymous threatened the Zetas by saying that they would expose the identities of key actors associated with the criminal organization in retaliation for the alleged kidnapping of one of its members. According to the group, the abduction took place in Veracruz during an Anonymous leaflet campaign known as "Paperstorm" (Genbeta.com 2011).

On October 6, 2011, Anonymous published an accusation against the Zetas through a YouTube video and some days later threatened to post a public list of government officials allegedly linked to the criminal organization if the hostage was not released by November 5 (Schiller 2011). In the end the Anonymous member was supposedly liberated and no list was posted, but in the process Anonymous obtained information about organized crime and activists from other social media users. This group of hacktivists would head the operation and concentrate information and confidential reports provided by other individuals, alleging that it was too dangerous for regular citizens to participate directly due to the much larger capacity and resources in the hands of organized crime.

According to Shannon Young, an independent journalist and editor of the South Notes blog, "this confrontation seemed to be more a 'false flag' operation through social media than a real fight between citizen groups and organized crime."[21] Operación Cartel could have been created with the intention of tracking the activity of cyber-activists and other social media users (including those connected with organized crime) and monitoring their locations and reactions to certain messages, in what could be considered an intelligence exercise in cyberspace. On the one hand, fear was spread among the virtual community through the announcement of an alleged kidnapping of a hacktivist by the Zetas and the claim of plausible further attacks against other social media users. On the other hand, Anonymous attempted to centralize SDR reports (Correa-Cabrera 2015b).

The main objective of #OpCartel could have been to gather intelligence from activists and then control, in some form, the flow of information circulating through cyberspace. Anonymous may have been used or infiltrated by a government agency to test intelligence and counterintelligence operations through social media, while at the same time generating a sense of terror among the virtual community with the aim of justifying the militarization of the security strategy in Mexico. This would help to legitimize the actions of the Mexican government in a situation that threatened the security of Mexican citizens, even in cyberspace.

According to Shannon Young, "#OpCartel was probably the first experiment of military intelligence and counterintelligence in social media, as part of Mexico's new civil war."[22] Interestingly, this experiment involved the Zetas organization.[23] It showed some elements of paramilitarism that are not easy to test but mirrored what was taking place in Mexico at that time.[24] It is worth mentioning that the arrival of paramilitaries in Veracruz occurred in the real world and in cyberspace at almost the same time. At the end of September 2011 the Mata-Zetas appeared in a video after dumping dozens of bodies on the streets of Boca del Río, Veracruz (*Animal Político* 2011). Operación Cartel took place a few days later. The epicenter was also Veracruz, and the enemy was the Zetas group.

VALOR POR TAMAULIPAS: CITIZEN, SELF-DEFENSE, OR PARAMILITARISM IN SOCIAL MEDIA?

In 2012 the infiltration of social media by cyberparamilitaries was noticeable due to the presence of actors who did not officially form part of the armed forces but displayed military tendencies in their language and social media profiles. A successful model of this type is represented by Valor por Tamaulipas, a cyber communications platform that replaced Blog del Narco as the preferred source of information on situations of risk in Tamaulipas.[25] This platform ended up monopolizing the reports of SDRs as well as of the activities of organized crime in an extremely violent Mexican state. Notwithstanding the alleged "citizen" character of this platform (Monroy-Hernández 2014; Hernández 2014), VxT seems to be a clear example of what is known as cyberparamilitarism.

The arrival of VxT in social media occurred in early 2012.[26] With considerable resources at hand and alleging citizen collaboration, this virtual platform considerably extended its influence through the whole state of Tamaulipas and accumulated a large number of followers. "Due to the type of reports and information it disseminated, VxT became an essential source for those who wished to know about the security situation in this northeastern Mexican state," a Twitter user based in Matamoros said.[27] This social media user communicated—in a more systematic way than any other source—important details about the extreme violence prevailing in Tamaulipas, showing it to be an unmanageable state that was extremely corrupt and largely under the control of organized crime. This insecurity presented by VxT would justify the use of the armed forces as the preferred public security strategy in Tamaulipas. In other words, the militarization of the state seemed to be an adequate measure to regain the control of the territories that were under the control of organized crime.

Through analysis of the content and messages and a deep investigation of the development of this account's profile, it is possible to question the citizen nature of VxT (Hernández 2013). The account displays several elements that show strong links to government agencies and in particular to the Mexican armed forces. From its inception, Valor por Tamaulipas seems to have been linked to the Mexican government. By closely following VxT's Facebook and Twitter messages (see https://twitter.com/ValorTamaulipas and https://www.facebook.com /ValorPorTamaulipas) and examining the language used in some of them, it is possible to identify elements and phrases related to the military and armed forces. Also, VxT is associated with other accounts that seem to have direct or indirect links to the Mexican army and navy. It is worth emphasizing VxT's use of images and messages promoting and glorifying the role of the armed forces in the battle against organized crime in Mexico (Correa-Cabrera 2015b).

OTHER FORMS OF CYBERPARAMILITARISM: SELF-DEFENSE GROUPS ON THE WEB

New patterns of cyberparamilitarism in Mexico have appeared in more recent times as Mexico's conflict has turned into a symmetric unconventional war in some parts of the country. The case of Michoacán is of special interest when looking at how cyberparamilitarism spread and adapted to local conditions. Valor por Michoacán (VxM) is a good example of this process; this platform appeared on Facebook ("Valor por Michoacán SDR" on https://www.facebook.com /ValorMichoacanSDR) and Twitter (@ValorMichoacan on https://twitter .com/ValorMichoacan) and focused on self-defense groups.

The Facebook page of VxM was created on August 14, 2013, the day of the arrest of forty-five members of the community police in the municipality of Aquila in Michoacán. Irregular armed groups then started to use social media to report on criminal groups' activities and to assess the involvement of government authorities in this conflict (García 2014). The role of VxM was particularly interesting because it advanced "collective action" in real and virtual arenas by promoting the activities of self-defense groups in their fight against the Knights Templar and other criminal actors. It was also used as a recruitment tool for self-defense groups (Monroy-Hernández 2014).

The VxT and VxM platforms show some basic differences but display a similar model and seem to be part of a common paramilitary strategy in cyberspace. As in the case of #OpCartel and the Mata-Zetas in Veracruz, paramilitarism on the ground in Tamaulipas and Michoacán coincides with cyberparamilitarism in the respective regions and the rise of the VxT and VxM accounts. In the case of Michoacán, paramilitary actions seem mainly to have involved self-defense groups. According to some, this seems to be an informal component of the government's security strategy against organized crime in this southwestern Mexican state (Correa-Cabrera et al. 2015). The case of Tamaulipas is more complex, because paramilitary actions have been apparently performed by irregular armed groups specializing in counterinsurgency operations, maybe trained by government forces or possibly involving actual government forces who fight without uniforms. This seems to resemble the case of Valor por Tamaulipas in cyberspace. There is no confirmation of this, but several elements hint at this possibility.

Fourth-Generation Warfare

Martin Van Creveld, author of *The Transformation of War* (1991), claims that due to the inefficiency of big armies in certain conditions, the control of a society can be exercised through a war strategy that incorporates a combination of propaganda, terror, and psychological manipulation. The battles that feature these elements are sometimes called fourth-generation wars, asymmetric wars, or wars without weapons. In such wars military operations can be replaced or complemented by operations that utilize media or psychological means and are led by experts in communications and mass psychology. All of these elements have complemented Mexico's modern war. The role of the media in this conflict has been crucial. In this sense, Paley (2013, par. 22) recognizes:

> The horrific actions carried out against civilians by criminal groups in the context of the drug war are regularly featured on TV, shared on social media, and printed in newspapers. Few media reports explain and contextualize the use of terror; instead, they portray it as random, wanton, out-of-control violence. . . . The reproduction of these media narratives on screens, iPhones, and tabloids across the region terrorizes the entire society.

Traditional media and social media have had a very important effect on Mexico's public opinion regarding this high-intensity armed conflict or new civil war. Many of the bloody images presented and the messages of out-of-control violence conveyed through these means could be interpreted as an attempt to justify the (continuing) militarization and (current) paramilitarization of the security strategy in the country. In this new phase of Mexico's drug war on the ground and in cyberspace, a greater presence of irregular armed actors with ties to law enforcement agencies can also be seen. At the same time, a desire by the government to be accepted and esteemed by Mexican society might be part of a strategy for generating trust and legitimizing the militarization of security in Mexico. This has been done through the delivery of positive messages supporting the armed forces, federal police, and government actions in general and through the development of a closer relation between public officials and civil society.

The dynamic of Mexico's drug war in cyberspace changes quickly. At present the strategy appears to focus on reconciling the state and civil society. For example, on May 8, 2014 the site "Unidos por los Valores en Tamaulipas" (https://www.facebook.com/#!/unidosporlos valoresentamaulipas/info) was created as a platform to promote a better relationship between the armed forces and civilians. SEDENA, SEMAR, the municipal government of Reynosa, the Tamaulipas government, PGR, and Mexico's Federal Police are all part of this exercise. The site posts information on dates and details about expositions, conferences, concerts, and events showcasing military equipment (aerial, sea, and land units), among other activities involving the government and the civilian population. The objective of this project could be to win the hearts of Tamaulipas society with the aim of legitimizing the government's operations in its fight against organized crime.

These actions seem to be inspired by the strategies developed by the former director of the Central Intelligence Agency (CIA), General David Petraeus, in Iraq and also by those implemented by the US Marine Corps in the Vietnam War (West 1972). The central element of these strategies revolves around the idea of "winning the hearts and minds" of the citizens living in war zones, which implies a closer relationship between the armed forces and the civilian population and a more peaceful coexistence between them.

SECTION III

LOS ZETAS INCORPORATED

The final section of this book assesses the impact of a modern civil war in Mexico on strategic economic activities and reforms, in particular on the hydrocarbon industry and energy reform. It analyzes who benefits from the Zetas' war and explains the links between criminal paramilitaries, civil society, the armed forces, and transnational energy companies. This analysis shows that Mexico's modern civil war seems to be more like a war for hydrocarbons. This argument is exemplified by analyzing the oil and gas–rich state of Tamaulipas, the "cradle" of the Zetas. In fact, violence in Mexico has been concentrated in areas rich in hydrocarbons and key to the future development of Mexico's energy sector. Many of these areas have been controlled by criminal paramilitaries or TCOs like the Zetas, the Knights Templar, La Familia Michoacana, the CJNG, Los Rojos (the Red Ones), Guerreros Unidos (United Warriors), and others. Military and paramilitary operations against organized crime have also been located in these zones.

CHAPTER 7

The Zetas' War and Mexico's Energy Sector

The present chapter analyzes the direct relationship that exists between violence and the presence of natural resources in the so-called time of Mexico's drug war. Through a series of maps this analysis demonstrates that the current conflicts in the country—involving the Zetas or groups that have followed the same model (such as the Knights Templar, the CJNG, and Guerreros Unidos) as well as Mexico's armed forces and paramilitary groups—have been located in regions with abundant natural resources, particularly hydrocarbons or alternate resources necessary for energy generation. This analysis also shows how militarization and current security policies interact with corporate capital and how they determine the protection of economic interests and establish priorities for resource extraction.

Mexico's War: A War for Hydrocarbons?

Resource Extraction and Civil Wars

As mentioned in chapter 6, civil wars have the dual function of extracting resources and increasing control. According to Paley (2014), we should take into consideration resource extractions as a driving force behind whatever the current dominant explications of the conflicts are. According to Gray (2008, 78), the role of natural resources in civil conflicts and the proliferation of armed groups can be exemplified in the case of Colombia, "a nation rich in oil, gas, coal, timber, cropland, gold, platinum, and emeralds." She points out that "the presence of oil, gemstones, illicit drugs, and other so-called war commodities fuels violence by eroding trust and discipline in armed groups, and prolongs conflict by giving weaker groups the means to keep fighting" (78):

Where resources that can be smuggled, mined, or logged are available, armed groups can use them to establish areas of de facto sovereignty and garner local support. . . . In the coal, oil, and gas sectors, the government has the advantage as far as the technology and capital required for extraction, but the energy sector is vulnerable to obstruction and the resources cannot be relocated, so energy firms have been known to undermine governments by paying off whatever armed group holds power locally.

Hence "resource development attracts armed groups seeking protection rents, thereby strengthening the groups that garner those rents and intensifying competition among rivals" (Gray 2008, 79). Extreme violence in Colombia coincided with a period of increased resource exploitation. It can be said that the driving force behind violence in this Andean country was not only drug cultivation but also the "licit development in the oil, mining, and agribusiness sectors" (79). The same thing has happened in Mexico in the time of the drug wars. "Looting" seems to be a recurrent element of the Mexican armed conflict; but, as Kalyvas (2001, 103) claims, it is unclear whether the concept of looting "refers to the causes of war" or "the motivations" of TCOs "(or both)." It might refer to both. Mexican TCOs—following the Zeta model—have waged war in order to loot and have looted to be able to wage war. In the end the actions of these groups have greatly influenced the recent transformation of Mexico's energy sector.

These phenomena are characteristic not only of Colombia and Mexico but of several regions of the world. Similar dynamics can be observed and documented in other parts of the hemisphere, such as in Guatemala and Honduras.[1] The internal conflicts in these Latin American countries have been concentrated in strategic areas for energy projects and resource extraction. Moreover, criminal paramilitarization, militarization, and paramilitarism coincide with regions that show important social and land conflicts, where some segments of the society oppose the imposition of mega-projects, particularly those related to oil and natural gas exploration or exploitation (Paley 2014). Violence has had the ultimate effect of restricting social mobilization and supporting private investments in a number of extractive industries.

Mexico's recent history provides a good example of these dynamics. Zones of potential resource extraction after energy reform have shown the highest levels of violence, experiencing first the arrival of criminal groups (following the Zeta model) and then the militarization and paramilitarization of security, allegedly implemented as a response to "drug-related violence" and the so-called cartel wars. However, drug trafficking was not the sole cause of this chain of violence—and maybe not even the most important one. Conflict involving the presence of Mexican armed forces and irregular armed groups has been mainly concentrated in Mexico's northeast, Chihuahua, the Gulf Coast states of Veracruz and Tabasco, Michoacán, Guerrero—and most recently, in Jalisco and Colima. These states are home of the most important ports in the country, and are key sites for energy production and transportation (see appendix 3).[2]

When analyzing the patterns of armed conflict, extreme violence, and potential resource extraction after energy reform, we could claim that Mexico's war has not been a war on drugs but a war for the control of territory—an area that is rich in hydrocarbons. Dominating these regions would assure the domination of most of the supply chains in Mexico's energy sector. Mexican TCOs, such as the Zetas, the Knights Templar, and CJNG, began establishing control over many of these zones. But in the end the resulting violence and government responses to it might bolster the participation of (and control by) new actors: transnational energy firms.

Energy in Mexico's Northeast and the Gulf Corridor

The patterns described above are quite visible in part of Chihuahua, Mexico's northeast (Coahuila, Nuevo León, and Tamaulipas), and the Gulf corridor (particularly Veracruz and Tabasco). These regions are rich in hydrocarbons and have abundant deposits of oil, natural gas, shale gas, and coal (see maps 7.1 and 7.2). The main zone of natural gas extraction in Mexico, the Burgos Basin, is located here. Veracruz and Tamaulipas are among Mexico's "most important states in terms of hydrocarbons development" and "house significant refining assets and some of Mexico's largest ports" (Daugherty 2015, par. 2). According to Mexico's Mining Chamber (Cámara Minera de México), the country produces 15 million tons of coal annually and almost 95 percent is mined in the state of Coahuila.

Important discoveries of oil and shale gas deposits were recently made in this region (see the section "A Fight for the Control of Territory and Natural Resources" below). Such discoveries were at the forefront of the debate for energy reform and will probably attract the majority of the private investment (foreign and national) that is projected

Map 7.1. Energy in Chihuahua, northeastern Mexico, and the Gulf corridor.
Sources: Pemex and SGM. Design by Mario Cruz and Carlos D. Gutiérrez-Mannix.

to come to develop Mexico's energy sector after the historic change in legislation. In fact a number of states in northern Mexico (like Coahuila, Nuevo León, and Tamaulipas) are drawing up plans to "provide qualified human capital and physical infrastructure to make their regions more attractive to investors" (O'Neil and Taylor 2014, par. 18).

Recent discoveries of shale gas in Mexico run from Matamoros, Tamaulipas, to Piedras Negras, Coahuila, in an area that shares a border with Texas. These shale deposits are an extension of the Eagle Ford Shale formation, which has been intensively developed over the past few years (O'Neil and Taylor 2014, par. 18). The new discoveries are recoverable through a process known as "fracking."[3] After Mexico's energy reform, foreign energy companies will be able to frack in these areas. Mexico's shale gas reserves are extensive and will plausibly make Mexico one of the world's leading natural gas producers.

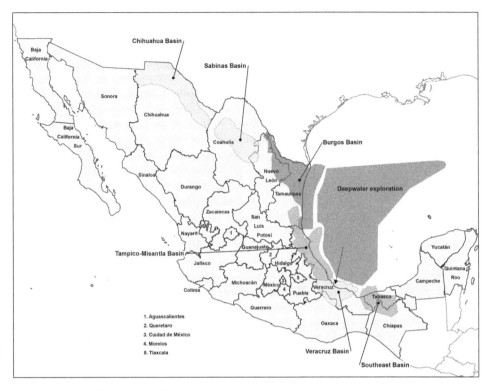

Map 7.2. Oil and gas in Mexico.
Source: *Milenio* newspaper, with information from Pemex. Design by Carlos D. Gutiérrez-Mannix.

Overall, the zones rich in shale gas in Mexico, where important investments are about to come, are located in the states of Chihuahua, Coahuila, Nuevo León, Tamaulipas, San Luis Potosí, Veracruz, and Tabasco (see map 7.3). Pemex recently identified important potential shale gas reserves in five geological areas: Sabinas, Coahuila; Burro-Picachos, Coahuila; Burgos (Tamaulipas, Nuevo León, and Coahuila); Tampico-Misantla (Tamaulipas and Veracruz); and Veracruz (Cruz Serrano 2011).

THE BURGOS BASIN: STRATEGIC GAS RESERVE

The Burgos Basin is just one of the oil- and gas-rich areas in northeastern Mexico. Officially called Activo Integral Burgos, it is Mexico's most important non-petroleum-associated gas reserve and is estimated to hold two-thirds of Mexico's technically recoverable shale

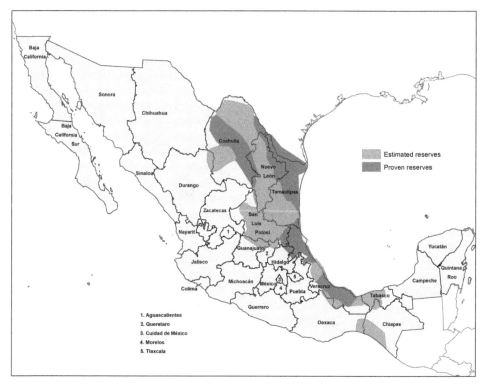

Map 7.3. Shale gas reserves in Mexico.
Source: EIA.

gas resources.[4] It has an extension of 70 thousand square miles and includes important areas in Tamaulipas, Nuevo León, and Coahuila (see map 7.4).[5] Soon after the signing of NAFTA, gas exploitation work was intensified at the Burgos Basin by partially allowing the participation of private businesses, such as Delta, Repsol, Petrobras, Schlumberger, and Halliburton, which have operated as contractors for Petróleos Mexicanos (Pemex) in this zone.[6] Since then the amount of investment in infrastructure for the extraction of gas has increased considerably (Meza 2010). Nevertheless, the hydrocarbons exploitation net is still very limited in relation to the richness of the region.[7] For example, in 2010 the neighboring state of Texas had more than 90,000 discovered deposits and over 10,000 were operating, while Tamaulipas had 11,000 explored deposits and only 1,900 were operating (Meza 2010). This will change with new private investments after the passage of energy reform.

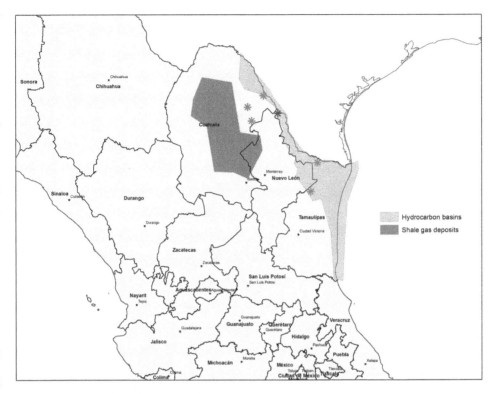

Map 7.4. Hydrocarbons in northeastern Mexico.
Source: Pemex. Design by Mario Cruz and Carlos D. Gutiérrez-Mannix.

Violence in Hydrocarbon-Rich Zones

Organized crime has had a strong impact on Mexico's energy sector, mainly in the northeastern region of the country, the Gulf corridor, and the state of Michoacán (see map 7.5). These regions are rich in hydrocarbons or natural resources that are integral for energy production (for example, iron ore in Michoacán). Northeastern Mexico—in particular the states of Coahuila, Nuevo León, and Tamaulipas—has been rocked by violence, especially where hydrocarbons are abundant (see map 7.4 and appendix 3). This has been the case for Ciudad Mier, Tamaulipas, and other cities located on or near the Burgos Basin and important mining zones in the state of Coahuila. The same phenomenon is observed in Chihuahua, where important oil and shale gas deposits are concentrated. Ojinaga, Chihuahua, for example, is one of the main oil regions of the state and is precisely where the Juárez Car-

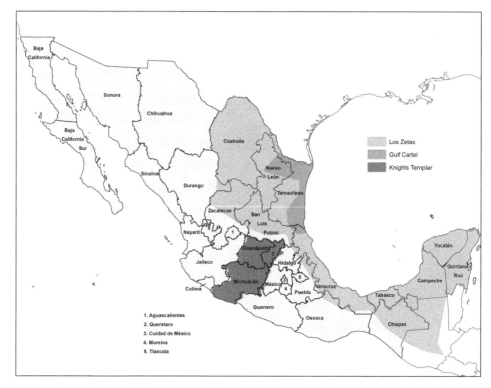

Map 7.5. Territorial control by three major TCOs, 2013.
Source: Correa-Cabrera 2015a. Design by Mario Cruz and Carlos D. Gutiérrez-Mannix.

tel was born. The Juárez Valley—also called Mexico's Murder Valley and considered by some to be "one of the deadliest places on earth" (Baverstock 2015)—has large petroleum and gas reserves and also has recorded the highest number of homicides in Mexico since 2008 as well as displacements of a large number of people (Mayorga 2014).

Violence in Mexico reached a peak in 2011, but investments in the energy sector did not stop. Indeed they increased. At the same time, the involvement of transnational criminal organizations in activities related to resource extraction grew (Cruz 2011). It is quite interesting that at some point the Zetas' areas of territorial control, with extremely high levels of violence fueled by militarization and other government strategies to fight organized crime, coincided with shale gas regions (see maps 7.3 and 7.5). Interestingly, "some of the most significant oil and gas deposits are located in—or just offshore of—areas that came to be known in Mexico as *zonas de silencio* or silence zones" (Young 2014, par. 22).

In silent zones criminal organizations "operate with little hindrance from local authorities; civilians face economic and physical violence; open criticism and adversarial journalism can be life-threatening; and impunity is systemic," explains journalist Shannon Young (2014, par. 23). Many of these zones are located in northeast Mexico as well as in the Gulf corridor, including areas in the states of Coahuila, Chihuahua, Nuevo León, Tamaulipas, San Luis Potosí, and Veracruz. As Paley (2014, 159) explains:

> These regions have all been militarized as part of a war on drugs. Some of them also have high levels of displacement because of violence linked to the war. Following a pattern set in Colombia, there is little doubt that the abilities of residents to organize or even protest against the thousands of wells to be drilled in the desert areas will be massively compromised by the intense violence that preceded the projects.

Natural Resources, Violence, and Businesses: The Cases of Coahuila and Michoacán

Government responses to violence related to organized crime in Mexico through military and paramilitary tactics further elevated violence, terror, and land displacement in zones rich in natural resources. The main losers in this process were small entrepreneurs who initially exploited these resources as well as land and property owners who had to flee these regions due to extreme violence, extortion, and scores of assassinations and disappearances by irregular armed groups (either criminal or linked to the government). Large transnational companies participating in such industries remained untouched and achieved great success during the most violent times in Mexico. What happened in Coahuila and Michoacán exemplified these dynamics as well as the role of different actors (losers and winners) involved in the generation of terror, forced displacements, and resource extraction. During this process, the armed forces, other law enforcement agencies, and transnational companies played key roles and maintained close relationships.

Coahuila: A Land Rich in Coal and Shale Gas

The case of Coahuila illustrates the links between organized crime, state violence, and resource exploitation and how such relationships end up benefiting multinational energy companies. The hostilities in this state mainly involved the Zetas, the armed forces, Coahuila's police, and paramilitary groups. The conflict was allegedly part of Mexico's drug war but in reality seemed to be a war for the control of coal extraction and use as well as for access to territories with large amounts of shale gas, since the state is located just south of the Texas Eagle Ford Shale play.

LOS ZETAS AND HYDROCARBONS IN COAHUILA

In recent years Coahuila, rich in coal and natural gas, has experienced many gruesome events, including the assassination of a former governor's son,[8] gunfights, and the discovery of bags of severed heads at a soccer stadium. It was also the site of the robbery of the alleged corpse of the second most-wanted criminal in the country, Heriberto Lazcano (aka Z-3), leader of Los Zetas. The Zetas arrived in Coahuila and consolidated their presence during the time when Humberto Moreira was governor of the state from 2005 to 2011 (January).[9] The group not only focused on trafficking drugs to the United States but started to get involved in the coal business. Its arrival in Coahuila was accompanied by a massive increase in the levels of violence (AFP 2012, par. 17). In order to infiltrate coal mines, the Zetas began to extort, kidnap, and even kill employees and owners of coal-mining companies (see map 7.6).

Areas with high concentrations of coal and shale gas registered the highest levels of violence in the state. Coal is important for the generation of electricity and for fueling the steel industry, while natural gas and shale gas compete with coal for electricity generation.[10] The most violent areas of Coahuila in the last few years have been the border region, the coal region (*cuenca carbonífera*), and Torreón and Saltillo (the capital city of the state). Today important industrial chains (coal/steel and coal/electricity) represent the greatest source of employment and economic activity in the coal region and in northern Coahuila (AHMSA 2016a). In the state's border region with Texas, just south of the Eagle Ford Shale formation, violence and terror were particularly intense. This area includes recently discovered important reser-

Map 7.6. Violence in Coahuila.
Source: Information provided by Ignacio Alvarado. Map designed by Carlos D.
Gutiérrez-Mannix and Wendy Macías.

voirs of natural gas that are highly valued, given the current conditions of North America's energy markets.

The Massacre of Allende in March 2011, when about three hundred people allegedly disappeared at the hands of Los Zetas, took
place in an area where natural gas and water are abundant. Allende
is located in a region called Los Cinco Manantiales (the Five Springs)

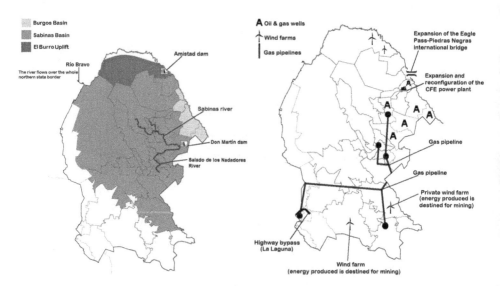

Map 7.7. Water, energy resources, and energy infrastructure in Coahuila. Sources: CFE, CRE, CONABIO, Pemex, SEGOB, SEMARNAT, and Universidad Autónoma de Coahuila. Design by Carlos D. Gutiérrez-Mannix.

due to the vast water springs that cover important parts of this area. This town and its surroundings have been a battlefield with their respective Zeta training camps and clandestine graveyards. According to Osorno (2014, par. 13), "No one lives in the area now and in its current state it resembles the surface of Mars. The only humans that are occasionally seen are the guys in orange jumpsuits that work for Geokinetics, a shale gas exploration and testing company based in Houston." Many oil and gas zones in Coahuila are among the driest in the Americas (Schneider 2015). But Los Cinco Manantiales has enormous potential. In order to exploit the potential of these hydrocarbon-rich areas, as Osorno (2014, par. 14) points out, "two things are needed: permission from the Mexican government and lots of water. With the recent reforms in Mexico, which allow foreign companies to invest in the country's energy [industry], permits are on their way. And, in the Five Springs, water is as abundant as fear."

"There is a close relationship between the energy industry, security, and new forms of organized crime in the northeastern part of the country," says journalist Ignacio Alvarado (see maps 7.6 and 7.7).[11] Official sources blame the Zetas for the extreme violence in Coahuila. However, the reactions of federal law enforcement agencies and the state government through the GATE (see chapter 6)—and allegedly by some paramilitary groups—caused even more violence that also contributed to displace small coal entrepreneurs and landowners from their original properties.

Now bigger companies and transnational corporations have a better chance of exercising further control over much of Mexico's energy production. Shale gas coexists with solar and wind energy to date, and its capacity has exponentially increased since 2008. However, it competes with coal to generate electricity (*Offnews.info* 2013, par. 3). Coahuila's northern lands are rich in both coal and shale gas (see map 7.7). The owners of the largest tracts of these lands will have a competitive advantage producing electricity, other forms of energy, and steel. It is worth noting that coal is an essential resource to produce steel, which plays a key role in the energy sector—for example, in the extraction and transportation of natural gas and other fuels.

ORGANIZED CRIME, CORRUPTION, AND TRANSNATIONAL BUSINESSES

In Mexico's most important coal zone, located in Coahuila, the Zetas, coal entrepreneurs, and the state's government had a close relationship. In recent years this criminal group started to extract and commercialize minerals, particularly coal. According to the state's former governor, Humberto Moreira, the Zetas stole this natural resource and sold it to "third parties, who then [re-sold] it to the Federal Electricity Commission (CFE)" (Paley 2014, 168). It is interesting to observe that PRODEMI (Promotora de Desarrollo Minero de Coahuila [Coahuila's Mining Development Promoter]), a company once owned by the state government of Coahuila, grew considerably during Moreira's administration. In the recent past this firm bought coal from eighty-seven companies—many of them allegedly illegal—and then sold this resource to CFE. In the view of journalist Sanjuana Martínez (2012, par. 2), "it is paradoxical" that the man who governed Coahuila some years ago and was ultimately responsible for the operations of PRODEMI suggested the existence of "coal narco-entrepreneurs" (*narcoempresarios del carbón*), who were the same actors with whom he had done important business. Moreira has actually been associated with this criminal group (García and Alvarado 2014). It has been claimed that he protected the Zetas and allowed them to operate in the state. It is worth noting that Moreira's declarations against narco-entrepreneurs (who allegedly have links to or leadership positions within the Zetas organization) were made after his son was purportedly assassinated by the Zetas.

According to Martínez (2012), Moreira's narco-entrepreneurs would not have been able to survive without the big businesses that allegedly bought their stolen coal. These firms include Altos Hornos de México (AHMSA), Beneficios Internacionales del Norte (BINSA), Compañía Minera El Progreso, Minera Díaz, Minería y Acarreos de Carbón, AlvaRam, El Sabino, and Industrial Minera México (IMMSA) (which belongs to the powerful Mexican business group Grupo México, the largest mining corporation in the country and the third largest copper producer in the world).[12] Among the owners of these businesses are some of the richest men in Mexico, such as Alfonso Ancira and Germán Larrea (Martínez 2012, par. 9).[13]

AHMSA: A SUCCESSFUL MEXICAN TRANSNATIONAL COMPANY

Some transnational businesses (both national and foreign) remained untouched by the violence that has gripped Mexico. While Los Zetas were growing as a business in Coahuila, another transnational company also became highly successful: Altos Hornos de México, SA (AHMSA). The two businesses grew significantly during the governorship of Humberto Moreira and were able to expand their market share and operations considerably.[14] AHMSA and the Zetas both loom large in the recent history of the state of Coahuila. AHMSA is a transnational company of Mexican origin that has grown enormously in the last few years. In this same period the Zetas consolidated their presence in Coahuila, to the extent that it was declared that "Coahuila [was] written with a 'Z'" (*Coahuila se escribe con Z*) (Riva Palacio 2012).

AHMSA is the largest integrated steelworks company in the country. Its corporate offices are located in Monclova, Coahuila. It "operates a vast industrial chain, from the extraction of iron ore and coal to the manufacturing of various steels." In 2016 the company operated "at a rate of close to 5 million metric tons of liquid steel annually and [had] a workforce of 19,000, including its mining subsidiaries" (AHMSA 2016b, pars. 1–3). The role of this firm has been central in the political and economic context of the state of Coahuila. AHMSA's influence has extended to the national level, including its sway over Mexico's energy reform. AHMSA was a big supporter of the constitutional changes that finally opened the oil sector to the private sector's participation. It also expressed a great interest in participating in shale gas exploitation (*El Diario de Coahuila* 2013).

Several companies in northeast Mexico related to the steel industry—mostly small and medium-sized ones—have received threats from organized crime groups that extract coal or iron ore illegally. Some of them have been severely affected financially, and others have been forced to close. AHMSA, however, seemed to thrive in spite of the violence and in spite of past financial problems. The company registered record numbers in production and shipment capacity during Coahuila's most violent years (*Zócalo Saltillo* 2013).[15] AHMSA's situation contrasted with that of most small businesses in the state, which were subject to frequent extortion and attacks by groups like the Zetas.

In sum, two very different realities have taken place simultaneously in the state of Coahuila in the last few years: rapid industrial development and the remarkable growth of transnational energy companies such as AHMSA and Los Zetas; and extreme violence that has mainly affected the most vulnerable groups in society, including small landowners and small- and medium-sized entrepreneurs who compete with transnational energy companies. Many of these smaller companies have closed, or their owners have been forced to flee due to threats and extortion. Their place will probably be occupied in the future by large corporations operating in several stages of the energy supply chain. The involvement of the Zetas and the responses to the groups' actions by the federal government and state forces seem to have facilitated this process.

Michoacán: Iron Ore and the Methamphetamine Trade

With a key port that connects Mexico to Asia (Lázaro Cárdenas), Michoacán has been strategic for drug trafficking. Both the Familia Michoacana and Los Caballeros Templarios have controlled areas in this state, with the second group dominating most of the illegal activities and self-defense groups recently joining the fray. Michoacán has become the epicenter of Mexico's production of synthetic drugs, which are exported internationally together with poppy and marijuana (Ángel 2014b, par. 1). At the same time, the state is strategic for drug entrepreneurs who import precursor chemicals from South America and Asia through the port of Lázaro Cárdenas. Criminal and illegal activities in Michoacán, however, are not centered solely on the drug trade. More recently, criminal groups have diversified their activities and have started extracting and trading minerals, particularly iron ore. Violence has followed these groups to areas with extensive iron ore reserves.

A NEW BUSINESS: IRON ORE EXTRACTION AND TRADE

The Knights Templar has been actively involved in illegal iron ore exports to Asia (Pérez and de Córdoba 2014). Iron ore is a key raw material in the production of steel and therefore is an essential resource in oil and gas supply chains. According to some, the trafficking of this mineral substance "and not drugs" is the real business of Michoacán's main criminal organizations (Beauregard 2013, par. 5). Illegal iron ore is shipped to Asia mainly through the Lázaro Cárdenas port, recently in the control of the Knights Templar and its predecessor criminal organization, La Familia Michoacana. The main destination of the iron ore in Asia is China, the biggest consumer of steel in the world and the largest importer of iron ore, with approximately 70 percent of the market share (Guillén 2012, par. 74).[16] Santiago Pérez and José de Córdoba (2014, par. 11) explain how illegal mines proliferated along Michoacán's coast in recent years "to feed Chinese hunger for minerals." As they observe, "While the Templars [shipped] out raw iron ore to China from Lázaro Cárdenas, they [received] shipments of precursor chemicals in return at the port that [enabled] them to dominate Mexico's methamphetamine trade—a key component of their illegal activities."

In the past thirteen years iron ore prices increased more than a thousand percent. Instead of representing good news for Michoacán, which is the largest iron ore producer in Mexico, the price surge initiated a very violent fight among criminal groups and other actors for the control of the mineral's extraction and trade. These groups included *ejido* landowners (*ejidatarios*),[17] self-defense groups, and criminal organizations like the Knights Templar, La Familia, the CJNG, the Zetas, important steel companies, and Chinese entrepreneurs. Due to a greater exploitation of iron ore in the state, as well as the very high prices of this natural resource, criminal groups started to intervene as intermediaries in the negotiation between landowners and steel companies (Sigler 2014).

What was going on in the iron ore industry in this state started to become obvious beginning in 2010. Four members of La Familia Michoacana were arrested in October 2010 and accused of illegally exporting 1,100,000 tons of iron ore that were valued at nearly $42 million. This accusation was widely covered by the media (Guillén 2012, pars. 9–10). Since that time it has become clear that armed criminal groups have been "involved in the whole process, from extraction to transport and shipping of minerals"; according to some estimates, they made "as much as 2 million dollars per vessel loaded with illegally extracted minerals—about 72 million [dollars] a year" (Pérez and de Córdoba 2014, par. 12). Others even calculated that at some point "between 50 and 75 percent of the iron ore shipped out of the port of Lázaro Cárdenas . . . was taken from mines operated by Knights Templar affiliates" (quoted in Paley 2014, 210–11).

What is interesting about this process is the close connection between criminal entrepreneurs and important legal companies. The Attorney General's Office (PGR) has accused groups like La Familia and the Knights Templar of establishing trade relationships with major international energy companies operating in Mexico and exporting minerals—iron ore in particular—to Asia (Guillén 2012, par. 11). It is worth noting that these activities are similar to those linking the Zetas to selling stolen natural gas condensate (coming mainly from the Burgos Basin in Tamaulipas) to US energy companies or to the illegal sale of coal by the Zetas to the state of Coahuila's company PRODEMI and other major energy companies operating there. According to some testimony, the "legal" companies that maintain commercial relations with criminal groups know that the hydrocarbons or minerals they buy are obtained through illegal methods (Paley 2014; Pérez 2012). They remain silent, however, plausibly because they greatly benefit from such operations—particularly from less government regulation and lower prices.

MILITARIZATION, PARAMILITARIZATION, MINERALS, AND CORPORATE INTERESTS IN MICHOACÁN

Extreme violence has been a constant in Michoacán since the beginning of this century. Los Zetas introduced new forms of violence and organized crime to the state and La Familia adapted the Zeta model to a particular regional reality. Calderón's drug war through the so-called Joint Operation Michoacán (Operativo Conjunto Michoacán) elevated the level of violence and helped weaken La Familia, which was immediately replaced by the Knights Templar as the major criminal organization in the state. Violence was not restrained; it continued to expand into new areas in the state even as federal forces and large expenditures tried to contain the criminal groups. As already explained (see chapters 2 and 5), self-defense groups appeared in vast zones of Michoacán as a response to the many abuses of the Knights Templar.

The appearance of self-defense groups and their violent confrontations with the Knights Templar resulted in the further militarization of the security apparatus in Michoacán. Again, the zones with a large amount of conflict coincided with places rich in natural resources (see map 7.8 and CNN México 2014). In other words, new forms of organized crime, militarization, and paramilitarism produced high levels of violence in strategic parts of Michoacán: the ports, nearby zones, and iron ore mining locations (Mexican Geological Survey 2013). This contributed to displacing locals from their land and might limit social dissent in the near future in a state that was once known for community organization and mobilization.

Large corporate interests in the mining and energy sectors might end up benefiting from these circumstances. Some of them have already profited from the current situation by buying minerals and hydrocarbons from criminals or illegal suppliers at lower-than-market prices. Most of these transactions appear to avoid tax collection. Lázaro Cárdenas is the second-largest container port in Mexico and occupies the third place in terms of merchandise value (after Manzanillo and Veracruz). But in regard to tax collection it is fourth nationally—even with its more than nine thousand transactions per day (Beauregard 2013, par. 9).

Today influential transnational companies hold significant concessions to exploit natural resources in Michoacán. Mining concessions covering more than 15 percent of the state's territory have been granted to companies such as Ternium, ArcelorMittal, Geologix Exploration, Endeavour Silver Corp., and AHMSA (Sigler 2014). Violence provoked by criminal groups, law enforcement agencies, self-defense groups, and other irregular armed actors in recent years does not seem to have affected these companies. None have been forced to leave the state, and some have even reported record levels of production and income during periods of intense violence in Michoacán. Ternium and Arcelor-Mitall provide two examples of how companies are thriving in this atmosphere.

TERNIUM

Ternium is a leading steel producer in Latin America. It manufactures "flat and long steel products with production centers in Argentina, Mexico, Colombia, Guatemala and the United States." This company "has become a preferred supplier in its local markets and more

Self-Defense Groups

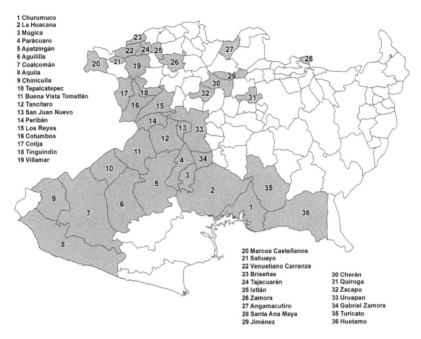

1 Churumuco
2 La Huacana
3 Múgica
4 Parácuaro
5 Apatzingán
6 Aguililla
7 Coalcomán
8 Aquila
9 Chinicuila
10 Tepalcatepec
11 Buena Vista Tomatlán
12 Tancítaro
13 San Juan Nuevo
14 Peribán
15 Los Reyes
16 Cotumbos
17 Cotija
18 Tinguindín
19 Villamar

20 Marcos Castellanos
21 Sahuayo
22 Venustiano Carranza
23 Briseñas
24 Tajacuarán
25 Ixtlán
26 Zamora
27 Angamacutiro
28 Santa Ana Maya
29 Jiménez
30 Cherán
31 Quiroga
32 Zacapu
33 Uruapan
34 Gabriel Zamora
35 Turicato
36 Huetamo

Mining

(continued)

Map 7.8. Violence, mining, and infrastructure in Michoacán.
Sources: self-defense: *Milenio* newspaper; mining: SGM; infrastructure: CFE,
Pemex, SEGOB, SENER; disappearances: RNPED. Design by Carlos D. Gutiérrez-
Mannix and Wendy Macías.

Infrastructure

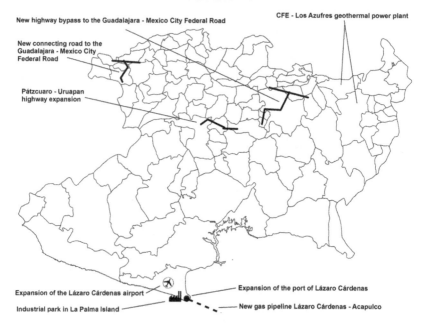

New highway bypass to the Guadalajara - Mexico City Federal Road

CFE - Los Azufres geothermal power plant

New connecting road to the Guadalajara - Mexico City Federal Road

Pátzcuaro - Uruapan highway expansion

Expansion of the Lázaro Cárdenas airport

Industrial park in La Palma Island

Expansion of the port of Lázaro Cárdenas

New gas pipeline Lázaro Cárdenas - Acapulco

Disappearances

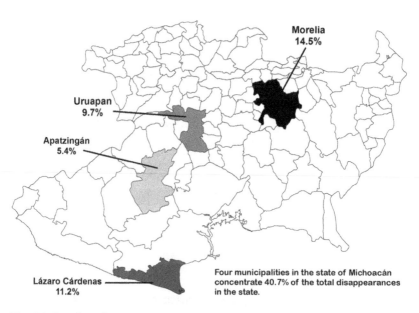

Morelia
14.5%

Uruapan
9.7%

Apatzingán
5.4%

Lázaro Cárdenas
11.2%

Four municipalities in the state of Michoacán concentrate 40.7% of the total disappearances in the state.

Map 7.8. (*continued*)

widely in the Americas where demand for its steel products is steadily increasing" (Ternium 2016, pars. 1–3). Ternium's mining operations in Mexico are located in the states of Colima, Jalisco, and Michoacán. The firm has concessions in two open-pit mines (one in Aquila, Michoacán, and the other in Cerro Náhuatl in Cuauhtémoc, Colima) and also in one underground mine located in the municipality of Pihuamo, Jalisco. Ternium owns 50 percent of Peña Colorada (ArcelorMittal owns the other 50 percent), which consists of an open-pit mine in Minatitlán, Colima, and a pellet plant in Manzanillo, Colima (Ternium 2014). Some of these territories have been contested by groups like the Knights Templar and the CJNG.

One of the most important mines that Ternium operates in Mexico is located in Aquila, Michoacán. In recent years the company has had serious conflicts with the owners of the *ejidos* and communal lands where the iron ore mine is located. The Mexican miners' union leader, Napoleón Gómez Urrutia,[18] claims that the conflict between Ternium and landowners is mainly because the firm had not paid a fair sum for using the land for more than twenty years. Gómez Urrutia claims other companies besides Ternium do the same thing when operating in Mexico (Gómez Urrutia 2013, par. 1).

It has been alleged that the landowners' efforts have been frustrated by the mining company, which has cooperated with local authorities and criminal groups acting as paramilitary groups. Gómez Urrutia (2013, par. 7) describes how Ternium announced by radio and local newspapers in April 2012 that it paid more than 18,000 Mexican pesos a month to each landowner for using the properties for extracting iron ore. This information attracted the attention of organized crime, which started to extort the proprietors (around 401 of them) and charged each of them approximately 2,000 Mexican pesos monthly. In such a complicated situation for small and communal landowners and for other members of Michoacán society, the community police appeared as a response to the multiple abuses committed by organized crime and the complicity and inaction of local authorities (Gómez Urrutia 2013, par. 8).

It is worth noting that while small proprietors and vulnerable people in Michoacán have suffered terror and abuses in recent years Ternium has expanded its operations and investments—in Michoacán and other states. For example, in 2013 Mexican president Enrique Peña Nieto inaugurated the Ternium Industrial Center in the municipality of Pesquería in Nuevo León, with an investment of $1.1 billion. Days before this event Ternium announced an additional investment of $1 billion to construct a thermoelectric power plant in Nuevo León that would utilize natural gas (Ramírez 2013).

ArcelorMittal is the world's largest steelmaker, operating in more than sixty countries and producing about 6 percent of all steel output. Its primary operations in Mexico are in Michoacán, "where it arrived in 1992, and now employs about 6,000 people." In 2014 the company invested approximately $2.4 billion in Mexico, "with its biggest plant in Michoacán responsible for about 5% of the company's total steel production." According to Pérez and de Córdoba (2014, par. 9), "The plant itself is about three times the size of New York's Central Park and is Mexico's largest corporate consumer of electricity and gas."

Like Ternium, ArcelorMittal has flourished in Mexico in recent years. It has not been affected by organized crime in the same way as smaller entrepreneurs, who have suffered extortions and all kinds of abuses by La Familia and the Knights Templar.[19] Many of these small businesses have been forced to close or are now owned by criminal organizations. ArcelorMittal has recently lost one of its employees, however, who allegedly found himself in the hands of a criminal group, in this case the Knights Templar. The employee was the director of institutional development of ArcelorMittal in Mexico, Virgilio Camacho Cepeda, who had reported the illegal trafficking of iron ore by the Templarios through the port of Lázaro Cárdenas—a venture that was valued at approximately $40 million (Sigler 2014).

According to Pérez and de Córdoba (2014, par. 4), "Mr. Camacho may have found himself caught in the crossfire between a firm with more than $80 billion in annual sales and a drug cartel that makes millions of dollars from illegal mining in an area where the company has exclusive mineral rights." They reported that a month after Camacho's murder in April 2013 "Lakshmi Mittal, the company chairman, met with President Peña Nieto and top security officials to discuss the killing." According to this version, "Mr. Mittal told the Mexican president that crime and violence were hobbling the firm's operations and threatening Lázaro Cárdenas' bid to become a leading commercial hub in the Pacific" (par. 14). After talks with ArcelorMittal's chairman, the federal government announced a reinforcement of security operations in Tierra Caliente in May 2013 and sent hundreds of members of the armed forces and federal police to the region. But the real protagonists in the subsequent months were the self-defense groups that started to regain territories that once were in the hands of the Knights Templar (see chapter 5). Irregular warfare turned into a symmetric nonconventional war in Michoacán at this point.

In early November 2014 Peña Nieto launched a military takeover of the port of Lázaro Cárdenas "in an effort to squeeze the Templars' supply lines." In this operation, "hundreds of army troops detained the city's 130 police officers, disarmed them, and sent them to an army base for 'evaluation and retraining.' Soldiers were soon patrolling the port city" (Pérez and de Córdoba 2014, par. 16). Civil authorities in charge of the port's administration (Administración Portuaria Integral) were replaced by members of the armed forces headed by Vice Admiral Jorge Luis Cruz (Beauregard 2013, par. 10). The militarization of the port and the appearance of self-defense groups were seemingly justified to end the abuses of the Knights Templar.

Corporate interests were apparently the biggest winners of the "war for Michoacán." Transnational companies like Ternium and Arcelor-Mittal extended their areas of influence within the state during extremely violent times. This process might have contributed to further the oligopolization of steel production in Mexico. The militarization of key zones in the state ultimately protected corporate capital as well as investments made by large companies. This is the reality of the port of Lázaro Cárdenas, where important economic interests are still at play.

On January 12, 2014—during a critical period in this region—the general coordinator of ports and merchant marine of the Secretariat of Communications and Transportation, Guillermo Ruiz de Teresa, declared that "the work to expand the port of Lázaro Cárdenas will turn it into Latin America's largest logistical center, thus contributing to social development and employment creation, particularly in the state of Michoacán" (Mexico, Secretariat of Communications and Transportation 2014, par. 1; see also Peña Nieto 2014). These efforts include the widening of Container Terminal 1 and some projects to improve Terminal 2 of this port.[20] Ruiz de Teresa explained that this new infrastructure would make the cargo management through the port's containers more efficient and would promote a greater interaction with Asia. He also assured people that the port of Lázaro Cárdenas "works well, on time and without problems," and that it continues growing, "has its own life," and has an autonomous economy (Mexico, Secretary of Communications and Transportation 2014, pars. 4–7). This statement was made at a time when the federal government was desperately trying to regain control of the port, which had been lost to the hands of organized crime.

A Fight for the Control of Territory and Natural Resources

Evidence demonstrates that irregular warfare and symmetric non-conventional war in Mexico were concentrated in places rich in hydro-carbons and other natural resources—most of them essential for energy generation. Recent violent conflicts in northeastern Mexico, the Gulf Coast states of Veracruz and Tabasco, and Coahuila and Michoacán show similar and consistent dynamics that end up benefiting big corporate interests. In all the examples mentioned above we can observe close business relationships between legal and illegal companies, extreme violence, militarization of security, paramilitarism, land displacements, and government protection of corporate capital and foreign investments.

All these territories rich in hydrocarbons and other natural resources initially felt the presence of criminal groups like the Zetas or others following the same criminal model (see appendix 3). Such groups made these territories "ungovernable," and the government responded to this phenomenon with more violence in order to regain control. It is plausible that in the end the control of these strategic lands for energy production will be concentrated in the hands of transnational corporations (both foreign and national) that already have important investments and interests in the area. Lands where recent discoveries of hydrocarbons (mainly oil and gas) have been made, as well as zones with abundant water and plentiful deposits of lithium, uranium, and other minerals, have similar dynamics. A central feature of the extreme violence recently observed in these areas of Mexico is the participation of "incorporated" legal and illegal businesses.

Recent Discoveries in Territories at War

In recent years oil and shale gas discoveries in northeastern Mexico and along the Gulf Coast have increased the significance of these regions in the global energy market. After the passage of Mexico's energy reform, these territories have acquired even more importance and have become more valuable. In October 2011 the secretary of energy, Jordy Herrera, confirmed the discovery of big natural gas deposits along the border with the United States (Cruz Serrano 2011).

These discoveries extend through a strategic border zone that goes from Matamoros, Tamaulipas, to Piedras Negras, Coahuila. In this new context Mexico could become a world leader in natural gas production (Cruz Serrano 2011).

In 2012 Pemex found two new oil reservoirs in the deep waters of the Gulf of Mexico, located close to the city of Matamoros, Tamaulipas. The first discovery of light crude oil in the Gulf of Mexico was made in August of that year. With this finding of well Trion-1, Pemex expects to certify new proven, possible, and probable reserves of 400 million barrels of crude oil. The second discovery took place in October of that same year. It was the Supremus-1 well, located 250 kilometers to the east of Matamoros and less than 40 kilometers south of the border with the United States. This new discovery in deep waters would add between 75 and 125 million barrels of crude oil in proven, possible, and probable reserves. At the same time it would "extend the potential range of the oil system that is located in the northern Gulf of Mexico in around 4,000 and 13,000 million barrels" (Sigler 2012, par. 2). According to former president Felipe Calderón, "this finding was probably the most important one made by Pemex in decades" (Sigler 2012, par. 4).

In 2014 Pemex found resources estimated in between 150 and 200 million barrels of crude oil in the Exploratus-1 well, also located in deep waters of the Gulf of Mexico. The well, which belongs to a zone known as Perdido, is the fourth discovery made in ultradeep waters and is situated 320 kilometers east of the border between Texas and Mexico (see maps 8.2 and 8.4) (*Crónica de Hoy* 2014, par. 1). In June 2015 Pemex announced five new shallow-water discoveries in the Gulf of Mexico; four were found off the coast of the state of Tabasco and another off the coast of the state of Campeche—close to the Cantarell complex (Pemex 2015, par. 3). All these fields are located near states where the Zetas had an important presence.

More recently, the discovery of a shale gas basin similar in size to the Burgos Basin was confirmed in the state of Chihuahua (Coronado 2015). According to some, the Chihuahua Basin is among the largest shale gas basins in northern Mexico, covering approximately 70,000 square kilometers. The Burgos Basin is about the same size, followed by the Tampico Basin, which covers nearly 50,000 square kilometers (see maps 7.1 and 7.2). It is worth noting that important segments of the territories occupied by these three basins have been marred by violence.

The recent oil and gas discoveries near Mexico's northeastern border generate great expectations because of the possibilities to increase the production of oil and natural gas significantly in the long term as well as to generate new investment and jobs. These possibilities have been linked to the energy legislation recently approved in Mexico, which opens up even more of Mexico's hydrocarbons industry to private transnational businesses.

It is interesting to observe that all these areas were once occupied by criminal groups that operated following the Zeta model, whose main intention was to control territories. Violence in these places was extreme, and so was the reaction of the Mexican government. Transnational corporations were key players in this process. Criminal transnational businesses (like the Zetas, the Knights Templar, and the CJNG) arrived in these lands first. Legal transnational energy, steel and mining companies—like AHMSA, Ternium, ArcelorMittal, Shell, and Halliburton—subsequently arrive or extend the presence that they already have in certain zones. The process described above has also taken place in other Mexican territories with large reserves of natural resources utilized in the energy industry, water, or highly valued minerals. This is the case, for example, in certain areas with lithium and uranium deposits.

LITHIUM, URANIUM, AND WATER

In the limits of the Mexican states of Zacatecas and San Luis Potosí is a huge lithium-potassium deposit that has not yet been developed. It is worth noting that the Zetas exercised territorial control over this region at some point. The resources that can be obtained from this deposit are frequently used for the production of lithium-ion batteries, used to "power battery electric vehicles, hybrid electric vehicles, and plug-in hybrid electric vehicles," and can also be used in more traditional industrial activities. This alternative form of energy has become more popular as a result of two key national worries in the "wealthy technologically advanced countries": oil dependency and environmental degradation. These two perceived fears have created "political and economic pressure to reduce the consumption of gasoline" (Wallace 2014, 1). Thus, under certain circumstances, lithium-ion batteries would be adequate energy substitutes.

Energy potential in the Burgos Basin is not limited to shale gas extraction. This contested territory possesses another highly valued resource: uranium. This silvery-white heavy metal can be used as an abundant source of concentrated energy and is frequently utilized to fuel nuclear power plants. Until 1985 the now defunct state company

URAMEX (Uranio Mexicano or Mexican Uranium) conducted uranium exploration and extraction in the Burgos Basin. One of the most important reservoirs of this metal in Mexico is located in this region, once controlled by organized crime. Near El Puerto ranch (situated in the municipality of General Bravo, Nuevo Léon, close to Reynosa, considered the capital of the Burgos Basin) is an open-pit uranium mine (Rivera 2013, pars. 29–31). After Mexico's energy reform, if market conditions allow it, private companies can participate in the uranium business as well.

Water is another resource that is key for the future development of the energy sector in Mexico and particularly for the production of natural gas. Shale gas extraction through fracking is possible in several areas in Mexico but requires access to significant amounts of water. Many of these regions are extremely arid and lack nearby water sources. This elevates the cost of producing natural gas. Therefore territories like the violent region of Los Cinco Manantiales in Coahuila are very valuable for private transnational energy and oil service companies that will eventually extract shale gas after a historic change in Mexico's energy legislation.

Mining

Paley (2014, 98) observes that "mining projects have been among the most conflictive sites of recent capitalist expansion in Mexico, and the majority of gold and silver production in the country takes place with some of the highest rates of violence." This phenomenon has occurred in key regions of Sonora, Chihuahua, Zacatecas, Guerrero, and Durango, many of which have been in control of the Zetas or similar groups and other irregular armed groups (including paramilitaries). At the same time the Mexican government has applied an unconventional security strategy in these areas and has sent the armed forces and federal police to regain control of these territories. Such actions have contributed to further violence and to displacing people from their resource-rich lands.

This pattern is evident if we analyze the location of iron ore deposits in Mexico. The Mexican Geological Survey in 2010 issued a document that shows iron's potential in the states of Jalisco, Colima, Michoacán, and Guerrero (SGM 2010). It is worth noting that the Jalisco New Generation Cartel (CJNG) is present in many of the regions identified in this study. This criminal group has exerted control over strategic areas of Jalisco, Colima, and Michoacán and has been recently confronted there by other criminal groups and by the Mexican federal police and armed forces, which have allegedly attempted to stop its rapid expansion.

It has been said that criminal organizations in the aforementioned regions are mainly interested in establishing labs for producing methamphetamines and other synthetic drugs (*narcolaboratorios*) to export them internationally. This might not be completely accurate. It is true that many of the chemical precursors to producing synthetic drugs arrive in Mexico through the ports of Manzanillo and Lázaro Cárdenas.[21] Nonetheless, labs for such drugs are not geographically bound to these ports and may be located anywhere in the country. For TCOs, controlling the two key ports might be crucial for another reason.

According to researcher Carlos Flores, "the main interest of criminal groups operating in the states of Jalisco, Colima, and Michoacán is the control of strategic territories and access routes with the ultimate goal of dominating resource extraction and most forms of illegal trade in these zones."[22] A very significant amount of the iron ore extracted illegally from these areas and sold to China, "the biggest consumer of this mineral in the world," is transported through the ports of Manzanillo and Lázaro Cárdenas (Guillén 2012, par. 3). China has been particularly interested in the iron ore that is extracted in zones that are closest to these two ports, because the transportation costs are considerably lower from that area (Guillén 2012, par. 67). Moreover, Chinese steel companies would probably be interested in establishing commercial relationships with groups such as the Knights Templar, which extract iron ore illegally and are willing to charge much lower prices.

The relationship between natural resources trade, legal transnational companies, and organized crime is also evident in the mining sector in Guerrero. Predatory criminal groups following the Zeta model, like Los Rojos and Guerreros Unidos, operate in key regions of this southern Mexican state. Particularly interesting is the case of the so-called Gold Triangle (Triángulo del Oro), where the second biggest gold mine in the country, Los Filos, is located. In recent years groups of heavily armed masked men arrived in this area—particularly in the town of Carrizalillo in the municipality of Eduardo Neri—and started to assassinate, kidnap, and charge extortion fees to those who rent their lands to Goldcorp, the Canadian mining company that manages the mine (Rama et al. 2015).

Most of the inhabitants of the town of Carrizalillo obtain their incomes by renting their lands to Goldcorp or working for this company, which produced 931,500 ounces of gold between 2012 and 2014. According to documents released by the news agency Reuters, approximately 175 families obtain an equivalent of $3 million annually by renting their lands to the mining company (Rama et al. 2015, pars. 4 and 6). This represents "a small fortune for the inhabitants of a small town like Carrizalillo" (par. 6). However, these people have not necessarily enjoyed the benefits of owning these gold-rich lands.

Organized crime violence is extreme in the zone near Los Filos mine, and small landowners here suffer constantly from extortions and all types of aggressions. Several mass graves recently have been found in this area. In less than a week, at the end of 2015, approximately sixty bodies were discovered in two clandestine graves located one and a half kilometers from Carrizalillo, which is located approximately one hour from Iguala, Guerrero, where forty-three students disappeared in 2014. Forced displacements in this zone are also very frequent. Hence the criminal dynamics in Guerrero's Gold Triangle are quite similar to the patterns observed in the Burgos Basin, Coahuila's coal region, and the iron ore-rich zones located close to the ports of Manzanillo and Lázaro Cárdenas. Hydrocarbons, minerals, and other natural resources seem to be the main forces that drive war and conflict.

CHAPTER 8

Energy and Security in Tamaulipas, Ground Zero for the Zetas

This chapter explains what has happened in Tamaulipas recently, exemplifying the dynamics described in the previous chapter and the patterns of criminal paramilitarization, militarization, and paramilitarism. The most violent zones of Tamaulipas are also zones rich in hydrocarbons, where forced displacements have been frequent and the opportunities for societal resistance have been eroded. Recently the government announced important discoveries of oil and shale gas reservoirs in this region (see chapter 7). Soon afterward an ambitious infrastructure plan was announced; the plan would facilitate the development of energy projects in this northern Mexican state. These developments will take place despite the very violent conflict involving the Zetas and its previous bosses, the Gulf Cartel, as well as the Mexican state.

The War in Tamaulipas

Tamaulipas is a strategic state due to its geographic location: economic interests, both legal and illegal, are central and the patterns of conflict and extreme violence involving TCOs, legal transnational firms, and the law enforcement agencies are quite evident. International trade, the energy industry, and organized crime coexist and are defining the future of this Mexican state. Tamaulipas has Mexico's largest petrochemical complexes and two of the country's major ports on the Gulf of Mexico. It is also one of the most violent states in Mexico and the state where the Zetas and Gulf Cartel began operating. The two crime groups started their extremely bloody battle there in 2010.

The Effects of the War in Tamaulipas

Probably in no other state in Mexico has the fight between the Gulf Cartel and its previous allies, the Zetas, been as violent and as pervasive as in Tamaulipas. There the levels of violence and terror were so intense that the already highly censored traditional media stopped reporting and the state seemed at times to have lost its monopoly on the legitimate use of violence. The two crime groups eventually dominated most aspects of the economy, social life, and politics in this northeastern state. This domination of key territories—mainly the border region, the capital city, and the lands bordering the Gulf of Mexico (see map 2.1)—was a defining aspect of this bloody armed conflict.

After the split from the Gulf Cartel, the Zetas started to invade *ejido* lands in key areas of the state. They stole and acquired by force "ranches, houses, shops, and all sorts of businesses and began to control the economic activity of certain zones, such as agriculture and livestock in Valle Hermoso and San Fernando and the fishing business in the Laguna Madre. This last site is the largest hypersaline lagoon in the world" and is also heavily used as a route to transport drugs into the United States (Martínez 2011, par. 4). The Gulf Cartel fought back, trying not to lose the territories that it had once dominated for trafficking drugs. The two groups then started to kidnap and assassinate. They were at war. "In some *ejidos* men almost disappeared" due to the confrontation and brutality exercised by the rival groups (Martínez 2011, par. 5).

As already mentioned, fear and terror impacted the traditional media, which stopped reporting on the violence and on organized crime groups, hoping to prevent further deaths and kidnappings of reporters (Mendieta 2014). The rate of murders and violent crimes increased exponentially during the first years of the war. Due to the absence of coverage by the media, however, it is difficult to describe accurately what happened and to report exact statistics. The material and human costs of the war in Tamaulipas were extremely high, but unfortunately it is not possible to calculate exactly how high.

While no one knows the exact toll on Tamaulipas, some statistics, although unconfirmed, can give us an idea of what the violence was like. The total number of homicides in Tamaulipas increased significantly in 2010–2012, the worst years of the war between the Gulf Cartel and its former enforcers, the Zetas (see table 8.1 and figure 8.1). According to INEGI data, collected by the Executive Secretariat of the

Table 8.1 Homicides in Tamaulipas (2000–2015)

Year	Homicides	Year	Homicides
2000	222	2008	308
2001	165	2009	288
2002	165	2010	721
2003	244	2011	855
2004	225	2012	1,016
2005	357	2013	556
2006	346	2014	628
2007	265	2015	763

Source: INEGI, with data from SESNSP of SEGOB.

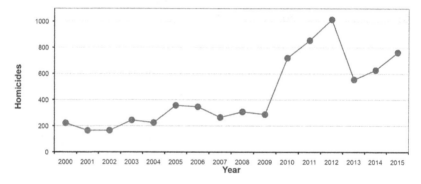

Figure 8.1. Homicides in Tamaulipas (2000–2015).
Source: INEGI, with data from SESNSP of SEGOB.

National System of Public Safety (SESNSP) of the Secretariat of the Interior (SEGOB), the total number of homicides was 288 in 2009 and reached 1,016 in 2012. Between 2011 and 2013 in this state 93 graves containing 258 unidentified bodies were found (distributed in 15 municipalities). This figure represents more than half of the total number of bodies found buried in graves in the whole country during the same period (488 corpses in 222 graves) (Mendieta 2014).

According to official statistics, Tamaulipas also had the highest number of disappeared people (*desaparecidos*) (see table 9.1). From 2006 to 2015 this state registered a total of 5,720 missing or disappeared persons—including foreigners and government officials (Mexico, RNPED 2015).[1] The number of displaced people from certain key areas of the state was also very significant during these years. In Ciudad Mier an exodus of hundreds of people began in November 2010; in the end, it was more than a half of the total population of the municipality.[2] Approximately 200 persons left the town of La Fé del Golfo in the municipality of Jiménez, and 250 people abandoned their properties and homes in the community of El Barranco, located in the municipality of Cruillas (Mendieta 2014).

In 2015 the state also registered the highest number of kidnappings in the country—327 according to a 2015 report of the Executive Secretariat of the National System of Public Safety (Mexico, SESNSP 2016, 2). It is worth noting that there were no records of kidnappings in Tamaulipas in 2004 but 262 ten years later, in 2014. Part of the reason for the very significant rise may be the fracturing of the Zetas and the Gulf Cartel, which weakened these groups and forced them to search for alternative sources of income. As they experienced a loss of leadership and control due to fighting each other and resisting government intervention, they further diversified their activities and found smaller businesses that require less logistical organization than international drug trafficking (Mejía 2014, par. 5).

The terror and violence prevalent in Tamaulipas during the worst years of the war (2010–2012) were reflected in the prison system. Four major breakouts from local prisons in Matamoros, Miguel Alemán, Nuevo Laredo, and Reynosa occurred between 2006 and 2008. In a five-year period 86 inmates were assassinated inside these four "security units." The situation in the Tamaulipas prison system deteriorated even more in recent years; 28 inmates escaped from prison from 2006 to 2008; this number increased to 377 from 2010 to 2013 (Mendieta 2014). Other violence has taken place in this Mexican state: 49 bodies were abandoned at parking lots of shopping malls and in front of local government buildings in 2012, such as the town halls of Mante and Nuevo Laredo (Mendieta 2014). Eight car bombs were found in different points of key Tamaulipas cities between August 2010 and July 2012, attacking businesses, the media, and civilians. Car thefts have also been a huge problem. In 2010, the first year of the war for Tamaulipas, 8,586 motor vehicles were stolen (Mendieta 2014).[3]

The government responded strongly to the violence. Initial efforts included the arrest of the main leaders of the two fighting criminal groups, the entrance of the federal forces (the army and the navy in particular) to reinforce public safety operations in the most violent regions of the state, and the creation of the "Single Police Command" (Mando Único Policial) in April 2013. Notwithstanding these forceful actions, the situation of extreme brutality and insecurity in Tamaulipas did not improve immediately or consistently. This became evident during March and April of 2014, when very violent episodes took place in different regions of the state, particularly in the cities of Ciudad Victoria, Matamoros, Reynosa, and the Tampico–Ciudad Madero–Altamira coastal corridor.

This period also saw the arrests of key leaders of criminal organizations as well as strong confrontations within the main crime groups and between these groups and government forces. These events left at least twenty-eight people dead just before Holy Week of 2014 (Frontera NorteSur 2014). Meanwhile other major crimes committed by the criminal organization continued, such as smuggling and trafficking of migrants. In recent years dozens of Central American migrants have been rescued from stash houses located in certain Tamaulipas border cities (such as Reynosa, Matamoros, and Miguel Alemán). Investigations related to these events have frequently linked organized crime with such activities.

The Zetas and the Gulf Cartel were also active in stealing and illegally selling fuel and a variety of hydrocarbons. And criminal acts of high impact continued to take place. The state police intelligence chief (chief of the Intelligence Unit of the Tamaulipas Secretariat of Public Safety), Colonel Salvador Haro Muñoz, was ambushed and killed in May 2014, allegedly by members of the "Accredited State Police" (Policía Estatal Acreditable). A few days after this event, the PGR ordered the arrest of José Manuel López Guijón, who was in charge of the personal security of the Tamaulipas governor (Guerrero 2014a).

Violence in this northern Mexican state has been close to locations where foreign transnational companies operate. In April 2014 about thirty workers for the Swiss oilfield services company Weatherford International Ltd. were escorted out of Ciudad Mier "by police after gunmen riddled their hotel with bullets" (Corchado and Osborne 2014, par. 29).[4] This gas-rich region located in the Burgos Basin "had already become a ghost town after most of its inhabitants had fled following [months] of bloodshed" (Cattan and Williams 2014, par. 1). After the event that frightened Weatherford employees, President Peña Nieto "beefed up the army presence in Tamaulipas," and soldiers began escorting Burgos workers "to and from their wells" (Cattan and Williams 2014, par. 17).

Overall, the number of high-impact crimes in Tamaulipas is above the national average (Wilson and Weigend 2014). In recent years the state has also occupied the first place nationally in number of investigations involving illegal arms and organized crime (Ángel 2014a). While the situation of insecurity has not visibly improved since 2010, when the Gulf Cartel and the Zetas began their open confrontation, it is worth noting that the dynamics have changed. Currently the main violent episodes in Tamaulipas have more to do with the conflict within the criminal organizations themselves and confrontations between these groups and Mexico's federal forces rather than with fights between the Gulf Cartel and the Zetas, which characterized the beginning of the war for Tamaulipas (see appendix 2).

Plan Tamaulipas: The Federal Government's Involvement in the War

Due to the failure of the security strategy implemented during the first years of the war and the high levels of insecurity and violence still prevalent in the state, the federal government decided to act more forcefully and designed a new strategy to combat organized crime. On May 13, 2014, in the border city of Reynosa, Miguel Ángel Osorio Chong, then secretary of the interior, met with Tamaulipas governor Egidio Torre Cantú, and announced the beginning of a new era in the state's security policy under what became known as Plan Tamaulipas (Tamaulipas Plan). This security program included three main objectives: (1) to dismantle criminal groups in the state; (2) to seal illicit trafficking routes of people, drugs, arms, and money; and (3) to guarantee efficient and trustworthy local institutions.

In order to achieve these goals, the state was divided into four areas (border, coast, center, and south), which would be protected by the Mexican army or the navy (Wilson and Weigend 2014). Federal prosecutors and military personnel were assigned to each zone (see map 8.1). Different actions were also designed to strengthen coordination among the different law enforcement agencies and to reinforce surveillance at airports, ports, customs, border crossings, highways, and state prisons. This plan also created the Institute of Police Training and Research (Instituto de Formación Policial e Investigación) for vetting and professionalizing the local police. As part of this plan, anonymous reports were encouraged (through a 088 emergency line) and actions to prevent crimes like extortion and kidnapping were strengthened.

Notwithstanding the implementation of this new strategy and the

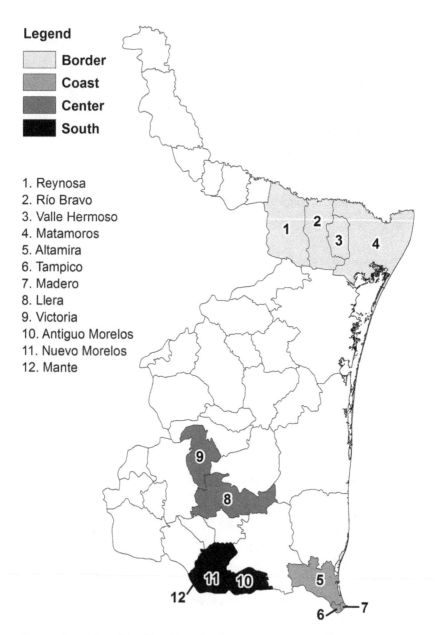

Legend

Border
Coast
Center
South

1. Reynosa
2. Río Bravo
3. Valle Hermoso
4. Matamoros
5. Altamira
6. Tampico
7. Madero
8. Llera
9. Victoria
10. Antiguo Morelos
11. Nuevo Morelos
12. Mante

Map 8.1. Tamaulipas Plan (Plan Tamaulipas).
Source: *El Universal*. Design by Carlos D. Gutiérrez-Mannix and Wendy Macías.

reinforcement of the presence of the federal forces in Tamaulipas, extreme violence, impunity, and a weak rule of law continued to characterize this northeastern Mexican state. Examples include the assassination of Ricardo César Niño Villarreal, police chief in the northern region of Tamaulipas, in November 2014 and the abduction and assassination of four people (one Mexican man and three US citizens—a woman and her two younger brothers) in October of that year, allegedly by local security forces in the community of Control (part of the municipality of Matamoros). This crime was attributed to a new tactical security unit, the so-called Grupo Hércules, which was introduced by the then mayor of Matamoros, Leticia Salazar.[5] The legality of this group had been strongly questioned since its formation, and it was dismantled soon after this incident.

Civil society in Tamaulipas has not been able to organize effectively after years of abuse and destruction by organized crime and government authorities. Unlike other states, Tamaulipas has not been able to face violence in an effective way (Guerrero 2014a, par. 30). As Paley (2011, 23–24) recognizes, "there is a basic absence of advocacy" in Tamaulipas. The state "doesn't have a proliferation of nongovernmental advocacy, research or aid organizations devoted to assisting victims of the conflict and their family members."

Guerrero (2014a, par. 30) notes how government officials and analysts in the states of Baja California, Chihuahua, and Nuevo León recognized that "the formation of ample citizen coalitions with enough power to demand an effective response from government authorities (and through an adequate participation of the business sector) was a decisive element to overcome the security crises experienced by the three states in earlier years." Unfortunately, as he points out, "organized civil society and the business community in Tamaulipas have not been able to form a comparable movement." The business community in important Tamaulipas cities, such as Tampico and Reynosa, was directly affected, and a number of small entrepreneurs were kidnapped or attacked physically. Thus several business owners decided to emigrate out of the country or to safer places in Mexico.

Extreme violence and militarization are not the only factors that have been observed in this state in the past few years. The brutal events already described (terror, forced displacements, and the government failure to control organized crime and assure stability in this strategic region) were accompanied by a series of economic developments (see appendix 1). Important discoveries of oil and gas were made during the most brutal periods in one of the most violent states of Mexico. At the same time, the Mexican government was extremely successful in providing the infrastructure that would promote trade and develop the energy sector after a historic reform.

Energy in Tamaulipas

Tamaulipas: A State Rich in Hydrocarbons

A Wilson Center report identified Tamaulipas as one of "Mexico's most important states in terms of hydrocarbons development." This state holds an important "portion of the country's oil and gas deposits, including offshore oil sites in the Gulf of Mexico and shale gas formations similar to those already being successfully developed in the [United States]" (Daugherty 2015, par. 2). Hence Tamaulipas will be an epicenter of energy production in Mexico after the country's recent change in the constitutional framework. The Government of Tamaulipas (2014a, 10) has noted that the state contains "two important assets for the exploration and exploitation of hydrocarbons" in Mexico: the Burgos Basin in the north and the Poza Rica-Altamira Asset, which is located in the Tampico-Misantla province and includes the southernmost region of Tamaulipas and part of Veracruz.

In the past few years, notwithstanding the violence and organized crime's control of certain regions of the state, important efforts have been made to discover, explore, and map all available energy resources in Tamaulipas. Oil and gas technicians have visited Reynosa and San Fernando in recent years and performed various geological, geochemical, and environmental studies in these hydrocarbon-rich regions (Dorantes 2014). Simultaneously, some key regions of Tamaulipas have experienced robust growth in gas and petroleum activity "in the form of incentive contracts with private foreign companies to engage in the exploration, extraction, and production activities of existing oil and natural gas fields" (Haahr 2015, 7). Particularly important are the developments in the Burgos Basin, where the country's most important gas reserves are located. It is worth mentioning that 26 percent of Mexico's natural gas production takes place in Tamaulipas, representing approximately "200 billion daily cubic feet and 18,000 barrels of condensed gas" (Haahr 2015, 7).

According to official figures, in 2014 approximately 65 percent of the 52.6 thousand million barrels of crude oil equivalent estimated by

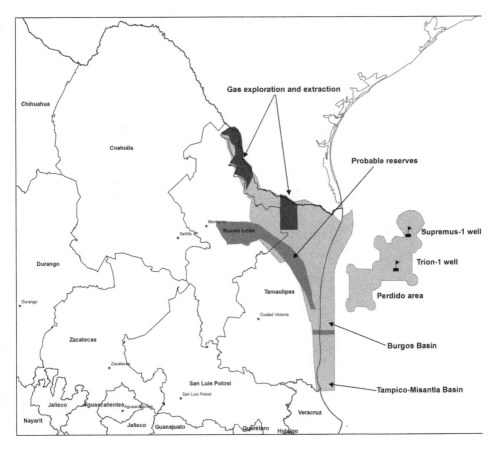

Map 8.2. Hydrocarbons in Tamaulipas I.
Source: Pemex. Design by Carlos D. Gutiérrez-Mannix.

Pemex as "conventional prospective resources" was located in Tamaulipas oil provinces, specifically in Burgos, Tampico-Misantla, and the deep waters of the Gulf of Mexico (Government of Tamaulipas 2014a, 10). According to some estimates, a little more than 60 billion barrels of crude oil equivalent (BBOE) of "unconventional prospective resources" are concentrated in four oil provinces (see map 8.2). Three of these provinces extend through some parts of Tamaulipas: Burgos and Tampico-Misantla occupy important zones of the state and Sabinas-Burro-Picachos extends through smaller regions (Government of Tamaulipas 2014a, 11).

At the end of the first decade of the present century Pemex identified 500 oil fields located along the Tamaulipas coastal zone (see map 8.3),

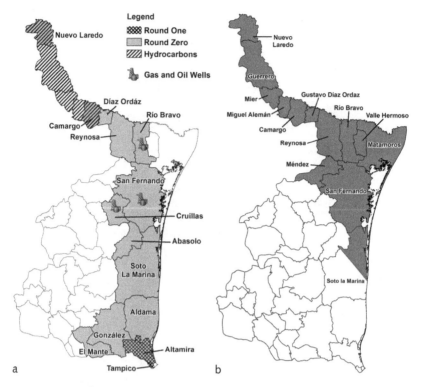

Map 8.3. (a) Hydrocarbons in Tamaulipas II. (b) Hydrocarbons in the Burgos Basin. Source: Pemex. Design by Carlos D. Gutiérrez-Mannix and Wendy Macías.

between the mouth of the Río Bravo in Matamoros and the locality of La Pesca in the municipality of Soto la Marina (*El Bravo* 2011, par. 1). During this time Mexico's government also found important mineral resources in this state and mapped them as part of a serious effort to systematize the information related to all these findings (see Mexican Geological Survey 2011).

Organized Crime, Violence, and Hydrocarbons in Tamaulipas

As Shannon Young (2013, par. 11) recognizes, "some of the most oil and gas rich areas of Mexico are also the most tightly controlled by irregular armed groups and government supported silence." This is exactly the case in Tamaulipas, where "some of Mexico's most significant oil and gas fields" are located. Some of these areas are dominated by organized crime or are secured by Mexican federal forces (the army, navy, or the federal police). This state is also characterized by its "lack of government transparency" and considered a "high-risk area" for traditional journalism. The same happens in other areas of Mexico (such as Veracruz and Guerrero), but these dynamics in Tamaulipas are very visible. Violence has been extreme in strategic zones of this state lately. All of these territories have very important oil or gas reservoirs or are important areas for the construction of new energy infrastructure and new gas pipelines (most of them connecting to the US gas pipeline network). After Mexico's energy reform, the control of many of these territories and the management of many of these resources and new investments will probably be in the hands of private transnational companies.

THE BURGOS BASIN

Organized crime has forced people working at the Burgos Basin to pay fees for protection. Some sources in Tamaulipas mention that armed groups have also threatened and kidnapped oil-field workers. Many of these groups are allegedly part of the Zetas organization, and they also have stolen fuel and natural gas from the state-owned company Pemex. This situation has certainly affected hydrocarbon production in the Burgos Basin. At the end of 2010 there were 2,737 active gas wells in this region that produced 1,400 million standard cubic feet of gas per day (mmscfd)—equivalent to a fifth of Mexico's gas production. Production has consistently declined since then due to security concerns over the presence of organized crime. Criminal groups have kidnapped dozens of oil and gas workers in the past few years (Pemex reported that sixteen of its employees were kidnapped in 2010 alone). They have also at times prevented Pemex workers and contractors from entering or crossing through certain key areas of the Burgos Basin (CNN Expansión 2011).

THE SAN FERNANDO VALLEY AND THE SMALL BORDER

As Shannon Young (2013, par. 8) observes, "What are considered to be Mexico's easiest to exploit shale gas formations are located in some of the most violent areas of Tamaulipas," specifically the San Fernando Valley and the Small Border (Frontera Chica) region between Nuevo Laredo and Reynosa.[6] San Fernando is well known for the massacre of seventy-two migrants in 2010 and the discovery of a series of mass graves in 2011. This region "marked a dividing line between Gulf Cartel and Zeta-controlled territory." The Frontera Chica also forms part of the Burgos Basin, and in 2010–2013 was an epicenter of violence in the state. These two regions of Tamaulipas register some of the highest rates of *desaparecidos* (disappeared people) and forced displacements in Mexico.

San Fernando is one of the most important municipalities in Mexico with regard to hydrocarbon production (Manilla 2012). It also has an enormous potential in terms of energy generation. It is difficult to imagine that such an important municipality for the energy industry was once controlled by the Zetas and has been among the most violent regions in the whole country. At some point (mainly in 2010–2012) the streets of San Fernando were empty and dozens of businesses were abandoned. The buildings of local law enforcement agencies were closed, and some of them had no personnel for months (Martínez 2011, par. 7).

The cities of the Small Border observed a similar situation during the same period. Nueva Ciudad Guerrero, Ciudad Mier, Ciudad Miguel Alemán, Ciudad Camargo, and Díaz Ordaz had very violent and continuous confrontations between the Gulf Cartel and the Zetas. This plight brought destruction, death, and fear to the inhabitants of these regions. Citizens of other nationalities were also affected by the extreme violence in these Tamaulipas territories. Consider, for example, the case of the Weatherford workers who were escorted out of Ciudad Mier by police in 2014. In September 2010 a US citizen named David Hartley was allegedly murdered by members of a criminal group while he was jet skiing with his wife and taking pictures of a historic church located on the Mexican side of Falcon Lake, close to Nueva Ciudad Guerrero.[7] During that time it was claimed that armed men used to assault, rob, or threaten fishers and boaters in this region. "The ultimate effect of this phenomenon was to discourage visitors and businesses from getting close to this area," affirms one citizen journalist based in Nueva Ciudad Guerrero.[8]

Also in 2010, organized crime took control of the Pemex-run Gigante-1 well, which produces natural gas and is located in Nueva Ciudad Guerrero, close to Nuevo Laredo. According to some versions, Pemex workers were beaten and threatened by a criminal group here; five of these workers were kidnapped. It is worth noting that the well and re-collection stations of this region were very productive at the time. Organized crime began to steal hydrocarbons in this area and allegedly sold them to people and companies on both sides of the border (*Reforma/El Norte* 2010). This pattern of crime and corruption extended through other municipalities of the Small Border, particularly to Mier and Camargo. It is worth noting that in more recent years investments in energy infrastructure in some of these regions have started to expand. Particularly important is the expansion of the gas pipeline network that passes through this zone, including the construction of the Los Ramones natural gas pipeline, which links the Texas Eagle Ford Shale formation to central Mexico and runs through Camargo, Tamaulipas.[9]

Hydrocarbon Theft in Tamaulipas

The hydrocarbons industry in Tamaulipas has become an extremely lucrative target for the TCOs operating there (Mejía 2014). As in other parts of the country—and as mentioned earlier (see chapter 3)—hydrocarbon theft in this state has represented an important opportunity for these groups to diversify their incomes. According to some estimations, organized crime now controls up to 15 percent of the gasoline business in the state and nationwide (Gurney 2014; Mejía 2014) and has developed a sophisticated illegal hydrocarbon distribution system.[10] In Tamaulipas "organized criminals control many secondary roads to gas fields." They have been stealing fuel massively from state-owned pipelines and have openly sold the stolen fuel "out of the backs of vans in border cities like Matamoros, Rio Bravo and Reynosa" (Young 2014, par. 24). In 2013 Pemex detected 491 illegal siphons in Tamaulipas, a more than 180 percent increase compared to the previous year and the highest number of any state in the country (Gurney 2014, par. 5).

Various key zones of this northeastern Mexican state have a high density of oil and gas pipelines that are on private ranches and *ejidos*. Hence the new criminal business represents a big problem for a number of private and social landowners. But hydrocarbon theft and related activities have mainly harmed Mexico's state-owned oil company. In recent years, as Guerrero (2014a, par. 26) notes, criminal organizations have intimidated and kidnapped Pemex engineers and other technicians in order to develop the knowledge required to perform their activities in this important industry. At the same time, the proximity of the US border has allowed these groups to utilize drug-trafficking networks to export stolen fuel from Pemex to Mexico's northern neighbor.[11] The Zetas and the Gulf Cartel are the two groups involved in these illegal activities in Tamaulipas. They are "well-financed and technically-savvy," and as Daugherty (2015, pars. 9–10) recognizes:

> Both organizations have the money and muscle to bribe or intimi-date oil workers into revealing pipeline network vulnerabilities. Those same assets are used to dissuade local government and security per-sonnel from interfering in oil theft operations. Criminals also report-edly operate extensive infrastructure including a fleet of tanker ships, oil trucks and cartel-controlled gas stations. . . . On top of stealing oil and gas, the Zetas and Gulf Cartel directly threaten oil company per-sonnel with kidnapping and often extort "narco-rents" from compa-nies operating in their areas of influence. The two groups have also been known to destroy oil and gas infrastructure and block transpor-tation routes, attempting to force financial losses on each other's black market fuel operations.

According to some accounts, the Zetas and the Gulf Cartel turned to hydrocarbon theft in Tamaulipas after they were both severely weakened and fragmented and after they lost their unified national leadership following their infighting and their battles against the Mex-ican government. Under such conditions, they would be "more likely to turn towards the local criminal economy as a source of income, rather than depending on activities like international drug trafficking, which require coordinated operations not just throughout Mexico but also all along transnational trafficking routes" (Gurney 2014, par. 8). But this explanation does not seem to be quite accurate. In this par-ticular region the stolen hydrocarbons business at some point became "a large scale criminal operation" (par. 7). In fact, compared to other crimes, these activities are "easy to carry out, lucrative, and there is an extremely low risk of being caught, making it ideal for criminal groups following the pattern of diversification of interests and reve-nues" (par. 7).

The Zetas' and the Gulf Cartel's expansion into hydrocarbon theft impacted Mexico's state oil company the most. Quoting a Wilson Cen-ter report, Daugherty (2015, par. 11) states that these groups used to "regularly set up 'narco-blockades' to capture and assassinate each other's members." These operations "stopped oil trucks from reaching refineries and even shut down Altamira international airport for a pe-riod in 2014."[12] Moreover, in parts of the state (for example, in certain zones of La Frontera Chica) Pemex and its contractors stopped some of their activities; a number of their employees simply left after kidnappings and extortion practices multiplied after 2010.

The Future of the Energy Sector in Tamaulipas

Tamaulipas: Land of Opportunities

In just a few years Pemex registered massive losses and became discredited due to the endemic corruption in the organization. This phenomenon contributed to the success of criminal organizations in the hydrocarbon theft business. Under the new framework posed by energy reform, Pemex will plausibly cease to be a protagonist in Mexico's energy sector and some key private players will occupy relevant spaces once occupied by the state monopoly. Tamaulipas offers important investment opportunities for private oil and gas companies linked to the recent discoveries of shale gas and oil in the deep waters of the Gulf of Mexico. These discoveries would probably benefit the private sector to a greater extent due to Pemex's recent deterioration and precarious financial situation.

As Daugherty (2015, par. 3) recognizes, after Mexico's historic reform, "a host of foreign firms have lined up to enter this newly opened market. Several firms have even revealed investment plans of a billion dollars or more." Notwithstanding visible insecurity in Tamaulipas, investment in the energy sector in this state is projected to grow considerably. As in other parts of the world, investment in Mexico will plausibly flow toward large-scale resource exploitation in "hot regions," as Gray (2008, 81) explains: these are "areas where the use of violence for private gain is rarely investigated, much less prosecuted. Though a small number of individuals and organizations are trying to expand the rule of law in such places, the work is extremely dangerous. And despite the security issues, the prospects for high returns on investments are strong." This happens in Colombia, and it seems that it will take place in Mexico too. Tamaulipas will probably be a perfect example of this pattern.

The government of Tamaulipas (2014d, par. 1) has praised recent constitutional changes that will greatly transform Mexico's energy sector. It claims that the changes will promote favorable developments that will generate important opportunities for the local communities and the state in general. Tamaulipas's authorities have argued that these reforms will further the participation of national oil and gas producers in hydrocarbon extraction and "will promote industrial activity, employment and a more effective utilization of the natural resources [and technology] that are located in South Texas" and northeastern Mexico. According to these sources, "the future is in unconventional reservoirs such as deep water fields, tertiary oil recovery and development of mature oil fields, in which Tamaulipas has a significant wealth it still needs to explore" (par. 3).

The energy sector in Tamaulipas is made up of more than a thousand oil and gas companies, manufacturing businesses, and electric, trade, and services companies, which employ more than 52,000 people. Official sources point to the potential of new growth and employment as well as increased foreign direct investment in the state, all derived from the recent constitutional changes (Government of Tamaulipas 2014a). In the past few years both the state and federal governments have unveiled plans to build massive new energy infrastructure in the Small Border, Reynosa, Matamoros, San Fernando, and Tampico-Madero-Altamira area and the Perdido area in the Gulf of Mexico (see map 8.4).

Potential energy developments in Matamoros are particularly important and will possibly be combined with further developments in the manufacturing industry (Ávila 2013). The recent deep-water oil discoveries located just offshore from this city might attract further foreign investments in this strategic area. It is worth noting that some have even claimed that these discoveries may have oil reservoirs that are close in size to those that exist in some countries of the Middle East (Ávila 2013, par. 8). Energy potential in this region has spawned important infrastructure investments, such as the construction of the West Rail Bypass Bridge between Matamoros and Brownsville, Texas. This is the first new rail crossing built between the United States and Mexico in more than a century (Ávila 2013; Embassy of the United States in Mexico 2014).

Infrastructure for the Energy Sector in Tamaulipas

The infrastructure network being developed in light of the huge energy potential in Tamaulipas will connect the state with the rest of the country, the United States, and other parts of the world.[13] It includes the recently constructed Mazatlán-Matamoros super highway and the completion of the Ciudad Valles–Tampico, Reynosa–Ciudad Mier,

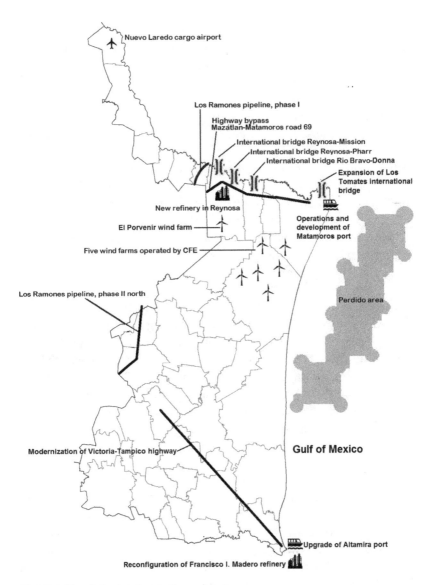

Nuevo Laredo cargo airport

Los Ramones pipeline, phase I

Highway bypass
Mazátlan-Matamoros road 69

International bridge Reynosa-Mission

International bridge Reynosa-Pharr

International bridge Rio Bravo-Donna

Expansion of Los
Tomates international
bridge

New refinery in Reynosa

El Porvenir wind farm

Operations and
development of
Matamoros port

Five wind farms operated by CFE

Los Ramones pipeline, phase II north

Perdido area

Gulf of Mexico

Modernization of Victoria-Tampico highway

Upgrade of Altamira port

Reconfiguration of Francisco I. Madero refinery

Map 8.4. New infrastructure in Tamaulipas.
Source: INEGI and SCT. Design by Carlos D. Gutiérrez-Mannix.

Matehuala–Ciudad Victoria, and Tuxpan-Tampico highways that will connect with the proposed Saltillo-Matehuala-Tula-Altamira highway. There also are plans to rehabilitate the port of Matamoros and modernize the Ciudad Victoria highway to connect Tamaulipas's capital city with Nuevo León.

Important energy investments are projected to be made in this Mexican state. At the same time, key infrastructure projects have already been created to encourage cross- and trans-border exchanges of hydrocarbons and other products. Consider, for example, the Anzaldúas (also called Reynosa-Mission) international bridge and the Donna–Rio Bravo international bridge inaugurated in 2010 as well as the West Rail Bypass Bridge. According to a Wilson Center report, the projected hydrocarbon export projects are set to "put Tamaulipas on the map as Mexico's most important energy state" (quoted in Daugherty 2015, par. 4). As Haahr (2015, 6) notes:

> The reform . . . will provide a significant push to Tamaulipas' oil and gas down- and mid-stream activities, including the chemical and electrical industries. . . . [F]oreign investors will look to invest predominantly in the state's petrochemical and chemical sectors along the border with Texas, where the Eagle Ford and Burgos Basin are located. Consequently, the Mexican Government anticipates that foreign investment will go a long way to build new, and consolidate existing, infrastructure projects for the purpose of moving crude and gas to Tamaulipas' ports for export, as well as pipelines to the U.S.

Also, according to Haahr (2015, 7), the National Infrastructure Plan (PNI 2014–2018) for this northeastern Mexican state "demonstrates the government's intention to revitalize its oil and gas infrastructure in preparation for private investment." For example, the plan seeks to "optimize output at the Francisco I. Madero refinery," improve the infrastructure of the Burgos Basin, establish the South Texas–Tuxpan (Marino) gas pipeline, construct the Los Ramones–Cempoala gas pipeline, and create a new storage and distribution terminal in the city of Reynosa.

GAS INFRASTRUCTURE

Among the most important energy projects proposed or underway in the state of Tamaulipas are those related to the gas industry. If market conditions allow, important efforts will be centered on the development of the shale gas industry. Some of the companies that have expressed interest in this venture are BP, Citgo, ExxonMobil, and LyondellBasell Industries. All of these companies are part of the Eagle Ford Shale Consortium (Dorantes 2014, par. 7).[14] Other gas projects in this Mexican northern state "include an offshore terminal to provide new supply routes, as well as a subterranean storage capability" (Haahr 2015, 6). In fact the main initial interest of US energy companies in the gas industry in Tamaulipas is to export gas from US shale fields to buyers in Mexico.

Shannon Young (2013, par. 10) notes that "[d]espite the seemingly unstable investment climate, US companies plan to expand the binational gas pipeline system to double capacity—mostly along the Texas border with Tamaulipas." The Los Ramones pipeline, which links the Texas Eagle Ford Shale formation to central Mexico, crosses Tamaulipas and is one of the main infrastructure projects recently created to promote the expansion of US natural gas exports to Mexico. Pemex has affirmed that this is the most important energy infrastructure project built in the country in the last fifty years (Macías 2013). It is worth noting that the Los Ramones pipeline crosses through some lands that have been controlled by organized crime or marred by extreme violence caused by the confrontation between the two main criminal organizations operating in the state of Tamaulipas.

Los Ramones is part of a big project involving wide extension of the natural gas pipeline network connecting the United States with Mexico in order to meet Mexico's growing natural gas demand. Tamaulipas is a key region that will interconnect an important segment of this network, which starts in Texas and goes to central and southern Mexico. The adequate and timely completion of the scheduled works in this Mexican border state is fundamental for the success of this binational energy project. Before the projected natural gas pipeline system coming from Texas is completed and operates at full capacity in Tamaulipas, natural gas imports will arrive in the ports of Altamira and Manzanillo and will be distributed from there. Additionally, the capacity in five gas compression plants will temporarily increase substantially. Four of these plants are located in Tamaulipas—two of them in Reynosa, one in Mier, and one in Argüelles (Macías 2013).[15] According to Haahr (2015, 6) the "construction of Los Ramones gas pipeline, together with the construction of gas compression plants coupled with the port of Altamira for petrochemical exports will put Tamaulipas on the map as Mexico's most important energy state."

WATER

The success of energy reform in Mexico will require the efficient use of water and ample access to it. In order for Tamaulipas to accomplish the "desired advances in industrial, economic and social development" under new conditions defined by the new energy legislation, the state also needs to assure the availability of enough water. Hence the state's government is now working on a number of projects to make this possible, including the construction of hydroelectric dams (Government of Tamaulipas 2014b, par. 1). These projects were discussed in the framework of "Tamaulipas Energy Agenda," designed during the administration of Egidio Torre Cantú (2011–2016). The idea was to build a number of storage dams. The main locations would include the once very violent region of San Fernando and the southern zone of the municipality of González (Government of Tamaulipas 2014b, par. 12).

Land and Energy in Tamaulipas

Extreme violence in Tamaulipas has caused a great number of forced displacements in key regions of the state. Some roads and highways were virtually abandoned at times, and some communities became almost ghost towns—the streets were emptied, businesses (mainly small ones) were closed, and many families abandoned their houses. Inhabitants of Nuevo Laredo, Ciudad Mier, Reynosa, Valle Hermoso, Matamoros, Tampico, Ciudad Mante, among other Tamaulipas cities, were particularly affected by clashes between the Zetas and the Gulf Cartel as well as by the reaction of the armed forces and federal police. Between Ciudad Victoria and Matamoros are hundreds of dirt roads, ranches, and *ejidos* where the control by organized crime was almost absolute at one point. During the past few years a considerable number of Tamaulipas landowners have been forced to leave their property; in many cases their lands have been taken by criminal groups (Martínez 2011, 2013). Paley (2014, 215) reports that approximately 5,000 farmers were displaced in this Mexican state by the end of 2010.[16]

Displacements have occurred most frequently along the border with

Texas, along the Gulf Coast, and in some municipalities in the center of the state. Forced displacements in the central region at times were so numerous that the state government designed a plan to identify the original landowners in abandoned *ejidos* and ranches with the aim of reinstating these properties. This plan was announced in 2014 by state secretary of public safety, General Arturo Gutiérrez, who declared that these efforts would involve the Accredited State Police (Policía Estatal Acreditable) and would initially take place in the municipalities of Güémez, Padilla, Hidalgo, and Victoria (Government of Tamaulipas 2014c). Farmers and ranchers have also left Tamaulipas because of threats, kidnappings, extortion, and all sorts of violent acts committed by criminal groups or by government forces.

According to press reports, some of the abandoned lands "were used for training camps" (Paley 2014, 215). However, the important question here is: Who would benefit in the long term from recent massive land displacements in Tamaulipas? Some of these lands have significant oil and gas reservoirs (see maps 8.3 and 8.4), and some of these territories will host key infrastructure projects to advance energy reform in Mexico (see map 8.4). For example, beneath the surface in the region of San Fernando is one of Mexico's most important shale gas reservoirs (see map 8.3). Many families have left this zone; some have abandoned their properties due to fear, and others have been forced to give up their lands as ransom payments in cases of kidnapping.[17]

Various parts of the Tamaulipas northern border region and those municipalities located along the Gulf Coast have important hydrocarbon reserves. It is worthwhile noting that many of the forced displacements from hydrocarbon-rich territories have taken place in *ejido* lands. Approximately 32 percent of land property in Tamaulipas is social—that is, communal or *ejido* lands (Mexico, INEGI 2007).[18] This percentage is different for northern Tamaulipas, where the portion of social property land seems to be substantially higher than the state's average (see map 8.5). In northern Tamaulipas *ejido* land represents 41 percent of the total area (Andrade et al. 2010, 73). It is more difficult to rent or purchase *ejidos* compared to private lands. After the war in Tamaulipas, some of these lands will be available and could be sold or leased at lower prices. Thus violence on the Tamaulipas border and forced displacement in this region might have a positive effect for private investment in the framework of Mexico's energy reform.

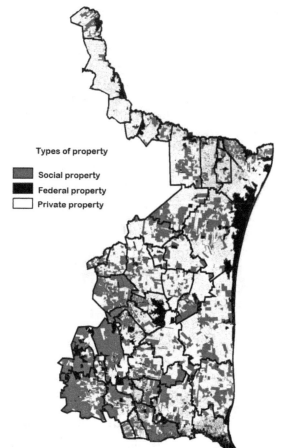

Map 8.5. Land property in Tamaulipas. Source: INEGI.

Guarding Interests: Militarization and Paramilitarism in Strategic Areas

According to Christopher Wilson and Eugenio Weigend (2014, 21), Tamaulipas experiences today severe security problems that are reinforced by the weaknesses of local, state, and federal law enforcement, the limited degree of civil society organization, and almost absolute media censorship in local spaces. This strongly restricts the government's capacity "to resist and respond [effectively] to both the crisis conditions and underlying challenges of governance, economic development, and social inclusion." Under conditions of extreme violence where corruption is endemic and organized crime is militarized, the Mexican government has found severe limitations in trying to maintain peace and stability. Violence and crime in Tamaulipas have not ceased, notwithstanding the militarization of security and recurrent efforts by and coordination between state and local forces (see appendix 2). Under these circumstances, civil society finds itself in a very vulnerable situation, where armed actors dominate the scene and there is no space for its participation—particularly in the field of security.

In fact the paramilitarization of organized crime in Tamaulipas brought with it the presence of the federal forces and the militarization of security in the state. The initial direct actions by Mexico's federal forces to fight organized crime included the arrests of the main (traditional) leaders of the rival Tamaulipas TCOs, which provoked the fragmentation of the two groups and their alleged implosion. At the same time, this process resulted in a transformation of organized crime patterns: a decrease of high impact crimes and an increase of regular crimes (Wilson and Weigend 2014). Thus crime was not reduced overall. The immediate government response to violence caused by the confrontation between the Gulf Cartel and the Zetas was ineffective. Then initial efforts were reinforced through the incorporation of further military personnel and federal police officers, who started to operate in specific zones and in a selective form (see map 8.1).

This new "administration" of criminal activities and a reinforced military presence through Plan Tamaulipas occurred essentially in the state's hydrocarbon-rich territories and where new energy infrastructure projects had been constructed or were projected to be built (see maps 8.3 and 8.4). Violence arrived in the state, and military personnel subsequently were assigned to guard economic interests in these strategic zones. The ultimate role of the armed forces would seem to be to protect transnational interests. Moreover, the discourse on the development of Mexico's energy sector after the reform overlaps with a discourse focused on the need for strengthening security to promote foreign investments.

Consider, for example, what was said during a visit to the city of Matamoros in July 2013 of Janet Napolitano, US secretary of homeland security. Those who participated in events at the time highlighted the potential developments in Mexico's energy sector as well as the alleged advances in terms of security and the need to continue strengthening them (Ávila 2013, par. 4). In fact the main aim of the 2013 meeting was to discuss some key details on border security operations and bilateral cooperation to reinforce security in the region, which was then considered "critical for strengthening national security and promoting economic competitiveness of both nations" (Ávila 2013, par. 6). Mexico's security strategy since then has focused on protecting economic interests and particularly on promoting investments in the energy sector. In 2014 Mexico's government even created a new police unit intended to protect the production chain and strategic regional industries known as the "gendarmerie." This group's efforts would be strengthened by the Mexican military.[19]

CHAPTER 9

Who Benefits from the Zetas' War?

What happened in Tamaulipas was unique to that state's geography and its political and economic history, but it also reflects the sea change that has been going on in Mexico in the time of drug wars. This chapter analyzes the overall effects of Mexico's war that can be characterized as a modern civil war related to the control of energy production. It identifies the groups that seem to have benefited the most (directly or indirectly) from the novel criminal scheme introduced by the Zetas, the Mexican government's reaction to it, and the resulting brutality. The main winners (or potential winners) appear to be corporate actors in the energy sector, transnational financial companies, private security firms (including private prison companies), and the US border-security/military-industrial complex.

The Real Effects of Mexico's Modern Civil War

Two-Way "Illegal" Flows

Historian and political activist James D. Cockcroft (2010) argues that, while Mexico's so-called drug war represents a failure in some regards, it is simultaneously a success in many ways. Essentially it has not reduced the drug trade or drug consumption, and this illegal business represents huge profits in the international drug market for exporting countries and their governments. Many of these profits are recycled in the international financial system and international arms markets, mainly benefiting banks and arms manufacturers (Pijamasurf 2011b, par. 18). The two-way illegal flow (*flujo ilegal de dos vías*) is constant. Arms and cash (originating in the United States) go south, while drugs, people, and other key natural resources like stolen hydro-carbons (originating in Mexico, Central America, and South America) go north to North America. As Tabor (2014, par. 22) notes, "the flow of drugs north enables a flow of cash south," which TCOs frequently "use to buy off police, politicians, and public officials, as well as to hire new recruits and purchase guns—lots of guns." These guns have been used in Mexico's twenty-first century war.

It is worth noting that the same dynamics have been taking place in some parts of Mexico's Pacific region. Consider, for example, the cases of Michoacán, Colima, and Jalisco and the involvement of groups like the CJNG, the Knights Templar, and the Familia Michoacana in il-legal activities. In this region interests in Asia end up crossing paths with interests in the United States. For example, illegal businesses here enable the flow of iron from Mexico to China and the flow of precur-sor chemicals from Asia to Mexico. These goods are needed to en-sure Mexico's drug supply to its northern neighbors. This context thus presents a series of transnational interests and intricate relationships that are either determined or fundamentally affected by the so-called drug wars.

Some of the key interests in these transnational processes are linked to the world energy sector. By mapping armed conflicts in nations (or regions) classified as failed states—mainly by US government officials and US mainstream political analysts—we can often observe the si-multaneous presence of organized crime violence, militarization, and exploitation of natural resources. Under the pretext of fighting crim-inal insurgent groups, militarization occurs and might end in a mod-ern civil war. Such a phenomenon, which involves a strong dose of vio-lence and terror, would eventually generate psychological warfare that could destroy social cohesion and undermine activism and all forms of social organization leading to resistance.

In sum, a thorough analysis of armed conflicts in the present era shows specific patterns that involve monopolies/oligopolies in resource exploitation as well as demobilized societies, social paralysis after years of war against drug-trafficking organizations, and the continued flow of drugs. Notwithstanding current efforts to eradicate drug trade and organized crime, neither violence nor drug consumption has been reduced. On the contrary, a vast drug supply is always guaranteed in the very large US market. Simultaneously, this illegal business has sig-nificantly benefited transnational banks in multimillion-dollar money-laundering operations.

Theories of War

Some experts believe that the aforementioned process of violence generation, militarization of organized crime and security, and resource extraction is part of a premeditated strategy involving transnational interests and the US government. This strategy, they say, causes destabilization, displacement, and territorial control by the armed forces in zones rich in hydrocarbons or other natural resources (such as water and gold). Those benefiting the most from these kinds of situations are transnational corporations—many of them headquartered in the United States. The main losers in this process are the state-owned company Pemex, small entrepreneurs located in strategic regions or participating in extractive industries, small and medium landowners, and the civil society in general.

In the view of Dawn Paley (2013, par. 7), the so-called drug war in Mexico is a political phenomenon or "a counter-revolution, 100 years late," which has decimated communities and destroyed "some of the few gains from the Mexican Revolution that remained after NAFTA was signed in 1994." According to her, this process was made possible through a number of simultaneous factors, such as the paramilitarization of organized crime and the militarization of security backed by the Mérida Initiative and the United States. For Paley, the militarization of criminal groups took place as a response to state militarization of drug-trafficking routes, and this process finally created a form of paramilitarism that would further the expansion of capitalism and essentially benefit extractive industries.

Cockcroft (2010, 38) claims that Mexico's drug war has been an excuse for militarizing the country. These events would prevent the rise of Mexican opposition, which at the same time would allow US companies "to gain greater control over Mexican oil, minerals, uranium, water, biodiversity, and immigrant labor" (40), which would "better U.S. chances of firming up energy security" and would represent "a new phase of contemporary imperialism" (37). For Professor Alfredo Jalife-Rahme, what is really at stake in Mexico's war is the control of oil resources. He argues that "when the United States has access to the Mexican oil" the terrible violence generated by this war—that promotes the looting of natural resources and seems to require an intervention—will end. He describes this as a consequence of "the voracity of the United States," which now knows that oil has reached its peak and will become a scarce resource. Hence for the United States to maintain its status as an empire, it must assure wide access to the remaining oil in the world (quoted in Pijamasurf 2011a, par. 9).

Following this same logic, journalist Carlos Fazio maintains that the new security model in Mexico focuses essentially on fighting "disguised cartels" that were actually activated by the state (quoted in Chávez 2013, par. 1). The ultimate goal of these actions would be to support transnational corporations by concentrating power in the government and eroding all sorts of regional autonomy, thus allowing these companies to control resource extraction and energy generation (par. 1). In this new context groups like the Zetas, the Knights Templar, and CJNG have played a key role in the war plan drafted by former president Felipe Calderón (and continued by Enrique Peña Nieto), because they were its main "justified" target due to their extremely violent practices and the menace that they represented for society. In Fazio's view, these groups were necessary to vindicate the Mexican government's "repressive policy that was applied under the cover of the war on drugs" (par. 6).

Fazio, a specialist in geopolitics, alleges that under the government of Enrique Peña Nieto this repressive policy also favored the selective collaboration between legal and illegal transnational businesses in export activities of strategic natural resources, including hydrocarbons and mining products. Fazio uses the example of the US Chiquita Brands (the successor to United Fruit Company), "which used paramilitaries in Colombia to displace farmers" in order to use those farming areas for its own benefit (Chávez 2013, par. 7). "Fazio also warns against the indiscriminate use of the term 'failed state,' a category that he claims comes from US think tanks and institutions like the CIA or the Pentagon and has often served as an excuse to destabilize countries" (par. 9).[1]

Fazio notes that the concept of failed state appeared in Mexico between the governments of George W. Bush and Barack Obama and recalls that secretary of state Hillary Clinton raised the question of the "existence of narco-insurgency in Mexico, attempting to compare groups of the criminal economy with the tactics of rebel armed groups" (Chávez 2013, par. 11). Under this logic, policies that should be implemented by the Mexican government to fight organized crime—backed by the United States—would require the usage of "counterinsurgency" tactics. The analyst recognizes that "these terms are linked to the policies of the CIA and the Pentagon, which have been tied to neo-colonial wars for the control of strategic resources" (par. 10). Cockcroft (2010,

40) agrees with this argument: "High officials of the U.S. government and its armed forces blather a lot about 'failed states.' We are told that these states are bleeding to death and only a transfusion of military intervention can save the patients."

IMPORTANT NOTE

The aforementioned theories are subject to verification. The "official" version of this conflict in Mexico contradicts such explanations. Mexican authorities allege independent and sovereign decision-making and deny purported intervention by foreign governments in the design and implementation of this unconventional security strategy. Instead, claiming a shared responsibility, they welcomed collaboration by the US government through the Mérida Initiative. Calderón declared a war on drugs allegedly to liberate the country from the problems caused by narcotics trade, extreme violence, and other forms of organized crime. He positioned himself (and is considered in some circles) as a firm leader who finally decided to undertake an urgent task to put a stop to those that were harming the nation—and other nations, particularly Mexico's northern neighbor.

The former president of Mexico initially justified his decision by declaring a frontal attack against drug trafficking. Subsequently he presented his security policy as a battle between "good" and "bad" (*buenos vs. malos*), as a struggle between the government authorities and the *narcos*, but the real situation seems to be much more complex than this. Many more actors with diverse agendas seem to be involved in Mexico's conflict. The intricacies of the current reality in the country show a confluence of national and international actors and interests collaborating or fighting for the control of territories, natural resources, and spaces of political power.

Obtaining all the supporting evidence for the critical theories discussed above can be somewhat difficult. However, it is possible to identify clear winners and losers from the so-called drug war. Regardless of whether the end results of Mexico's modern civil war were premeditated or not, some powerful groups have greatly profited from the country's armed conflict.

The present study does not allege a conspiracy by transnational economic actors and foreign governments for the ultimate control of Mexican hydrocarbons and other key natural resources. There is not enough evidence yet to substantiate related theories or to affirm that all this was premeditated. However, certain lines of investigation and unequivocal relationships among actors and events (like the ones presented here) might lead some to believe in a conspiracy. The processes and connections analyzed here show that among the major (potential) winners of Mexico's war are large energy and security companies. Destabilization, displacement, and the control of territories by armed actors (criminal groups, paramilitaries, and regular armed forces) have been benefiting—or will greatly benefit—these transnational private actors.

A War Against the People

Journalist Ioan Grillo (2011, 273) posed "an imaginary scenario" in which Mexico's drug war "could escalate into a broader civil war over the country's natural and financial resources." In such a setting, paramilitary squads would be securing "oil installations and mines and fighting off enemies trying to seize them. Such a conflict could draw in hundreds of thousands of people and have a devastating human cost." As Dawn Paley notes, this scenario "is perhaps not as far off as Grillo imagined."[2] Without analyzing geopolitics per se and mainly talking about drugs and drug cartel wars, Grillo recognized the severe human cost of Mexico's conflict. Paley (2014, 29) goes further, carefully analyzing how the so-called drug wars have greatly transformed the economies of Colombia, Mexico, and Central America. She sees these types of armed conflicts as wars "against people" (*guerras contra los pueblos*).

According to Paley (2014, 42), "people living through the impacts of the war on drugs in the US and elsewhere understand that it is a war on them and their communities." Hence, in the case of Mexico as well, the victims of this modern civil war "are poor people, migrants, and indigenous and peasant farmers" (55). Another important point that Paley (2013, par. 31) makes is that these types of wars are "about so much more than drugs." Some of the TCOs that are involved in Mexico's armed conflict "are responsible for carrying out actions that have little or nothing to do with drug trafficking, including attacks and extortion against civilians, migrants, journalists, and activists." Hence, in Paley's view (2014, 41), "the term war on drugs is definitely problematic": this phenomenon "is very clearly a war against people, waged with far wider interests than controlling substances." Similarly, according to Cockcroft (2010, 37), "the real targets of [the] plans for the international coordination and militarization of the struggle against alleged *narcos*" are "immigrants, original peoples, guerrilla resistance, political dissidents, and social movements against transnational corporations taking over natural resources, including water, and causing mining pollution."

A Major Loser: The National Oil Industry

As shown by the situation in Tamaulipas, the theft of hydrocarbons has become increasingly problematic in various regions in Mexico (see chapter 3). Organized crime has started to control whole areas transited by oil pipelines and fuel trucks. In fact, in some parts of the country, "Mexican crime groups have virtually taken over the pipeline system of Mexico's state oil [company], stealing growing amounts of fuel and gaining an important source of new revenue as they fight other gangs and Mexico's government" (Harrup and Luhnow 2011, par. 1).[3] According to Grayson (2014b, 24), the "largest robberies have taken place in Pemex installations in Villahermosa, Ciudad del Carmen, Veracruz, Poza Rica, and Reynosa." He attributes the majority of such operations to the Zetas.

The scale of the problem is unclear. Estimates of the losses in Mexico's energy sector as a result of the security crisis vary. From 2000 to 2013 Pemex reported an increase of 1,548 percent in the number of illegal pipelines transporting oil. In 2014 it was calculated that nearly ten thousand barrels were stolen daily (Alvi 2014a, par. 10). In that same year Pemex estimated that losses from oil theft were around 65 thousand million pesos. Oil has been sold in the black market to a number of clients, including individuals, gas stations, industries, and even transnational energy companies (Alvi 2014a, par. 3).

Between 2012 and 2013 over 1,500 illegal fuel taps allegedly caused about $1.1 billion in losses, according to some Mexican officials. Sinaloa and Veracruz were cited as the most affected states in those years (EIA 2014, 7). According to public Pemex records, in 2013 alone approximately 9.3 million barrels of oil and gasoline were stolen (Montes and Althaus 2014, par. 14). The Mexican Association of Gasoline Entrepreneurs (Asociación Mexicana de Empresarios Gasolineros, AMEGAS) estimates that organized crime controls approximately 20 percent of the national fuel market (González 2015).

As mentioned earlier, a phenomenon that has gained particular attention in recent years is the theft of natural gas condensate from the

Burgos Basin for its sale in the United States.[4] Pemex internal reports also show that the theft and illegal sales of natural gas condensate have spread to wide zones of northeastern Mexico.[5] This clearly demonstrates the absence of adequate surveillance mechanisms and the possible involvement of public state officials. It is also worthwhile noting that the recent security crisis in the country has affected the production of hydrocarbons in specific zones. As noted in chapter 8, for example, the presence of organized crime and violent activity severely affected the Burgos Basin's gas production in 2010 and 2011; of the existing deposits, half stopped their activities (Correa-Cabrera 2014a).

The number of victims linked to the state oil company has increased in many regions in Mexico (Alvi 2014a, par. 4). In 2012 "an entire eight-man crew from a private Mexican oil-service firm [working for Pemex] went missing while working on well heads down river from Nuevo Laredo. . . . Neither the company nor Mexico's government ever commented on the disappearance" (Montes and Althaus 2014, par. 7). According to a document from the attorney general's office obtained through Mexico's transparency institute, "in the six years between January 2008 and March 2014, [twelve] Pemex workers were kidnapped" (par. 9). As in Tamaulipas, Pemex employees and contractors in other parts of the country have been assassinated, kidnapped, or been victims of extortion in recent years. These practices have not been exclusive to groups like the Zetas or the Gulf Cartel. Other criminal organizations, like the CJNG—following the same paramilitary model—have also entered these very profitable businesses (Ángel 2015).

From the Burgos Basin to the Campeche Sound, violence and fear are present in oil regions. Oil municipalities such as Reynosa in Tamaulipas, Paraíso in Tabasco, Ciudad del Carmen in Campeche, and Coatzacoalcos and Poza Rica in Veracruz have been particularly infiltrated by criminal paramilitary groups (Pérez 2010b). This same pattern takes place in maritime zones, refineries, and hydrocarbon storage and distribution terminals, where suppliers and service providers of all Pemex subsidiaries are obliged to pay protection payments (*derecho de piso*) in order to avoid executions by those who call themselves Zetas or are alleged to be members of groups such as the Gulf Cartel, CJNG, or Knights Templar (Pérez 2010b).

Overall, hydrocarbon theft and related activities have mainly harmed Mexico's state-owned oil company, Pemex. The current security strategy has not been effective in preventing these crimes. On the contrary, during the years of the drug war, looting grew exponentially and the image of Pemex greatly deteriorated due to alleged corrupt practices that allowed the large-scale occurrence of these illegal activities. At the same time, criminal organizations needed additional resources to wage a war against government forces; stealing oil and gas from the state company facilitated such a task. In the end Pemex's poor image would favor the entrance of new, private players into the hydrocarbon industry. Pemex's severe problems could further public support for potential private investors, who might appear to be much more efficient, more effective in containing crime, and less corrupt than Pemex.

Who Benefits from Mexico's Modern Civil War?

Overall, the main losers from Mexico's modern civil war seem to be the national oil industry and the country's most vulnerable people—those who did not have the resources to flee or defend themselves against extortion, kidnappings, and other forms of brutality by criminal groups, paramilitaries, and government forces. Their spaces are being occupied by private companies—mostly transnational and very powerful. Forced displacements, massive disappearances, and militarization in key parts of the country have emptied strategic lands and left them available for future investments, many in the energy sector. At the same time, the war in Mexico—like any other war in the world—has become a big business for private actors who provide security services to the government, entrepreneurs, and even criminal groups.

Forced Displacements: A War for the Land

According to the United Nations Educational, Scientific and Cultural Organization (UNESCO 2015, par. 3), internally displaced persons are individuals "or groups of persons who have been forced to flee, or leave, their homes or places of habitual residence as a result of armed conflict, internal strife, and habitual violations of human rights, as well as natural or man-made disasters involving one or more of these elements, and who have not crossed an internationally recognized state border." Mexico's recent armed conflict left many people in this situation. But who benefits from these displacements, which have also occurred in other parts of the hemisphere? Analyzing the case of Colombia, Professor Carlos G. Vélez-Ibáñez (quoted in Paley 2014, 103) states:

> Forced displacement in Colombia is not a casual by-product of the internal conflict. Armed groups attack the civil population to strengthen territorial strong hold, expand territorial control, weaken support of the opponent, and accumulate valuable assets (e.g., land or extraction of natural resources). Forcing out population as a war strategy aims at impeding collective action, damaging social networks, and intimidating and controlling the civilian population.

In fact, when "people have been forced off their land and are living in camps and slums, it becomes much more difficult for them to effectively organize to control their territories" (Paley 2014, 103). Paley also notes that "violence deployed by the state and justified with claims of combating trafficking can lead to urban and rural populations being displaced, clearing territory for corporations to extract natural resources, and impacting land ownership and property values" (47). In other words, "moving people off of the lands, new territories are opened up for [the] so-called frontier investments" (103). Such dynamics have been present in Colombia and Mexico. For example, Gray (2008, 81) found some links between business interests and violence in Colombia: "ranchers and plantation owners in Córdoba and Urabá funded paramilitary campaigns that caused mass displacements, and then the 'freed up' lands became ranches and plantations." What happened in Mexico also illustrates this point.

A study published by the Mexican Commission for the Defense and Promotion of Human Rights (Comisión Mexicana de Defensa y Promoción de los Derechos Humanos, CMDPDH) shows that at least twelve states have witnessed a population exodus as a result of the conflict in Mexico. Between 2011 and 2014 approximately 280,000 persons were forcibly displaced, mainly from Chihuahua, Nuevo León, Tamaulipas, Sinaloa, Durango, Michoacán, Guerrero, and Veracruz (Rubio 2014, 120). According to this same study, Chihuahua, Tamaulipas, Michoacán, Guerrero, and Veracruz registered the greatest number of massive internal displacements (those involving more than ten families). It is worth noting that all of these are places where the Zetas or similar groups (which follow a paramilitary model) operated or have been operating and where the militarization of security has been more intense.[6]

As mentioned in chapter 8, Tamaulipas has registered a very large number of forced displacements—particularly in hydrocarbon-rich municipalities located along the border region and the Gulf Coast. Inhabitants of these territories have denounced this situation and a series of incidents that have driven people out of their lands.[7] Government inaction has prevailed in these zones. For example, an old man who lives in an *ejido* near Reynosa (located in the Burgos Basin area) reported "a chain of anomalies and corruption in the regions of the Burgos Basin" that mainly affected *ejido* landowners (*ejidatarios*), whose lands have been easily invaded due to their poverty conditions and their lack of organization and resources to defend their properties (Meza 2010, par. 13).

A similar situation has taken place in Chihuahua's Juárez Valley, a region that has registered the highest rate of homicides, kidnappings, extortions, and forced displacements in the state. Some have attributed this phenomenon to state militarization (Alvarado 2015), but official sources simply refer to "cartel wars." On the surface it seems that violence results from a fight for drug-trafficking plazas, but this might not necessarily be the case (Alvarado 2015). La Línea and Gente Nueva are two very violent criminal groups that have had a strong presence in Chihuahua and have operated as armed wings of the Juárez Cartel and the Sinaloa Cartel, respectively. Both criminal groups allegedly have recruited former military personnel. The criminal paramilitaries have also followed the Zetas model and have recently become the target of government forces in Chihuahua's regions that are rich in natural resources, particularly hydrocarbons (see appendix 3). Home of the recently discovered Chihuahua Basin, the state is strategic for the new energy developments and megaprojects in the framework of Mexico's energy reform.

"Chihuahua is becoming a key state for the transportation of natural gas," secretary of energy Pedro Joaquín Coldwell said in 2015. Important projects in this area are now being built and will be completed in the next few years. Coldwell mentions, for example, the El Encino–Topolobampo pipeline and "the construction of pipelines in Waha–San Elizario, Waha-Presidio, Ojinaga–El Encino–La Laguna." These projects will "bring cheaper natural gas from the United States" to the whole state of Chihuahua (quoted in Alvarado 2015, par. 47). Under this plan, the El Encino locality in Chihuahua "will be one of the main interconnection points to distribute [natural gas] in the northeast and central parts of the country."

Map 9.1. Mexican states at risk of "expropriation."
Source: Martínez Huerta (2014).

According to agrarian leader Martín Solís,[8] the areas most unin-
habited because of violence in Chihuahua "are exactly the same as
those planned for the development of these megaprojects" (quoted in
Alvarado 2015, par. 49). Solís observes an initial "emptying of [these
areas] by means of violence, which brought a depreciation in the value
of ranches and great expanses of desert land." In this new context,
transnational private investors can "purchase these properties at very
cheap prices because they are now abandoned." Such a situation applies to many other regions of the country that will be key for energy
development under the new context of Mexico's energy reform.

The projected massive exploration and extraction of shale gas and
other natural resources essential for energy production would require
access to large expanses of land. According to some critics and activists, this can encourage the (temporary or permanent) expropriation of
ejido, communal, and small private lands and ultimately favor transnational energy corporations (for example, see Saxe-Fernández 2014).[9]
Such actions would be possible due to the recent changes in legislation
related to land ownership and use in Mexico.[10] In 2014 PRD senator
Luis Sánchez claimed that energy reform puts the properties of millions
of Mexicans at risk of expropriation in twelve states. These territo-

ries possess hydrocarbons in their subsoil or will host important infrastructure projects for energy generation or distribution. According to a study sponsored by the senator, communities at risk can be found in the states of Chihuahua, Coahuila, San Luis Potosí, Nuevo León, Tamaulipas, Veracruz, Puebla, Hidalgo, Tabasco, Oaxaca, Chiapas, and Campeche (see map 9.1) (Martínez Huerta 2014, par. 14).

These twelve states where potential affected communities are located include approximately 260 municipalities. These lands represent more than 400,000 square kilometers of the national territory (Martínez Huerta 2014). A great portion of the resources that can be extracted in these territories are within communal and *ejido* lands (Chávez 2014, par. 5). It is also worthwhile noting that these specific areas of the country have registered the presence of Zetas or similar criminal groups that use paramilitary tactics for exercising territorial control (see map 2.2, map 7.5, and appendix 3). The extreme violence generated by these groups and the responses by the Mexican government have emptied strategic lands, thus facilitating the consolidation of energy reform and reducing the need for land expropriations to some extent.

Disappearances and Forced Disappearances

Since 2006 more than 27,000 people have disappeared in Mexico (see table 9.1).[11] According to Italian journalist Federico Mastrogiovanni (2014), a number of these should be considered "forced disappearances," because they directly involve government forces. The use of the term "forced disappearance" in reference to what happened in Mexico can seem problematic, because there is no systematic state policy and no military junta behind these events.[12] On several occasions, however, migrants or young people living in conditions of poverty were those who went missing, allegedly at the hands of municipal police, state police, federal police, or the military.[13] In Mexico disappearances seem to be part of a strategy of terror, starting with the so-called drug war. It is obvious that not all of these cases are linked to government actions—some are perpetrated by private actors or organized crime members (Mastrogiovanni 2014).[14]

Perhaps the most important result of these disappearances is the fear generated in society as a whole, preventing people from organizing and mobilizing against key policies. In Mastrogiovanni's opinion, this has happened in Mexico, particularly in certain areas where

Table 9.1. The Disappeared in Mexico (2006–2015)

State	2006	2007	2008	2009	2010	2011
			Common jurisdiction			
Aguascalientes	0	25	7	19	18	27
Baja California	0	7	25	11	8	19
Baja California Sur	0	0	2	1	3	2
Campeche	0	0	5	0	1	0
Chiapas	0	1	0	0	1	3
Chihuahua	17	92	110	168	228	247
Coahuila	1	58	105	125	242	279
Colima	0	0	2	1	10	20
Distrito Federal	0	2	2	92	35	202
Durango	2	10	16	30	148	59
Estado de México	19	92	58	123	97	184
Guanajuato	4	54	30	61	34	94
Guerrero	4	19	19	9	24	57
Hidalgo	3	10	17	18	24	56
Jalisco	4	54	55	93	148	290
Michoacán	3	18	33	61	96	117
Morelos	0	0	0	1	2	4
Nayarit	0	0	1	4	0	4
Nuevo León	3	74	54	122	642	635
Oaxaca	4	24	53	6	13	24
Puebla	0	3	30	44	37	54
Querétaro	0	4	0	5	19	16
Quintana Roo	1	7	18	13	7	9
San Luis Potosí	0	0	0	1	8	29
Sinaloa	3	49	75	50	199	212
Sonora	1	14	37	48	58	63
Tabasco	0	3	1	4	2	1
Tamaulipas	8	74	63	197	957	1,275
Tlaxcala	0	0	0	2	0	2
Veracruz	2	5	6	2	31	83
Yucatán	0	1	1	2	4	3
Zacatecas	0	2	7	26	35	45
Unspecified	0	1	2	2	1	5
Total	**79**	**703**	**834**	**1,341**	**3,132**	**4,120**

Source: Mexico, RNPED (2015).

	Common jurisdiction				Federal juris-diction	Common juris-diction	Global total
2012	2013	2014	2015	Before 2006			
12	13	55	98	0	9	274	283
126	163	502	0	394	22	1,255	1,277
3	5	4	4	0	0	24	24
0	5	11	5	1	0	28	28
5	5	4	5	0	6	24	30
221	205	231	129	31	19	1,679	1,698
149	234	107	0	130	53	1,430	1,483
38	43	22	6	1	0	143	143
111	108	53	26	15	42	646	688
41	22	10	9	4	1	351	352
164	361	631	909	24	26	2,662	2,688
73	98	191	222	9	5	870	875
63	139	261	216	48	247	859	1,106
29	7	2	4	39	4	209	213
291	540	460	176	2	24	2,113	2,137
169	286	156	76	4	49	1,019	1,068
5	27	45	0	8	15	92	107
0	6	2	0	0	2	17	19
240	126	111	203	14	25	2,224	2,249
5	40	23	4	3	31	199	230
55	91	242	274	5	1	835	836
25	33	51	127	5	3	285	288
5	38	40	3	0	5	141	146
2	11	3	3	1	6	58	64
189	310	319	321	9	20	1,736	1,756
113	164	300	128	7	25	933	958
1	3	8	9	0	6	32	38
1,129	759	777	247	97	137	5,583	5,720
2	5	4	0	0	4	15	19
45	117	223	4	2	165	520	685
9	17	17	41	0	2	95	97
22	47	62	50	1	15	297	312
4	2	2	1	2	20	22	42
3,346	4,030	4,929	3,300	856	989	26,670	27,659

important natural resources have been discovered. In his opinion, if a transnational company arrives in the country and wants to exploit hydrocarbons or other natural resources and needs access to big extensions of land to do so, it would be much easier to achieve this if the population is terrified. Massive disappearances seem to facilitate this process. Mastrogiovanni mentions what has happened in Tamaulipas as an example of this strategy.

Mastrogiovanni raises important questions about Tamaulipas, wondering why this border state, rich in hydrocarbons with a strategic location, is still controlled by organized crime. He does not understand why it seems impossible to stop what is happening there. "How can it be that in such an important geostrategic place, the State has not been able to retake control and provide [the needed] security for the people living there?" (quoted in Martínez 2014, par. 18). Hence, thinking of the experience in other developing countries possessing abundant natural resources, Mastrogiovanni hypothesizes a phase of artificially generated violence benefiting big transnational interests and promoting organized crime. Nonetheless, "the [government] does not necessarily need to be an accomplice of these groups" (par. 18). Simply by not acting, Mexico's government would collaborate indirectly in this new scheme of capital concentration through the anticipated generation of terror, which would be the true value of "omission." The government, organized crime, and transnational economic interests need not be direct allies but can reinforce each other's objectives.

Mastrogiovanni identifies common patterns of massive and forced disappearances in key areas of Monterrey, Tamaulipas, and Coahuila and tries to find a coherent explanation of the events. He concludes that some people living in these areas feel pressured to leave their lands and keep silent due to the terror generated by criminal groups and the government's inaction. These empty territories can then be utilized by others for resource extraction. Mastrogiovanni's investigation found that the largest numbers of disappearances were in the states of Tamaulipas, Coahuila, Nuevo León, Guerrero, and Michoacán. He also mentions the cases of Baja California (the Tijuana area), Veracruz, Sinaloa, and the State of Mexico. Again, many of these areas had criminal paramilitaries and were epicenters of a modern civil war.

Official data on missing persons in Mexico have been gathered by the National Registry of Data of Missing or Disappeared Persons (RNPED) (Lara 2014b).[15] According to these figures, Tamaulipas registered the largest number of missing or disappeared persons (see table 9.1). Following Tamaulipas were the State of Mexico, Nuevo León, Jalisco, Sinaloa, Chihuahua, and Coahuila, which have also recorded high numbers of disappearances in the past few years. All these states also had a disproportionate number of forced disappearances. During the Calderón administration, three out of ten cases (overall disappearances) occurred in Tamaulipas or Guerrero. During the first two years of the Peña Nieto administration, these same states accounted for two out of ten disappearances (Merino et al. 2015, par. 21).

Of the ten municipalities registering the highest rates of disappearances in the country, seven are located in Tamaulipas: Mier, Guerrero, Jiménez, Miguel Alemán, Abasolo, Matamoros, and Valle Hermoso (Merino et al. 2015, par. 22). It is worth noting that these incidents happen frequently in Mexico's border towns. Official data show that only four out of the thirty-eight border municipalities reported zero disappearances between 2006 and 2014. In the other thirty-four municipalities a significant number of people were reported missing during Mexico's war. Matamoros has the largest number (1,378), followed by Nuevo Laredo (918) and Reynosa (848). Considering population size, Mier registered the highest rate, with an average of 128 missing per 100,000 inhabitants, followed by Guerrero (92) and Miguel Alemán (38). All of these municipalities are located in Tamaulipas (Merino et al. 2015, par. 40).

Winners of Mexico's War

Like all armed conflicts, Mexico's new civil war has benefited specific groups or actors (national, foreign, and transnational). Overall, the biggest winners of Mexico's drug war seem to be transnational actors that operate in different areas—particularly transnational security and energy firms. Many of these companies are headquartered in the United States. Moreover, "dominant factions in the [Mexican] state apparatus stand to benefit. State military power, policing, and the prison system are strengthened through increased aid and cooperation with the world's military superpower" (Paley 2014, 117). Extreme violence in Mexico has promoted the militarization of security in the country and along the US southern border, thus benefiting essentially US arms-producing companies and private security contractors. Hence Mexico's northern neighbor has profited from the so-called drug war through its border-security/military-industrial complex.[16]

Mexico's violent spiral has had positive effects on US border security and the border economy. Crime rates in US border counties have decreased significantly in the past few years due to enhanced border enforcement (Correa-Cabrera 2013a). At the same time, forced displacements in Mexico have modified to some extent migration patterns from Mexico to the United States. In fact the extreme violence that "has pervaded Mexico's border states has produced a marked change in immigration dynamics between the two countries as a greater number of relatively more skilled and wealthier Mexicans are legally emigrating from afflicted border areas in Mexico to the United States in search of a better and more peaceful life" (Correa-Cabrera 2013a, 73). Hence the effects of the war on Mexico-US migration dynamics seem to be positive for the US economy.

ARMS-PRODUCING COMPANIES

Among the major winners of Mexico's armed conflict are US arms-producing companies. In fact the United States sells more weapons to Mexico than any other country in the world.[17] Mexico's drug war has represented a very big business for US arms manufacturers and intermediaries. Calderón drastically elevated purchases of arms and military equipment to fight a war against organized crime. Criminal groups were forced to do the same in order to respond effectively to the government's offensive. The paramilitarization of organized crime and the growing conflicts among different criminal groups for control of Mexico's key territories had already significantly increased illegal imports of arms and military equipment into Mexico. Hence a vast amount of legal and illegal arms arrived in Mexico in the framework of its most current security conflict.

According to Joshua Partlow (2015, par. 12), *Washington Post* correspondent in Mexico, arms buying is "a sign of the intensity of the war against [drugs]." He also notes that "the Mexican military has aggressive operations ongoing in several states such as Tamaulipas, on the Texas border, and Jalisco" and that "these operations have driven a rapid increase in defense spending over much of the past decade." He reported that from 2006 to 2015 "spending has tripled, from $2.6 billion to $7.9 billion" (par. 12) and that more than $1 billion in US military equipment was sold to Mexico in only two years (2013 and 2014) (par. 2). According to Íñigo Guevara, a Mexican defense consultant based in Washington, from the end of the Calderón administration until 2015, "Mexico has purchased about $1.5 billion in equipment through the government's military sales program, plus $2 billion more through U.S. companies" (quoted in Partlow 2015, par. 10). Additionally, he noted that defense spending also increased sharply under Felipe Calderón and that it reflects the "maturing military-to-military relationship at the institutional level, regardless of who is in power" (par. 11).

SECURITY CONTRACTORS

Mexico's war promotes private security businesses and is part of a set of contract schemes that include consulting services, training, and the massive sale of weapons. These services can be offered to TCOs as well as to law enforcement agencies. The Mexican modern civil war can be compared in some ways to the wars in Iraq and Afghanistan, which are considered to be two important promoters of private security contractors. In such conflicts these specialized private companies have been hired by the US government or by other transnational private businesses to protect their facilities, personnel, and interests in areas of extreme violence and confrontations. The privatization of security—including the privatization of the prison system—seems to be a worldwide trend.[18]

After the most violent years of the war in Mexico and in the context of energy reform, the situation in some areas of the country continues to be delicate. The consolidation of energy reform and the development of key energy projects require visible improvements with regard to security in strategic and still very violent regions. Alternatively, those private transnational energy firms eyeing Mexico's energy markets might end up hiring private security. However, Mexico's legislation is currently unclear regarding the participation of foreign security contractors. Currently (as Rodríguez and Nuche [2015, par. 13] recognize), "security implementation [has been] provided by the state," which has "retained the monopoly of the industry which fell under the responsibility of the Armed Forces as it was seen as a matter of national security." With new players in the energy industry, private investors might pressure for the approval of new legislation that would allow the participation of foreign private security firms.

THE TRANSNATIONAL CORPORATE SECTOR

As mentioned repeatedly in the course of this work, one key actor that has visibly benefited from Mexico's security policies is the transnational corporate sector. As Paley (2014, 117) observes, this sector has experienced "improved conditions for investment thanks to reforms as well as an increasingly paramilitarized and repressive social context that allows a freer hand to pursue . . . controversial mega projects."[19] These policies and reforms, according to Paley, have been supported by the Mérida Initiative, which was designed to disrupt drug trafficking "while transforming Mexico in three key ways: introducing a new legal system and promoting structural reforms, increasing levels of militarization, and, as a by-product of the latter, encouraging the formation of paramilitary groups" (211). According to this view, the main aim of this initiative is "the creation of more welcoming investment policies and legal regulations" (118).

The application of this set of policies to combat organized crime, according to Paley (2013, par. 14), has "more to do with improving the conditions for foreign direct investment and encouraging the expansion of capitalism than it does with stemming the flow of drugs." More specifically, in the case of Mexico the militarization of security as a response to the presence of groups like the Zetas seems to have more to do with protecting transnational economic interests—mainly in the energy sector—than with fighting organized crime. In several regions of Mexico the militarization of security seems to have contributed to further natural resource exploitation by multinational companies. Hence extractive industries—many of them based in the United States—are the big winners in this new security strategy supported by Mexico's northern neighbor.

It is worth noting that forced displacements, disappearances, and depreciation of land values in key areas of Mexico have not halted investment in energy and commercial infrastructure (see chapter 7). Energy contractors have not stopped working; the expansion of large investment projects continues despite the high risk posed by organized crime and the large number of disappearances. It is also interesting to observe that while Los Zetas and groups following the same criminal paramilitary model have affected small and medium entrepreneurs in the hydrocarbon industry as well as Pemex, they have hardly touched other transnational interests. This might make possible the oligopolization of all the energy supply chain by specific corporate players.

In other words, it is plausible that in the future some key transnational firms will control the extraction, transportation, commercialization, and distribution in Mexico of most resources essential for energy generation, such as oil, natural gas, coal, iron, and other fuels. Controlling most energy production processes would give these companies further market power and thus a greater capacity to exercise control over prices.[20] Los Zetas and similar groups might have "unintentionally" helped these companies to augment their influence in the world energy markets.

The United States: A Key "Indirect" Winner of Mexico's War

The process through which disappearances, forced displacements, and paramilitarism have cheapened lands and benefited the transnational corporate sector has had a very positive impact on the economy of Mexico's northern neighbor. The war in Mexico coincides with the process of achieving US/North American energy independence and with the so-called shale gas revolution. These developments will essentially benefit extractive industries, especially the energy sector in the United States. Hence Mexico's security crisis—which facilitated the passage of key reforms and displaced people from key territories— might help the United States to achieve its immediate economic goals. After the worst years of the war, the core of the debate in Mexico focused on energy reform and the benefits that it would bring to the two neighboring nations through greater bilateral cooperation.

US Energy Independence and the "Shale Gas Revolution"

In the past few years there has been an important shift in the dynamics of the US energy industry. Thanks to its large reserves of unconventional hydrocarbons and new technology, the United States is projected to emerge in the coming years as the world's largest oil producer and as a global leader in gas production (Page 2012). According to recent estimations by the US Energy Information Administration (EIA), the United States will drastically reduce its oil imports in the next two decades and will even become a gas exporter. The United States—which currently imports about 20 percent of all the energy it needs—will be almost self-sufficient by 2035.[21] Under these new circumstances, the United States "could remain as the world's largest economy longer than expected (to the detriment of China) and could redefine its foreign policy by reducing oil imports from the Middle East to almost zero" (Page 2012, par. 1).

Recently the United States became the main protagonist of a new energy boom, which stalled in 2015 due to a drastic decrease in oil and gas prices. Notwithstanding the current adverse conditions of the world energy markets, it is quite plausible that the United States will continue improving its position within the industry.[22] It has some of the largest unconventional energy reserves (light crude and shale gas) in the world. These resources were once considered to be very difficult to exploit, but US companies have developed adequate technology to extract these hydrocarbons "more easily and at reasonable prices." The access to more efficient techniques to obtain "unconventional hydrocarbons has become a key factor in the development of the US energy sector."[23] It is thus possible that in the near future the United States will become a "global energy power" (Page 2012, par. 2). Its successful incursion into the Mexican market will also contribute to this goal. The war in Mexico has already emptied some key hydrocarbon-rich lands that are now available for potential energy investors.

The path toward US energy independence coincides with what has been called the "shale revolution," which has stimulated significantly the production of oil and particularly of natural gas in the United States. The revolution was possible because of "advances in oil and natural gas production technology—notably, a new combination of horizontal drilling and hydraulic fracturing. These technological advances combined with high oil and gas prices [in the recent past] increased production of [hydrocarbons] in the United States" (Brown and Yücel 2013, 1). Rising shale gas production, in particular, has been significantly transforming the US economy, environment, and energy policy (*Offnews.info* 2013).[24]

This shale gas boom greatly altered the forecasts regarding the future of the US energy sector and the global energy landscape. Less than a decade ago the consensus was that the United States was beginning to run out of economically recoverable natural gas and that the country would have to import large quantities of this resource from abroad. This has not yet happened, and now it seems that Mexico's northern neighbor is flooded with natural gas.[25] US natural gas production increased almost 30 percent from 2005 to 2012. In 2011 about a third of that production was shale gas, compared with only 11 percent in 2008. Today shale gas represents approximately 40 percent of all the natural gas produced in the United States (*Offnews.info* 2013). By 2035, according to a study conducted by the research firm IHS Global Insight, shale gas will account for nearly 60 percent of total US natural gas production (O'Keefe 2012).

It is also worth noting that "national oil companies from emerging economies have fallen out of favor on stock markets over the past year relative to western energy groups, as the North American shale revolution continues to attract investors" (Crooks 2014, par. 1). It seems that the boom in US shale gas production "has created an alternative for investors concerned about the risk in state-controlled companies" (par. 6). In this new context, large energy corporations like Schlumberger, Halliburton, and Baker Hughes have thrived as they have acquired "the skills and technology needed for shale oil and gas production" (par. 12).[26] It is quite plausible that companies like these would end up dominating the energy market in Mexico, occupying spaces that were once reserved for Pemex. Today the state oil company is in a very difficult financial situation due to a severe reduction in oil and gas prices, long-term mismanagement, and extreme corruption. Moreover, organized crime and Mexico's war (as noted) have particularly affected the former energy monopoly. Thus large transnational energy companies will have great advantages in a revamped Mexican market.

US/North American Energy Independence, Mexico, and the Shale Revolution

The idea of energy independence does not only apply to the United States but extends to North America (including Mexico and Canada).[27] Some have even seen the possibility of building a new hemispheric energy coalition. Chris Faulkner, chief executive of the Dallas-based Breitling Energy Corporation, for example, proposed the creation of a "North American energy confederation," with the aim of achieving "North American energy independence," to become "the second largest oil producing coalition in the world next to OPEC" (Schneider 2015, par. 47). To achieve this goal, Mexico would be a key actor. When Mexico had just approved energy reform and prices were much more favorable, David Goldwyn et al. (2014, 37) wrote the following in a report of the Atlantic Council:

> Mexico's revival will . . . positively impact global energy security. Market analysts who projected Mexican production declines will now factor in rising production, creating downward pressure on the need for OPEC production and oil prices more broadly, and positioning Mexico to take advantage of rising demand across the Pacific. Mexico's deepwater program should produce significant volumes by 2025, the point at which many forecasters have targeted as the peak of US unconventional production. Mexico therefore will become a strate-

234 Los Zetas Inc.

gic supplier of oil just as US production plateaus, extending the run of North American energy self-sufficiency at an optimum moment.

A key component in achieving North American energy independence is the development of the natural gas industry. In fact, US president Barack Obama, through the Department of State led by Hillary Clinton from 2009 to 2013, promoted the use of fracking worldwide under the argument that the development of the shale gas industry could help rewrite global energy politics (*SinEmbargo* 2014; Blake 2014). Clinton personally defended the technique of hydraulic fracturing in meetings with foreign ministers and representatives from different countries held in Washington, where she talked about US plans to help promote fracking worldwide. She also advanced the "Global Shale Gas Initiative, which aimed to help other nations develop their shale potential" (Blake 2014, par. 7).

As part of these efforts, Clinton appointed a lawyer named David Goldwyn as US State Department special envoy and coordinator for international energy affairs. One of his tasks was "to elevate energy diplomacy as a key function of US foreign policy" (Blake 2014, par. 5). After leaving office, Goldwyn collaborated on a report produced by the Atlantic Council, a Washington, DC–based think tank, in which the authors expressed great support for Mexico's energy reform (Goldwyn et al. 2014). According to the report, this historic legislative change would promote foreign investment and significantly increase production levels of oil and gas in Mexico. The report also underscored the importance of investment opportunities in pipeline infrastructure. When it was released in August 2014, Goldwyn asserted that "natural gas is the lynchpin of the energy reform." He also claimed that the "key to delivering lower cost and more reliable electric power to Mexico is increasing access to natural gas first by pipeline from the U.S., and then over time from indigenous production."[28]

This thinking is in line with what was expressed in a minority staff report prepared for the use of the Committee on Foreign Relations of the US Senate issued on December 21, 2012, titled "Oil, Mexico, and the Transboundary Agreement." This report—completed before Mexico's energy reform was passed—concluded by claiming that "the potential benefits of the United States and Mexico working more closely on their respective national energy goals have never been higher" (US Senate 2012, 16). The document also says that for the United States, "thoroughly understanding Mexico's oil prospects is also vital for [the country's] energy security outlook." In sum, according to this analysis, energy reform is an opportunity to ensure US/North American energy security, so the United States should negotiate with the Mexican government with this issue at the center of the bilateral agenda of both countries.

It is worth noting that "shale gas exploration is one of the recurring themes in the document" (Estrop 2013, par. 10). In fact the US government has a notable interest in investing in the extraction of this hydrocarbon. Moreover, the report is adamant that because of the large reserves of shale gas in Mexico it should be a priority for the United States to establish closer trade links with its southern neighbor and thus gain more access to its energy sector (Estrop 2013, par. 11). Mexico is key in the recent US energy development plans due to its strategic location and the availability of unexplored energy resources—mainly oil and shale gas reservoirs located in northeastern Mexico and the Gulf corridor.

Similarly, the exploitation of gas in the border region seems to be part of the Mexican government's bet for the development of some states, such as Coahuila, Nuevo León, and Tamaulipas. However, it is projected that the United States would first become Mexico's natural gas provider. In this context the Mazatlán area in Sinaloa and Mexico's northeastern border region would experience increased commercial activity. At the same time, Michoacán and the Gulf region—the areas that were hardest hit by recent violence in Mexico—would receive a large amount of investment resources, mostly from transnational private firms, as energy reform moves forward.

As mentioned earlier, violence has contributed to lowering the price of land through forced displacements in strategic energy regions. If Mexico's energy reform "proceeds as planned, it will create a large new market in which U.S. companies can utilize their cutting edge technologies for oil and gas drilling and production" (Regoli and Polley 2014, par. 19). It seems that under this new reality the two countries are "interested in consolidating a strategy of cooperation with the aim of securing the supply of Mexican oil and the exploitation [of] shale gas, which will be crucial in the coming years" (García and Verza 2013, par. 10).

Texas: One of the Biggest Winners

As noted, extractive industries—many of them based in the United States—will possibly be the major winners of Mexico's war and recent energy policies in the two countries. Among these companies, the ones headquartered in Texas will probably benefit the most due to their location (just north of the new hydrocarbon discoveries in northern Mexico), wide experience, and advances in this field. Texas energy companies "are not taking a wait-and-see approach, but have already begun positioning themselves to take advantage of this potential new market" (Regoli and Polley 2014, par. 20). In this regard Ray L. Hunt, chief executive officer of Dallas-based Hunt Consolidated, mentioned the following in an interview with journalists Alfredo Corchado and James Osborne (2014, pars. 1–3):

> [E]xpectations are high, especially for Texas companies that likely will play a leading role in the development. . . . I think all the stars are in alignment this time . . . Mexico has a significant natural resource. And I think 10, 15, 20 years from now you're going to see huge changes along the border. . . . The obstacles are numerous, from oil at the deepest depths of the Gulf of Mexico to gas shale formations in cartel-controlled territory along the 1,200-mile border with Texas. . . . Mexico is seeking to model its oil and gas development in the border region after the booming development on the Texas side, but there are many obstacles, including lack of security and infrastructure.

This is a good summary of the challenges and opportunities that US energy companies, and Texas firms in particular, are identifying today. South Texas, for example, is a region of great opportunities for energy development that can easily take advantage of what is supposedly about to happen in Mexico. According to the US Department of Energy, a number of South Texas areas have very large reserves of shale oil and gas and could eventually become the largest unconventional production areas of the planet (Michel 2014, 13).[29] The Eagle Ford Shale formation in South Texas recently has become one of the most productive oil and gas plays in the United States. It is allegedly responsible for more than half of Texas's recent energy boom.[30] The production boom here and in other shale fields of North Dakota and west Texas (all "made possible by horizontal drilling and hydraulic fracturing") has "lowered the country's dependence on imported oil by more than a third in recent years" (Krauss 2014, par. 7).

Many think that this success could be extended to Mexico, which is also among the countries that possess the largest shale gas reserves in the world.[31] In fact, as Víctor Hugo Michel (2014, par. 14) notes, "all maps containing the Eagle Ford Shale formation show a kind of

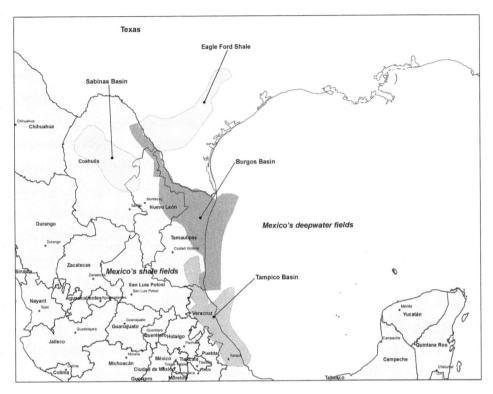

Map 9.2. The Eagle Ford Shale formation and Mexico's basins.
Source: Pemex and EIA. Design by Carlos D. Gutiérrez-Mannix.

horn that starts as a slim line south of Dallas and widens as it approaches the Mexican border, where it acquires its maximum width approximately from Nuevo Laredo, Tamaulipas, to Piedras Negras, Coahuila" (see map 9.2). These deposits do not stop at the Rio Grande (Río Bravo). They extend to important zones of northeastern Mexico, specifically to the Burgos Basin. According to some, South Texas and northeastern Mexico can take great advantage of shale oil and gas developments in the Burgos Basin (Taylor 2014). Actually the Burgos Basin and the gas fields of South Texas are part of the same geological province. Hence some have proposed that Mexico try to "replicate the kind of shale bonanza taking place in Texas. . . . Drilling in Mexico would seem a natural next move for the thousands of wildcatters who have brought a boom to Texas" (Cattan and Williams 2014, par. 4).

The Burgos Basin area—recently marred by violence and terror that displaced dozens of families—is apparently "well positioned [now] to take advantage of unconventional extraction techniques" because of its dimensions and "its close proximity to major shale field development in South and West Texas" (Wood et al. 2015, 7). With regard to this region, Representative Henry Cuellar (D-Laredo) has envisaged "another Eagle Ford right across the border" (McCumber Hearst 2015, par. 9). Del Mar College president Mark Escamilla has even affirmed that energy production in the Burgos Basin will be "eight times bigger than that of Eagle Ford Shale" (*Rio Grande Guardian* 2014, par. 1).

Henry Cuellar observes that "the Burgos Basin offers similar positive economic results" as Eagle Ford and that if "the Mexicans are able to develop their side," as the United States has, then this "border area will be the epicenter" of important hemispheric energy developments (McCumber Hearst 2015, par. 9). Now that energy reform is approved—and after a war that displaced people from strategic territories—it would be a logical step for companies that are already operating successfully in the Eagle Ford Shale to cross into Mexico. According to David Porter, chair of the Texas Railroad Commission, it "would just be a matter of moving pipelines, infrastructure, and people to the other side of the river in order to connect it to the American system" (Michel 2014, 20).

Four Successful Business Models in an Era of Modern Civil Wars

A new civil war in Mexico for the control of hydrocarbons and energy production in the North American region had the Zetas as one of its protagonists. Los Zetas, with a corporate structure and sophisticated business model (see chapter 3), transformed the panorama of organized crime in Mexico. Its presence contributed to justify an extremely violent armed conflict—involving irregular and symmetric nonconventional warfare in some regions of the country. Violence in Mexico's war had a dual function of extracting resources and increasing control by the government and criminal groups. This study shows how resource extraction has been a driving force behind Mexico's so-called drug war. Mexico's modern civil war benefited businesses (legal and illegal, national and transnational), banks, and the arms industry in particular. As highlighted in chapters 7 to 9, transnational energy businesses and security contractors have profited greatly from this new criminal model inspired and extended by the Zetas and, above all, from government responses to it.

But where is the organization today? What is the current role of the Zetas in the criminal world and the transnational legal and illegal economy? What has happened to this extremely violent transnational criminal organization that transformed organized crime in the hemisphere and had a fundamental role in Mexico's new civil war? From 2000 to the summer of 2013—when the group's then leader, Miguel Ángel Treviño Morales (aka Z-40), was arrested—Los Zetas was a protagonist in Mexico's criminal world. Immediately after Treviño's arrest, the Zeta organization lowered its public profile. Many have argued that this had to do with the group's demise or evident decline as a result of a successful government strategy against its "public enemy number one." But no one is certain about this. We do not hear much about this transnational criminal group nowadays, but the model that it inspired seems to be alive and still dominant in the Mexican crime world (consider, for example, the CJNG, Rojos, and Guerreros Unidos, which follow this model). Moreover, some of the Zetas' main activities are still being performed (including stealing gasoline, drug trafficking through Nuevo Laredo, kidnappings, and extorting small businesses). Who is performing such activities? How has the Zetas' model changed in recent years?

This concluding chapter suggests that the Zetas may still operate today as a transnational corporation—possibly with a different name and with a modified structure—and explains how this illegal group is linked to other legal corporations, particularly to those participating in extractive industries. Moreover, this transnational criminal organization seems to share a number of characteristics with legal transnational businesses that operate in the energy and private security industries. Thus this final chapter compares the Zetas with three other corporate entities participating in these sectors: Exxon Mobil Corporation, Halliburton Company, and Constellis Holdings, LLC (Constellis). Such a comparison seems useful to achieve a better understanding of the Zetas' role in the areas of energy and security in Mexico and in other parts of the continent. The present analysis also depicts different plausible scenarios that predict the future of the Zetas as well as the potential for the security and energy industries in the Americas.

It is important to mention that this study does not necessarily allege a very close relationship between the Zetas and these three companies (or similar ones). It does not suggest causation, intentionality, or a conspiracy by transnational energy and security companies with the aim of generating a chaotic situation in Mexico that would end up furthering their corporate interests. Any similarity between the Zetas' business model and these particular corporations is merely coincidental, but a comparison is useful to understand how criminal corporations operate.

Los Zetas and Three Successful Corporate Models

ExxonMobil: Transnational Corporation with Multiple Subsidiaries

Exxon Mobil Corporation is the world's largest publicly traded oil and gas company and one of the world's biggest companies in any industry. Its "core businesses include oil and gas exploration and production, petroleum refining and chemical production, and the marketing of petroleum and chemical products" (Carpenter 2015, pars. 1–2). A direct descendant of Standard Oil Company (founded in 1870 by John D. Rockefeller), ExxonMobil is the largest refiner in the world. This multinational oil and gas corporation is headquartered in Irving, Texas, and was formed on November 30, 1999, by the merger of Exxon and Mobil (once Standard Oil of New Jersey and Standard Oil of New York).[1]

ExxonMobil owns hundreds of subsidiaries, including ExxonMobil Energy Ltd., ExxonMobil Finance Co. Ltd., ExxonMobil International Services, ExxonMobil Abu Dhabi Offshore Petroleum Co. Ltd., Esso Pipeline Investments Ltd., Esso Petroleum Co. Ltd., Imperial Oil Ltd., Mobil Producing Texas & New Mexico Inc., Mobil Producing Nigeria Unlimited, RasGas Company Ltd., Aera Energy LLC, and XTO Energy Inc. Each subsidiary participates in a certain field or activity in the energy industry: production, refining, transportation, and so forth. In other words, they are all specialized. A subsidiary focused on transportation is not going to interfere with a subsidiary in charge of exploration and production, for example. However, they all work together to create a successful energy company.

In sum, ExxonMobil is a transnational corporation owning multiple subsidiaries divided by field of specialization but also by nation and geographic area. Structuring by subsidiaries insulates ExxonMobil from general lawsuits, as each subsidiary is fully responsible for the mistakes that it makes. For example, if a transportation subsidiary breaks the law, it can be sued. But all the other units of the company will remain untouched, as they have nothing to do with this particular business. Also, if someone sued one of ExxonMobil's refineries in Venezuela, the entire refining operation would be unaffected, as the company has several refining subsidiaries across the world and even in one nation. Moreover, the company is not liable beyond each subsidiary's assets.

The Zetas can arguably be seen in the same light as ExxonMobil. This criminal company is also divided by field of specialization and subsidiary (see chapter 3). The different criminal subsidiaries seem to work with relative independence from each other. Members of one unit of this criminal enterprise are almost always unaware or know very little about the activities and strategies of other units in the organization. Hence if a subsidiary of this criminal transnational corporation does poorly or gets in legal trouble for any reason (*sicariato* in Nuevo León, coal theft in Coahuila, drug trafficking along the Tamaulipas Small Border, and so forth), the other existing subsidiaries will plausibly remain untouched. Similarly, if one subsidiary stops being profitable for any reason, it might simply disappear, while other lucrative criminal activities will still be performed (such as the theft of hydrocarbons and extortion of migrants, for example).

The Zetas' structure is very horizontal and different from traditional drug-trafficking organizations, which operate over large areas and are tightly controlled by leaders at the top. The Zetas do not focus exclusively on trafficking narcotics. Different cells of the group are dedicated to varied activities, and leaders of each cell seem to operate with relative independence (see table 3.1). Thus if the government dismantled one drug-trafficking cell of the Zetas in Nuevo Laredo, for example, other Zeta cells would remain unaffected. It might also be the case that drug-trafficking operations of this criminal group would not suffer considerably in other states along the Gulf of Mexico, in southeastern Mexico, and in Central America. At the same time, it is highly plausible that subsidiaries dedicated to human smuggling, gasoline theft, and the control of other informal markets (such as music piracy) would remain untouched. It is also possible that operations in a specific city or region (plaza) would only be affected temporarily, while the leadership regrouped and restarted its activities. If one local operation was down, another subsidiary from the surrounding area would fill the gap momentarily.

Halliburton: Multiple Holding Companies and Oilfield Services

Halliburton, founded in 1919, is the world's second-largest oilfield services company and the largest provider of hydraulic fracturing services in the United States (Blumenthal 2014; McCarthy 2014).[2] "With more than 80,000 employees, representing 140 nationalities in over 80 countries, the company serves the upstream oil and gas industry throughout the lifecycle of the reservoir—from locating hydrocarbons and managing geological data, to drilling and formation evaluation, well construction and completion, and optimizing production through the life of the field" (Halliburton 2015).

Halliburton, like ExxonMobil, owns hundreds of subsidiaries, affiliates, brands, and divisions worldwide (Halliburton 2015). This company also divides its services by country and by type of service.

That enables the company to organize its assets and protect itself in case of a lawsuit. Halliburton owns many holding companies as well (companies created to buy and possess the shares of other companies), which the oilfield-services company then controls. Halliburton's name may not be directly related to these companies, but they indirectly become part of its business structure. As explained in chapter 3, the Zetas' organization also possesses holding companies, through which the group essentially conducts its money-laundering operations.

Halliburton is not an oil company but works very closely with oil companies. It is a provider of products and services to the energy industry. Halliburton includes thirteen product service lines that "are primarily responsible and accountable for strategy, technology development, process development, people development and capital allocation" (Halliburton 2015, par. 2).[3] Overall, the company helps its customers to meet the world's demand for energy. Halliburton has operated as an important Pemex contractor in recent years and will probably expand its activities in Mexico after the passage of Mexico's energy reform. During the last few years Halliburton has been working in some regions close to areas where the Zetas controlled important plazas and where this criminal group has stolen large amounts of fuel and gas (for example, the Burgos Basin).

Apart from its corporate structure and ownership of subsidiaries and holding companies, Los Zetas resembles companies like Halliburton in one activity that has been quite important to this criminal group in the past few years: supplying key products to the energy industry. The Zetas form part of a mafia that has built an industry parallel to Pemex by providing products to transnational energy companies. In recent years this transnational criminal organization has been stealing and selling crude oil, gasoline, diesel, and a series of lubricants and other refined oil products.[4] The most popular product in this illegal market is natural gas condensate, due to its high demand in energy markets (Pérez 2012, par. 4).[5] In the past few years large amounts of natural gas condensate have arrived in US energy markets, where it is in demand for the production of high-quality fuels (par. 5).

Oil and gas theft from Mexico's pipelines has created a multimillion-dollar underground industry. Recent reports and investigations show how organized crime has accessed Pemex's pipeline system to steal oil and gas, and sells these hydrocarbons to a number of transnational energy companies (Alvi 2014a; Cattan and Williams 2014; Pérez 2012). Texas companies, in particular, have benefited from buying large amounts of stolen hydrocarbons from criminal organizations like the Gulf Cartel and Los Zetas. It is worth noting that these transactions require the existence of sophisticated corruption networks that involve Pemex employees, contractors, private companies, law enforcement agents, customs brokers, and customs officers who are connected to Mexican TCOs (Pérez 2012, par. 13).

Between 2008 and 2009 an investigation by the US Department of Justice, the DEA, the FBI, and Immigration and Customs Enforcement (ICE) named Project Reckoning revealed the involvement of important US-based transnational energy corporations in the acquisition of hydrocarbons—particularly natural gas condensate from the Burgos Basin—sold by organized crime groups. By that time the main provider was "the Company," at the time made up of the Gulf Cartel and the Zetas (Pérez 2012, par. 15). This investigation also discovered the involvement of senior business executives and company representatives, who admitted these illegal purchases. For example, one key person in this illegal network of operators and buyers was Joshua Crescenzi—once a news liaison for former president George W. Bush and former vice president Dick Cheney, who was at one point Halliburton's largest individual shareholder (Pérez 2012).

Moreover, Pemex has filed three lawsuits against US energy and chemical companies, alleging that they bought enormous amounts of stolen natural gas condensate from Mexican TCOs.[6] According to these court cases, more than $300 million in stolen natural gas condensate from the Burgos Basin was smuggled across the US border by Mexican TCOs from 2006 to 2010.[7] It is worth noting that fuel-theft losses have risen significantly since then. In the lawsuits Pemex established that the sales of stolen natural gas condensate required the existence of a corrupt network operating on the US side of the border that transported the products across the border and within the country, laundered its source, and fraudulently distributed and sold the product to the final consumer (Pérez 2012, par. 46).

According to Pemex's lawsuits, between 2010 and 2012 nearly twenty energy companies of all sizes—small, medium, and even transnational—were implicated in illegal transactions that involved the purchase of stolen hydrocarbons. The accusations incriminate importing firms, transportation companies, operators of pipeline networks and refineries, hydrocarbon trading companies, and firms in the chemical industry (Pérez 2012, par. 7). Among these companies were BASF Corporation, Big Star Gathering LLP Ltd., Conoco Phillips, F & M

Transportation Inc., FR Midstream Transport, Marathon Petroleum, Murphy Energy Corporation, Royal Dutch Shell, Sunoco Marketing Partners LP, and others. These companies were accused of buying (directly or indirectly) stolen condensate (Pérez 2012).[8] Hence the Zetas operated in this instance as a provider of products and services to the energy industry, just like Halliburton and similar enterprises.

Academi (Blackwater) and Constellis: Transnational Security Services

Due to the nature of its activities, one transnational corporation that might serve as a model to understand the business structure and some forms of Los Zetas operation is Constellis. This group of companies includes a company once named Blackwater, which has been one of the US government's biggest providers of training and security services. Blackwater was founded in 1997 by Al Clark and former navy SEAL (Sea, Air, Land) Erik Prince to provide training support to the military and law enforcement agencies. Blackwater was one of several private security firms employed in the US war in Afghanistan and the Iraq War. Subsequently the company was hired by the US State Department to provide protective services in Afghanistan, Bosnia, Iraq, and Israel. *Wall Street Journal* reporter Nathan Hodge (2011, par. 3) notes that "Blackwater cultivated a special-operations mystique." But this company "was tarnished by a string of high-profile incidents, including a deadly 2007 shoot-out in Iraq that ultimately led to its reorganization and rebranding as Xe Services."

In 2009 Blackwater changed its name to Xe Services LLC as part of a company-wide restructuring plan. In 2010 a group of private investors purchased Xe's main assets and built a new company around what was once Blackwater, named Academi. The new security firm specializes in "personnel training, critical infrastructure protection, maritime security, unmanned aircraft systems (UAS), government services, security technology and logistics" (Academi 2014, 4). Some of the services provided by Blackwater-Xe-Academi resemble the Zetas' functions in one of its subsidiaries involving protection services (see chapter 3). Moreover, a group like the Zetas, in terms of human resources, might need the services of a firm like Academi if its training capacities fall short and it wants to continue its expansion. This proposed collaboration seems to be implausible, due to the different natures of the two types of companies (one legal and one illegal). However, Academi could find a profitable market in groups like the Zetas.

Finally, Academi stopped working independently and started to form part of a larger group named Constellis Holdings, LLC (Constellis) that includes several companies providing "services within the global security market" (Constellis 2014, par. 3). Its main services consist of "delivering mission support, integrated security solutions, training and advisory services at home and abroad." With more than 8,000 personnel, Constellis recruits and retains the industry's most experienced and trained employees, most of whom are military or law enforcement veterans (par. 2). Jason DeYonker, chief executive officer of Constellis, explains how the group provides "critical support capabilities for government and commercial clients" and utilizes "Academi's world-class training facility, the largest and most comprehensive private training center in the United States" (par. 4).

Business and Politics

When Academi was created after the purchase of Xe, the "new ownership instituted a board of directors and entirely new management system, including a full compliance and governance program" (Constellis website, no longer posted). Some members of Academi's board of directors became part of the board of Constellis.[9] Past and present board members of Constellis have vast experience in both the public and private sectors, and some of them held key positions in the US government. For example, John Ashcroft served as the 79th US attorney general in the George W. Bush administration. Also former board member retired admiral Bobby R. Inman served as director of the National Security Agency and CIA deputy director; and Jack Quinn was former White House counsel and vice-presidential chief of staff.

It is always advantageous for businesses to have personalities of this caliber as members of their boards of directors due to their wide experience and access to high-level political connections. The case of Constellis seems to be particularly telling, due to the nature of the firm and the involvement of people like Ashcroft and Inman, who were once protagonists in US security policy. Companies like Constellis would probably benefit from the political connections of members of their board, although they are not necessarily more prone to be involved in corrupt practices or conflicts of interest. However, in some cases big and influential businesses with close links to the US power structure have been involved in notorious corruption scandals. Consider, for example, the case of Kellogg Brown and Root (KBR), a former subsidiary of Halliburton, which was once run by Dick Cheney, vice-president of the United States from 2001 to 2009. Recently KBR has been plagued by claims of corruption, cronyism, and financial mismanagement.[10] However, its connections with US government officials at the highest levels probably represented significant advantages for the company at one time.

Business and politics might work well together, benefiting mainly corporate interests and those making the key decisions for certain companies. This also applies to illegal businesses. The Zetas and similar groups found a way to advance their businesses through corrupt links with government authorities at all levels. Important money-laundering cases filed in US federal courts have documented the involvement of key state and local politicians in activities that have greatly benefited organized crime. Consider, for example, the cases that link the former governors Fidel Herrera (of Veracruz), Tomás Yarrington and Eugenio Hernández (of Tamaulipas), and Humberto Moreira (of Coahuila) with the Company or simply with the Zetas.

State and local officials in Michoacán have been accused of colluding with and facilitating the activities of organized crime, particularly La Familia Michoacana and the Knights Templar. Near the end of April of 2014 the mayor of Lázaro Cárdenas, Arquímides Oseguera, was arrested due to his alleged connection with organized crime and was also "accused of kidnapping and extortion. His arrest was part of a broader government crackdown aimed at purging Mexico's Michoacán state of Knights Templar members and allies" (Matich 2014, par. 1). On April 17, 2014, another mayor, Uriel Chávez of Apatzingán, was also arrested on suspicions of links with criminal syndicates.

Chávez's arrest came ten days after Jesús Reyna—interim governor of Michoacán from April to October 2013—was placed under house arrest due to evidence of meetings with members of the Knights Templar organization (Matich 2014). Reyna appeared in videos with Servando Gómez Martínez (aka La Tuta), a former leader of La Familia and the Knights Templar, and was arrested in April 2014. Rodrigo Vallejo Mora, son of former governor of Michoacán Fausto Vallejo, has also been accused of links with the main criminal organization in the state.[11] In fact the very large and profitable business activities of the Knights Templar in Michoacán—such as the operation of iron ore mines and its involvement in the methamphetamine trade—require more than access to material resources. It "would be difficult to conduct an illegal iron ore mining and smuggling operation of such magnitude without extensive ties to local and state governments" (Matich 2014, par. 10).

The Future of Los Zetas

In Mexico's contemporary corporate world that connects politics and legal and illegal businesses, what is the current status of the Zetas organization? What are the prospects for its participation and development in different markets? Is its role still relevant for the present and future of organized crime in Mexico? Some analysts have noted the demise or decline of this organization that has transformed the face of organized crime in the country since the beginning of the twenty-first century (see chapter 2). Is this a correct description of the current status of the Zetas organization? As mentioned earlier, available analyses of the Zetas and similar groups have mainly focused on drug-trafficking trends, drug policy, and drug war casualties (see chapter 3). This does not seem to be an appropriate approach to understand the current status of this transnational criminal corporation and to forecast what is next for it. Los Zetas Inc. has apparently been losing influence and power in the criminal world of Mexico and Central America. Other dynamics might be taking place, however, and the criminal corporation may just be reorganizing, transforming, or reinventing itself.

By analyzing the Zetas' future through a business administration framework, it may be possible to gain a better understanding of the development of this group (and similar groups) as well as the effects of its business model in regional security and economic development. Los Zetas may not be on the decline, as many have argued, but may only have entered into a new phase in which they continue doing business in an effective and efficient but more silent manner. It is also possible that the group has abandoned some activities (or sold some subsidiaries) to dedicate itself to new ones or to reinforce the most profitable ones. It is possible to make some predictions regarding the Zetas' future by analyzing the three companies mentioned above. Transnational businesses like Los Zetas Inc., ExxonMobil, Halliburton, and Academi/Constellis Holdings Inc. can be compared in some ways, especially in areas like mergers and acquisitions, selling subsidiaries, rebranding, and changing names. The Zetas seem to have recently lowered their profile and could rebrand, merge, or establish different connections with other groups.

Rebranding

Before becoming part of Constellis and changing its name and image, the private security firm Blackwater was involved in a series of scandals. In 2007 a group of its employees killed seventeen Iraqi civilians and injured twenty in Nisour Square, Baghdad.[12] After that incident the company "was excluded from one of the most lucrative markets for private security" and the Iraqi government stripped it of its operating license (Hodge 2011, par. 6). As a result, and in order to recover its important share of the market, the company was sold, rebranded, and renamed Xe Services in 2009. Despite new ownership, a new board, and new management, the security firm "could never shake a troublesome" past (Hodge 2011, par. 1). So the company again changed its name and brand and became Academi. Very few people know about these changes. Most are unfamiliar with the new name or are unaware that it is part of Constellis. It seems that Blackwater's bad reputation finally has been forgotten; but the company is still alive. This could also happen with the Zetas; they could change their name and rebrand, after lowering their profile substantially and maintaining silence.

Selling Subsidiaries

In order to adapt to new market conditions related to the illicit activities in which the Zetas participate, and especially when some of these activities stop being profitable, the criminal organization could do what the three legal businesses analyzed here do in similar circumstances: sell the subsidiaries that do not represent a profitable business anymore. For example, in June 2008 ExxonMobil decided to phase out of the directly served retail market, due to the difficulty of running gas stations with rising crude oil costs. Similarly, in November 2006 Halliburton began selling the KBR engineering and construction unit and had completely sold off this major subsidiary by February 2007. KBR "had been accused of everything from overcharging in Iraq to bribery in Nigeria" (Blumenthal 2014, par. 1).

The Zetas could make similar decisions due to scandals or decreasing profits. Today, for instance, it seems that the criminal organization has left the migrant smuggling business along Mexico's eastern migration routes in the hands of a number of local criminal groups and corrupt law enforcement agents. Once the Zetas used to control these migration routes and the business of human trafficking. They used to charge *derecho de piso* to all other groups that operated throughout the routes, either smuggling or trafficking migrants. Things have recently changed in this regard.

Divide and Merge Again

Los Zetas Inc. might also divide itself into smaller companies, which eventually would reunite to form an even larger transnational criminal organization. ExxonMobil is a good example of this pattern. In 1911 John D. Rockefeller's Standard Oil trust was dissolved and split into more than thirty companies. In 1999 the two largest companies that were once part of Standard Oil—Exxon (previously Standard Oil Co. of New Jersey) and Mobil (previously Standard Oil Co. of New York)—reunited and formed Exxon Mobil Corporation. This reunion resulted in the largest merger in US corporate history. This is also a plausible process that the Zetas could go through if it became convenient for their interests. At some point the Zetas and the Gulf Cartel formed part of the Company. Even though the Company was dissolved in 2010 and the two former allies started a bloody fight for important parts of the Mexican territory, there is no reason to believe that they could not start working together again. In late 2014 factions of Los Zetas and the Gulf Cartel "announced the two criminal groups have formed an alliance, which, if true, would be a game changer in Mexico's underworld by ending one of the country's bloodiest criminal feuds" (Gagne 2014, par. 1).

In a joint statement that circulated on November 11, 2014, leaders of factions of the two organizations announced that they would stop fighting, affirming: "Those that kept the war going are either dead or in jail" (Gagne 2014, par. 2). They also declared that the groups had agreed to the alliance because they wanted peace. Thus the organizations would "allegedly stop criminal activities that put at risk the general population such as kidnapping and extortion, and revert to 'old school' ways, like drug trafficking" (Gagne 2014, par. 3). This statement was allegedly signed by the then head of the Gulf Cartel's Los Rojos faction, Juan Reyes Mejía González (aka R-1), as well as one of the original founders of the Zetas, Rogelio González Pizaña (aka El Kelín) (who was released from prison that same year). According to this communiqué released by Blog del Narco, these two criminal groups are not currently fighting among themselves anymore; they are "more united than before" and want to achieve peace, particularly in Tamaulipas (Padilla 2015, par 21).

Joint Ventures and Other Strategic Alliances

With the aim of expanding their share of key markets and taking advantage of new business opportunities, transnational corporations usually form joint ventures or build strategic alliances with a number of similar or complementary firms. ExxonMobil is related to various firms in different ways. For example, it holds 70 percent ownership of Imperial Oil Ltd., which is Canada's second-biggest integrated oil company. In August 2011 ExxonMobil announced a $3.2 billion joint venture with Russian oil company Rosneft to develop two offshore oilfields in Russia. The company also formed a joint venture with Royal Dutch Shell for manufacturing and marketing lubricant and fuel additives; the name of this joint venture is Infineum. Another example is the case of Constellis, the world's largest security services company. In 2014 Academi became a division of Constellis along with Triple Canopy and other security companies as the result of an acquisition.

Thus "Constellis combines the legacy capabilities and experience of Academi, Edinburgh International, Olive Group, Strategic Social and Triple Canopy and all of their affiliates" (formerly posted on the Constellis website in 2015). In November 2014 it was announced that Halliburton Company would buy Baker Hughes Inc. in a stock-and-cash deal valued at nearly $35 billion, "ending weeks of discussions and merging the world's second- and third-largest oilfield services companies" (Chen 2014, par. 1). The two companies operate in more than eighty countries and have a combined revenue of more than $50 billion and more than 136,000 employees worldwide. The aim of this operation was to create an oilfield services company that would compete with Schlumberger, the world's largest oilfield services company.[13]

The Zetas and similar groups also have formed joint ventures or built strategic alliances with other criminal organizations. Consider, for example, the alliance between the Zetas and the Beltrán Leyva family or the case of the Company and the Federation. Some of these operations have been extremely successful, such as the Jalisco New Generation Cartel (CJNG), which today maintains a key role in certain illicit businesses in some parts of Mexico, including the production and commercialization of synthetic drugs, and stealing hydrocarbons. In the past five years the CJNG's influence has been growing significantly. Born as a remnant of other groups and once working in alliance with groups like the Sinaloa Cartel, the CJNG has recently become one of the most powerful criminal organizations in Mexico. Forming strategic alliances with a number of criminal syndicates, the CJNG has expanded from Jalisco to Guanajuato, Michoacán, Colima, and Veracruz (Ángel 2015, par. 3).[14]

Four Business Models in Practice in Mexico

The (legal and illegal) transnational companies mentioned above not only share some key features but also interact and do business together in the areas of energy and security. Transnational criminal groups like the Zetas have provided some products and services to energy companies. In this new era of energy reform in Mexico TCOs, transnational energy companies, and private security firms will most probably coincide and collaborate even more. The Zetas model and the effects of a modern civil war declared by the Mexican government generate incentives for a closer relationship between extractive industries and security corporations. These corporations have worked closely in conflict areas in other parts of the world. As Paley (2014, 122) recognizes, "they are today at work in Mexico promoting policy reforms designed to improve the experience for transnational corporations and investors seeking to do business in Mexico. Their programs are unfolding at the same time as the country undergoes militarization and paramilitarization."

Transnational Energy Firms and Oilfield Service Companies in Mexico after a Historic Reform

Oil and gas and oilfield service companies have operated in Mexico together with the Zetas and the Mexican state-owned petroleum company Pemex in the past few years, including during the most violent times. Many of these firms have benefited from Pemex contracts,[15] and some of them have allegedly taken advantage of the illegal sale of hydrocarbons by organized crime. Most of these businesses will continue to benefit and expand their activities in Mexico after the passage of energy reform. Under the new framework all of these companies will have incentives to remain in the country and extend their presence. Many more new players are expected to enter Mexico's energy industry in the very near future. Oilfield services companies like Halliburton will benefit from less restrictive fee-for-service contracts, and major international oil companies like ExxonMobil will probably greatly increase their share in Mexico's market, as in other parts of the world, since they will now be able to book oil and gas reserves for financial reporting purposes (Jalife-Rahme 2014).[16]

Apart from the very favorable conditions under which these companies will operate after a historic reform in Mexico, "they have good allies in the country." Mexican journalist Jesús Ramírez (2013) identifies a number of former government officials who currently work for transnational companies and investment banks connected to the energy sector—former Pemex directors and heads of the ministries of finance and energy during the administrations of Carlos Salinas de Gortari (1988–1994), Ernesto Zedillo (1994–2000), and the PAN presidencies of Vicente Fox and Felipe Calderón (2000–2012). These people are recognized as adamant supporters of the reforms in articles 27 and 28 of the Mexican Constitution; they have intensely lobbied for the total opening of the energy sector to private participation and for the sale of Pemex's assets (Ramírez 2013, par. 2).

Some of them worked for Mexico's public sector in key positions during the most difficult times for the national energy monopoly, when groups like the Zetas were taking control of an important part of the sector through massive looting of hydrocarbons. One interesting example mentioned by Ramírez (2013) is Jesús Reyes-Heroles, secretary of energy in 1995–1997, Mexican ambassador to the United States in 1997–2000, and head of Pemex from 2006 to 2009. It was during this last period when stealing hydrocarbons became a major business of transnational criminal groups like the Zetas and Pemex corruption reached unseen levels that facilitated the actions of TCOs.

Instead of being charged for his responsibility as head of the national energy monopoly after leaving his position, Reyes-Heroles widened his consulting firm and in 2012 announced a strategic business partnership with Morgan Stanley Private Equity to promote investment projects in Latin America's energy sector (StructurA 2016, par. 2).[17] This business holding, according to Ramírez (2013, par. 9), "would allow Reyes-Heroles to take advantage of his 'connections' in order to negotiate contracts between Pemex and his clients and partners." It is worth noting that Reyes-Heroles currently serves on the board of directors of OHL Mexico and on the advisory board of Energy Intelligence Group (EIG), among others—some connected directly or indirectly to the energy industry.

Further cases of former public servants who are currently close allies of private energy firms in Mexico include Juan José Suárez-Coppel, Pemex director from 2009 until 2012, who left his position and became independent director of Jacobs Engineering Group Inc., an international technical professional services firm that participates in the energy sector. Ramírez (2013, pars. 29 and 35) notes that transnational companies such as Schlumberger, Halliburton, and Weatherford received the largest number of contracts in Mexico during Suárez-Coppel's administration.

Similarly, Georgina Kessel—who served as Mexico's secretary of energy from 2006 and 2011—became part of the advisory board of the Spanish firm Iberdrola after leaving her position. This company has important investments in Mexico's energy sector. In her position as secretary of energy and president of Pemex's board of directors, Kessel participated in the awarding of very important contracts to Iberdrola for more than a thousand million euros (Ramírez 2013, par. 41). In July 2014 former president Felipe Calderón became a member of the board of directors of Iberdrola's subsidiary Avangrid Inc.[18] Ramirez (2013, par. 19) also highlighted the case of Emilio Lozoya-Austin, Pemex director from 2012 to 2016, who in 2012 still participated as a member of the board of directors of the Spanish firm OHL Mexico. This company operates in the area of transportation infrastructure and recently entered the energy industry, allegedly with the help of Lozoya-Austin. OHL-Mexico obtained important contracts with Pemex during the tenure of its former employee.

The current climate in Mexico is extremely favorable for transnational energy companies and for any firm that provides products and services for the energy industry. Mexico offers important incentives and new opportunities for those who are able to enter its energy market. New energy legislation, abundant natural resources, and a deliberate set of policies and strategies—including the militarization of Mexico's security strategy and the eventual protection of transnational interests through government actions—provide fertile ground for massive investments in the hydrocarbon sector (Jalife-Rahme 2014). Thus, after the passage of the historic reform, the country is prepared for the arrival of a number of transnational companies, many of which have been extremely successful in other parts of the world, even in regions where the security situation has been a central issue (such as Iraq).

Security Contractors

In violent environments transnational energy companies and oilfield services firms have coexisted with security contractors. Companies like ExxonMobil, Halliburton, and Blackwater/Xe Services/Academi (through some of their subsidiaries) have worked together in a number of conflict zones, including the Middle East. They might meet in Mexico as well if the security situation does not visibly improve in the near future. Private security contractors might be the new players in Mexico's pacification process after its modern civil war. A number of companies within the Constellis umbrella—Academi, for example— might find interesting business opportunities in Mexico in the coming years.[19] The current legal framework might need to be modified in order to accept the participation of foreign private security contractors bearing arms in Mexico, but this is a possibility.

It is indeed plausible that foreign energy companies will invest in and enter the Mexican market even with the extended presence of irregular armed actors in violent zones (such as Tamaulipas). This will depend of course on the future trends of world oil and gas prices. As Shannon Young (2014, par. 25) recognizes, "experiences in Iraq, which de-nationalized its oil reserves after the U.S.-led invasion, have shown that some American energy companies are willing to do business in violence-plagued areas if the reserves and the potential gains from them seem to justify the risks." In fact, in a context of high hydrocarbon prices, violence and insecurity would not be an issue for energy investors. "While multinational [energy] firms would prefer stable operating environments, they are no strangers to conflict zones and have experience in mitigating risks and violence, and are willing to pay a lot of money for private security" (Daugherty 2015, par. 21).

Hence new and potential investors in Mexico's energy sector might call for private security. The creation of the gendarmerie and other government efforts to secure economic interests might be considered insufficient to assure the level of security that many companies would want before taking big risks. Global trends seem to promote the privatization of security. The forthcoming situation in Mexico could resemble in some ways recent "pacification" attempts in places like Iraq. Here some key companies "made money off the war by providing support services as the privatization of what were former US military operations rose to unprecedented levels" (A. Young 2013, par. 1).[20] Reliance on security contractors is a trend observed in the United States. According to Professors Deborah D. Avant and Renée de Nevers (2011, 88), "More than one half of the personnel the United States has deployed in Iraq and Afghanistan since 2003 have been contractors." In Iraq the United States "hired more private companies . . . than in any previous war, and at times there were more contractors than military personnel on the ground" (Fifield 2013, par. 6).[21]

Therefore it seems plausible that foreign security contractors will enter Mexico's market as oil, gas, and oilfield service companies ramp up their operations (Fifield, 2013, par. 25). The real impact of the participation of these armed actors on the country's levels of violence and security cannot be anticipated. Transnational companies have an impact on security under situations of extreme violence (Avant and Haufler 2012). The presence of further irregular armed actors might have negative consequences for the stability and security of certain communities located in zones rich in hydrocarbons or natural resources related to energy generation. As Deborah D. Avant and Virginia Haufler (2012, 254) recognize, "the strategies these transnational non-state actors pursue in response to violence, [might] affect security for both themselves and the societies in which they operate."

Overall, under certain circumstances, transnational corporations are provided with resources that can be "diverted to fund violence" by governments, rebels, and other irregular armed actors (Avant and Haufler 2012, 258). "These organizations are often believed to have undermined stability." Working in violent environments, transnational businesses seem to constitute "additional security 'nodes.' Providing security is not their main mission, but in attempting to achieve their missions, they influence the governance of security" (274). This seems to have already happened in some Mexican regions: the Burgos Basin, Coahuila's coal region, the ports of Colima and Lázaro Cárdenas, Michoacán's iron ore belt, the Juárez Valley in Chihuahua, and Guerrero's Gold Triangle, for example. Further regions might experience similar dynamics, especially if foreign private security companies arrive on the scene in the near future.

Interestingly, the presence of important transnational business interests coexisting with regular and irregular armed groups can be identified in all the regions mentioned above. The paramilitarization of organized crime and criminal business models inspired by the Zetas model are a constant in these zones. Criminal groups like the Zetas, Gulf Cartel, CJNG, Knights Templar, Los Rojos, and Guerreros Unidos are allegedly the enemies to fight in the first place. The actual leaders of these organizations are not just criminals but entrepreneurs. And these groups are not simply what people commonly refer to as drug cartels: they are transnational criminal businesses that coexist with and support big legal transnational businesses in a context of modern civil war. It is difficult to allege intentionality by corporate interests when analyzing the development of the conflict and trying to find its main instigators. However, it is evident that those who have benefited (or will benefit) the most from Mexico's civil war are extractive industries and, plausibly, private security firms.

Energy Reform and the Zetas' Expansion (Timeline)

Date	Event
December 23, 1992	Reform of article 3 of the Energy Electric Power System Public Service Act is enacted. This allows Independent Power Producers (IPPs) to sell and generate electricity for the Federal Electricity Commission (CFE), Mexico's state-owned electric utility.
January 1, 1994	NAFTA goes into effect.
May 11, 1995	Reform of the regulatory law of article 27 of the Mexican Constitution to allow the participation of social and private capital in the production, transportation, storage, and distribution of natural gas.
October 21, 1995	The Energy Regulatory Commission (CRE) Act is created.
1995–1996	Proyectos de Inversión Diferida en el Registro del Gasto (Investment Projects with Deferred Expenditure Registration, PIDIREGAS) is created by the Mexican government with the aim of financing long-term infrastructure projects for hydrocarbon exploitation and electricity generation.
November 13, 1996	Reform of the regulatory law of article 27 of the Mexican Constitution to allow production, transportation, storage, and distribution of oil derivatives that can be used as basic industrial raw materials.

February 2, 1999	President Ernesto Zedillo (1994–2000) submits an initiative to reform articles 27 and 28 of the Mexican Constitution. The passage of this reform would allow the participation of the private sector in electricity generation, transmission, distribution, and commercialization. It does not pass.
late 1999	Osiel Cárdenas consolidates his position as leader of the Gulf Cartel. The group ceases to be a traditional DTO and begins expanding and diversifying its activities to become a TCO. Cárdenas incorporates the Zetas as the Gulf Cartel's enforcers.
December 1, 2000	Vicente Fox of the PAN becomes president of Mexico after 71 years of PRI rule.
January 19, 2001	Joaquín (aka El Chapo) Guzmán, leader of the Sinaloa Cartel, escapes from prison. His criminal organization grows considerably in subsequent years and becomes an important rival of the Zetas.
early 2001	As a response to the Zetas' growing influence and rapid advancement, four important DTOs meet and form La Federación, including the Sinaloa Cartel, the Juárez Cartel, the Colima Cartel (also called the Cartel of the Amezcua-Contreras Family), and the Milenio Cartel (or the Cartel of the Valencia Brothers).
January 2002	The first Zeta commando unit arrives in Nuevo Laredo. The expansion of the group begins after this event. The Zetas gradually extend their presence throughout Nuevo León, Coahuila, Veracruz, Tabasco, and Campeche.
June 20, 2002	Multiple Services Contracts (CSM) are introduced in Mexico. Through these instruments, Pemex contracts the services of the private sector for the exploitation of nonassociated natural gas deposits in northern Mexico, particularly in the Burgos Basin.

August 21, 2002	Vicente Fox submits to the Mexican legislature his energy reform initiative that includes (1) reforms to articles 27 and 28 of the Mexican Constitution; (2) reforms to the Energy Electric Power System Public Service Act; (3) reform to the CRE Act; (4) an initiative to change CFE's Organic Law; and (5) an initiative to modify the Organic Law of the National Center for Energy Control. This reform is aimed at opening Mexico's electricity sector to the participation of private investment.
November 21, 2002	Arturo Guzmán Decena (aka Z-1) is killed by Mexican armed forces in Matamoros. Alejandro Lucio Morales Betancourt (aka Z-2) was arrested a year before, so Heriberto Lazcano (aka Z-3) becomes the leader of the armed wing of the Gulf Cartel.
March 14, 2003	Osiel Cárdenas is arrested in Matamoros. The Zetas start to expand aggressively and an era of terror in northeastern Mexico begins.
October 7, 2003	Reform of article 27 of the Mexican Constitution (par. 6) related to the transportation, distribution, and provision of electrical energy is proposed.
2004	PGR reports a strong presence of Los Zetas in Michoacán. It is believed that professional Zeta hit men were sent to Michoacán to train gunmen of La Empresa, who eventually became La Familia Michoacana. The influence of the Zetas later becomes noticeable in the style in which La Familia conducts mass executions, decapitations, and shoot-outs.
June 11, 2005	President Vicente Fox initiates an operation called "Safe Mexico" (México Seguro) against organized crime.
2006	The Familia Michoacana starts to seek independence from the Zetas and tries to forge an alliance with the Sinaloa Cartel.
January 12, 2006	Reform of the regulatory law of article 27 of the Mexican Constitution (art. 6 regarding petroleum) and reform of Pemex's Organic Law and subsidiary bodies (art. 3).
January 19, 2007	Osiel Cárdenas is extradited to the United States.

November 28, 2008	President Felipe Calderón's energy reform and reforms of articles 25, 27, and 28 of the Mexican Constitution are enacted. Particularly important is a reform of the regulatory law of article 27 in the area of oil and the creation of the National Hydrocarbons Commission (CNH).
September 22, 2009	The new Reglamento de la Ley Reglamentaria del Artículo 27 Constitucional en el Ramo del Petróleo (Regulation of the Regulatory law of Article 27 of the Mexican Constitution concerning Petroleum Affairs) is published in the *Official Gazette of the Federation* (*Diario Oficial de la Federación*). It dictates the execution of the Regulatory Law.
January 18, 2010	In Reynosa, Tamaulipas, gunmen loyal to CDG member Samuel Flores Borrego (aka El Metro 3) kill Sergio Peña Mendoza (aka El Concord 3) of Los Zetas. The war between the Gulf Cartel and the Zetas begins.
August 25, 2010	The Mexican Army finds the bodies of 72 migrants killed in a ranch in San Fernando, Tamaulipas, which turns out to be an orchestrated mass homicide by the Zetas. This event is known as the "San Fernando Massacre."
November, 2010	More than half of the population of Ciudad Mier, Tamaulipas, suddenly abandons the municipality due to extremely violent confrontations between the Zetas and the Gulf Cartel.
March 2011	A massacre in Allende, Coahuila, leaves 300 dead and the town in ruins.
March 2011	The Knights Templar appear on the map as a new criminal organization formed from the vestiges of the Familia Michoacana.
April 6–7, 2011	Between 145 and 193 bodies are retrieved from mass graves in San Fernando, Tamaulipas.
August 25, 2011	An attack on the Casino Royale in the city of Monterrey, Nuevo León, ends with the death of 52 people. It is believed to have been planned by a high-ranking Zeta boss.

September 2011	Los Mata-Zetas (the Zeta-Killers), part of the Cartel de Jalisco Nueva Generación (CJNG), appears on the scene. The CJNG is believed to have been formed in 2009 by the remaining leaders of the Milenio Cartel after the death of Ignacio Coronel, one of the leaders of the Sinaloa Cartel.
September 20, 2011	The CJNG, in one of its first blatantly violent actions, executes 35 members of the Zetas and dumps the bodies on a busy street in the city of Boca del Río, Veracruz. A few days later 14 more bodies turn up in the cities of Veracruz and Boca del Río. This happens during a convention of the nation's top state and federal prosecutors.
October 6, 2011	Another 35 bodies are found in Boca del Río, Veracruz, believed to be members of the Zetas. The CJNG is now seen as a serious threat. In just 18 days approximately 100 executions are carried out by this organization. As the dispute for territory against the Zetas becomes more violent, the CJNG—with a structure and behavior similar to those of the Zetas—consolidates its power and begins to be recognized as one of the strongest TCOs operating in Mexico.
February 20, 2012	The US-Mexico Transboundary Hydrocarbons Agreement is signed in Los Cabos, Baja California. The Mexican Senate ratifies the agreement on April 12, 2012. The US Senate approves it on December 19, 2013, and President Obama signs it into law on December 23, 2013, as part of the Bipartisan Budget Act.
May 13, 2012	Along a highway connecting Monterrey with Reynosa 49 corpses are discovered by military personnel in Cadereyta, Nuevo León. They are believed to be members of the Gulf Cartel, who allegedly died at the hands of the Zetas while still in Tamaulipas and were then transported to Cadereyta. Others believe they were migrants.
July 2012	Infighting within the Zetas apparently is starting to debilitate the organization. The factions are divided by those loyal to Heriberto Lazcano (aka Z-3) and those loyal to Miguel Ángel Treviño Morales (aka L-40 or Z-40).

October 3, 2012	José Eduardo Moreira, son of the former Coahuila governor Humberto Moreira, is executed by the Zetas.
October 7, 2012	Heriberto Lazcano (aka Z-3) is killed in a shoot-out with the Mexican navy.
July 15, 2013	Miguel Treviño Morales (aka Z-40) is arrested by the Mexican navy.
October 12, 2013	Gerardo Jaramillo (aka El Yanqui) is arrested in Guatemala. He is believed to be the regional boss of the Zetas in Guatemala.
December 20, 2013	Mexico's Congress passes far-reaching constitutional reforms to open the energy sector to private participation and worldwide investment after 76 years of state monopoly.
2013	In 2012 and 2013 Guerrero becomes the state with the highest rate of homicides in the country. The violence is believed to be the result of a dispute between Guerreros Unidos and Los Rojos (factions of the Beltrán Leyva Brothers' Cartel).
April 30, 2014	President Enrique Peña Nieto petitions secondary legislation for Mexico's energy reform.
May 9, 2014	Galindo Mellado Cruz (aka El Mellado) is killed in a shoot-out with the Mexican army. He was an original (founding) member of the Zetas.
August 11, 2014	Secondary legislation of Mexico's energy reform is approved by Mexico's Congress.
August 13, 2014	Ronda Cero (Round Zero) of Mexico's energy reform takes place. In this stage of the reform, Pemex has priority over choosing what hydrocarbons and in what amounts it wants to explore and extract. Once Pemex chooses the amount of hydrocarbons that it will extract, Ronda Uno (Round One) goes into effect.
August 30, 2014	Rogelio González Pizaña (aka El Kelín) is released from prison. He is also a founding member of the Zetas. He was accused by the DEA of threatening US federal agents in 1999.

September 26–27, 2014	Members of the Guerreros Unidos criminal organization allegedly kidnap 43 students (8 students are killed, 25 are injured, and 43 remain missing). It is believed that the Mexican state was complicit in the executions. This event is remembered by the Mexican citizenry as the "Ayotzinapa Massacre."
March 4, 2015	Omar Treviño Morales (aka Z-42), head of the Zetas, is arrested by the Federal Police and the Mexican army in San Pedro Garza García, Nuevo León.
April 2015	As infighting exacts its toll and regional and national leaders are arrested or killed, the Zetas begin a process of fragmentation. Criminal bands loyal to the group become independent. According to some accounts, allied criminal groups such as La Familia Michoacana and the Beltrán Leyva Brothers' Cartel allegedly disappear, as their leaders are either killed or arrested.
May 1, 2015	A helicopter belonging to the Mexican army is shot by members of the CJNG and forced to land in order to avoid an accident.
July 2015–December 2016	Ronda Uno (Round One) of Mexico's energy reform takes place. In this stage of the reform private companies are able to bid for exploration and extraction of hydrocarbons. When the process is completed, then bidding results are published and made public. Note: Round One consists of five different calls for proposals.
October 5, 2015	Los Rojos, a criminal organization originally attached to the Beltrán Leyva Brothers' Cartel, come onto the national stage. The public security commissioner, Alejandro Rubido, says in an interview that he believes the group to be highly dangerous, alleging that they are behind multiple homicides, kidnappings, and extortions.
2017	Gasoline prices are liberated from government regulation.

History of Organized Crime in Tamaulipas: Timeline of Key Events

Date	Event
1930s	Juan N. Guerra starts what would later become the Gulf Cartel by smuggling whiskey along the Tamaulipas-US border.
May 17, 1984	A convoy of commandos is involved in a shoot-out in Matamoros for the first time. The goal is to assassinate Casimiro (aka El Cacho) Espinoza, one of the heads of the Gulf Cartel while he is at the Raya Clinic.
1987	Juan García Ábrego takes partial control of the Gulf Cartel and starts business dealings with the Colombian Cali Cartel.
1987	Juan N. Guerra is arrested. Juan García Ábrego takes complete control of the organization. The Gulf Cartel then gradually begins to take a violent and confrontational attitude toward other criminal syndicates in Mexico.
Beginning of 1990	The Gulf Cartel expands, according to some, thanks to the protection of Raúl Salinas de Gortari (brother of the then president) and Mario Ruiz Massieu.
1993	Peace in northern Mexico is achieved after negotiations with El Azul, ending a series of massacres and executions from Rio Grande City to Ciudad Juárez.
January 14, 1996	Juan García Ábrego is arrested, and according to some accounts, Salvador Gómez Herrera (aka Chava Gómez) becomes the new head of the Gulf Cartel.
1997	Arturo Guzmán Decena is recruited by Osiel Cárdenas of the Gulf Cartel.

1998	Heriberto Lazcano joins the Gulf Cartel after leaving the army.
1999	Miguel Ángel Treviño Morales joins the Gulf Cartel.
1999	Osiel Cárdenas takes control of the Gulf Cartel and recruits 31 former members of the Special Forces Airmobile Group (GAFE) under the command of Arturo Guzmán Decena, who was in charge of the execution of Salvador Gómez Herrera in July of the same year.
1999	The Zetas are born, commanded by Z-1 (this term allegedly comes from a radio code used by Arturo Guzmán Decena). The Gulf Cartel's structure begins to resemble a business model with a private army as it moves into new areas and lines of business.
July 1999	Gregorio Sauceda (aka El Caramuela or Don Goyo) arrives in the plaza of Reynosa as a designated operator of Osiel Cárdenas. He initiates the strategy of paying for protests and blockades against the army.
July 1999	Osiel Cárdenas breaks a truce with the Sinaloa Cartel and the Juárez Cartel. The war is reborn.
November 18, 1999	Osiel Cárdenas threatens DEA and FBI agents, which puts him in the crosshairs of the United States. This foreshadows his capture four years later.
2000	Vicente Fox Quezada becomes president of Mexico.
2000	The fight for the Tamaulipas border starts with a failed alliance between a local smuggler (Edelio López Falcón aka El Yeyo) and drug-trafficking organizations operating along the Pacific Coast (the Sinaloa Cartel and the Juárez Cartel), which attempt to dominate the most profitable territory of the Gulf Cartel and its armed wing, the Zetas.
November 2000	El Yeyo flees from Miguel Alemán to Monterrey, which ends the conflict in La Ribereña, with the Gulf Cartel taking control of the area.
2001	The Federation is created through an alliance of the Sinaloa, Juárez, Colima, and Milenio Cartels. This is to counteract the strength of the Zetas and the Gulf Cartel.
January 27, 2002	The first Zeta commando unit arrives in Nuevo Laredo. The expansion of the Zetas begins.

2002	Private transportation companies begin to steal oil from Pemex's pipelines in the Burgos Basin. They then start to smuggle and sell it.
April 9, 2002	A court in Houston, Texas, opens a criminal investigation against Osiel Cárdenas.
November 21, 2002	Arturo Guzmán Decena (aka Z-1) is killed by Mexican armed forces in Matamoros, Tamaulipas. Since Alejandro Lucio Morales Betancourt (aka Z-2) was arrested a year before, Heriberto Lazcano (aka Z-3) becomes the leader of the armed wing of the Gulf Cartel.
March 14, 2003	Osiel Cárdenas is arrested in Matamoros. A violent expansion of the Zetas and an era of terror starts with this event.
2003	The Gulf Cartel, the Tijuana Cartel, and Los Texas win a battle for control of Nuevo Laredo, beating the Sinaloa Cartel, the Juárez Cartel, and Los Chachos.
January 14, 2004	The United States files for the extradition of Osiel Cárdenas.
October 10, 2004	The media becomes aware of Édgar Valdez Villarreal (aka La Barbie), who works for Arturo Beltrán Leyva.
November 6, 2004	The Zetas arrive in Acapulco to fight the Sinaloa Cartel for control of this plaza.
2005	La Barbie forms an elite commando unit called Los Negros to fight the Zetas in Nuevo Laredo.
January 19, 2007	Osiel Cárdenas is extradited to the United States.
July 2007	Pemex tries to control massive oil and gas theft that has now turned into a business under the Gulf Cartel.
October 9, 2008	The first massive escape of TCO members from a prison takes place in Reynosa, Tamaulipas.
December 2009	Heriberto Lazcano calls for a massive meeting of Zetas in Matamoros to decide whether to end or continue their alliance with the Gulf Cartel, which is starting to negotiate with the Sinaloa Cartel.
January 18, 2010	The war between the Zetas and the Gulf Cartel begins after the killing of Metro 3 (Gulf Cartel member) by Concord 3 (Zeta member).
February 4, 2010	The DEA warns intelligence agencies about a new configuration of organized crime in Mexico.
February 23, 2010	Conflict between the Zetas and the Gulf Cartel starts with a fight for control of Valle Hermoso, Ciudad Mier, and Miguel Alemán.

February 24, 2010	A US judge sentences Osiel Cárdenas to 25 years in prison.
February 25, 2010	Social media start to fill the information void left by the mainstream media after they were silenced by the government and criminal groups.
February 25, 2010	The US consulate office in Reynosa closes in the face of increasing violence.
February 27, 2010	The government of Reynosa opens a Twitter account to issue alerts on "situations of risk."
February 27, 2010	The city of Camargo experiences one of the most violent shootings in the Small Border area. A citizen uploads a video of this event, which goes viral.
February 28, 2010	A number of reports are released regarding ghost towns and municipal presidents living in the United States.
March 3, 2010	In Tamaulipas 8 journalists are missing.
March 6, 2010	Ciudad Mier cancels its annual festivities. Other cities in Tamaulipas follow suit.
March 11, 2010	Attacks on Tamaulipas police stations begin.
March 17, 2010	The City Hall (Presidencia Municipal) of Hidalgo is the target of grenades and shootings.
March 18, 2010	The Tamaulipas war spreads to the state of Nuevo León.
March 21, 2010	Propaganda against the Gulf Cartel begins as the Zetas deliver flyers and give out money in Ciudad Mante.
March 22, 2010	Gulf Cartel members arrive in Ciudad Mante to fight for control of the plaza.
March 25, 2010	In Matamoros 41 inmates escape from a prison.
March 31, 2010	The battle for control of the city of San Fernando forces the Zetas to move to the states of Nuevo León and Coahuila.
April 3, 2010	The Zetas take back the plaza of San Fernando.
April 3, 2010	While a Zeta armed commando raids a Nuevo Laredo prison, 13 inmates escape.
April 4, 2010	The Zetas' battle for territory reaches Tampico.
April 4, 2010	Two children die in an alleged military attack against civilians on the Ribereña highway between Guerrero and Ciudad Mier.
April 11, 2010	The entire state of Tamaulipas becomes a "war zone."

April 12, 2010	Juan (Reyes) Mejía González (aka R-1 or El Quique) begins a strategy that includes kidnapping of families (*levantones*) and burning houses, cars, and businesses owned by members of rival groups.
April 15, 2010	The first hangings as a form of murder occur in Altamira.
April 20, 2010	The Zetas start throwing grenades as a strategy to stir up trouble in plazas controlled by the Gulf Cartel.
May 13, 2010	José Mario Guajardo, PAN candidate for the Municipal Presidency (mayorship) of the city of Valle Hermoso, is killed.
May 20, 2010	Dozens of migrants who were allegedly kidnapped are released as the trafficking of undocumented migrants in the Small Border increases and becomes more visible.
May 31, 2010	Reports show that the prices of rural properties are rapidly decreasing in zones where conflict is high.
June 11, 2010	The first multiple execution occurs in Ciudad Madero: 20 people are found assassinated after a raid by an armed group.
June 15, 2010	A violent confrontation between irregular armed groups and Mexico's armed forces starts in Nuevo Laredo.
June 28, 2010	In Ciudad Victoria the PRI candidate for governor (and potential winner), Rodolfo Torre Cantú, is murdered.
June 30, 2010	Egidio Torre Cantú, brother of the murdered candidate, is chosen as the new candidate for the Tamaulipas governorship.
July 4, 2010	Egidio Torre Cantú wins the Tamaulipas election.
August 1, 2010	A grenade is thrown at Televisa's buildings in Nuevo Laredo, sparking the first of many attacks on the media and newspapers in Tamaulipas.
August 6, 2010	The first multiple execution in a Tamaulipas prison occurs: 14 inmates are executed.
August 25, 2010	The Mexican army finds the bodies of 72 migrants killed on a ranch in San Fernando, later known to be an orchestrated mass homicide by the Zetas. This event is known as the "San Fernando Massacre."
August 27, 2010	Two car bombs detonate in Ciudad Victoria. These are the first events of this kind in Tamaulipas.
August 28, 2010	The leading investigator of the San Fernando Massacre, Roberto Jaime Suárez, is assassinated.

August 29, 2010	In Reynosa 19 citizens are injured in the downtown area as a grenade attack targets the population.
September 30, 2010	A US citizen, David Hartley, is murdered by members of a criminal group while jet skiing with his wife and taking pictures of a historic church located on the Mexican side of Falcon Lake on the US border.
October 1, 2010	The US Consulate in Matamoros issues an alert to avoid travel to Tamaulipas.
October 12, 2010	The lead Mexican investigator of Hartley's case, Rolando Armando Flores, is assassinated and beheaded. His severed head is delivered to the Mexican military in a suitcase.
November 5, 2010	Antonio Ezequiel Cárdenas (Tony Tormenta) [Osiel Cárdenas's brother] is killed in Matamoros by the Mexican army and navy. This sparks infighting for control of the Gulf Cartel between those loyal to Eduardo Costilla Sánchez (aka El Coss) and those loyal to Mario Cárdenas (also brother of Osiel Cárdenas).
November 11, 2010	More than a half of the total population of the municipality of Ciudad Mier abandons the city.
November 13, 2010	Rancher Alejo Garza Tamez, 77, confronts an armed convoy after being threatened and asked to turn over his property to the criminals. He dies in the shoot-out, leaving 4 of his aggressors dead and 2 seriously wounded. News of his last stand circulates in the national and international media. A number of ranchers in the area start to leave due to fears of similar incidents.
November 14, 2010	200 members of the ministerial police in Tamaulipas resign.
December 17, 2010	141 inmates flee a Nuevo Laredo prison.
January 1, 2011	The elected governor, Egidio Torre Cantú, takes office; 11 army generals are appointed to local police departments in Tamaulipas.
January 18, 2011	A plaza leader and founder of the Zetas, Flavio Méndez Santiago (aka El Amarillo), is captured.
January 31, 2011	The government of Tamaulipas recommends no travel at night in the state.
February 2, 2011	In Nuevo Laredo 25 children are found abandoned after their parents are kidnapped.

February 4, 2011	General Manuel Farfán Carriola is killed along with 4 of his escorts after being recently named chief of police in Nuevo Laredo.
February 16, 2011	The Zetas group blames the Gulf Cartel for attacks on civilians.
February 26, 2011	The PGR reveals that Tamaulipas has the highest number of kidnappings in the country.
March 15, 2011	A car bomb goes off on the premises of the police department in Ciudad Victoria.
March 21, 2011	The Cameron County assistant district attorney, Arturo José Íñiguez, is found dead in Matamoros.
March 21, 2011	It is reported that sales have fallen 50% in Tamaulipas because of a significant decrease in tourism.
March 24, 2011	Bus passengers start to get kidnapped in San Fernando.
March 26, 2011	A trailer loaded with weapons is burned in Nuevo Laredo when it is about to be searched by the military.
March 27, 2011	After the loss of a trailer with weapons, 11 informants (*halcones*) are found killed in Nuevo Laredo.
March 29, 2011	Reports of bus passenger kidnappings continue in San Fernando.
April 2, 2011	The first mass graves are found in San Fernando.
April 6, 2011	PRG confirms the finding of mass graves in San Fernando.
April 7, 2011	At least 113 cadavers are counted in the San Fernando mass graves.
April 8, 2011	Raúl Zúñiga Hernández, secretary of the government of the city of Hidalgo, is murdered by a criminal group.
April 9, 2011	The US Consulate in Matamoros alerts its nationals to avoid driving on Tamaulipas highways.
April 12, 2011	Federal police officers claim that all Tamaulipas highways, not only those in the San Fernando area, are controlled by organized crime.
April 13, 2011	The federal government sends more troops to Tamaulipas.
April 16, 2011	Omar Martín Estrada (aka El Kilo), the alleged mastermind behind the murder of more than 200 people in San Fernando, is captured by members of the navy.
April 21, 2011	The Zetas enter Ciudad Miguel Alemán and burn businesses.

May 12, 2011	The federal government sends 500 army officers to replace state police officers.
May 25, 2011	At least 17 inmates escape from prison in Reynosa.
June 4, 2011	Tanks belonging to criminal syndicates are seized in Camargo.
June 25, 2011	2,790 military officers arrive in Tamaulipas to strengthen security.
July 2, 2011	In Matamoros a priest, Father Marco Antonio Durán, is severely injured after getting caught in crossfire between members of organized crime and the military.
July 12, 2011	In Nuevo Laredo members of the Mexican army take preventive security measures after 900 members of local and transit police were suspended.
July 15, 2011	At least 7 inmates die and another 59 flee after a prison altercation in Nuevo Laredo.
July 20, 2011	After six months local citizens who escaped from violence return to Ciudad Mier.
August 16, 2011	Governor Egidio Torre supervises the construction of military barracks in Ciudad Mier.
August 21, 2011	Ricardo Cruz García, secretary of government of Ciudad Mante, is killed in his vehicle.
August 21, 2011	The San Fernando security complex is attacked.
September 2, 2011	Samuel Flores Borrego (aka El Metro 3), chief of the plaza of Reynosa, is found dead.
September 10, 2011	The Gulf Cartel's internal conflict begins. Bars in Río Bravo are attacked with grenades. Attacks then spread to other businesses in Reynosa.
September 15, 2011	A car bomb detonates in Ciudad Victoria.
September 24, 2011	Social media user María Elizabeth Macías (known as "La Nena de Laredo") is killed after she denounces organized crime in online reporting. Her body was found decapitated at a well-known stone monument of Nuevo Laredo (La Glorieta de Colón).
October 7, 2011	The first clash among opposing groups inside the Gulf Cartel occurs in Reynosa.
October 24, 2011	652 members of the "105 infantry battalion" arrive at the barracks of Ciudad Mier.
October 26, 2011	The second clash among enemy factions within the Gulf Cartel occurs in Reynosa.

October 31, 2011	The Gulf Cartel sends a message to the Zetas by leaving 7 beheaded Zetas' bodies in a pickup truck in Ciudad Mante.
November 17, 2011	167 members of the municipal police in Matamoros test positive after drug tests were administered to 560 agents.
December 2, 2011	Rival groups within the Gulf Cartel clash for the third time.
December 16, 2011	A car bomb detonates in Ciudad Victoria.
December 25, 2011	A truck with 15 bodies is left in Tampico.
December 29, 2011	8,000 soldiers are sent to Tamaulipas to strengthen security.
January 2, 2012	1,500 federal police officers are sent to Tamaulipas.
January 4, 2012	A riot in the Altamira penitentiary orchestrated by the Zetas leaves 31 members of the Gulf Cartel dead.
January 11, 2012	After a commando attack at the downtown facilities of the Ministerial Police (Policía Ministerial) in Ciudad Madero, 1 person dies and 6 others are injured.
January 19, 2012	650 military officers arrive at the new barracks in San Fernando.
January 30, 2012	The Mexican government investigates former governors of Tamaulipas Eugenio Hernández, Tomás Yarrington, and Manuel Cavazos Lerma for corruption. Authorities are instructed to record every instance in which the former governors, their families, and their political associates leave the country.
February 8, 2012	The US Consulate issues a new alert about the dangers in the Tamaulipas border area.
February 9, 2012	After more than six months of advertising for new local police officers, San Fernando authorities lack applicants.
February 19, 2012	Rivals in the Gulf Cartel clash for the fourth time in Reynosa. A civilian reporting the shooting on Facebook dies.
February 21, 2012	Tamaulipas is reported to have the highest rate of kidnappings of all Mexican states.
March 2012	Restructuring among the Zetas causes kidnappings (*levantones*) and confrontations.
March 5, 2012	A grenade launched in a Walmart in Ciudad Victoria hurts 10 civilians.

March 6, 2012	The Gulf Cartel's internal conflict spreads to Río Bravo with a series of grenade attacks.
March 6, 2012	The US government officially investigates former Tamaulipas governor, Tomás Yarrington.
March 17, 2012	An explosive device goes off in the morning in front of Ciudad Victoria's City Hall.
March 19, 2012	An attack, presumed to be a car bomb, damages the facilities of the *Expreso* newspaper in Ciudad Victoria.
March 26, 2012	Joaquin (aka El Chapo) Guzmán challenges Heriberto Lazcano (aka Z-3) and Miguel Ángel Treviño Morales (aka Z-40) in Nuevo Laredo, leaving a message and beheading people.
March 31, 2012	The US Consulate issues an alert regarding the violence in Ciudad Victoria.
April 14, 2012	15 dismembered people are found: 10 in Ciudad Mante and 5 in Ciudad Victoria.
April 17, 2012	14 dead bodies inside 10 plastic bags are found in a vehicle in front of Nuevo Laredo's City Hall.
April 22, 2012	Authorities and union leaders reveal that petitions from teachers who want to transfer to other locations have skyrocketed during the year in Tamaulipas as a result of crime and violence.
April 24, 2012	A car bomb explodes in front of the local police building in Nuevo Laredo.
May 2, 2012	The Independent Peasant Confederation (Central Campesina Independiente, CCI), an NGO, reveals that 11 percent of Tamaulipas *ejidos* have been abandoned between the end of 2011 and the first four months of 2012 due to fear of violence.
May 9, 2012	The federal government and Tamaulipas authorities sign the "Safe Tamaulipas" (Tamaulipas Seguro) agreement, through which the federal forces ratify their commitment toward working to assure security in the state.
May 13, 2012	49 corpses are discovered by military personnel in Cadereyta, Nuevo León, along a highway connecting Monterrey with Reynosa.
May 24, 2012	A car bomb explodes in Nuevo Laredo.

June 6, 2012	The former secretary of government of Tamaulipas during Eugenio Hernández's term as governor, Pedro Argüelles Ramírez, is apparently kidnapped by members of an organized crime group.
June 7, 2012	15 dismembered bodies are abandoned in front of Ciudad Mante's City Hall.
June 7, 2012	Grenades are thrown at 2 car dealerships in Ciudad Victoria.
June 12, 2012	The US Consulate in Matamoros issues a new alert warning of the possibility of increasing violence in Tamaulipas.
June 13, 2012	Army members capture one of the main Zeta operators, who is allegedly responsible for several grenade attacks against schools, media outlets, businesses, and military buildings in Matamoros.
June 23, 2012	A bus with 14 cadavers inside is found at a mall in Ciudad Mante.
June 25, 2012	Grenades are launched into a bus station and local police offices in Ciudad Victoria.
July 1, 2012	A body is found inside an icebox on the main square of the municipality of Padilla.
July 3, 2012	A car bomb explodes outside of the house of the Tamaulipas public security secretary, Rafael Lomelí, in Ciudad Victoria; 2 police agents are killed and 7 police and civilians are injured.
July 29, 2012	Infighting among the Zetas is starting to debilitate the organization. The factions are divided into those loyal to Heriberto Lazcano (aka Z-3) and those loyal to Miguel Ángel Treviño Morales (aka L-40 or Z-40).
August 1, 2012	After threats allegedly from the Zetas, citizens abandon the city of Güémez.
August 12, 2012	Rafael Lomelí admits that despite the state's deficit of more than 3,000 police officials, the main issue of this agency is the process of vetting (*control de confianza*).
August 14, 2012	Alleged members of an organized crime cell detonate at least 6 explosive devices in different areas of Matamoros at night; 2 of the explosions occur outside 2 malls and leave 4 people injured.

August 17, 2012	Blas Castillo, president of the Council of Financial Institutions of Southern Tamaulipas (Consejo de Instituciones Financieras del Sur de Tamaulipas, CIEST), reveals that cash flow problems and assaults have impacted close to 3,000 businesses in the southern area of the state, thus causing higher unemployment rates and business closings.
August 21, 2012	The Twitter account of the US Consulate in Matamoros starts posting alerts on "situations of risk."
September 3, 2012	Mario Cárdenas (Osiel Cárdenas's brother) is captured in Altamira. He is believed to have been the leader of the Gulf Cartel after the death of his brother Antonio Ezequiel Cárdenas (aka Tony Tormenta).
September 12, 2012	The marines capture Juan Gabriel Montes Sermeño (aka El Sierra or Gaby Montes), right-hand man of José Eduardo Costilla, top leader of the Gulf Cartel, who is also arrested this day.
September 27, 2012	The Mexican navy arrests Iván Velázquez Caballero (aka Z-50 or El Talibán), a presumed member of the Zetas thought to be the third-ranking leader of the organization.
October 7, 2012	Heriberto Lazcano dies in a confrontation with Mexican security forces in the state of Coahuila.
October 8, 2012	The Mexican navy arrests Salvador Alfonso Martínez Escobedo (aka La Ardilla), presumed to be regional chief of the Zetas in Tamaulipas, Nuevo León, and Coahuila.
November 3, 2012	In Reynosa 2 big clashes between 2 cells of the Gulf Cartel occur without the intervention of federal law enforcement agencies.
December 5, 2012	Organized crime members launch 2 grenades in front of the house of the governor of Tamaulipas, Egidio Torre Cantú. No injuries are reported.
January 2013	Tensions among different factions of the Gulf Cartel become more visible.
January 15, 2013	Gulf Cartel member Héctor Salgado (aka Metro 4) is killed. Versions of his death vary; some point to a possible execution by the Zetas, while others believe that it was the result of infighting within the Gulf Cartel.

March 10, 2013	A three-hour shoot-out in Reynosa (for the control of this city) between 2 rival factions of the Gulf Cartel (followers of Mario Ramírez Treviño [aka El Pelón] and followers of Miguel Villarreal [aka El Gringo]) leaves a possible death toll of 40 people. Miguel Villarreal and his allies may have lost their lives in this gun battle. Rumors of a Gulf Cartel reconsolidation become widespread.
May 6, 2013	A shoot-out in Tamaulipas between the Zetas and the Gulf Cartel leaves 17 dead, including Comandante Gallo of the Gulf Cartel.
July 15, 2013	Miguel Ángel Treviño Morales (aka Z-40) is arrested by the Mexican navy.
August 2, 2013	All international bridges that connect Laredo, Texas, and Nuevo Laredo are closed due to a bomb threat.
August 17, 2013	Mario Ramírez Treviño is arrested in Reynosa, Tamaulipas. He was allegedly the leader of the Gulf Cartel at the time.
August 17, 2013	Homero Cárdenas (brother of Osiel Cárdenas) allegedly takes control of the Gulf Cartel.
January 31, 2014	Authorities in Gómez Farías find a mass grave that contains 30 bodies and 10 metal barrels with human remains.
May 4, 2014	Galindo Mellado Cruz (aka El Mellado), an original founder of the Zetas, is killed in Reynosa in a shoot-out with the Mexican army.
May 5, 2014	Salvador Haro Muñoz, state police intelligence chief of Tamaulipas, is assassinated in Ciudad Victoria, allegedly by members of the Accredited State Police (Policía Estatal Acreditable).
May 14, 2014	"Plan Tamaulipas" is enacted by the federal government, dividing the state into four areas. Ports, airports, and border crossings become a focus of the security plan.
August 30, 2014	Rogelio González Pizaña (aka El Kelín), a founder of the Zetas, is released from prison. He was accused by the DEA of threatening 2 US federal agents in 1999.
October 15, 2014	María del Rosario Fuentes Rubio (also known as @Miut3 or Felina), a Twitter user and former collaborator of Valor por Tamaulipas, is kidnapped and killed.

October 31, 2014	4 people (1 Mexican man, and 3 US citizens—a woman and her 2 younger brothers) are abducted and assassinated, allegedly by local security forces in the community of Control (a municipality of Matamoros). This crime is attributed to a new tactical security unit, the so-called Grupo Hércules, introduced by the mayor of Matamoros, Leticia Salazar.
November 3, 2014	General Ricardo César Niño Villarreal, police chief in the northern region of Tamaulipas, is assassinated while driving along the Monterrey–Nuevo Laredo highway.
December 10, 2014	A detailed report by the PGR explains how the municipal police in San Fernando assisted the Zetas in kidnapping and killing 72 migrants and 193 bus passengers.
March 4, 2015	Omar Treviño Morales (aka Z-42), head of the Zetas, is arrested by the Federal Police and the Mexican army.
March 18, 2015	José Manuel Saldívar Farías (aka Z-31), believed to be the Zeta member in charge of drug trafficking in Mexico's northern region and South Texas, is arrested.
March 24, 2015	Ramiro Pérez (aka El Rama), believed to be a possible successor to Omar Treviño Morales (Z-42), is arrested.
March 31, 2015	José Guadalupe Reyes Rivera (aka El Sasi), believed to be directly related to the massacre of the 72 migrants in San Fernando, is arrested.
April 2015	As infighting exacts its toll and regional and national leaders are arrested or killed, the Zetas begin a process of fragmentation. Criminal bands loyal to the group become independent. Allied criminal groups such as La Familia Michoacana and the Beltrán Leyva Brothers' Cartel allegedly disappear, as their leaders are either killed or arrested.
May 6, 2015	A shoot-out between the Metros and the Ciclones (Gulf Cartel factions fighting for control of territory in the state) occurs in the community of Lucio Blanco in the municipality of Matamoros.
July 7, 2015	Shoot-outs between the Metros and the Ciclones take place in multiple municipalities of Tamaulipas. As the battle becomes increasingly violent, the Mexican army intervenes.
November 16, 2015	Ángel Eduardo Prado Rodríguez (aka Ciclón 7) is arrested in Matamoros by the Mexican army. His detention sparks a series of shoot-outs and road blockades in this city.

Map of Criminal Paramilitaries and Natural Resources in Mexico

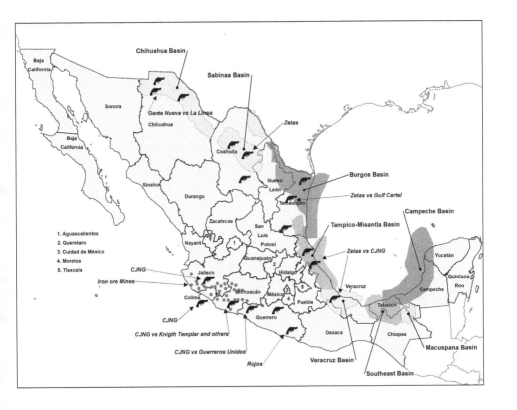

El disfraz de la guerra (The War's Disguise): Communiqué by Residents of La Ribereña

Note: This document was sent anonymously to me on January 20, 2014. It was allegedly written by a group of citizens who live in different cities of the Tamaulipas Small Border—also known by many as "La Ribereña" region.

The inequality in our country, caused by the brutality of the Spanish conquest and its irreversible consequences to our people, directly feeds the war between drug lords and the federal government. We have lost our identity, our values, and our convictions. We have experienced repeated failed governments, inefficient public administration, and a poorly performing Mexican education system.

Hundreds, if not thousands, of teenagers and young adults between the ages of fifteen and twenty-five have aligned themselves with Mexican criminal groups. They have joined the drug-trafficking ranks without any forethought. As a consequence these criminal groups have grown exponentially, and the violence that characterizes them seems to have no end.

Every day young people and children who come from dysfunctional families, detached from their social surroundings, commit themselves to criminal organizations, with blind obedience, faithfulness, and loyalty to the heads of these violent groups. Women and housewives who lack education and who apparently have no social and ethical values have joined this useless war for unknown reasons. Most of the new additions to these criminal groups have no real understanding of what they are doing and are often promised only a meager salary that in most cases they never receive because they are assassinated or disappear while on their first assignment.

A mix of poverty, lack of education, unemployment, the rampant practice of well-organized corruption, and the tremendous drug appetite of our northern neighboring country has created these dismal circumstances, which have been decisive factors in the development of the current violence in Mexico. The war was declared in 2006 and reached its violent peak by the end of the first decade of the new century (2010–2011). This moment of intense violence also characterized the first decade of the past two centuries (the Independence movement in 1810 and the Revolution in 1910).

Since its inception as a nation, Mexico has been in a complex, disadvantaged relationship with the United States in regard to topics of mutual interest, including commerce, human relations, diplomacy, and security. Sharing a border of more than three thousand kilometers with the most powerful country in the world, which is the prime producer and distributor of arms, the biggest consumer of drugs per capita, and the most attractive destination in the world for migrants, undoubtedly contributes to the loss of our young people to a drug war of massive proportions and consequences.

Historically, the reasons for war—territory, economic interests, differences of beliefs and ideologies, the simple desire to acquire more power—have varied. War, the most serious sociopolitical form of conflict between two or more human groups, is a political instrument serving a state or other politically affiliated organization. The rules of war have varied throughout history. The two most frequent scenarios are (1) a general population of civilians, generally young people, in conflict with each other or (2) permanent troops of professional soldiers supported by government joined by volunteers and mercenaries (source: Wikipedia).

Today, more than [ten] years since the "war on drugs" commenced, as front-row spectators from the northern Tamaulipas border, we know in our minds and in our hearts that the fight against drug trafficking has just been an excuse for the war. The flow of drugs has not been interrupted even momentarily, nor has its path to the US border been shortened, yet the number of criminal groups that dominate our towns grows. Nevertheless, the constant fighting among criminal groups and the never-ending attacks from federal authorities have contributed to the apparent weakening of the powerful criminal groups. According to many experts, the drug market in the United States has been saturated to the point where conditions of supply and demand have caused a decrease in price, but this has not affected marketing and consumption.

There is no consistency between the acts and episodes of terror and death presented throughout this conflict. The real reasons for the war are unknown, and many more doubts than answers are left with regard to the identity of the true immediate beneficiaries and the final objective that this war pursues. As [Mexican writer and journalist Armando Fuentes Aguirre] Catón said (October 2010):

> The worst part is that Mexico is fighting a battle that is not even its own; this battle belongs to the United States. It is there where the drugs are consumed and where weapons are manufactured and sold, almost without any control. The Americans are not fighting these problems; they are fought in Mexico at the expense of so many untold lives. The real problem is theirs, and they are demanding that we solve it. The problems in Mexico are the result of the vices of the American society. However, nobody in the United States seems to realize what an injustice this represents. We consider that Mexicans should fight their own battles against poverty, unemployment, and all forms of setbacks that we suffer, instead of fighting the battles of others with so much effort and so many resources.

As usual, everything has been perfectly manipulated by the beneficiaries of the war. Paradoxically, the comfort and vice of millions of US citizens are directly proportional to the size of the misfortune in Mexico.

Newspaper publications and other media coverage about the war have been vague and brief. Biased reporting tends to be the norm. Only when you [live the tragedy] do you realize the inconsistencies and lies told publicly. Unfortunately, very little news has had real substance and truthfulness when purportedly reporting the facts.

It is evident that all the information has been manipulated by good and bad actors of high rank who participate in the conflict. The truth has been hidden, with or without reasons, but without much analysis, strong political, economic, and social interests can be perceived. These interests cannot be completely hidden, especially from the sector of society not participating in the armed conflict, and it is that sector of society that has suffered the worst misfortunes in their individual lives. From their own perspective of terror, these people have had the opportunity to analyze the causes and origins, actors, events, places, and consequences of this war where there is seemingly no beginning or end and no winners or losers.

After years of conflict between government and drug dealers, we can conclude that:

- Drug trafficking has not been reduced.
- Revenues from this illicit activity have remained untouched.
- The high consumption of drugs in the United States has not declined.
- Arrests and apprehensions have not been proportionate to the magnitude of the war as related to the shootings and seizures on both sides of the border, crimes against public health, kidnappings, homicides, and related human suffering.
- The great majority of arrests by federal forces have been of those in the lower levels of the criminal organizations.
- Assassinations, kidnappings, extortions, robberies, assaults, lootings, raids, and surveillance activities have intensified disproportionally.
- Most of the complaints made by affected innocent people have not been resolved.
- Local economic conditions—low employment and job creation and investment shortages—persist.
- Highways in some regions of the country have not been reestablished for free and safe transit.
- Mexican federal forces are only part of the equation, with no plan of action, minimal or no investigation, a lack of intelligence strategy, and no coordination between the police and military.
- The criminals' power and capacity of organization and reorganization is far more efficient than government and tends to anticipate the reactions and actions of government officials.
- The Mexican government has relied on the cartels to destroy themselves by infighting, without caring how and when this will occur.

It seems as if criminals are now motivated by the challenge to face the military or the marines and propel themselves into history fighting for a cause unknown to them, all of this while accepting as payment franchises granted by criminal groups that have increased the type and quantity of common crimes.

What is all this about? What is the reality of this conflict? Who have been the direct beneficiaries of hundreds of millions of dollars that the Mexican government and criminals have spent to acquire weapons and ammunition to fuel this fight? If drug trafficking continues, so does the consumption of narcotics. If there are only a few high-profile arrests, the criminal structure remains strong and able to reorganize, to commit new crimes with the aim of obtaining easy money. Then what is the real reason behind this war where external interests are perverse and unclear?

The attention has been focused on Mexican cities and towns using civilians as shields, especially in regions with oil, tourism, agriculture, ports, industries, malls, and national highways.

- The case of the Burgos Basin is an example. Identified as the largest and most important area of exploration and production of gas administered and operated by Petróleos Mexicanos (Pemex), it was the scene of the first armed attack that deliberately targeted hundreds of workers. Production efforts in this area were partially stopped by Pemex at some point, and so far only [a fraction of them] have been reactivated. Meanwhile, in the neighboring state of Texas, in Zapata and Webb Counties, there are 70 wells producing natural gas for each well producing this resource on the Mexican side of the border—in the municipalities of Mier and Guerrero, Tamaulipas. The two regions share the same geological formation that is divided, on the surface, by the Rio Grande and the International Falcon Dam.
- In some kidnapping cases where the victims have been fortunate enough to be released, they have provided details about the modus operandi of criminal groups. These descriptions tend to reveal the fact that some of their captors only spoke and gave instructions in English. It is worth mentioning that the captors were not inexperienced children, as it was once believed. They were well-trained and well-equipped adults. This provides some evidence that the armed fighting between criminal groups has been planned and organized for other purposes than just disputing strategic territories for drug-trafficking purposes—for example, to weaken and undermine political, social, and economic structures in some regions of the country.
- Hundreds of undocumented migrants from Central America and Mexico are kidnapped and forced to join the ranks of criminal groups. This makes us suspect a planned measure intended to control the flow of undocumented migrants who pass through Mexico, wishing to enter the United States.
- The exodus of hundreds of Mexican families from war-torn cities and towns to Texas and other US states became more prevalent and legally easier. Some of them with large amounts of capital from questionable sources were received with open arms by US immigration authorities without much

prescreening or investigation prior to the issuing of legal investment visas. These people who migrated alone or with family were rapidly included in the American society and business world without much difficulty.

- The massive influx of US manufactured assault weapons and high-caliber ammunition to Mexican criminal groups has been one of the most perverse and harmful actions directed toward our country through many years of rocky and two-faced relations.

- Horrendous shoot-outs between criminals were occurring for several hours nightly in the streets of our communities for several months in past years. On some occasions, it was surprising to listen to planes—which we supposed were unmanned aerial vehicles or drones that flew over the areas of conflict—while the Mexican military remained in their barracks. Were they localizing, controlling, inspecting, directing, leading, or supporting the conflict? They were hardly there by chance.

- The Mexican military presence and performance only occurs at the end of the armed conflicts between criminals. When any military officer arrives at the scene to secure the area, he will boast about how the criminal groups had been detected moving from one site to another, as if spotting the movement of criminals was enough. These types of encounters leave civilians wondering about the efficacy of the military forces. They have just been mere spectators throughout this conflict.

- In most of the confrontations between armed criminal groups, some of the rival groups need to travel distances of up to 50 kilometers along highways or side roads to the place where fighting occurs. These journeys have been done with vehicles with rustic bulletproofing at slow speed or with caravans of recent-model trucks with cargoes of tons of ammunition, weapons, and gasoline. However, these caravans are not usually detected or confronted by federal authorities, even if they know that civilians will be caught in the middle of the battle. The worst part happens at the end of the confrontations, when, after shooting thousands of bullets and after exploding hundreds of bombs that could be heard in a ten-mile radius for more than four or five hours, the survivors will go back to their dens at dawn in the same way they had arrived, with free access to side roads and highways without worrying about being intercepted or bothered by anybody.

- New attacks on civilians and the incursions of rival groups have been intentionally spread by the criminals from all sides through social media and word of mouth. . . . Seldom has one group surprised the other; and when one has, some members have hidden while the visiting rival group has destroyed and shot at private houses and businesses in town in order to demonstrate their criminal power to the entire society, with, of course, the distant supervision and willingness of the federal forces.

Infiltration by organized crime at all levels of government and the social disorder in diverse sectors of the country are signs pointing toward the possible intended destabilization of the weakened Mexican society and the dismantling of its main economic and political elements.

In recent years Mexico has had a favorable environment for the development of armed conflict. This phenomenon started in January 2007 on the pretext of fighting organized crime and its main activity: drug trafficking. The idea was furthered by the United States, which ended up benefiting from the conflict and destruction in our county. For the most part, social, political, and economic structures in different zones of Mexico have been dismantled. Time and money have been lost trying to fix a conflict that is not ours. Now we have to face a setback of several years. In this new social reality we need to redefine our priorities and develop the areas that really matter for the country's growth and Mexicans' well-being: health, education, employment, and housing.

Organizational Charts:
Constellis Holdings, LLC, and Los Zetas Inc.

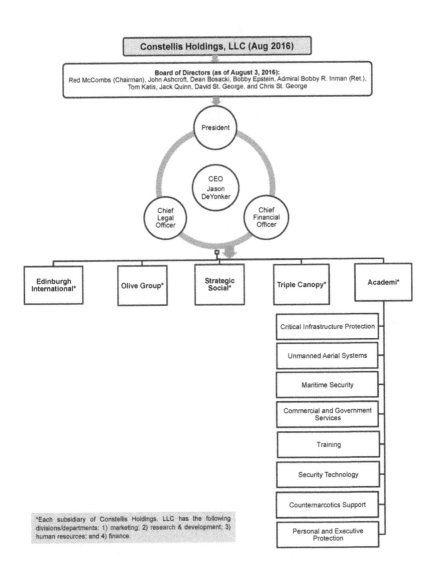

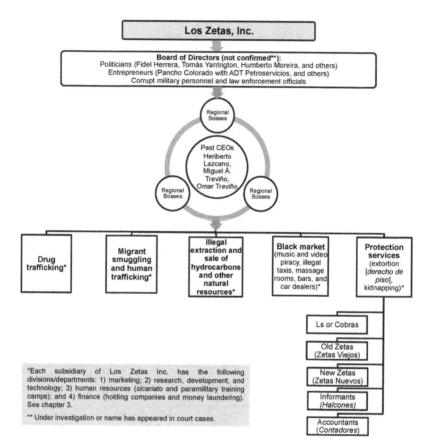

*Each subsidiary of Los Zetas Inc. has the following divisions/departments: 1) marketing; 2) research, development, and technology; 3) human resources (*sicariato* and paramilitary training camps); and 4) finance (holding companies and money laundering). See chapter 3.

** Under investigation or name has appeared in court cases.

APPENDIX 6

Areas of Dominant Influence of
Major TCOs in Mexico, 2015

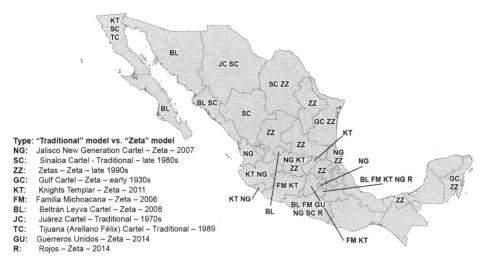

Type: "Traditional" model vs. "Zeta" model
NG: Jalisco New Generation Cartel – Zeta – 2007
SC: Sinaloa Cartel - Traditional – late 1980s
ZZ: Zetas – Zeta – late 1990s
GC: Gulf Cartel – Zeta – early 1930s
KT: Knights Templar – Zeta – 2011
FM: Familia Michoacana – Zeta – 2006
BL: Beltrán Leyva Cartel – Zeta – 2008
JC: Juárez Cartel – Traditional – 1970s
TC: Tijuana (Arellano Félix) Cartel – Traditional – 1989
GU: Guerreros Unidos – Zeta – 2014
R: Rojos – Zeta – 2014

Sources: *El Universal* newspaper and PGR. Design by Carlos D. Gutiérrez-Mannix.

Notes

Introduction

1. Important information and statistics about security in Mexico during this period can be found in *Atlas de la seguridad y la defensa de México* for 2009 and 2012 (see Benítez et al. 2009; Benítez and Aguayo 2012).

2. Official sources report more than 70,000 deaths related to organized crime during the Calderón administration. Some say that this conflict has claimed many more lives than reported by Mexico's government (Molloy 2013; O'Reilly 2012). The National Institute of Statistics and Geography (INEGI) reports 157,429 homicides in the period 2007–2015 (see table 4.2); this number does not separate deaths related to organized crime from the rest.

3. On the recent transformation of organized crime in Mexico and new corruption networks that have allowed its expansion, see Valdés (2013).

4. The terms "state" and "government" are not used interchangeably in this text. On the distinction between state and government, see Robinson (2013). Making use of international legal scholarship, Robinson defines states as "juridical entities of the international legal system," while for him "governments are the exclusive legally coercive organizations for making and enforcing certain group decisions" (556). Simply put, the government designs and implements laws and policies in a society. The state is the geographic entity where a government can exercise its powers. State is a broader concept; government is an element of the state. In this text the term "government" is mostly used to describe and analyze specific actions designed to fight organized crime in Mexico. In the theoretical parts of this text (for example, when explaining paramilitarism or different types of war) references are made to the state.

5. The usage of the term "paramilitary" when referring to the Zetas and other similar TCOs and their tactics does not seem to conform to the strictest meaning of the word. This concept implies direct or indirect links to the state, while TCOs and the state are antagonists according to general wisdom. However, various elements support the usage of the term "paramilitary" when characterizing the Zetas and other related criminal syndicates. Some evidence indicates a relationship between some of these groups and the state that has

taken different forms at certain moments throughout the conflict. See chapters 4 and 5 for further details.

6. *Drug War Capitalism* (Paley 2014) does analyze these aspects for the cases of Colombia, Mexico, and Central America. Paley's text breaks the official discourse on the so-called drug wars in the Americas and opens up a new narrative that enables her to speak about violence and organized crime in this region. This book applies some of Paley's main ideas to Mexico. It goes further than *Drug War Capitalism* by analyzing the winners and losers of Mexico's recent armed conflict, with special emphasis on the energy sector and the role of formal and informal transnational and multinational corporations.

7. Notwithstanding the aforementioned limitations, these texts are useful to understand the historical trends of organized crime in Mexico as well as the evolution of the major criminal organizations that have operated in the country. These manuscripts include some valuable material utilized to provide some context for the present work. See also Saldaña and Payán (2016), who present a timeline of the evolution of TCOs in Mexico from 1980 to 2015 and a useful list of references that provides key details of the historic trends and main leaders of these groups.

8. An example of this type of analysis can be found in Wainwright (2016).

9. There is an important debate regarding the usage of this type of literature to analyze cases like the Mexican one. The classic concepts on revolutions and civil wars do not necessarily apply to what has been called "Mexico's drug war." However, contemporary social scientists have developed analytical frameworks that could place Mexico—during the Calderón years at least—in the category of a civil war. For further details on this debate, see chapter 6.

10. Many sources that report organized crime activity do not always provide reliable information. I have tried to select the most credible informants and sources. Whenever questions about the veracity of specific sources or media outlets arose, I compared the coverage of the same event by several web platforms and media outlets.

11. These interviews were part of a project entitled "Violence on the 'Forgotten' (Texas-Tamaulipas) Border: Unemployment, Corruption, and the Paramilitarization of Drug Cartels in Mexico's 'New Democratic' Era" that took place during the period from August 1, 2011, to July 31, 2012. This project was supported by the Open Society Institute, the Social Science Research Council, the International Development Research Centre (IDRC), and Universidad de los Andes through a Drugs, Security and Democracy (DSD) Post-Doctoral Fellowship.

12. Some members of organized crime groups may not relish journalistic or scholarly attention and may retaliate against persons that they believe are providing information about their criminal activities.

13. Part of the analysis in chapter 6 was done in collaboration with a well-known social media user, @MrCruzStar, who reports situations of risk in Tamaulipas via Twitter and has "curated" information on Mexico's so-called drug war and organized crime in Tamaulipas during the past six years. He is an active participant in the hashtag #Reynosafollow.

14. In other words, information acquired through social media can only be considered valid if there is an adequate process of social media content "curation." This process requires the constant participation in specific social media networks (such as Twitter) through horizontal reporting platforms—where users write with total freedom, avoiding hierarchies and differentiated material incentives—to obtain valuable and consistent information through the identification of reliable sources and reports. This procedure is part of a citizen platform and is the result of a collective effort. For further information on social media curation, see Correa-Cabrera (2015b), Monroy-Hernández (2013), and Monroy-Hernández et al. (2012).

15. Despite this, these sources are still useful because they provide some basic background to understand the origins of these groups, their business trends, and details about their leadership (past and present).

16. Grayson (2014b), for example, centered his attention on what he calls the "sadistic personality disorder (SPD)" of the Zetas' leaders.

17. The kingpin strategy is a methodology developed by the Drug Enforcement Administration (DEA) in 1992 to target and eliminate, by death or by capture, the command-and-control elements or key leaders of major drug-trafficking organizations (Cockburn 2015).

18. See also appendix 1, which includes a timeline of events depicting key changes in Mexico's energy legislation since the early 1990s as well as the transformation of criminal organizations following the Zeta model.

Chapter 1

1. Some of the quoted material in this book is translated from Spanish (including this quotation). All translations are my own unless otherwise noted.

2. However, according to 1960 reports of the extinct Federal Directorate of Security (Dirección Federal de Seguridad, DFS), García Ábrego did traffick in narcotics. Carlos Flores, Skype interview, October 26, 2016.

3. Carlos Flores, Skype interview, October 26, 2016.

4. On the history of drug trafficking in Mexico, see Astorga (2016) and Valdés (2013).

5. On the links between the Gulf Cartel, García Ábrego, and the federal government, see Figueroa (1996).

6. García Ábrego was arrested by Mexican police outside the city of Monterrey—at his ranch located at Villa Juárez, Nuevo León—in an operation that involved no shooting. The next day, allegedly due to the possibility that he would escape from prison, García Ábrego was extradited to the United States, where he was sentenced to life imprisonment (Guerrero 2014a).

7. According to Professor Carlos Flores (Skype interview, October 26, 2016), Cárdenas was not strictly Ábrego's successor. He claims they led two different organizations, which were wrongly considered to be the same by the media and government authorities. Flores has not found a clear line of continuity or verifiable heritage.

8. Cárdenas established contact with the Zetas when he worked in the

Federal Judicial Police (Policía Judicial Federal) and met Arturo Guzmán Decena (aka Z-1).

9. Among these groups are the Special Forces Airmobile Group (GAFE), the Special Forces Amphibious Group (GANFE), and the Parachute Rifle Brigade (BFP). Subsequently the Zetas incorporated some members of the Maras and Kaibiles. At present recruits wanting to join the Zetas face no requirements of previous military training. The Zetas are now open to almost anyone who wants to join the organization.

10. On the origins and expansion of the Zetas, see Reyes (2009b). The Zetas were allegedly created at the end of the 1990s. The exact date of their creation is unknown, but their first public appearance was after the assassination of Arturo Guzmán Decena on November 21, 2002, in the city of Matamoros. To indicate the place where Guzmán Decena was killed, members of the organization left flowers and a note saying: "You will always be in our hearts: From your family, the Zetas" (*Te llevaremos siempre en el corazón: De tu familia, de Los Zetas*). Guzmán Decena's leadership role in the group was taken by Heriberto Lazcano (aka Z-3), who started to appear aggressively in the agendas of communication media and law enforcement agencies in 2003.

11. These versions have not been officially confirmed but are taken for granted in most journalistic accounts analyzing the Zetas and their history.

12. The term "Praetorian Guard" (*praetoriani* in Latin) comes from the name given to a military body used to protect Roman emperors.

13. While the creation of this criminal organization is generally attributed to Osiel Cárdenas, this does not mean that their creation was the idea of only one man. However, Cárdenas took advantage of the circumstances presented to him in the form of highly trained and poorly paid former military personnel, who used to work as federal agents during the mid- to late 1990s in the framework of the so-called Sealing Operation (Operación Sellamiento) (Nava 2011, 17). This operation was part of the antinarcotics collaboration between Mexico and the United States; it took place in Mexico's northern and southern border areas.

14. UEDO was then part of the Attorney General's Office (PGR) and disappeared in January 2003 due to a restructuring process of the Mexican agency.

15. The term "plaza" in this context refers to a defined drug marketplace, smuggling point, or corridor.

16. Nuevo Laredo is connected to Laredo, Texas, through four international bridges, one rail bridge (Laredo International Railway Bridge) and three road bridges: the Gateway to the Americas International Bridge (Bridge 1), Juárez-Lincoln International Bridge (Bridge 2), and World Trade International Bridge.

17. It is difficult to verify these numbers. Some analysts consider these figures relatively high. Carlos Flores, Skype interview, October 26, 2016.

18. The Kaibiles were created in the 1970s and were allegedly trained with the support of the United States. The members of this group are trained in counterinsurgency operations and are characterized by their resistance, adap-

tation capacities, and cruelty. They are taught to survive and fight under extreme conditions.

19. More details of this process can be found in Valdés (2013).

20. This type of alliance does not last for long periods. Criminal syndicates collaborate with different groups for short lapses of time in special circumstances, and betrayals are common. Further details of these criminal groups and their main developments and alliances can be found in Valdés (2013) and Astorga (2016).

21. The Company and the Tijuana Cartel started to work with "Los Texas," the group led by the brothers Guillermo and Arturo Martínez Herrera, while the Federation allied with "Los Chachos," an old local organization founded by Dionisio Román García-Sánchez (Alvarado 2004).

22. By this time the role of the Juárez Cartel in this alliance had changed. The Carrillo Fuentes family decided to ally with the Company, its former adversaries. Actually, the objectives of some key members of the Federation had shifted and included ending up with the hegemony of the Carrillo Fuentes family in the Juárez Cartel (Ochoa 2005). Therefore the leadership of this organization decided to switch alliances.

23. See chapter 2 to understand the origins of La Familia Michoacana.

24. This information was found in the blog "Daño Colateral" (Collateral Damage), administered in Tamaulipas by an anonymous person who used the name "Reynowarrior."

25. The *Dallas Morning News* was the first media outlet to publish this video. Some parts of it were censored due to the extremely bloody scenes presented there.

26. In August 2005 a cell of the Sinaloa Cartel allegedly activated two fragmentation grenades inside a *palenque* (cockfighting arena) in Tonalá, Jalisco, thus causing terror among the numerous persons present at the event. Four people died, and at least twenty-five people were severely wounded. This was possibly the first attack perpetrated in a public space by a drug-trafficking organization (Reynowarrior 2010). Events of this type were considered part of what has been called narcoterrorism.

27. In January 2008 Alfredo Beltrán Leyva (aka El Mochomo) was arrested. His brother, Arturo Beltrán, alleged a betrayal by El Chapo Guzmán, then leader of the Sinaloa Cartel, and decided to separate from this group. A new criminal group was then created, which incorporated La Barbie and Los Negros.

Chapter 2

1. @MrCruzStar, personal interview; December 1, 2013, Reynosa, Tamaulipas.

2. On this event and the Mata-Zetas, see chapter 5.

3. The category "disappeared" applies to people who were kidnapped, murdered, or detained and who never resurfaced, either dead or alive.

4. The Allende massacre took place very close to where the military was stationed in Piedras Negras: it operated a checkpoint outside of Allende (García and Alvarado 2014, par. 6).

5. La Libertad is one of the fourteen municipalities that form the department of El Petén.

6. The main leaders of the Enterprise were Carlos Rosales Mendoza (aka El Tísico), Nazario Moreno González (aka El Chayo), and José de Jesús Méndez Vargas (aka El Chango).

7. This region extends to the state of Guerrero.

8. The attack was not officially attributed to either of the two groups in particular, but both of them blamed each other for this fatal incident.

9. "Third-generation gangs" are those organizations involved in a wide range of criminal activities—drug trafficking, human smuggling and trafficking, kidnapping, arms trafficking, among others—that "use violence and bribery to neutralize state institutions and gain a free hand in pursuing their illegal enterprises" (Brands 2009a, par. 32).

10. Nonetheless, the security situation still remained fragile in several parts of Mexico, including the Zetas' birth state, Tamaulipas (Nelsen 2015).

11. The Zetas were the TCO most affected by the actions of Mexico's federal government during the administration of Felipe Calderón and in the first two years of Enrique Peña Nieto's six-year term. In March 2015 the PGR reported 832 arrests of members of this organization since 2007. The highest number of arrests (227) took place in 2009 (Ramírez 2015).

12. Lazcano was allegedly killed when he was watching a baseball game in Progreso, Coahuila, in 2012. It is worth noting that an armed commando spirited his body from the funeral home in Sabinas, Coahuila, just hours after his death.

13. Z-40 allegedly was arrested in Tamaulipas without a shot being fired (Beith 2013). He was captured on a dirt road near Nuevo Laredo.

14. On March 4, 2015, Z-42 was captured in a wealthy suburb of Monterrey, Nuevo León.

15. On Valor por Tamaulipas, see chapter 6.

16. Apparently the Central American gangs were the ones that provided the Zetas with "a model to achieve territorial control and for building a long-term economic strategy that is not tied to drug shipments" (Paley 2014, 227).

Chapter 3

1. In 2007, for example, journalistic sources quote file PGR/SIEDO/UEIDCS/014/2007, which contains the testimonies of informants "Karen, Rufino, Rafael, Gabriel and Yeraldín," who provide some details on how and where the Zetas are trained and how they allegedly operate (Gómez 2008).

2. Among the Old Zetas are El Mamito, El Hummer, El Comandante Mateo, El Rex, El Caprice, El Tatanka, El Lucky, El Paguita, El Cholo, El Ostos,

El JC, El Cachetes, El Pita, El Bedur, El Cuije, El Chispa, El Chafe, El Tizoc, El Tejón, and El Flaco, among others (Gómez 2008). These are nicknames of deserters from the Mexican army who ended up founding the Zetas.

3. Miguel Ángel Treviño Morales (aka Z-40) and his family formed part of this group. They have been key leaders of the Zetas but had no military training.

4. Examples of these works are Ravelo 2013; Grayson 2014b; Grayson and Logan 2012; and Fernández Menéndez 2007.

5. According to Ríos and Dudley (2013, par. 10), the Zetas inaugurated criminal operations in 249 municipalities of the Mexican Republic.

6. Rincón-Rincón was finally convicted. The jury returned its verdict quickly after seven days of trial and less than two hours of deliberation (FBI 2012, par. 1).

7. See *USA v. Cardenas-Vela et al. U.S. Courts Opinion*, Case 1:11-cr-01022, filed in US District Court for the Southern District of Texas.

8. José Nava, personal interview, March 2, 2012, Matamoros, Tamaulipas.

9. @MrCruzStar, personal interview, January 17, 2014, Reynosa, Tamaulipas.

10. Therefore it would be possible to use business administration academic literature to study transnational organized crime. TCOs like the Zetas seem to operate like transnational corporations, so in order to understand the market strategies and development of these powerful criminal groups we could utilize Michael E. Porter's "five competitive forces" model (Porter 1980, 2008). The model originated from Porter's 1980 book *Competitive Strategy: Techniques for Analyzing Industries and Competitors* and is a "frequently used tool for analyzing a company's industry structure and its corporate strategy." The five forces are the (1) threat of new entrants; (2) power of suppliers; (3) power of buyers; (4) availability of substitutes; and (5) competitive rivalry. These five forces seem to shape every industry and market and help us to analyze everything from the intensity of competition to the profitability and attractiveness of an industry (*Investopedia*: http://www.investopedia .com/terms/p/porter.asp, pars. 1–3). The Zetas, like any transnational company, share some common traits and could be analyzed and compared by making use of this model.

11. See the proposed organizational charts in appendix 5.

12. According to the *Business Dictionary* (www.businessdictionary.com), companies "have holdings in other companies when they own enough voting stock in another company to control its policies and management." Parent or holding companies "also exist for the sole goal of becoming bigger and diversifying into different sectors of the economy."

13. Eloy Garza, personal interview, August 2, 2011, Monterrey, Nuevo León.

14. Citizen journalist (anonymous), Skype interview, August 2, 2011.

15. Some details about the operation of this network were known through a DEA-led investigation called "Project Reckoning," intended to weaken the Company (the Zetas and the Gulf Cartel).

16. According to some sources, the Zetas have even forced undocumented migrants to collaborate with them in this type of activity (see the section "Migrant Smuggling and Human Trafficking" below).

17. The Zetas are not the only TCO that has subcontracted gangs for the *sicariato*. The Sinaloa Cartel contracted earlier gang units (*clicas,*) allegedly belonging to the Mara Salvatrucha 13 (MS-13) for its operations in Chiapas and Tamaulipas. The Salvadoran gang members were coordinated by Los Pelones, former military personnel who participated as the enforcers of the Sinaloa Cartel (Nájar 2005).

18. According to the PGR, in 2014 the Zetas worked with nine gangs: Sangre Zeta (Coahuila and Nuevo León); Operativo Zetas (Mante, Soto la Marina, and Ciudad Victoria, Tamaulipas); Comando Zetas (Nuevo Laredo, Mier, Miguel Alemán, Díaz Ordaz, Reynosa, and Matamoros, Tamaulipas); El Círculo and El Extranjero (Jiménez, Ciudad Victoria, Ciudad Madero, and Abasolo, Tamaulipas); Unidad Zetas (Nuevo Laredo, Tamaulipas); Néctar Lima (Nuevo Laredo); Delta Zeta (Valle Hermoso, Tamaulipas); Los Negros (Irapuato, Guanajuato); and Fuerzas Especiales (Cárdenas, Huimanguillo, and Centro, Tabasco, and Cancún, Quintana Roo) (Aguilar 2014, par. 5).

19. *Investopedia*: http://www.investopedia.com/terms/h/holdingcompany.asp, par. 1.

20. On December 4, 2012, the US Department of Justice pressed charges against four additional persons involved in this same case. Two of them utilized an account opened at JPMorgan Chase & Co. to transfer $600,000 from Mexico (*Animal Político* 2012).

21. Melissa del Bosque, personal interview; November 2, 2014; Austin, Texas.

22. Carlos Flores, personal interview; August 13, 2013; Mexico City.

23. *Investopedia*: http://www.investopedia.com/terms/b/boardofdirectors.asp, par. 1.

24. Initially, Francisco Colorado was sentenced to twenty years of prison in the United States, but in March 2015 a federal appeals court acquitted him, overturning the 2013 jury's conviction, and ordered a new trial for him. Finally, in a retrial in March 2016, Colorado got a twenty-year sentence.

25. These opportunistic connections are not new. We should remember the alleged links between federal authorities and the Company in the early 1990s, when this organization grew significantly. Some investigations have linked very high-level politicians with the Gulf Cartel—even Raúl Salinas de Gortari, brother of former president of Mexico, Carlos Salinas de Gortari (Flores 2013b; Figueroa 1996).

26. *United States of America v Tomás Yarrington Rubalcava and Fernando Alejandro Cano Martínez*, US District Court, Southern District of Texas, Brownsville Division, May 22, 2013, Kenneth Magidson, indictment No. B-12-435-S1.

27. *Investopedia*:   http://www.investopedia.com/terms/s/subsidiary.asp, pars. 1–2.

28. According to this report, the 'Ndrangheta dominates the cocaine market in Europe thanks to its links with Colombian drug-trafficking organiza-

tions, but particularly because of its recent ties to the Zetas (*Proceso* 2013c, par. 9).

29. The relationships between the two criminal groups have been demonstrated by investigations conducted by the Reggio Calabria antimafia district prosecutor's office, in a region where the 'Ndrangheta operates (*Proceso* 2013c; Libera 2012).

30. The report explains that the "narco-flights" to Europe frequently make stops at airports in West Africa that are not totally controlled by the relevant authorities and whose management is prone to corruption (*Proceso* 2013c, par. 13).

31. Jennifer Bryson Clark, personal interview, September 2, 2014, Harlingen, Texas.

32. See the section "The Real Effects of Mexico's Modern Civil War" in chapter 9 for more information on this subject.

33. Raúl Benítez, personal interview, October 23, 2014, Mexico City. See also Pérez (2010a).

34. On this new business, see Cruz Serrano (2012).

35. According to Mexico's Mining Chamber, in 2012 the country produced 15 million tons of coal annually, valued at approximately $3.8 billion (AFP 2012).

36. It has been said that Heriberto Lazcano, the alleged top Zeta leader at one point, had his own coal business and mines in Progreso, Coahuila, where he was finally killed by the Mexican navy on October 7, 2012 (AFP 2012).

37. I conducted interviews in Saltillo and Torreón, Coahuila, from February 24 to March 1, 2016.

Chapter 4

1. On this debate and fundamental critique of making this comparison, see the Wilson Center report titled *One Goal, Two Struggles: Confronting Crime and Violence in Mexico and Colombia* (Arnson and Olson 2014).

2. It is worth noting that reference is made here to some parts of the state but not to the state as a whole.

3. Citizen journalist (anonymous), Skype interview, November 18, 2011.

4. This idea is linked to the theory of Molly Molloy and Charles Bowden, who refer to "social cleansing"—or elimination of drug addicts, indigents, and poor people in general—by criminal paramilitaries and government forces in Ciudad Juárez. See Molloy and Bowden (2010) and Bowden (2010).

5. See, for example, Benítez (2009, 2011). Benítez and others criticize the usage of terms like "failed state," "criminal insurgency," "narcoinsurgency," and "narcoterrorism" when referring to the Mexican case. Benítez (2011) contends that the use of such concepts is helpful for US think tanks and consulting firms that wish to obtain contracts from the US State Department, Department of Defense, Department of Homeland Security, and Department of Justice to design programs of bilateral cooperation with Mexico. In Benítez's

view, these companies benefit from maximizing the threat that Mexico represents for US national security.

6. For a detailed overview and thoughtful analysis of the security strategy in Mexico during the Calderón administration, see Astorga (2015). He also provides an assessment of the security situation in the country and state of organized crime groups before Calderón's arrival to power.

7. Mexican military veteran (anonymous), personal interview; January 24, 2015; Matamoros, Tamaulipas.

8. The Mérida Initiative began in Fiscal Year 2008 (FY2008). From FY2008 to FY2015, the US Congress appropriated approximately $2.5 billion in Mérida Initiative assistance for Mexico. See Seelke and Finklea (2015).

9. Former secretary of public security Genaro García Luna identified the limitations of the kingpin strategy. He even acknowledged that removing the top leaders from the main TCOs operating in the country did not result immediately in their destruction and recognized that the power in these criminal syndicates was only transferred to new, more numerous, and more violent leaders (Beittel 2013, 33).

10. Homicides related to organized crime increased from 62 in December 2006, to 2,826 in 2007, to 6,837 in 2008, to 9,814 in 2009, to 15,273 in 2010, and 12,903 in the first nine months of 2011.

11. These statistics were released by the Office of the Presidency (Oficina de la Presidencia de la República) during Calderón's administration (downloaded on December 11, 2011, at http://www.presidencia.gob.mx/?DNA=119). These numbers were compiled by the National Center of Planning, Analysis, and Information for Combating Delinquency (CENAPI), with information provided by Mexico's Secretariat of Defense, Secretariat of the Navy, Secretariat of Public Safety, and Secretariat of the Interior. It is worth mentioning that this database ended in September 2011 and is not available today.

12. We must look at these figures with caution, because most crimes in Mexico are neither investigated nor prosecuted, according to many scholarly and even official sources. Therefore it is very difficult for the president's office to determine which murders were caused by organized crime and which were perpetrated by government forces. On the reliability of homicide figures in Mexico, see Molloy (2013). More crime statistics and a useful discussion of these numbers and murder trends can be found in Benítez et al. (2009) and Benítez and Aguayo (2012).

13. Tony Payán, personal interview, April 17, 2014, Houston, Texas.

14. See Frontera List at Google Groups for more information (https://groups.google.com/forum/#!forum/frontera-list).

15. On trends in US security assistance to Mexico and Latin America in general, see Biron (2014) and Isacson et al. (2013).

16. USNORTHCOM was established on October 1, 2002, with the aim of conducting "homeland defense, civil support and security cooperation to defend and secure the United States and its interests." Its area of responsibility "includes air, land, and sea approaches and encompasses the continental United States, Alaska, Canada, Mexico, and the surrounding water out to approximately 500 nautical miles. It also includes the Gulf of Mexico, the

Straits of Florida, and portions of the Caribbean region, including the Bahamas, Puerto Rico, and the US Virgin Islands. The commander of USNORTH-COM is responsible for theater security cooperation with Canada, Mexico, and The Bahamas" (US Northern Command 2014, pars. 1–4).

17. Jacoby served as the fifth Commander of USNORTHCOM and the twenty-second commander of the North American Aerospace Defense Command (NORAD).

18. These data are reported by the National Institute of Statistics and Geography (INEGI), which collects information from the Executive Secretariat of the National System of Public Safety (SESNSP) of the Ministry of the Interior.

19. Sergio Aguayo, personal interview; November 11, 2011, Mexico City. The continuous participation of these agencies in matters of public safety has resulted in major human rights abuses after Calderón's period. Two recent examples are the military's massacre of disarmed gunmen in Tlatlaya, State of Mexico, in June 2014 and the alleged forty-three extrajudicial killings by the federal police in Tanhuato, Michoacán, on May 22, 2015.

Chapter 5

1. Examples of companies that allegedly contracted extralegal violence during these years are Chiquita Brands International and Coca Cola.

2. José Nava, personal interview, March 2, 2012, Matamoros, Tamaulipas.

3. At the beginning of 2010 the Milenio Cartel split into La Resistencia and the CJNG after their leader was captured.

4. According to the United Nations Development Programme (UNDP), the municipality of San Pedro Garza García registered the highest human development index in the state of Nuevo León and the second highest at the national level in 2010. It was also the municipality with the lowest levels of extreme poverty in the nation according to the National Council for the Evaluation of Social Development Policy (CONEVAL) (Machuca 2014).

5. Obed Campos, personal interview, August 3, 2012, Monterrey, Nuevo León.

6. This group of industries includes Cemex, Alfa, Vitro, Femsa, Gruma-Banorte, and Villacero-Afirme, among others.

7. The contributions were made in cash, so there is no exact number or official trace of such transactions.

8. In 1861 Benito Juárez decreed the creation of four corps of the rural police under the command of the Ministry of War. This is the historical reference for the current communitarian police groups that operate in some rural zones of Mexico (Gil Olmos 2013).

9. Salvador Maldonado, public lecture, May 3, 2016, El Colegio de México, Mexico City.

10. Mexican military veteran (anonymous), personal interview, January 24, 2015, Matamoros, Tamaulipas.

11. Carlos Flores, personal interview, August 13, 2013, Mexico City.

12. In 2006 the PGR linked Farías to Zhenli Ye Gon, a successful pharmaceutical businessman, after the seizure of almost twenty tons of ephedrine acetate. Farías is known for establishing the first self-defense group in Tepalcatepec in efforts to remove the Zetas from the state. In 2009 he was arrested by SEDENA, identified as a drug trafficker, and detained for forty days. The reason for his release is unknown (*Reforma/El Norte* 2014; Machuca 2014).

13. Los Viagras were the first Knights Templar splinter group, splitting in 2013.

14. Mireles was arrested on June 27, 2014, for allegedly violating Mexico's Federal Law of Firearms and Explosives. The reason behind this arrest may have been political.

15. María Machuca, personal interview, March 5, 2013.

16. Salvador Maldonado, public lecture, May 3, 2016, El Colegio de México, Mexico City.

17. On January 30, 2014, attorney general Jesús Murillo Karam said that the Mexican government had arrested two members of self-defense groups who had supposedly acquired weapons from the CJNG (Fausset and Sánchez 2014).

Chapter 6

1. Some elements of these theories can be found in Clausewitz (1989), Daase and Davis (2015), and Benítez (1986).

2. Finally in November 2016, Colombia signed a peace agreement with FARC after "five decades of war" (Casey 2016). As of today, the agreement has not been signed or approved by a majority of Colombian citizens.

3. Villalobos (2011, 10) recognizes that in order to understand the recent security crisis in Mexico "it is necessary to define organized crime and establish the difference between a problem of public safety and a threat against national security." This has not always been done properly.

4. Raúl Benítez, personal interview, July 28, 2016, Mexico City.

5. The main premises of this school differ from the perspectives of the classical school of civil wars and revolutions. See Clausewitz (1989) and Benítez (1986).

6. It is worth noting that Villalobos did not characterize Mexico's drug war as a civil war due to the apparent lack of political agendas of drug-trafficking organizations.

7. A detailed explanation of the actual winners of this war can be found in chapter 9.

8. Raúl Benítez, personal interview, July 28, 2016, Mexico City.

9. @MrCruzStar, personal interview, January 17, 2014, Reynosa, Tamaulipas.

10. On narcoinsurgency and US counterdrug policy, see Brands (2009b).

11. There have been several detentions related to this event, but none of them has helped to clearly identify the actual leaders and their true motivations.

12. Citizen journalist (anonymous), Skype interview, November 4, 2012.

13. See Monroy-Hernández (2013) and Monroy-Hernández et al. (2012) for more information on collective action using different electronic platforms and social media content "curation," which refers to the action of filtering the most interesting information on a subject across the web and sharing the best news, articles, photos, and videos on individual social channels.

14. These terms refer to members of civil society who were not trained as professional journalists but have actively reported dangerous and violent events. They have done so anonymously to protect their safety while working in situations of danger and extreme violence. For further information on this concept, see Correa-Cabrera (2015a, 2015b).

15. Citizen journalist (anonymous), personal interview, December 17, 2013, Nuevo Laredo, Tamaulipas.

16. Citizen journalist (anonymous), Skype interview, March 5, 2013.

17. Citizen journalist (anonymous), personal interview, December 16, 2013, Reynosa, Tamaulipas.

18. @MrCruzStar, personal interview, January 17, 2014, Reynosa, Tamaulipas.

19. "Hacktivism" is the use of digital tools and massive participation in social media with a political purpose. Hacktivists perform as political activists in cyberspace.

20. "Anonymous" is a group of cyberactivists operating worldwide. They started as a group of "street" activists that transitioned into social media, where the best weapon that they have is their anonymity. Their current agendas are somewhat related to those of street activists, and they operate hand in hand with them on some themes with the purpose of achieving specific goals; sometimes they are even used as "clash groups" (*grupos de choque*). At present, Anonymous only uses virtual activism and is considered a group of hacktivists. Hacktivism had its highest peak a few years ago in different parts of the world, but these trends arrived to Mexico later, when groups such as Anonymous ceased having a determinant political influence; now this group attracts public attention just for brief periods of time. The community of Anonymous-México operates basically in central and southern states of the country. They are dedicated to the development of free software and digital security and conduct themselves with a neo-Zapatista ethic.

21. Shannon Young, Skype interview, March 12, 2013.

22. Ibid.

23. Another experiment involving the same group of hacktivists and the Zetas took place in Ciudad Acuña, Coahuila, with the creation of the chapter Anonymous Free Acuña, which was dedicated to denouncing the Zetas' activities in this city and their connections with local politicians, particularly those belonging to the PRI (Buch 2013).

24. The paramilitary element of #OpCartel is not limited to the alleged links between Anonymous and Mexican government authorities. There is a

possibility that foreign agencies participated as well. It is important to remember the wide participation of the English-speaking virtual community in
#OpCartel, including the foreign press and in particular the US security think
tank Stratfor.

25. Blog del Narco is an internet platform launched in March 2010 that
documented the drug war by featuring "raw photos and videos of executions,
and gun battles uploaded by anonymous contributors." At some point this
blog "was one of the most visited websites in Mexico with 3m monthly visitors" (del Bosque 2013, par. 3).

26. The Facebook account of Valor por Tamaulipas was created on January 1, 2012, while the Twitter account appeared a month and a half later, on
February 16 of the same year.

27. Citizen journalist (anonymous), Skype interview, March 5, 2013.

Chapter 7

1. See detailed evidence of these patterns in *Drug War Capitalism* (Paley
2014).

2. Consider, for example, the ports of Altamira and Tampico, Tamaulipas;
Tuxpan and Coatzacoalcos, in the state of Veracruz; Lázaro Cárdenas, Michoacán; and Manzanillo, Colima.

3. Fracking, also known as "hydraulic fracturing," is a technique designed
to recover gas and oil from shale rock. It involves a process of drilling and in-
jecting fluid into the ground at a high pressure in order to fracture shale rocks
and release the hydrocarbons that are contained inside.

4. See Mexico, National Commission of Hydrocarbons (2012). In this document the commission makes a full assessment of the Burgos Basin regarding
its possibilities in terms of exploration, exploitation, information technology,
industrial security, environmental regulations, and several other aspects.

5. The Burgos Basin is bordered on the north by the US-Mexico border
and on the east by the Mexican Ridges and part of the Perdido fold belt in the
deep waters of the Gulf of Mexico.

6. Other energy companies that have also collaborated with Pemex in this
region under the umbrella of Multiple Services Contracts (Contratos de Servicios Múltiples, CSM) are Petrobras, Teikoku Oil, Techint-Tecpetrol, and D&S
Petroleum. On CSM, see Lajous (2004) and appendix 1.

7. The existence of this "richness" has been known for years. For example, in 2004 the government of the United States had a plan to gain access to
Mexican natural gas from Tamaulipas to Tabasco with the aim of guaranteeing a supply until 2030, thus increasing the natural gas reserves approximately
425 percent. This analysis was presented by the US secretary of energy, Abra-
ham Spencer, to his Mexican counterpart at the time, Felipe Calderón, and
president George W. Bush. This proposal was backed up by the National Petroleum Council (NPC) and the Department of State as well as by the directors of the main energy industries: American Electric Power, British Petroleum, Chevron Texaco, ConocoPhillips, Schlumberger Limited, ExxonMobil,

Halliburton Company, Kinder Morgan Energy Partners, Marathon Oil Corp., Valero Energy Corporation, and Shell Oil (Cruz Serrano 2004).

8. On October 3, 2012, José Eduardo Moreira, the eldest son of Coahuila's ex-governor, Humberto Moreira, was assassinated. His body was found in the municipality of Acuña.

9. Moreira became president of the PRI in March 2011 and had to resign in December of the same year amid allegations of corruption and opacity in the management of public finances of his home state. In January 2016 he was arrested in Madrid and charged with money laundering and embezzlement but was soon released. He has been frequently touted as a major ally of the Zetas during his period as governor of Coahuila.

10. Natural gas is considered by many to be a cleaner fuel than coal, because it produces less carbon dioxide per unit energy than coal does. However, "natural gas is predominantly composed of methane, a much more potent greenhouse gas than carbon dioxide, and it is thought that leaks at drilling fields could outweigh its potential benefit" (Cartwright 2015, par. 4).

11. Ignacio Alvarado, personal interview, March 2, 2016, Mexico City.

12. Grupo México owns Ferrocarril Mexicano (Ferromex), the company that operates the largest railroad network in the country.

13. Alfonso Ancira is chairman of the board and controlling shareholder of AHMSA. Germán Larrea is the chief executive officer of Grupo México.

14. Humberto Moreira was indirectly succeeded by his brother Rubén, who was elected as governor of Coahuila from 2011 to 2017. Actually, Rubén succeeded interim governor Jorge Juan Torres López as the leader of Coahuila's government.

15. AHMSA's production, net income, and new investments have increased considerably in the past few years. The years 2013 and 2014 were particularly good for this company. On July 18, 2013, AHMSA inaugurated the "Fenix Project" (Proyecto Fénix), which included the construction of a new Steckel mill containing important properties—from iron and coal mines to steel plants. The company has also increased its internal railway network considerably.

16. In the past few years thousands of tons of iron ore have been transported from this Mexican state to the Chinese ports of Qingdao and Tianjin (Guillén 2012, par. 4).

17. An *ejido* is a unique Mexican form of collective ownership. See further explanation in chapter 8.

18. This controversial union leader has lived in exile in Vancouver, Canada, since 2006 after fleeing Mexico amid fraud allegations, as the leader of the Mining and Metalworkers' National Union (Sindicato Nacional de Trabajadores Mineros y Metalúrgicos, SNTMM). He became a Canadian citizen in 2014.

19. For example, in January 2012 ArcelorMittal announced that "it would not cancel its plans of growth in Mexico notwithstanding the situation of insecurity that prevailed in the country" (Beltrán 2011, par. 1). ArcelorMittal's reduction in production took place until 2015, when the company announced a 90 percent decrease in its generation of steel and an indefinite technical stop-

page in its Las Truchas mine. It is worth noting that this decision had nothing to do with insecurity but was based on the strong reduction of steel prices in the world markets and the overflow of related products in Mexico coming from China, Brazil, and Russia.

20. This second stage requires an investment of $1.2 billion (Mexico, Secretariat of Communications and Transportation 2014, par. 2).

21. Manzanillo is Mexico's largest container seaport.

22. Carlos Flores, personal interview, February 12, 2016, Mexico City.

Chapter 8

1. In a period of four years (between 2010 and 2014) 69 public officials were reported to have disappeared; 90 percent of them belonged to law enforcement agencies (Mendieta 2014).

2. On this incident, see Casey and de Córdoba (2010).

3. See the chronology in appendix 2.

4. Corchado and Osborne (2014, par. 29) report that "it was not clear whether the workers were being targeted."

5. On the formation of this group, see Carreón (2014).

6. On the Small Border and its municipalities, see chapter 1.

7. Soon afterward the lead Mexican investigator of this case, Rolando Armando Flores, was assassinated and beheaded. His severed head was delivered to the Mexican military in a suitcase. David Hartley's body was never found.

8. Citizen journalist (anonymous), Skype interview, August 2, 2011.

9. On the economic benefits of the Los Ramones pipeline, see de la Cruz and García (2015).

10. Consider, for example, the case of the natural gas condensate extracted from the Burgos Basin. Recent investigations show how the condensate was allegedly transported from this big reservoir to the border with Texas. The shipments crossed through formal customs by utilizing false documentation that classified them as NAFTA cargo. They were then taken to terminals and warehouses in Texas for their temporary storage and later distribution to US buyers (Pérez 2012, par. 14).

11. See the concluding chapter.

12. Daugherty is quoting a Wilson Center report.

13. The region that encompasses the city of Reynosa and its surroundings has been especially dynamic in this sense in the last few years. Reynosa is a key point of economic integration in the eastern part of the US-Mexico border because two very important highways converge here. This border city is part of the interstate corridor (I-69), which starts in Canada, connects several states of the United States, and ends in this Mexican region, and today is linked to the center of the country and to the Pacific coast by the Mazatlán-Matamoros superhighway.

14. In 2014 the consortium's operations in Mexico were valued at more than $10 billion (Dorantes 2014, par. 7).

15. The fifth is located in San Isidro, Chihuahua. There is also a liquefied

natural gas (LNG) terminal in Altamira, which began functioning in 2006. This terminal has been used by CFE to supply fuel for electricity generation. Mexico is reevaluating the terminal's functions and exploring the possibility of using it for exporting LNG (Haahr 2015, 6).

16. This figure was found in a report prepared by Mexico's intelligence agency (Center for Investigation and National Security [Centro de Investigación y Seguridad Nacional, CISEN]).

17. Shannon Young, Twitter post, August 23, 2014, 11:30 A.M., https:// twitter.com/SYoungReports.

18. Article 27 of the Mexican Constitution recognizes three types of land ownership: private, public, and social. Private land ownership is "limited to the use of the surface of the land with no rights over subsoil resources." Public property refers to land "whose use is in the hands of governmental agencies." Social land ownership "includes communal lands, generally associated with indigenous communities, and a unique Mexican form of collective ownership known as the *ejido*." *Ejido* landowners were initially "entitled to use and work these lands to their benefit, but could not sell or use them for collateral." A reform of land tenure rules in 1992 enabled *ejidatarios* to lease or sell their plots if a majority of members of their *ejido* agreed (Payán and Correa-Cabrera 2014b, 2).

19. On the gendarmerie, see Chalk (2013).

Chapter 9

1. It is worth mentioning that Tamaulipas has often been referred to as a failed state (Hale 2010).

2. Dawn Paley, personal interview, February 14, 2012, La Paz, Baja California.

3. This problem became so widespread and serious that in February 2015 Pemex decided to "stop moving gasoline via pipeline to curb theft." The company would "transport mostly processed gasoline and diesel fuel through its pipelines" and finish processing the fuels at its storage terminals (Reuters 2015, par. 2). The move is aimed at dissuading the country's motorists and industrial users from buying stolen gasoline from nonauthorized sellers.

4. See the concluding chapter for further details on this phenomenon.

5. According to recent estimations, organized crime groups steal up to 40 percent of the condensates extracted from Mexico's northern border region and sell it on the US black market (Pérez 2010b, 2011a). Suroosh Alvi (2014b) reports that in the first decade of the present century ninety-seven Pemex employees and ten contractors were linked to these illegal activities.

6. The areas of territorial control by the Zetas and similar groups can be found in appendix 6.

7. See appendix 4.

8. Solís is the head of El Barzón Chihuahua, one of the most important agricultural and political organizations in the state.

9. On the different types of land ownership in Mexico, see article 27 of the

Mexican Constitution. A brief description of these types is also included in chapter 8 of this book.

10. See Mexico, SENER (2014a, 2014b).

11. Although the Secretariat of the Interior (SEGOB) acknowledges the disappearance of 27,659 persons in Mexico, the existence of multiple databases makes it impossible to know with certainty the real number of missing people in the country. At the federal level there are three different databases for missing persons: SEGOB's National Registry of Data of Missing or Disappeared Persons (RNPED), the database disseminated by the "Support Program for Relatives of Lost, Kidnapped, or Missing Persons" (Programa de Apoyo a Familiares de Personas Extraviadas, Sustraídas o Ausentes), and the "Dar Contigo" (Finding You) database. The three databases show completely different numbers (Lara 2014a).

12. The strategy of forced disappearance is not exclusive to dictatorships, although it is often found in those contexts (Mastrogiovanni 2014).

13. Among the disappeared in Mexico should be countless numbers of migrants. The actual figures for disappeared persons would not include many of the missing migrants, however, since their families frequently do not have the resources to report their loss in Mexico.

14. The United Nations International Convention for the Protection of All Persons from Enforced Disappearance considers enforced disappearance as taking place when "persons are arrested, detained or abducted against their will or otherwise deprived of their liberty by officials of different branches or levels of Government, or by organized groups or private individuals acting on behalf of, or with the support, direct or indirect, consent or acquiescence of the Government, followed by a refusal to disclose the fate or whereabouts of the persons concerned or a refusal to acknowledge the deprivation of their liberty, which places such persons outside the protection of the law" (http://www.un.org/en/events/disappearancesday/background.shtml). According to this definition, a significant number of the disappearances in Mexico—many more than those officially reported—would count as enforced disappearances.

15. RNPED's website (https://rnped.segob.gob.mx/) contains the official database of missing persons in the whole country. It includes information collected by the PGR and is administered by the Executive Secretariat of the National System of Public Safety (SESNSP).

16. On the drug war, increasing militarization, and new border security dynamics, see Payán (2016).

17. Most of these weapons come from Texas, California, and Arizona.

18. See, for example, Mercier (2011).

19. Another important factor that has supported Mexico's drug war is money laundering. In fact, a huge portion of the Mexican economy is based on narco-related businesses or other enterprises associated with organized crime and further illegal activities. And the money obtained through these illegal operations is laundered precisely in the transnational financial sector.

20. This situation is similar to the one observed in the past with the Standard Oil Company, now ExxonMobil. Controlling all stages of production and commercialization—through a secret majority share in a multitude of in-

termediate companies—Standard Oil managed to dominate the US oil market first before taking on its rivals in other parts of the world (Lepic 2005, par. 4).

21. The EIA projects that the access to abundant shale gas and oil reserves, along with energy efficiency improvements to reduce consumption, will allow the United States to become a net exporter of gas by 2020 and to slash its crude imports in the coming decades. This will reduce US dependence on foreign oil and encourage lower oil prices by increasing supply. At the same time, to achieve energy independence, the United States is interested in enhancing conventional offshore and deepwater production (Page 2012).

22. The significant recent increase in oil production in the United States as well as substantial energy savings have contributed to a drastic reduction in oil prices in the world. This could effectively limit OPEC's influence in the world energy markets (Zhu 2013, par. 1).

23. The technology needed for the extraction and processing of shale gas was developed only about two decades ago. Important advances in this regard have taken place in the United States.

24. Natural gas now competes with coal, nuclear energy, and other forms of renewable energy.

25. This is explained by the important amount of hydrocarbons being exploited in Texas and North Dakota, including natural gas extracted in some states of the East Coast (Vargas 2014, par. 7). The notorious production increase came mainly from deposits like the Texas Eagle Ford Shale and Bakken Shale in North Dakota (Zhu 2013, par. 3).

26. These transnational businesses have increased their investments in this sector and have focused their recent efforts on the shale gas business. For example, in 2010 ExxonMobil bought XTO Energy, a company focused on the production of unconventional resources (Carroll 2011). Exxon's acquisition of XTO "made the company the largest producer of natural gas in the U.S.; among U.S. integrated oil companies, it is the one that has bet the most on the value of unconventional natural-gas production" (DiColo and Fowler 2012, par. 6). Halliburton, the largest provider of fracking services in the United States, has made recent additions to its hydraulic fracturing fleet and logistics capabilities (Blumenthal 2014). The company recently announced that it "would establish a joint venture company focused on hydraulic fracturing and production enhancement services in China with an affiliate of SPT Energy Group Inc." (McCarthy 2014, par. 7). Halliburton also recently stated its intention to buy Baker Hughes (but the merger agreement was terminated in March 2016). Similarly, Schlumberger has acquired twelve North American companies that "specialize in boosting production from oil and gas wells." This firm has also become "a leader in extracting liquids from shale basins through what's known as artificial-lift operations, part of the booming business in hydraulic fracturing that's reshaping the industry" (Ward 2014, par. 1).

27. This analysis was written prior to the 2016 US presidential election. As a result, the situation projected here may be slightly different due to the Trump administration's approach to the US-Mexican border, US-Mexican relations, and the concept of North America.

28. http://www.atlanticcouncil.org/publications/reports/mexico-s-energy
-reform-ready-to-launch (par. 1).

29. Consider, for example, the cases of Cotulla and Carrizo Springs,
which are turning into "thriving communities" during this energy boom in
Texas (Corchado and Osborne 2014).

30. As Krauss (2014, par. 3) explains, the South Texas Eagle Ford Shale
in 2014 was "providing more than a million new barrels of oil supplies to
the world market every day." Before energy prices went down considerably,
United States refinery production "reached record highs and left supply de-
pots flush, cushioning the impact of all the instability surrounding traditional
global oil fields." This new bonanza "doubled the state's crude production
over [2012 and 2013], suddenly making Texas a bigger producer than either
Kuwait or Venezuela" (par. 6).

31. Estimations vary; sources place Mexico between third and sixth in
terms of size of shale gas reserves.

Conclusion

1. ExxonMobil has been considered to be a truly successful economic empire. It has been able to influence US foreign policy through a huge lobbying
operation in Washington (Coll 2012; Pindar 2013).

2. The largest oilfield services company is Schlumberger.

3. These product service lines operate in two divisions: (1) drilling and
evaluation and (2) completion and production.

4. See more details on these activities in chapter 3.

5. It is worth noting the massive theft of natural gas condensate initiated
at the end of Vicente Fox's administration (2000–2006).

6. The lawsuits were filed in July 2010, May 2011, and April 2012. The
cases are *Pemex Exploracion y Produccion v. BASF Corp. et al* (case number
10-1997), *Pemex Exploracion y Produccion v. Big Star Gathering Ltd.* (11-
2019), and *Pemex Exploracion y Produccion v. Murphy Energy Corp. et al*
(12-1081). All are in the US District Court for the Southern District of Texas.

7. It has been said that the amount of natural gas condensate stolen is
close to 40 percent of the total production of condensates in the Burgos Basin
(Pérez 2012, par. 47).

8. Pemex lost these cases. See Linares and Montalvo (2016).

9. Constellis's board of directors in August 2016 included Red McCombs
(chair), John Ashcroft, Dean Bosacki, Bobby Epstein, Adm. Bobby R. Inman
(ret.), Tom Katis, Jack Quinn, David St. George, and Chris St. George (see appendix 5). The board has already changed. Constellis is a transnational business group in constant transformation.

10. KBR recently participated in conflicts in Iraq, Libya, Kuwait, and the
Balkans. The company was given nearly forty billion dollars in Iraq-related
contracts over the first decade of the twenty-first century, "with many of the
deals given without any bidding from competing firms, such as a $568-million
contract renewal in 2010 to provide housing, meals, water and bathroom ser-

vices to soldiers" (A. Young 2013, par. 5). In January 2006 KBR was awarded a $385 million contingency contract by the Department of Homeland Security to build detention camps in the United States (Evans et al. 2010).

11. In April 2014 a video showing Vallejo Mora speaking with La Tuta was made public.

12. In 2003 Blackwater signed its first contract with the US Department of Defense to participate in Iraq (approximately $28 million).

13. On May 1, 2016, the companies announced the termination of their merger agreement after opposition from US and European antitrust regulators (Halliburton 2016).

14. The US government has also noted that this group has influence in the State of Mexico, Nayarit, and Guerrero (Ángel 2015, par. 4).

15. Pemex already operates various production contracts together with ExxonMobil, Weatherford International, Halliburton, Schlumberger, and Baker Hughes. For several years Halliburton has been one of the biggest contractors of Pemex (Pérez 2011b).

16. On booking oil reserves, see Estévez (2014).

17. Reyes-Heroles is executive president of StructurA, a group of consulting firms that includes MBD Desarrollo de Negocios (MBD Business Development), PRoA Communicación Integral (PRoA All-Round Communication), and EnergeA.

18. Avangrid was formed through the 2015 merger between UIL Holdings and Iberdrola USA.

19. Academi performs global operations focused on assessment, training, and protection; it trains and deploys with global reach, including Mexico City. Academi's global operations are international training, international counter narcotic support, border police training, and personal and executive protection (Academi 2014).

20. During the conflict these companies have worked "in supplying support services, security, reconstruction and the oil industry" (Fifield, 2013, par. 17).

21. At one point none of these companies benefited more than KBR, which was then part of Halliburton (Fifield 2013, par. 4).

References

Academi. 2014. "ACADEMI: Elite Training, Trusted Protection." https://academi.s3.amazonaws.com/uploads/document/document/57/ACADEMI_Brochure.pdf.

ADN Político (staff). 2013. "El cártel de Los Zetas no ha sido desmantelado." *ADN Político*, October 24. http://www.adnpolitico.com/gobierno/2013/10/24/stratfor-el-cartel-de-los-zetas-aun-no-ha-sido-desmantelado.

Agence France-Presse (staff; AFP). 2012. "El carbón, nuevo lucrativo negocio para el cartel mexicano de Los Zetas." *El Deber*, November 16. http://www.scivortex.org/single-post/2016/06/11/El-carb%C3%B3n-nuevo-lucrativo-negocio-para-el-cartel-mexicano-de-Los-Zetas-1.

Aguilar, Rubén. 2014. "Grupos asociados a los cárteles." *El Economista*, September 23. http://m.eleconomista.mx/columnas/columna-especial-politica/2014/09/23/grupos-asociados-carteles.

Aguilar, Rubén, and Jorge G. Castañeda. 2009. *El narco: La guerra fallida.* Mexico City: Santillana.

Aguilar Camín, Héctor. 2014. "México 2014: Narco para principiantes." *El País*, March 25. http://elpais.com/elpais/2014/03/17/opinion/1395083669_842358.html.

———. 2015. "La guerra perdida de México." *Milenio*, March 6. http://www.milenio.com/firmas/hector_aguilar_camin_dia-con-dia/guerra-perdida-Mexico_18_476532362.html.

Altos Hornos de México (AHMSA). 2016a. "Minera del norte." *AHMSA's website.* Accessed February 2, 2016. http://www.ahmsa.com/minera-del-norte.

———. 2016b. "Profile." http://www.ahmsa.com/en/company/profile.

Alvarado, Ignacio. 2004. "Nuevo Laredo: La otra guerra del 'narco.'" *Almargen*, March 29. http://www.almargen.com.mx/news/imprime.php?IDNOTA=612 (no longer available).

———. 2012. "Una historia de narco política." *El Universal*, June 17. http://www.eluniversal.com.mx/notas/853903.html.

———. 2014. "Tamaulipas y el estado mafioso." *Diario 19*, January 20. http://diario19.com/archivos/554.

―――. 2015. "Mexico's Ghost Towns: Residents Seeking Asylum in U.S. Fear Returning to Deadly Juárez Valley." *Al Jazeera America*, June 17. http://projects.aljazeera.com/2015/09/mexico-invisible-cartel/.

Alvi, Suroosh. 2014a. "¿A dónde se van los 10 mil barriles diarios que saquea el narco a Pemex?: Empresas de EU y México los compran." *VICE Mexico/ SinEmbargo*, July 30. http://www.sinembargo.mx/30-07-2014/1072896.

―――. 2014b. "Petroleras de EU y criminales, con ayuda de empleados y contratistas, participan en el robo masivo a Pemex." *VICE Mexico/Sin-Embargo*, July 31. http://www.sinembargo.mx/31-07-2014/1073918.

―――. 2014c. "Un 'pequeño olvido' en la reforma energética: Nada sobre cómo detener el robo masivo a Pemex." *VICE Mexico/SinEmbargo*, August 1. http://www.sinembargo.mx/01-08-2014/1075085.

Andrade, Elizabeth del Carmen, Martín Espinoza, and Francisco Belmonte. 2010. *La región agrícola del norte de Tamaulipas (México): Recursos naturales, agricultura y procesos de erosión*. Murcia, Spain: Ediciones de la Universidad de Murcia (Editum).

Ángel, Arturo. 2014a. "Lidera Tamaulipas en armas, crimen organizado y drogas." *24 Horas*, October 23. http://www.24-horas.mx/lidera-tamauli pas-en-armas-crimen-organizado-y-drogas/.

―――. 2014b. "Michoacán, epicentro de producción de drogas." *24 Horas*, January 22. http://www.24-horas.mx/michoacan-epicentro-de-produccion -de-drogas/.

―――. 2015. "¿Cómo se enriquece el cártel de Jalisco?: Cinco estadísticas lo revelan." *Animal Político*, May 7. http://www.animalpolitico.com/2015/05 /como-se-enriquece-el-cartel-de-jalisco-cinco-estadisticas-lo-revelan.

Animal Político (staff). 2011. "Suman 49 los cuerpos arrojados en calles de Veracruz en 48 horas." *Animal Político*, September 23. http://www .animalpolitico.com/2011/09/suman-49-los-cuerpos-arrojados-en-calles -de-veracruz-en-48-horas/#axzz33ce6Hu4m.

―――. 2012. "Los Zetas lavan dinero en JP Morgan: EU." *Animal Político*, December 13. http://www.animalpolitico.com/2012/12/los-zetas-lavan-di nero-en-jp-morgan/.

Arnson, Cynthia J., and Eric L. Olson (with Christine Zaino), eds. 2014. *One Goal, Two Struggles: Confronting Crime and Violence in Mexico and Colombia*. Washington, DC: Wilson Center.

Associated Press (staff). 2014. "Feud Splits Mexico 'Self-Defense' Forces." *USA Today*, March 11. http://www.usatoday.com/story/news/world/2014/03/11 /mexico-vigilantes-knights-templar-drug-gang/6297291/.

Astorga, Luis A. 2015. *¿Qué querían que hiciera?: Inseguridad y delincuencia organizada en el gobierno de Felipe Calderón*. Mexico City: Grijalbo.

―――. 2016. *El siglo de las drogas: Del Porfiriato al nuevo milenio*. New edition. Mexico City: Debosillo.

Avant, Deborah D., and Virginia Haufler. 2012. "Transnational Organisations and Security." *Global Crime* 13, no. 4: 254–275.

Avant, Deborah D., and Renée de Nevers. 2011. "Military Contractors and the American Way of War." *Daedalus, the Journal of the American Academy of Arts and Sciences* 140, no. 3: 88–99.

Ávila, Eleazar. 2013. "Matamoros un paraíso de oro negro." *Hoy Tamaulipas*, July 22. http://www.hoytamaulipas.net/notas/90113/Matamoros-un-paraiso-de-oro-negro.html.

Bailey, John. 2011. "Los Zetas y McDonald's." *El Universal*, November 5. http://www.eluniversalmas.com.mx/editoriales/2011/11/55520.php.

Baverstock, Alasdair. 2015. "Inside the Ghost Towns of Mexico's 'Murder Valley'—One of the Deadliest Places on Earth." *Daily Mail*, January 21. http://www.dailymail.co.uk/news/article-2916766/Two-murders-day-horrific-kidnappings-police-don-t-dare-enter-Inside-ghost-towns-Mexico-s-Murder-Valley-one-deadliest-places-earth.html.

Beauregard, Luis Pablo. 2013. "Lázaro Cárdenas: Puerto de aguas turbulentas." *Nexos*, December 1. http://www.nexos.com.mx/?p=15593.

Beith, Malcolm. 2013. "The Current State of Mexico's Many Drug Cartels." *CTC Sentinel* 6, no. 9: 18–20.

Beittel, June S. 2013. *Mexico's Drug Trafficking Organizations: Source and Scope of Violence*. Washington, DC: Congressional Research Service.

Beltrán, Harvey. 2011. "ArcelorMittal mantiene planes de crecimiento a pesar de inseguridad." *Business News Americas*, January 27. http://www.bnamericas.com/es/news/metales/arcelormittal-mantiene-planes-de-crecimiento-a-pesar-de-inseguridad.

Benítez, Raúl. 1986. "El pensamiento militar de Clausewitz." *Revista Mexicana de Ciencias Políticas y Sociales* 126: 97–123.

———. 2009. "La crisis de seguridad en México." *Nueva Sociedad* 220: 173–189.

———. 2011. "Estados fallidos e insurgencias criminales: Falacias conceptuales." *Foreign Affairs Latinoamérica* 11, no. 2: 32–41.

Benítez, Raúl, and Sergio Aguayo, eds. 2012. *Atlas de la seguridad y la defensa de México 2012*. Mexico City: Colectivo de Análisis de la Seguridad con Democracia (CASEDE) and Open Society Foundations.

Benítez, Raúl, Abelardo Rodríguez, and Armando Rodríguez, eds. 2009. *Atlas de la seguridad y la defensa de México 2009*. Mexico City: CASEDE.

Biron, Carey L. 2014. "La militarización policial de EEUU tiene tentáculos en América Latina." *Inter Press Service*, August 19. http://www.ipsnoticias.net/2014/08/la-militarizacion-policial-de-eeuu-tiene-tentaculos-en-america-latina/.

Blake, Mariah. 2014. "How Hillary Clinton's State Department Sold Fracking to the World." *Mother Jones*, September/October. http://www.motherjones.com/environment/2014/09/hillary-clinton-fracking-shale-state-department-chevron.

Blumenthal, Robin G. 2014. "Some See Upside for 'New' Halliburton: For Better or Worse, It's in Fracking." *Wall Street Journal*, July 26. http://online.wsj.com/articles/some-see-upside-for-the-new-halliburton-1406419418.

Bowden, Charles. 2010. *Murder City: Ciudad Juárez and the Global Economy's New Killing Fields*. New York: Nation Books.

Brands, Hal. 2009a. "Los Zetas: Inside Mexico's Most Dangerous Drug Gang." *Air and Space Power Journal*, October 1. http://www.airpower.maxwell.af.mil/apjinternational/apj-s/2009/3tri09/brandseng.htm.

———. 2009b. *Mexico's Narco-Insurgency and U.S. Counterdrug Policy.* Carlisle Barracks, PA: Strategic Studies Institute.

Brown, Stephen P. A., and Mine K. Yücel. 2013. "The Shale Gas and Tight Oil Boom: U.S. States' Economic Gains and Vulnerabilities." *Council on Foreign Relations*, Energy Brief, October 1. Washington, DC: Council on Foreign Relations Press.

Buch, Jason. 2013. "Zetas Have Anonymous Foes." *San Antonio Express-News*, May 31. http://www.expressnews.com/news/local_news/article /Zetas-have-Anonymous-foes-4566921.php.

Canales, Rodrigo. 2013. "The Deadly Genius of Drug Cartels." *TEDSalon NY2013* video (17:56), October. https://www.ted.com/talks/rodrigo _canales_the_deadly_genius_of_drug_cartels?language=en.

Carlsen, Laura. 2012. "Mexico's False Dilemma: Human Rights or Security." *Northwestern Journal of International Human Rights* 10, no. 3: 145–153.

Carpenter, J. William. 2015. "Top 5 Companies Owned by Exxon Mobil." *Investopedia*, November 6. http://www.investopedia.com/articles/markets /101315/top-5-companies-owned-exxon-mobil.asp.

Carrasco, Jorge. 2014. "La 'biblia' militar de la 'guerra' de Calderón." *Proceso*, July 12. http://www.proceso.com.mx/377063/la-biblia-militar-de-la -guerra-de-calderon-2.

Carreón, Ramón. 2014. "En informe Lety Salazar presenta a Grupo Hércules." *Milenio*, September 7. http://www.milenio.com/politica/informe_Lety _Salazar-grupo_hercules-informe_matamoros_0_368363378.html.

Carrizales, David. 2009. "NL: Desata polémica la propuesta de crear comando ilegal en Garza García." *La Jornada*, November 4. http://www .jornada.unam.mx/2009/11/04/estados/029n1est.

Carroll, Joe. 2011. "Exxon Trails BP after $35 Billion XTO Natural-Gas Gamble Amid Supply Glut." *Reuters*, May 23. http://www.bloomberg .com/news/ (article no longer available).

Cartwright, Jon. 2015. "Natural Gas Vs. Coal: The Verdict." *Environmental Research Web*, March 2. http://environmentalresearchweb.org/cws/article /news/60392.

Casey, Nicholas. 2016. "Colombia Signs Peace Agreement with FARC after 5 Decades of War." *New York Times*, September 26. http://www.nytimes .com/2016/09/27/world/americas/colombia-farc-peace-agreement.html.

Casey, Nicholas, and José de Córdoba. 2010. "Northern Mexico's State of Anarchy. Residents Abandon a Border Town as Vicious Drug Cartels Go to War." *Wall Street Journal*, November 20. http://online.wsj.com/article /SB10001424052748704104104575622840256881122.html.

Cattan, Nacha, and Adam Williams. 2014. "Drug Gangs Attacking with Tanks Block Mexican Shale Boom." *Bloomberg*, June 12. http://www .bloomberg.com/news/2014-06-12/drug-gangs-attacking-with-tanks -block-mexican-shale-boom.html.

Cepeda, César. 2014. "FBI investiga a 'Los Rudos.'" *Reporte Índigo*, September 10. http://www.reporteindigo.com/reporte/monterrey/fbi-investiga-los -rudos.

Chalk, Peter. 2013. "Mexico's New Strategy to Combat Drug Cartels: Evaluating the National Gendarmerie." *CTC Sentinel* 6, no. 5: 16–18.

Chávez, Adazahira. 2013. "Michoacán, el laboratorio peñista para acabar con las autonomías: Carlos Fazio." *Desinformémonos Periodismo de Abajo*, November 3. http://desinformemonos.org/2013/11/michoacan-el-laboratorio-penista-para-acabar-con-las-autonomias-carlos-fazio.

———. 2014. "México: La reforma agraria: Tiro de gracia a la propiedad social de la tierra." *Desinformémonos Periodismo de Abajo*, February 2. https://desinformemonos.org/la-reforma-agraria-tiro-de-gracia-a-la-propiedad-social-de-la-tierra-en-beneficio-del-extractivismo.

Chen, Angela. 2014. "Halliburton Agrees to Buy Baker Hughes." *Wall Street Journal*, November 17. http://online.wsj.com/articles/halliburton-to-buy-baker-hughes-for-34-6-billion-1416226472.

Chernick, Marc W. 1998. "The Paramilitarization of the War in Colombia." *NACLA Report on the Americas* 31, no. 5: 28–33.

Clausewitz, Carl von. 1989. *On War* (1832). Edited and translated by Michael Eliot Howard and Peter Paret. 1989. Princeton: Princeton University Press.

CNN Expansión (staff). 2011. "El narco acecha a contratistas de Pemex." *CNN Expansión*, February 15. http://www.cnnexpansion.com/negocios/2011/02/15/pemex-narco-pago-seguridad-zeta-cartel.

CNN México (staff). 2014. "¿Dónde hay autodefensas en Michoacán?" *CNN México*, February 15. (no longer available).

Cockburn, Andrew. 2015. "The Kingpin Strategy." *Huffington Post*, April 28. http://www.huffingtonpost.com/andrew-cockburn/the-kingpin-strategy_b_7161690.html.

Cockcroft, James D. 2010. *Mexico's Revolution: Then and Now*. New York: Monthly Review Press.

Coll, Steve. 2012. *Private Empire: ExxonMobil and American Power*. New York: Penguin Books.

Collier, Paul. 1999. "Doing Well Out of War." Paper prepared for Conference on Economic Agendas in Civil Wars, London, April 26–27. http://siteresources.worldbank.org/INTKNOWLEDGEFORCHANGE/Resources/491519-1199818447826/28137.pdf.

———. 2000. "Rebellion as a Quasi-Criminal Activity." *Journal of Conflict Resolution* 44, no. 6: 839–853.

Collier, Paul, and Anke Hoeffler. 2007. "Civil War." In *Handbook of Defense Economics*, edited by Todd Sandler and Keith Hartley, 2:711–739. 2 vols. Amsterdam: Elsevier.

Constellis. 2014. "Constellis Holdings, Inc. Acquires Constellis Group, Inc." *PRNewswire*, June 6. http://www.prnewswire.com/news-releases/constellis-holdings-inc-acquires-constellis-group-inc-262388561.html.

———. 2015. "About." *Constellis website*. http://www.constellisgroup.com/about (no longer available).

Contreras, Guillermo, and Jason Buch. 2015. "Former Mexican Border Governor Indicted." *San Antonio Express-News*, June 19. http://www.expressnews.com/news/local/article/Former-Mexican-border-governor-indicted-6337757.php.

Corchado, Alfredo. 2015. "Fierce Mexican Cartel's Likely New Chief Once Lived near Dallas." *Dallas Morning News*, March 4. http://res.dallasnews .com/interactives/border_energy/.

Corchado, Alfredo, and James Osborne. 2014. "The New Border: Eyes Are on Mexico's Untapped Potential." *Dallas Morning News*, July 13. http:// res.dallasnews.com/interactives/border_energy/.

Coronado, Martín. 2015. "Confirman en el estado cuenca de gas shale similar a la de Burgos." *El Diario de Juárez*, October 19. http://mobile.diario .mx/Local/2015-10-19_77c1991c/confirman-en-el-estado-cuenca-de-gas -shale-similar-a-la-de-burgos/.

Correa-Cabrera, Guadalupe. 2012. "A Business Perspective on Violence and Organized Crime." *Voices of Mexico* 94: 19–22.

———. 2013a. "Security, Migration, and the Economy in the Texas-Tamaulipas Border Region: The 'Real' Effects of Mexico's Drug War." *Politics and Policy* 41, no. 1: 65–82.

———. 2013b. "Violencia en el noreste mexicano: El caso Tamaulipas: Estado, sociedad y crimen organizado." In *Violencia e inseguridad en los estados fronterizos del norte de México en la primera década del siglo XXI*, edited by Vicente Sánchez Munguía, 139–162. Puebla: Universidad Autónoma de Puebla.

———. 2014a. "Inequalities and Global Flows in Mexico's Northeastern Border: The Effects of Migration, Commerce, Hydrocarbons, and Transnational Organized Crime." DesiguALdades.net, Working Paper 64. Berlin: Lateinamerika-Institut of the Freie Universität Berlin.

———. 2014b. Review of *La guerra de los Zetas: Viaje por la frontera de la necropolítica*, by Diego E. Osorno. *Critical Reviews on Latin American Research* 3, no. 1: 350.

———. 2014c. "Violence on the 'Forgotten' Border: Mexico's Drug War, the State, and the Paramilitarization of Organized Crime in Tamaulipas in a 'New Democratic Era.'" *Journal of Borderlands Studies* 29, no. 4: 419–33.

———. 2015a. "An Emerging Field after Mexico's 'Drug War': Energy, Security and Business-led Cross-border Governance." Paper presented at the annual meeting for the Association for Borderlands Studies (ABS), Portland, Oregon, April 8–11.

———. 2015b. "La guerra contra las drogas en redes sociales: El ciberespacio, el nuevo campo de batalla." Paper presented at the annual meeting for the Latin American Studies Association (LASA), San Juan, Puerto Rico, May 27–30.

———. 2017. "Métodos y experiencias de investigación en la frontera este (Tamaulipas-Texas): Paramilitarización del crimen organizado, violencia extrema y redes sociales." In *El arte de la investigación: Métodos y experiencias en contextos transfronterizos*, edited by Tony Payán and Consuelo Pequeño. Ciudad Juárez: Universidad Autónoma de Ciudad Juárez (UACJ)/ Eón (forthcoming).

Correa-Cabrera, Guadalupe, Michelle Keck, and Jose Nava. 2015. "Losing the Monopoly of Violence: The State, a Drug War, and the Paramilitarization of Organized Crime in Mexico (2007–2010)." *State Crime Journal* 4, no. 1: 77–95.

Correa-Cabrera, Guadalupe, María F. Machuca, and José Nava. 2015. "'New' Forms of Paramilitarism and a 'Modern' Civil War in Mexico (2006–2014)." Working paper, January 15. Brownsville: University of Texas at Brownsville.

Correa-Cabrera, Guadalupe, and José Nava. 2013. "Drug Wars, Social Networks and the Right to Information: The Rise of Informal Media as the Freedom of Press's Lifeline in Northern Mexico." In *A War That Can't Be Won: Binational Perspectives on the War on Drugs*, edited by Tony Payán, Kathleen Staudt, and Z. Anthony Kruszewski, 96–118. Tucson: Arizona University Press.

Crónica de Hoy (staff). 2014. "Encuentra Pemex rico yacimiento." *La Crónica de Hoy*, January 28. http://www.cronica.com.mx/notas/2014/811340 .html.

Crooks, Ed. 2014. "Emerging Market Oil Groups out of Favour." *Financial Times*, January 26. http://www.ft.com/intl/cms/s/0/4b6de976-8699-11e3 -aa31-00144feab7de.html?siteedition=intl#axzz3D4PaNtnl.

Cruz, Mónica. 2011. "Su adicción por el crudo robado: El narco abastece a Estados Unidos de su otra droga." *Emeequis*, September 19, 18–28.

Cruz Serrano, Noé. 2004. "Desde 2004 quiere EU gas natural de México para garantizar abasto." *El Universal*, April 2. http://www.quiminet.com /noticias/quiere-eu-gas-natural-de-mexico-para-garantizar-abasto -1656770.htm.

———. 2011. "Hallan yacimientos de gas en Tamaulipas." *El Universal*, October 25. http://archivo.eluniversal.com.mx/finanzas/90533.html, consultado el 5 de agosto de 2013.

———. 2012. "El carbón, nuevo lucrativo negocio para el cartel mexicano de Los Zetas." *El Universal*, November 25. http://www.eluniversal.com.co /cartagena/internacional/el-carbon-nuevo-lucrativo-negocio-para-el-cartel -mexicano-de-los-zetas-98439.

Daase, Christopher, and James W. Davis, eds. 2015. *Clausewitz on Small War*. Oxford: Oxford University Press.

Dal Bó, Ernesto, Pedro Dal Bó, and Rafael Di Tella. 2006. "'Plata o Plomo?': Bribe and Punishment in a Theory of Political Influence." *American Political Science Review* 100, no. 1: 41–53.

Daugherty, Arron. 2015. "Why Success of Mexico's Oil Security Plan May Not Matter." *InSight Crime*, February 3. http://www.insightcrime.com /news-analysis/why-success-of-mexico-oil-security-plan-may-not-matter.

Daugherty, Arron, and Steven Dudley. 2015. "How the U.S. Government Gets It Wrong with the Zetas." *InSight Crime*, March 20. http://www .insightcrime.org/news-analysis/us-govt-gets-it-wrong-mexico-zetas -leaders.

de Córdoba, José. 2013. "U.S. Indicts Ex-Mexico Governor for Bribes." *Wall Street Journal*, December 2. http://www.wsj.com/articles/SB10001424052 7023048548045792346833321327214.

———. 2014. "Mexico Reaches Pact with Vigilante Groups." *Wall Street Journal*, January 27. http://online.wsj.com/news/articles/SB100014240527 0230400750457934717092436970.

De la Cruz, Antonio, and Ángel García. 2015. "'Detona' el gasoducto la eco-

nomía." *Expreso.press*, July 3. http://expreso.press/2015/07/03/detona-el
-gasoducto-la-economia/.

De la O, Ricardo. 2011. *Genealogía del narcotráfico* (Parts 1–5). Tijuana:
Peninsular Digital.

del Bosque, Melissa. 2013. "Why Blog del Narco Has Become the Most Important Website in Mexico." *Guardian*, April 3. http://www.theguardian
.com/world/2013/apr/03/mexico-drugs-blog-del-narco.

del Bosque, Melissa, and Jazmine Ulloa. 2014. "Bloodlines: How the Scion
of a Texas Horse Racing Empire Became an Informant on Mexico's Most
Feared Cartel." *Texas Observer*, August 7. http://www.texasobserver.org
/bloodlines-how-the-scion-of-a-texas-horse-racing-empire-became-an
-informant-on-mexicos-most-feared-cartel.

DiColo, Jerry A., and Tom Fowler. 2012. "Exxon: 'Losing Our Shirts' on
Natural Gas." *Wall Street Journal*, June 27. http://online.wsj.com/news
/articles/SB10001424052702303561504577492501026260464.

Dorantes, David. 2014. "Oil Sir, Welcome to Tamaulipas." *El Financiero*,
April 8. http://www.elfinanciero.com.mx/monterrey/oil-sir-welcome-to
-tamaulipas.html.

Dufort, Philippe. 2014. "The Dual Function of Violence in Civil Wars: The
Case of Colombia." *Colombia Internacional* 81: 205–235.

Dyer, Dwight, and Daniel Sachs. 2013. "Los Zetas' Spawn: The Long Afterlife
of Mexico's Most Ruthless Drug Gang." *Foreign Affairs*, August 5. http://
www.foreignaffairs.com/articles/139626/dwight-dyer-and-daniel-sachs
/los-zetas-spawn.

Egremy, Nydia. 2007. "Comando del Norte engulle a México." *Contralínea*, January 1. http://www.contralinea.com.mx/archivo/2007/enero/htm
/comando_norte_mexico.htm.

———. 2010. "Fuerzas armadas mexicanas se alinean al Comando Norte."
Contralínea, May 2. http://contralinea.info/archivo-revista/index.php
/2010/05/02/fuerzas-armadas-mexicanas-se-alinean-al-comando-norte/.

El Bravo (staff). 2011. "Hayan yacimientos frente a la playa." *El Bravo*, August 11. http://www.skyscrapercity.com/showthread.php?t=804136&page
=78.

El Diario de Coahuila (staff). 2013. "AHMSA apuesta al gas shale en México." *El Diario de Coahuila*, June 20. http://www.eldiariodecoahuila
.com.mx/activos/2013/6/20/ahmsa-apuesta-shale-mexico-370515.html.

El Economista (staff). 2010. "Financia IP 'Grupo Rudo' Contra el Crimen en NL: Fernández Garza." *El Economista*, February 26. http://
eleconomista.com.mx/seguridad-publica/2010/02/26/financia-ip-grupo
-rudo-contra-crimen-nl-fernandez-garza.

El Universal (staff). 2010. "Mauricio Fernández disuelve Grupo 'Rudo.'" *El
Universal*, April 21. http://www.eluniversal.com.mx/notas/674593.html.

———. 2012. "Comando Norte apoya estrategia militar en México." *El Universal*, March 13. http://www.eluniversal.com.mx/notas/835766.html.

———. 2013. "El ocaso de los Zetas?: Áreas de influencia." *El Universal*,
September 6. http://www.eluniversal.com.mx/graficos/graficosanimados12
/EU-LosZetas/influencia.html.

Embassy of the United States in Mexico. 2014. "Ambassador Applauds New

Rail Bridge across U.S.-Mexican Border." Press release, September 12. https://mx.usembassy.gov/ambassador-applauds-new-rail-bridge-across -u-s-mexican-border.

Escalante, Fernando. 2009. "¿Puede México ser Colombia?: Violencia, narco-tráfico y estado." *Nueva Sociedad* 220: 84–96.

Estévez, Dolia. 2014. "Booking Oil Reserves Is an 'Attractive Incentive' for Foreign Companies in Mexico, Says U.S." *Forbes*, September 4. http://www.forbes.com/sites/doliaestevez/2014/09/04/booking-oil-reserves-is -an-attractive-incentive-for-foreign-companies-in-mexico-says-u-s.

Estrop, Armando. 2013. "Desde E.U. les dictan la reforma." *Reporte Índigo*, December 10. http://www.reporteindigo.com/reporte/mexico/desde -eu-les-dictan-la-reforma.

Etcharren, Laura. 2006. "Maras, Kaibiles y Zetas." *Offnews.info*, June 29. http://www.offnews.info/verArticulo.php?contenidoID=5003.

Evans, Gary, Peter D. Scott, and Maureen Farrell. 2010. "Homeland Security Contracts KBR to Build Detention Centers in the U.S." *Project Censored*, April 29. http://projectcensored.org/14-homeland-security-contracts-kbr -to-build-detention-centers-in-the-us.

Fausset, Richard, and Cecilia Sánchez. 2014. "Mexico Official Says Some Vigilante Arms Supplied by Drug Cartel." *Los Angeles Times*, January 30. http://www.latimes.com/world/worldnow/la-fg-wn-mexico-vigilante -drug-cartel-20140130-story.html#axzz2zadFY9xO.

Fearon, James. 2007. "Iraq's Civil War." *Foreign Affairs* (March/April). http://www.foreignaffairs.com/articles/62443/james-d-fearon/iraqs-civil-war.

Federal Bureau of Investigation (FBI). 2012. "Jury Convicts Gulf Cartel Plaza Boss." *U.S. Attorney's Office, Southern District of Texas*, September 28. http://www.fbi.gov/sanantonio/press-releases/2012/jury-convicts-gulf -cartel-plaza-boss.

Federal Government of Mexico. Office of the Presidency. 2005. "Ordena Presidente Vicente Fox puesta en marcha del 'Operativo México Seguro' contra el crimen organizado." *Presidency of Mexico*, June 11. http://fox .presidencia.gob.mx/actividades/orden/?contenido=18872.

———. 2010. "Base de datos de fallecimientos ocurridos por presunta rivali-dad delincuencial." http://www.presidencia.gob.mx/base-de-datos-defalle cimientos (no longer available).

Fernández Menéndez, Jorge. 2007. *De Los Maras a Los Zetas: De Colombia a Chicago: Los secretos del narcotráfico de Colombia a Chicago*. Mexico City: Grijalbo-Mondadori.

Fifield, Anna. 2013. "Contractors Reap $138bn from Iraq War." *Financial Times*, March 18. http://www.ft.com/intl/cms/s/0/7f435f04-8c05-11e2 -b001-00144feabdc0.html#axzz3D4PaNtnl.

Figueroa, Yolanda. 1996. *El capo del Golfo: Vida y captura de Juan García Ábrego*. Mexico City: Grijalbo.

Flores, Carlos A. 2013a. *Historias de polvo y sangre: Génesis y evolución del tráfico de drogas en el estado de Tamaulipas*. Mexico City: Centro de In-vestigaciones y Estudios Superiores en Antropología Social (CIESAS).

———. 2013b. "Political Protection and the Origins of the Gulf Cartel." In *A War That Can't Be Won: Binational Perspectives on the War on Drugs*, edited by Tony Payán, Kathleen Staudt, and Z. Anthony Kruszewski, 119–148. Tucson: Arizona University Press.

Forsyth, Jim. 2013. "Mexican Drug Cartel Money Laundering Trial Begins in Texas." *Reuters*, April 15. http://www.reuters.com/article/2013/04/15/us-usa-drugcartel-trial-idUSBRE93E15520130415.

Friedman, George. 2008. "Mexico: On the Road to a Failed State?" *Stratfor*, May 13. http://www.stratfor.com/weekly/mexico_road_failed_state.

Friesendorf, Cornelius. 2011. "Paramilitarization and Security Sector Reform: The Afghan National Police." *International Peacekeeping* 18, no. 1: 79–95.

Frontera NorteSur. 2014. "Border Narco War Returns." *Frontera NorteSur*, April 16. http://fnsnews.nmsu.edu/border-narco-war-returns.

Gagne, David. 2014. "Announced Zetas, Gulf Alliance Could Change Mexico's Criminal Landscape." *InSight Crime*, November 12. http://www.insightcrime.org/news-briefs/new-zetas-gulf-cartel-alliance-in-mexico.

García, Imelda. 2014. "Redes sociales, el otro campo de acción de las autodefensas." *ADN Político*, January 15. http://www.adnpolitico.com/gobierno/2014/01/14/redes-sociales-el-otro-campo-de-batalla-de-las-autodefensas.

García, Jacobo G., and María Verza. 2013. "México y EEUU cambian el discurso." *El Mundo*, February 5. http://www.elmundo.es/america/2013/05/02/mexico/1367476168.html.

García, Michelle, and Ignacio Alvarado. 2014. "Closer Look at Massacre in Mexico Reveals Glimpse of Corruption." *Al Jazeera America*, July 5, 2014. http://america.aljazeera.com/articles/2014/7/5/closer-look-at-massacreinmexicorevealsglimpseofcorruption.html.

Genbeta.com (staff). 2011. "Los Zetas secuestran a un activista de anonymous." Genbeta.com, October 30. http://www.genbeta.com/activismo-online/los-zetas-secuestran-a-un-activista-de-anonymous?utm_source=twitterfeed&utm_medium=twitter.

Gil Olmos, José. 2011. "'Los Matazetas' o el cogobierno del crimen organizado." *Proceso*, September 28. http://www.proceso.com.mx/?p=282649.

———. 2013. "Autodefensa civil, en el filo de lo paramilitar." *Proceso*, February 23. http://www.proceso.com.mx/?p=334505.

———. 2014. "La guerra entre michoacanos." *Proceso*, January 22. http://www.proceso.com.mx/?p=363015.

Goldwyn, David L., Neil R. Brown, and Megan Reilly Cayten. 2014. *Mexico's Energy Reform: Ready to Launch*. Washington, DC: Atlantic Council.

Gómez, Francisco. 2008. "Los 'Zetas' por Dentro: Los entrenan en Coahuila." *Vanguardia*, August 17. http:// www.vanguardia.com.mx/ (article no longer available).

Gómez, Francisco, and Alberto Torres. 2011. "Lucha encarnizada por las plazas." *El Universal*, July 12. http://www.eluniversal.com.mx/estados/81170.html.

Gómez Urrutia, Napoleón. 2013. "En Aquila: Empresa minera que alienta el conflicto social." *La Jornada*, August 22. http://www.jornada.unam.mx/2013/08/22/opinion/019a1pol.

González, Nayeli. 2015. "Pemex ya no usará ductos para gasolinas; se enfrenta a delincuencia." *Excélsior*, February 18. http://www.excelsior.com.mx/nacional/2015/02/18/1008966.

Government of Tamaulipas. 2014a. *Agenda energética de Tamaulipas*. Ciudad Victoria: Government of Tamaulipas.

——. 2014b. "Aseguran agua para desarrollo energético." September 11. http://tamaulipas.gob.mx/2014/09/aseguran-agua-para-desarrollo-energetico.

——. 2014c. "Impulsa la SSPE 'Rescate de Predios' en Tamaulipas." August 13. http://tamaulipas.gob.mx/2014/08/impulsa-la-sspe-rescate-de-predios-en-tamaulipas.

——. 2014d. "Impulsará la Reforma Energética la inversión extranjera." September 14. http://tamaulipas.gob.mx/2014/09/impulsara-la-reforma-energetica-la-inversion-extranjera.

Grant, Will. 2014. "Michoacan: Mexico's Failed State?" *BBC News*, January 17. http://www.bbc.co.uk/news/world-latin-america-25774430.

Gray, Vanessa J. 2008. The New Research on Civil Wars: Does It Help Us Understand the Colombian Conflict? *Latin American Politics and Society* 50, no. 3: 63–91.

Grayson, George W. 2009. *Mexico: Narco-Violence and a Failed State?* New Brunswick, NJ: Transaction Publishers.

——. 2013. *The Impact of President Felipe Calderón's War on Drugs on the Armed Forces: The Prospects for Mexico's "Militarization" and Bilateral Relations*. Carlisle Barracks, PA: Strategic Studies Institute, US Army War College.

——. 2014a. "Cartel Violence Anew in Mexico and Los Zetas Push for a Comeback." *Mexidata.info*, May 19. http://www.mexidata.info/id3889.html.

——. 2014b. *The Evolution of Los Zetas in Mexico and Central America: Sadism as an Instrument of Cartel Warfare*. Carlisle Barracks, PA: Strategic Studies Institute, US Army War College.

Grayson, George W., and Samuel Logan. 2012. *The Executioner's Men: Los Zetas, Rogue Soldiers, Criminal Entrepreneurs, and the Shadow State They Created*. New Brunswick, NJ: Transaction Publishers.

Grillo, Ioan. 2011. *El Narco: Inside Mexico's Criminal Insurgency*. New York: Bloomsbury Press.

Guerrero, Eduardo. 2010. "La guerra por Tamaulipas." *Nexos*, August 1. http://www.nexos.com.mx/?p=13889.

——. 2012a. "Epidemias de violencia." *Nexos*, July 1. http://www.nexos.com.mx/?p=14884.

——. 2012b. "La estrategia fallida." *Nexos*, December 1. http://www.nexos.com.mx/?p=15083.

——. 2014a. "El dominio del miedo." *Nexos*, July 1. http://www.nexos.com.mx/?p=21671.

——. 2014b. "La dictadura criminal." *Nexos*, April 1. http://www.nexos.com.mx/?p=20026.

Guillén, Alejandra. 2012. "La fiebre del hierro ilegal." *Verdebandera Perio-*

dismo Ambiental, November 27. http://verdebandera.com.mx/la-fiebre
-del-hierro-ilegal.

Gurney, Kyra. 2014. "Mexico Criminal Groups Running Sophisticated
Distribution Networks for Stolen Oil." *InSight Crime*, June 18. http://
www.insightcrime.org/news-briefs/mexico-criminal-groups-running
-sophisticated-distribution-networks-for-stolen-oil.

Haahr, Kathryn. 2015. "Addressing the Concerns of the Oil Industry: Security
Challenges in Northeastern Mexico and Government Responses." Mexico
Institute, Working Paper, January. Washington, DC: Wilson Center.

Hale, Gary. 2010. "A 'Failed State' in Mexico: Tamaulipas Declares Itself Ungovernable." James A. Baker III Institute for Public Policy, Working Paper
Series, July 26. Houston: James Baker Institute, Rice University.

Halliburton. 2015. "Corporate Profile." About Us. http://www.halliburton
.com/en-US/about-us/corporate-profile/default.page?node-id=hgeyxt5p.

———. 2016. "Halliburton and Baker Hughes Announce Termination of
Merger Agreement." Press release, May 1. http://www.halliburton.com
/public/news/pubsdata/press_release/2016/halliburton-baker-hughes
-terminate-merger.html.

Harrup, Anthony, and David Luhnow. 2011. "Bandas Criminales Expanden
el Robo de Combustible de Pemex." *Wall Street Journal*, June 17. http://
online.wsj.com/article/SB10001424052702303823104576392220037322
128.html.

Hernández, Daniel. 2013. "Facebook Page in Mexico Draws Attention for
Post on Security Risks." *Los Angeles Times*, February 19. http://articles
.latimes.com/2013/feb/19/world/la-fg-wn-mexico-facebook-page-security
-20130218.

Hernández, Luis G. 2014. "@ValorxTamaulipas: La otra autodefensa." *Emeequis* 321: 24–33.

Hodge, Nathan. 2011. "Company Once Known as Blackwater Ditches Xe
for Yet Another New Name." *Wall Street Journal*, December 12. http://
online.wsj.com/news/articles/SB10001424052970204319004577089021757803802.

Hultman, Lisa. 2012. "Attacks on Civilians in Civil War: Targeting the Achil-
les Heel of Democratic Governments." *International Interactions* 38,
no. 2: 164–181.

Isacson, Adam, Lisa Haugaard, Abigail Poe, Sarah Kinosian, and George
Withers. 2013. *Time to Listen: Trends in U.S. Security Assistance to Latin
America and the Caribbean.* Washington, DC: Center for International
Policy (CIP); Latin America Working Group Education Fund (LAWGEF);
Washington Office on Latin America (WOLA).

Jalife-Rahme, Alfredo. 2014. *Muerte de Pemex y suicidio de México.* Mexico
City: Orfila Valentini.

Kalyvas, Stathis N. 2001. "'New' and 'Old' Civil Wars: A Valid Distinction?
(Research Note)." *World Politics* 54 (October): 99–118.

———. 2006. *The Logic of Violence in Civil War.* New York: Cambridge
University Press.

———. 2007. "Civil Wars." In *The Oxford Handbook of Comparative Poli-*

tics, edited by Carles Boix and Susan C. Stokes, 416–434. Oxford: Oxford University Press.

Kalyvas, Stathis, and Ana Arjona. 2005. "Paramilitarismo: Una perspectiva teórica." In *El poder paramilitar*, edited by Alfredo Rangel, 25–45. Bogotá: Planeta.

Knox, Colin. 2002. "'See No Evil, Hear No Evil': Insidious Paramilitary Violence in Northern Ireland." *British Journal of Criminology* 42, no. 1: 164–185.

Krauss, Clifford. 2014. "A New American Oil Bonanza." *New York Times*, August 28. http://mobile.nytimes.com/2014/08/29/business/energy-envi ronment/shale-oil-in-texas-keeps-gas-prices-affordable.html?referrer =&_r=0.

Lajous, Adrián. 2004. "La cuenca de Burgos y los contrato de servicios múltiples." *La Jornada*, March 17. http://www.jornada.unam.mx/2004/03/17 /per-cuenca.html.

Lara, Catalina. 2014a. "Desaparecidos: Nadie sabe cuántos son." *El Universal*, October 5, 2014. http://www.eluniversal.com.mx/periodismo-datos /2014/ni-el-gobierno-sabe-cuantos-son-95415.html.

———. 2014b. "RPNED actualiza información." *El Universal*, November 24, 2014 (no longer available).

Lepic, Arthur. 2005. "Exxon-Mobil, proveedor oficial del imperio." *Voltaire Net*, April 16. http://www.voltairenet.org/article124563.html.

Libera (Pace Per Il Messico). 2012. *Messico, la guerra invisibile: Storie, cifre e affari dei cartelli criminali dei narcotrafficanti*. Rome, Italy: Libera.

Linares, Raúl, and Tania L. Montalvo. 2016. "Pemex perdió 300 millones de dólares en juicios por robo de combustible en Estados Unidos." *Animal Político*, November 16. http://www.animalpolitico.com/2016/11/pemex -robo-combustible-narcotrafico.

Llamas, Mercedes. 2014. "¿Autodefensa? ¿Paramilitares? JODIDOS de todas formas." *SinEmbargo*, January 22. http://www.sinembargo.mx/opinion/22 -01-2014/20975.

Lu, Lingyu, and Cameron G. Thies. 2011. "Economic Grievances and the Severity of Civil War." *Civil Wars* 13, no. 3: 215–231.

Lund, Joshua. 2011. "The Poetics of Paramilitarism." *Revista Hispánica Moderna* 64, no. 1: 61–67.

Machuca, María F. 2014. "From Militarization to New Forms of Paramilitarism in Mexico." Master in Public Policy and Management (MPPM) Professional Report, University of Texas at Brownsville.

Macías, Teresa. 2013. "Invertirán 3mmdd en nuevo gasoducto." *Conexión Total*, February 5. http://conexiontotal.mx/2013/02/05/invertiran-3 -mmdd-en-nuevo-gasoducto (no longer available).

Manilla, Enrique. 2012. "Es municipio líder de hidrocarburos." *El Mañana*, August 16. http://www.elmanana.com/diario/noticia/san_fernando /tamaulpas/es_municipio_lider_de_hidrocarburos/1727453.

Mansfield, Edward D., and Jack Snyder. 2007. *Electing to Fight: Why Emerging Democracies Go to War*. Cambridge, MA: MIT Press.

Manwaring, Max G. 2010. *Gangs, Pseudo-militaries and Other Mercenar-*

ies: New Dynamics in Uncomfortable Wars. Norman: University of Oklahoma Press.

———. 2011. *A "New" Dynamic in the Western Hemisphere Security Environment: The Mexican Zetas and Other Private Armies.* CreateSpace Independent Publishing Platform. http://www.strategicstudiesinstitute.army .mil/pdffiles/pub940.pdf.

Martínez, Marco Antonio. 2014. "Escritor italiano acusa a trasnacionales de orquestar desapariciones en México, para adueñarse de riqueza." *SinEmbargo*, June 8. http://www.sinembargo.mx/08-06-2014/1017871.

Martínez, Sanjuana. 2011. "En la ruta de la muerte." *La Jornada*, April 17. http://www.jornada.unam.mx/2011/04/17/politica/006n1pol.

———. 2012. "Los Moreira y los narcoempresarios." *SinEmbargo*, October 29. http://www.sinembargo.mx/opinion/29-10-2012/10391.

———. 2013. "Matamoros y la violencia silenciada." *Hilo Directo*, November 12. http://hilodirecto.com.mx/matamoros-y-la-violencia-silenciada.

Martínez Huerta, David. 2014. "La reforma energética traerá desalojos y expropiaciones en 260 municipios, alertan investigadores y senadores." *SinEmbargo*, April 6. http://www.sinembargo.mx/06-04-2014/952404.

Mastrogiovanni, Federico. 2014. *Ni vivos ni muertos: La desaparición forzada en México como estrategia de terror.* Mexico City: Random House Mondadori.

Matich, Teresa. 2014. "On Iron Ore and Drug Lords: Mexico's Continued Battle with the Knights Templar." *Iron Investing News*, May 12. http:// resourceinvestingnews.com/70622-on-iron-ore-and-drug-lords-mexicos -continued-battle-with-the-knights-templar.html.

Mayorga, Patricia. 2014. "Narco 'ablandó' zona de Chihuahua rica en gas shale: Morena." *Proceso*, August 21. http://www.proceso.com.mx/?p =380107.

Mazzei, Julie. 2009. *Death Squads or Self-Defense Forces?: How Paramilitary Groups Emerge and Challenge Democracy in Latin America.* Chapel Hill: University of North Carolina Press.

McCarthy, Erin. 2014. "Halliburton Names New President, Profit Rises 20%." *Wall Street Journal*, July 21. http://online.wsj.com/articles /halliburton-names-new-president-profit-rises-20-1405942988.

McCleskey, Claire O'Neill. 2013. "200,000 People Involved in Mexico 'Death Squads': Congressman." *InSight Crime*, July 4. http://www .insightcrime.org/news-briefs/200000-people-involved-in-mexico-death -squads-congressman.

McCrummen, Stephanie. 2013. "In Mexico, Self-Defense Groups Battle a Cartel." *Washington Post*, September 9. http://www.washingtonpost.com /world/the_americas/in-the-hills-of-michoacan-self-defense-groups -battle-a-mexican-drug-cartel/2013/09/09/6947e47a-119f-11e3-a2b3 -5e107edf9897_story.html.

McCumber Hearst, David. 2015. "Another Eagle Ford South of the Border?" *Laredo Morning Times*, January 31. http://m.lmtonline.com/business /article_9c9a3a5c-a9a2-11e4-aace-076fd54814a3.html?mode=jqm.

Mejía, Camilo. 2014. "Rise in Tamaulipas Kidnappings Points to Lack of

Mexico Govt Control." *InSight Crime*, August 21. http://insightcrime .com/news-briefs/rise-tamaulipas-kidnappings-lack-mexico-govt-control.

Mendieta, Eduardo. 2014. "Violencia en Tamaulipas es como un parte de guerra: Investigador." *Milenio*, August 12. http://www.milenio.com /monterrey/inseguridad_Tamaulipas-violencia_Tamaulipas-guerra_narco _Tamaulipas_0_352764740.html.

Mercier, Gilbert. 2011. "Iraq War: US Troops are Out, But Blackwater and Halliburton Will Stay." *News Junkie Post*, December 18. http:// newsjunkiepost.com/2011/12/18/iraq-war-us-troops-are-out-but-black water-and-halliburton-will-stay.

Merino, José, Jessica Zarkin, and Eduardo Fierro. 2015. "Desaparecidos." *Nexos*, January 1. http://www.nexos.com.mx/?p=23811.

Mexican Geological Survey (SGM). 2010. *Potencial de hierro en México: Estados de Jalisco, Colima, Michoacán y Guerrero*. Mexico City: Secretary of Energy, Government of Mexico.

———. 2011. *Panorama minero del estado de Tamaulipas*. Mexico City: Secretary of Energy, Government of Mexico.

———. 2013. *Panorama minero del estado de Michoacán*. Mexico City: Secretary of Energy, Government of Mexico.

Mexico. Executive Secretariat of the National System of Public Safety (SESNSP). 2016. *Informe de víctimas de homicidio, secuestro y extorsión 2015*. Mexico City: SEGOB.

———. National Commission of Hydrocarbons (CNH). 2012. *Dictamen del Proyecto Integral de Burgos*. Mexico City: Government of Mexico.

———. National Institute of Statistics and Geography (INEGI). 2007. *Censo agropecuario 2007: VIII censo agrícola, ganadero y forestal 2007*. Aguascalientes, Mexico: INEGI.

———. National Registry of Data of Missing or Disappeared Persons (RNPED). 2015. *Database of Missing or Disappeared Persons, 2006–2015*. Mexico City: RNPED, SESNSP, SEGOB. https://rnped.segob.gob.mx.

———. Secretariat of Communications and Transportation (SCT). 2014. "El Puerto de Lázaro Cárdenas será el más grande de América Latina: Ruiz de Teresa." Press release, January 12. http://www.sct.gob.mx/despliega -noticias/article/el-puerto-de-lazaro-cardenas-sera-el-mas-grande-de -america-latina-ruiz-de-teresa.

———. Secretariat of Energy (SENER). 2014a. "La reforma energética establece condiciones de equidad para el uso y ocupación de la tierra: Pedro Joaquín Coldwell." Press release, August 27. https://www.gob.mx/sener /prensa/la-reforma-energetica-establece-condiciones-de-equidad-para-el -uso-y-ocupacion-de-la-tierra-pedro-joaquin-coldwell?idiom=es.

———. 2014b. "Promulgación de la reforma energética. Leyes Secundarias." Press release, August 11. http://www.energia.gob.mx/webSener/leyes _Secundarias (no longer available).

———. Secretariat of the Navy (SEMAR). 2012. "El Comando Norte de Estados Unidos de América entrega reconocimiento al Secretario de Marina." Press release 227, November 27. http://2006-2012.semar.gob.mx /component/content/article/2293-comunicado-227-2012.html.

Mexico Gulf Reporter. 2011. "DEA Says the Dreaded 'Derecho de Piso' Has Arrived in the United States. *Mexico Gulf Reporter*, 24 December. http:// mexicogulfreporter.blogspot.com/2011/12/dea-says-the-dreaded-derecho -de-piso.html.

Meza, José Manuel. 2010. "Cuenca de Burgos: Riqueza abajo, miseria arriba." *Contralínea*, June 1. http://contralinea.info/archivo-revista/index .php/2010/06/01/cuenca-de-burgos-riqueza-abajo-miseria-arriba.

Michel, Víctor Hugo. 2014. "Riqueza estilo saudí . . . A una hora de Ta- maulipas." *Telediario*, January 21. http://www.telediario.mx/politica /riqueza-estilo-saudi-a-una-hora-de-tamaulipas.

Milenio (staff). 2015. "Las empresas atrás del lavado de dinero de Los Ze- tas." *Milenio*, March 4. http://www.milenio.com/policia/empresas_lavado _dinero_Los_Zetas-Z42_Omar_Trevino_Morales-Los_Zetas_lavan _dinero_0_475152728.html.

Miroff, Nick. 2013. "Soldiers Re-occupy Mexico's Hot Land." *Washing- ton Post*, May 21. http://www.washingtonpost.com/world/the_americas /soldiers-re-occupy-mexicos-hot-land/2013/05/21/b0f694ae-c25a-11e2 -9642-a56177f1cdf7_story.html.

Molloy, Molly. 2013. "The Mexican Undead: Toward a New History of the 'Drug War' Killing Fields." *Small Wars Journal*, August 21. http:// smallwarsjournal.com/jrnl/art/the-mexican-undead-toward-a-new -history-of-the-"drug-war"-killing-fields.

Molloy, Molly, and Charles Bowden, eds. 2010. *El Sicario: The Autobiogra- phy of a Mexican Assassin*. New York: Nation Books.

Molzahn, Cory, Viridiana Ríos, and David A. Shirk. 2012. *Drug Violence in Mexico: Data and Analysis through 2011*. San Diego: Trans-Border Insti- tute, University of San Diego.

Monaghan, Rachel, and Peter Shirlow. 2011. "Forward to the Past?: Loyal- ist Paramilitarism in Northern Ireland since 1994." *Studies in Conflict and Terrorism* 34, no. 8: 649–665.

Monreal, Ricardo. 2013. *Escuadrones de la muerte en México*. Mexico City: House of Representatives.

Monroy-Hernández, Andrés. 2013. "The New War Correspondents: The Rise of Civic Media Curation in Urban Warfare." *Social Media Collec- tive Research Blog*, January 8. http://socialmediacollective.org/2013/01/08 /civic-media-curation-in-urban-warfare.

———. 2014. "Facebook 'Courage' Page versus the Knights Templar's Car- tel." *Social Media Collective Research Blog*, March 3. http://social mediacollective.org/2014/03/03/facebook-courage-page-versus-the-knight -templars-cartel.

Monroy-Hernández, Andrés, Emre Kiciman, Danah Boyd, and Scott Counts. 2012. "Narcotweets: Social Media in Wartime." Proceedings of the Amer- ican Association for Artificial Intelligence (AAAI) International Con- ference on Weblogs and Social Media (ICWSM '12), June 4–7. http:// research.microsoft.com/pubs/160480/ICWSM12-093.pdf.

Montes, Juan, and Dudley Althaus. 2014. "Drug Cartels Will Challenge En- ergy Investors As Mexico Opens Sector to Outsiders the Gangs Present

Hurdle." *Wall Street Journal*, December 18. http://www.wsj.com/articles
/mexican-drug-cartels-pose-challenge-to-energy-investors-1418936709.

Moon of Alabama. 2011. "U.S. Special Operations in Mexico." *moonof
alabama.org* (blog), October 25. http://www.moonofalabama.org/2011
/10/us-special-operations-in-mexico.html.

Moreno, Felipe. 2008. "Azul 'Z': La guerra de los generales en el ejército de
México." *Despertar de Tamaulipas*, January 25. http://www.despertarde
tamaulipas.com/nota/87978 (no longer available).

Mullins, C. W., and D. L. Rothe. 2008. *Blood, Power, and Bedlam: Violations of International Criminal Law in Post-Colonial Africa*. New York:
Peter Lang Publishing.

Muñoz, Juan M. 1996. "México detiene y entrega a Estados Unidos a su prin-
cipal narcotraficante." January 16. http://elpais.com/diario/1996/01/16
/internacional/821746813_850215.html.

MVS Research Unit. 2014a. "Empresa de Pancho Colorado, Ligada a los 'Zetas', Operaba en Canadá . . . y en Pemex" *Aristegui Noticias*, September 2.
http://aristeguinoticias.com/0209/mexico/empresa-de-pancho-colorado
-ligada-a-los-zetas-operaba-en-canada-y-en-pemex.

———. 2014b. "Expediente de Pancho Colorado: 'Zetas' pagaron protec-
ción en Veracruz." *Aristegui Noticias*, September 9. http://aristeguinoticias
.com/0909/mexico/expediente-de-pancho-colorado-zetas-pagaron
-proteccion-en-veracruz.

Nájar, Alberto. 2005. "Dos toneladas de coca, en el inicio de la disputa por
Nuevo Laredo: La guerra del narco por dentro." *La Jornada*, July 10.
http://www.jornada.unam.mx/2005/07/10/mas-najar.html.

———. 2006. "Otra guerra de narcos este 2006: La sangre que falta por co-
rrer." *La Jornada*, January 8. http://www.jornada.unam.mx/2006/01/08
/mas-najar.html.

Nava, José. 2011. "Gagging the Media: The Paramilitarization of Drug Trafficking Organizations and Its Consequences on the Freedom of Press in
the Texas-Tamaulipas Border Region." M.A. thesis, University of Texas at
Brownsville.

———. 2013. "Trickling Policies: Mexico's 'New' Paramilitarism." MPPM
Professional Report, University of Texas at Brownsville.

Navarro, Santiago. 2014. "Michoacán Self-Defense Groups Celebrate 1st
Anniversary." *Americas Program*, March 5. http://www.cipamericas.org
/archives/11586.

Nelsen, Aaron. 2014. "Fear Spreads in Twitter Community in Mexico."
San Antonio Express-News, October 26. http://www.mysanantonio.com
/news/us-world/border-mexico/article/After-kidnapping-fear-spreads-in
-Reynosa-twitter-5849248.php.

———. 2015. "Spasm of Intense Violence Engulfs Tamaulipas." *San Antonio Express-News*, February 4. http://www.expressnews.com/news/local
/article/Spasm-of-intense-violence-engulfs-Tamaulipas-6063167.php.

Nieto, Pedro R., and Pablo R. García. 2008. "Las autodefensas y el paramilitarismo en Colombia (1964–2006)." *CONfines* 4, no. 7: 43–52.

Ochoa, Jorge O. 2005. "Las bandas del narco en México." jorgeoctavio

ochoa.wordpress.com (blog), June 24. http://jorgeoctavioochoa.wordpress
.com/2005/06/24/las-bandas-del-narco-en-mexico.

Offnews.info (staff). 2013. "Era del shale: Transformaciones en Estados Unidos." *Offnews.info*, August 1. http://www.offnews.info/verArticulo.php
?contenidoID=46536.

O'Keefe, Brian. 2012. "Exxon apuesta todo al shale gas." *CNN Expansión*.
April 18. http://www.cnnexpansion.com/negocios/2012/04/17/la-gran
-nueva-apuesta-de-exxon.

O'Neil, Shannon K., and James S. Taylor. 2014. "A Primer: Mexico Energy
Reforms." *Vianovo*, March 16. http://vianovo.com/news/a-primer-mexico
-energy-reforms.

O'Reilly, Andrew. 2012. "Mexico's Drug Death Toll Double What Reported,
Expert Argues." *Fox New Latino*, August 10. http://latino.foxnews.com
/latino/news/2012/08/10/mexico-drug-death-toll-double-what-reported
-expert-argues.

Ortega, Yemeli. 2015. "New Gang on the Rise in Troubled Mexico: Los
Viagras." *AFP*, January 22. http://news.yahoo.com/gang-rise-troubled
-mexico-los-viagras-212415104.html.

Osorno, Diego E. 2012. *La guerra de los Zetas: Viaje por la frontera de la necropolítica*. Mexico City: Grijalbo.

———. 2013. "Entrevista con un Zeta." *Gatopardo*, October 1. http://www
.gatopardo.com/reportajes/entrevista-con-un-zeta.

———. 2014. "How a Mexican Cartel Demolished a Town, Incinerated Hundreds of Victims, and Got Away with It." *Vice News*, July 10. https://news
.vice.com/article/how-a-mexican-cartel-demolished-a-town-incinerated
-hundreds-of-victims-and-got-away-with-it.

Otero, Silvia. 2007. "'Las Estacas,' escoltas de los 'Capos' del Golfo." *El Universal*, December 17. http://www.eluniversal.com.mx/nacion/156552.
html.

Pachico, Elyssa. 2014. "Testimony Describes Zetas' Ties to Mexico Governor." *InSight Crime*, September 11. http://www.insightcrime.org/news
-briefs/testimony-zetas-ties-veracruz-mexico-governor.

Padgett, Humberto. 2013a. "¿Vive el líder de la mafia michoacana?" *Sin-
Embargo*, July 30. http://www.sinembargo.mx/30-07-2013/703683.

———. 2013b. "Yo maté con el Z-40: La historia de 'Karen.'" *SinEmbargo*,
July 17. http://www.sinembargo.mx/17-07-2013/689011.

Padilla, Jesús. 2015. "¿Quién será el jefe de Los Zetas?" *Reporte Índigo*,
March 13. http://www.reporteindigo.com/reporte/monterrey/quien-sera
-el-jefe-de-los-zetas.

Page, David. 2012. "La revolución que cambiará el mapa energético mundial." *Expansión*, November 15. http://www.expansion.com/2012/11/14
/empresas/energia/1352908050.html.

Paley, Dawn. 2011. "Off the Map in Mexico." *Nation* 292, no. 21: 20–24.

———. 2013. "Repressive Memories: Terror, Insurgency, and the Drug War."
Occupied London no. 5: 22–32.

———. 2014. *Drug War Capitalism*. Oakland, CA: AK Press.

Partlow, Joshua. 2015. "What's behind Mexico's Military Buying Binge?

Washington Post, June 15. http://www.washingtonpost.com/news/world views/wp/2015/06/15/whats-behind-mexicos-military-buying-binge.

Payán, Tony. 2016. *The Three U.S.-Mexico Border Wars: Drugs, Immigration, and Homeland Security*. 2nd ed. New York: Praeger.

Payán, Tony, and Guadalupe Correa-Cabrera. 2014a. "Energy Reform and Security in Northeastern Mexico." Mexico Center, Issue Brief, May 6. Houston: James Baker Institute, Rice University.

———. 2014b. "Land Ownership and Use under Mexico's Energy Reform." Mexico Center, Issue Brief, October 29. Houston: James Baker Institute, Rice University.

Pemex. 2015. "Pemex Announces the Discovery of New Oil Deposits in the Gulf of Mexico." Press release, June 10. http://www.pemex.com/en/press _room/press_releases/Paginas/2015-053-national.aspx.

Peña Nieto, Enrique. 2014. "Modernización y equipamiento del Puerto de Lázaro Cárdenas." Mexico's Presidency (blog), September 10. https://www .gob.mx/presidencia/articulos/modernizacion-y-equipamiento-del-puerto -de-lazaro-cardenas.

Pérez, Ana Lilia. 2010a. *Camisas azules, manos negras: El saqueo de Pemex desde los Pinos*. Mexico City: Grijalbo Mondadori.

———. 2010b. "Crimen organizado somete a Pemex." *Contralínea*, July 25. http://contralinea.info/archivo-revista/index.php/2010/07/25/crimen -organizado-somete-a-pemex.

———. 2011a. *El Cartel Negro: Cómo el crimen organizada se ha apoderado de Pemex*. Mexico City: Grijalbo Mondadori.

———. 2011b. "México, paraíso de transnacionales del soborno." *Contralínea*, October 12. http://contralinea.info/archivo-revista/index.php/2011 /10/12/mexico-paraiso-de-trasnacionales-del-soborno.

———. 2012. "Ordeña de gas condensado en la Cuenca de Burgos." *Contralínea*, May 8. http://contralinea.info/archivo-revista/index.php/2012/05/08 /ordena-de-gas-condensado-en-la-cuenca-de-burgos.

Pérez, Juan C. 2014. "¿Qué pasó con los Zetas, el cartel más temido de México?" *BBC Mundo*, May 19. http://www.bbc.co.uk/mundo/noticias /2014/05/140518_mexico_cartel_zetas_que_paso_jcps.

Pérez, Santiago, and José de Córdoba. 2014. "Executive Slaying Sparks New Fears. Murder in Mexico: Drug Cartel behind Killing of Foreign Company Official, Intelligence Officials Say." *Wall Street Journal*, January 10. http:// www.wsj.com/articles/SB10001424052702304887104579304332314623 614.

Petrich, Blanche. 2011. "Para EU, la lucha contra el crimen en Tamaulipas 'es insostenible.'" *La Jornada*, June 14. http://wikileaks.jornada.com.mx /notas/para-eu-la-lucha-contra-el-crimen-en-tamaulipas-es-insostenible.

Pijamasurf (staff). 2011a. "Alfredo Jalife-Rahme analiza plan de Estados Unidos de obtener el petróleo mexicano escenificando guerra contra el narco." *Pijamasurf*, March 9. http://pijamasurf.com/2011/03/alfredo-jalife-rahme -analiza-el-plan-de-estados-unidos-de-obtener-el-petroleo-mexicano -escenificando-guerra-contra-el-narco/.

———. 2011b. "El verdadero motivo detrás de la guerra contra el narco (la invasión silenciosa de un estado fallido)." *Pijamasurf*, February 3. http://pijamasurf.com/2011/02/el-verdadero-motivo-detras-de-la-guerra-contra-el-narco-blackwater-y-el-plan-para-un-estado-fallido/.

Pindar, Ian. 2013. "Private Empire: ExxonMobil and American Power by Steve Coll—Review." *Guardian*, May 31. http://www.theguardian.com/books/2013/may/31/private-empire-exxonmobil-book-review.

Pineda, Manuel. 2003. "La hidra del narco ajusta cuentas." *Contralínea*, July 14. http://www.contralinea.com.mx/c14/html/sociedad/la_hidra.html.

Porter, Michael E. 1980. *Competitive Strategy: Techniques for Analyzing Industries and Competitors*. New York: Free Press.

———. 2008. "The Five Competitive Forces That Shape Strategy." *Harvard Business Review* 86, no. 1: 78–93.

Proceso (staff). 2013a. "Difunden en YouTube supuesta ejecución de colaborador de Valor por Tamaulipas." *Proceso*, February 21. http://www.proceso.com.mx/?p=334226.

———. 2013b. "Grupo criminal quiere la cabeza del administrador de una página en Facebook." *Proceso*, February 13. http://www.proceso.com.mx/?p=333503.

———. 2013c. "Se extienden a 43 países los tentáculos de Los Zetas." *Proceso*, May 8. http://www.proceso.com.mx/?p=341387.

Rama, Anahi, Lizbeth Díaz, and Frank Jack Daniel. 2015. "Oro y narcotráfico, combinación que alimenta caos en estado mexicano de Guerrero." *Reuters*, December 6. http://lta.reuters.com/article/topNews/idLTAKBN0TP0LG20151206.

Ramírez, Jesús. 2013. "Los políticos mexicanos que son socios de petroleras extranjeras." *Vanguardia*, December 10. http://www.vanguardia.com.mx/lospoliticosmexicanosquesonsociosdepetrolerasextranjeras-1900041.html.

Ramírez, Julio. 2015. "Los Zetas: El cártel más golpeado." *Reporte Índigo*, August 5. http://www.reporteindigo.com/reporte/mexico/los-zetas-el-cartel-mas-golpeado.

Raphael, Sam. 2009. "Paramilitarism and State Terror in Colombia." In *Contemporary State Terrorism: Theory and Practice*, edited by Richard Jackson, Eamon Murphy, and Scott Poynting, 164–180. London: Routledge.

Ravelo, Ricardo. 2009. *Osiel: Vida y tragedia de un capo*. Mexico City: Grijalbo.

———. 2011. *El narco en México: Historia e historias de una guerra*. Mexico City: Grijalbo.

———. 2013. *Zetas: La franquicia criminal*. Mexico City: Ediciones B.

Redner, Harry. 1990. Beyond Marx-Weber: A Diversified and International Approach to the State. *Political Studies* 38, no. 4: 638–653.

Reforma/El Norte (staff). 2010. "Toma narco gigante-1: Controla grupo armado un pozo en Burgos." *Reforma/El Norte*, June 10: 1.

———. 2013. "Revelan en EU operación de Zetas." *Reforma/El Norte*, June 3: 8.

———. 2014. "Abre comisionado planes ante capo." *Reforma/El Norte*, February 8: 1.

Regoli, Natalie, and Brian Polley. 2014. "EnergyBuzz: Mexico's Energy Reform to Tackle Declining Production." *Texas Lawyer*, August 21. http://www.texaslawyer.com/home/id=1202667670164.

Resa Nestares, Carlos. 2004. "Nuevo Laredo: Crimen desorganizado." *El comercio de drogas ilegales en México—Nota de investigación*, January 2004. http://www.uam.es/personal_pdi/economicas/cresa/nota0104.pdf.

Reuters. 2015. "Mexico Pemex to Stop Moving Gasoline Via Pipeline to Curb Theft." February 17. http://www.reuters.com/article/2015/02/18/mexico-pemex-theft-idUSL1N0VS00X20150218.

Reyes, Itzel, and Mónica Villanueva. 2014. "Inundan al país fosas clandestinas." *24 Horas*, February 13. http://www.24-horas.mx/inundan-al-pais-fosas-clandestinas.

Reyes, José. 2009a. "DEA, FBI, PGR: Osiel controló Tamaulipas." *Contralínea*, August 23. http://contralinea.info/archivo-revista/index.php/2009/08/23/dea-fbi-pgr-osiel-controlo-tamaulipas.

———. 2009b. "Las operaciones secretas del cártel del Golfo." *Contralínea*, August 30. http://contralinea.info/archivo-revista/index.php/2009/08/30/las-operaciones-secretas-del-cartel-del-golfo.

———. 2014. "Caballeros Templarios, entrenados por Estados Unidos, Egipto e Israel." *Contralínea*, September 28. http://contralinea.info/archivo-revista/index.php/2014/09/28/caballeros-templarios-entrenado-estados-unidos-egipto-e-israel-familia-michoacana-guerra-inteligencia-trasiego-droga-lavado-de-dinero-expediente-pgr-martin-rosales-magana-testigo-protegid.

Reynowarrior. 2010. "La Barbie: Padre del narcoterrorismo en México." Daño Colateral (blog), December 7. http://reyno-warrior.blogspot.mx/2010/12/la-barbie-padre-del-narcoterrorismo-en.html.

Rio Grande Guardian (staff). 2014. "Escamilla: Burgos Basin Will Be Eight Times Bigger Than Eagle Ford Shale." *RGV Newswire*, August 21. http://riograndeguardian.com/escamilla-burgos-basin-will-be-8-times-bigger-than-eagle-ford-shale/.

Ríos, Viridiana, and Steven Dudley. 2013. "La marca Zeta." *Nexos*, September 1. http://www.nexos.com.mx/?p=15461.

Riva Palacio, Raymundo. 2012. "Coahuila se escribe con Z." *Vanguardia*, October 14. http://www.vanguardia.com.mx/columnas-coahuilaseescribe conzeta-1396212.html.

Rivera, Jesús. 2013. "La zona noreste del país, que abarca parte de los estados de Tamaulipas, Nuevo León y Coahuila, es de las más ricas a nivel mundial en yacimientos de gas shale." *La Prensa*, August 18. http://laprensa.mx/notas.asp?id=221432.

Robinson, Edward H. 2013. "The Distinction between State and Government." *Geography Compass* 7, no. 8: 556–566.

Rodríguez, Gerardo, and Asael Nuche. 2015. "¿Existe una agenda de seguridad nacional para la industria energética?" *Animal Político*, March 2. http://www.animalpolitico.com/blogueros-c-al-cubo/2015/03/02/existe-una-agenda-de-seguridad-nacional-para-la-industria-energetica.

Rodríguez, Julián. 2014. "Los Zetas son la franquicia criminal más violenta,

dice Ricardo Ravelo." *SinEmbargo*, February 3. http://www.sinembargo
.mx/03-02-2014/893059.

Rodríguez, Marco A. 2006. "El poder de los 'Zetas.'" Monografías.com 28.
http://www.monografias.com/trabajos28/poder-zetas/poder-zetas.shtml.

Rolston, Bill. 2005. "'An Effective Mask for Terror': Democracy, Death
Squads and Northern Ireland." *Crime, Law and Social Change* 44, no. 2:
181–203.

Rost, Nicolas. 2011. "Human Rights Violations, Weak States, and Civil
War." *Human Rights Review* 12, no. 4: 417–440.

Rubio, Laura. 2014. *Desplazamiento interno inducido por la violencia: Una
experiencia global, una realidad mexicana*. Mexico City: CMDPDH.

Saab, Bilal Y., and Alexandra W. Taylor. 2009. "Criminality and Armed
Groups: A Comparative Study of FARC and Paramilitary Groups in Colombia." *Studies in Conflict and Terrorism* 32, no. 6: 455–475.

Saldaña, Juan Diego, and Tony Payán. 2016. "The Evolution of Cartels in
Mexico, 1980–2015." Mexico Center, James A. Baker III Institute for
Public Policy, Timeline, May 11. Houston: James Baker Institute, Rice
University.

Saxe-Fernández, John. 2014. "Defensa del petróleo, defensa de la tierra." *La
Jornada*, January 23. http://www.jornada.unam.mx/2014/01/23/opinion
/024a1eco.

Schiller, Dane. 2011. "Online Hackers Threaten to Expose Cartel's Se-
crets." *Houston Chronicle*, October 28. http://www.chron.com/news
/houston-texas/article/Online-hackers-threaten-to-expose-cartel-s-secrets
-2242068.php?utm_source=feedburner&utm_medium=feed&utm
_campaign=Feed:+houstonchronicle/topheadlines+%28chron.com+-+Top
+Stories%29.

Schneider, Keith. 2015. *Water Scarcity Could Deter Energy Developers from
Crossing Border into Northern Mexico*. Traverse City, MI: Circle of Blue,
and Wilson Center.

Scobell, Andrew, and Brad Hammitt. 1998. "Goons, Gunmen, and Gendarmerie: Toward a Reconceptualization of Paramilitary Formations." *Journal of Political and Military Sociology* 26, no. 2: 213–227.

SDP Noticias. 2014. "En Michoacán el gobierno enfrenta al monstruo
que creó." *SDP Noticias*, January 15. http://www.vanguardia.com.mx
/enmichoacanelgobiernoenfrentaalmonstruoquecreo-1924496.html.

Seelke, Clare Ribando, and Kristin Finklea. 2015. *U.S.-Mexican Security Cooperation: The Mérida Initiative and Beyond*. Washington, DC: Congressional Research Service.

Sherman, Christopher. 2012. "Crime at the US-Mexico Border Goes Corporate." *Associated Press*, September 29. http://bigstory.ap.org/article
/crime-us-mexico-border-goes-corporate.

Shirk, David, and Alexandra Webber. 2004. "Slavery without Borders: Human Trafficking in the U.S.-Mexican Context." *Hemisphere Focus* 12,
no. 5: 1–5.

Sigler, Édgar. 2012. "Pemex encuentra nuevo yacimiento." *CNN Expansión*,
October 5. http://www.cnnexpansion.com/economia/2012/10/05/aguas
-profundas-proyecto-felipe-calderon.

———. 2013. "Ley energética abre negocio a mineras." *CNN Expansión*, December 18. http://m.cnnexpansion.com/negocios/2013/12/17/mineras -pisan-zonas-de-shale-gas.

———. 2014. "Hierro 'forja' narcoguerra en Michoacán." *CNN Expansión*, January 15. http://www.cnnexpansion.com/economia/2014/01/13/hierro -forja-narcoguerra-en-michoacan.

SinEmbargo (staff). 2014. "De cómo Washington impulsó el fracking por el mundo, y ahora su enviado especial da bendición a reforma de EPN." *SinEmbargo*, September 13. http://www.sinembargo.mx/13-09-2014 /1114121.

Snyder, Jack. 1984. *The Ideology of the Offensive: Military Decision Making and the Disasters of 1914*. Ithaca: Cornell University Press.

Spener, David. 2009. *Clandestine Crossings: Migrants and Coyotes on the Texas-Mexico Border*. Ithaca: Cornell University Press.

Steinberg, Nik. 2011. "The Monster and Monterrey: The Politics and Cartels of Mexico's Drug War." *Nation* 292, no. 24: 27–34.

Stewart, Scott, and Tristan Reed. 2013. "Mexico's Zetas Are Not Finished Yet." *Stratfor*, October 24. http://www.stratfor.com/weekly/mexicos-zetas -are-not-finished-yet#axzz3Nrx0ZGCG.

Stillman, Sarah. 2015. "Where Are the Children?: For Extortionists, Undocumented Migrants Have Become Big Business." *New Yorker*, April 27. http://www.newyorker.com/magazine/2015/04/27/where-are-the-children.

StructurA (staff). 2016. "Jesús Reyes-Heroles G. G." *Nuestra Gente* (EnergeA). http://structura.com.mx/energea/nuestra-gente/jesus-reyes-heroles-g-g.

Tabor, Damon. 2014. "Radio Técnico: How The Zetas Cartel Took Over Mexico with Walkie-Talkies—Inside the Communications Infrastructure of the Ultraviolent Syndicate." *Popular Science*, March 25. http://www .popsci.com/article/technology/radio-tecnico-how-zetas-cartel-took-over -mexico-walkie-talkies?src=SOC&dom=tw.

Taylor, Steve. 2014. "Burgos Shale Consortium to Be Launched Today." *Rio Grande Guardian*, November 7. http://riograndeguardian.com/burgos -shale-consortium-to-be-launched-today.

Ternium. 2014. Mexico: Desarrollo minero, locaciones. October 12. http:// www.ternium.com.mx/desarrollo-minero-locaciones (no longer available).

———. 2016. "Our Company: Who We Are." http://www.ternium.com/en /about-us (no longer available).

Texas Department of Transportation (TxDOT). 2014. "SH 68 Project: Fact Sheet." *TxDOT*, November 1. http://ftp.dot.state.tx.us/pub/txdot-info/phr /projects/sh68/fact-sheet.pdf.

Ulloa, Jazmine. 2013. "Cartels' Influence in Austin Growing in Size, Complexity." *Austin American-Statesman*, April 14. http://www.mystatesman.com /news/news/crime-law/cartels-influence-in-austin-growing-in-size-comple /nXL8k.

——— 2015. "Businessman: Zetas Cartel Told Me to Buy Horses or Face Death." *Austin American-Statesman*, January 30. http://www.mystates man.com/news/news/crime-law/businessman-zetas-cartel-told-me-to-buy -horses-or-/nj2Kd/#1aa31759.3708363.735629.

United Nations Educational, Scientific and Cultural Organization

(UNESCO). 2015. "Displaced Person/Displacement." Social and Human Sciences: International Migration. http://www.unesco.org/new/en/social -and-human-sciences/themes/international-migration/glossary/displaced -person-displacement.

US Army and Marine Corps. 2007. *The U.S. Army/Marine Corps: Counter-insurgency Field Manual.* Chicago: University of Chicago Press.

US Department of Defense. 2010. *Department of Defense Dictionary of Military and Associated Terms* (Joint Publication 1-02). November 8. http://www.dtic.mil/doctrine/new_pubs/jp1_02.pdf.

US Department of State. 2012. *Trafficking in Persons Report 2012.* Washington, DC: US Department of State.

———. 2013. *Trafficking in Persons Report 2013.* Washington, DC: US Department of State.

US Energy Information Administration (EIA). 2014. "Country Reports: Mexico." April 24. http://www.eia.gov/countries/analysisbriefs/Mexico/mexico .pdf (no longer available).

US Northern Command. 2014. "About USNORTHCOM." Northcom.mil, March 1. http://www.northcom.mil/AboutUSNORTHCOM.aspx.

US Senate. Armed Services Committee. 2012. *Statement of General Charles H. Jacoby, Jr.,* United States Army Commander, United States Northern Command and North American Aerospace Defense Command before the Senate Armed Services Committee, March 13. Washington, DC: US Government Printing Office.

———. Committee on Foreign Relations. 2012. *Oil, Mexico, and the Transboundary Agreement.* A Minority Staff Report Prepared for the Use of the Committee on Foreign Relations, United States Senate, 112th Congress, 2nd Session, December 21. Washington, DC: US Government Printing Office.

Valdés, Guillermo. 2013. *Historia del narcotráfico en México.* Mexico City: Aguilar.

Van Creveld, Martin. 1991. *The Transformation of War: The Most Radical Reinterpretation of Armed Conflict since Clausewitz.* New York: Free Press.

Vanguardia. 2012. "Los Zetas es el Cártel con Mayor Presencia." , February 1. http://www.diariopresente.com.mx/section/nacional/50926/zetas -cartel-mayor-presencia/.

Vargas, Esther. 2012. "La historia incompleta de la periodista mexicana asesinada por informar en las redes sociales." *Clasesdeperiodismo.com,* February 8. http://www.clasesdeperiodismo.com/2012/02/08/la-historia -incompleta-de-la-periodista-mexicana-asesinada-por-informar-en-las -redes-sociales.

Vargas, Gustavo Adolfo. 2014. "Estados Unidos y su frenética carrera energética." *La Jornada,* January 28. http://www.lajornadanet.com/diario /opinion/2014/enero/28.php#.UugvqZPXxWI.twitter.

Villalobos, Joaquín. 2011. "De los Zetas al cártel de La Habana." *Foreign Affairs Latinoamérica* 11, no. 2: 10–21.

Vulliamy, Ed. 2014. "HSBC Has Form: Remember Mexico and Laundered

Drug Money." *Guardian*, February 15. http://www.theguardian.com/com
mentisfree/2015/feb/15/hsbc-has-form-mexico-laundered-drug-money.

Wainwright, Tom. 2016. *Narconomics: How to Run a Drug Cartel*. New York: Public Affairs.

Wallace, Robert B. 2014. "Lithium, A Strategic Element for Energy in the World Market." Working Paper. Mexico City: Post-graduate Department of Economics, National Autonomous University of Mexico (UNAM).

Ward, Sandra. 2014. "Schlumberger's North American Push." *Wall Street Journal*, August 23. http://online.wsj.com/news/article_email/schlumberger
-shares-set-for-a-boost-from-north-america-1408839395-lMyQjAxMTA0
MDIwOTEyNDkyWj.

Weber, Max. 1919. *Politics as a Vocation*. http://anthropos-lab.net/wp/wp
-content/uploads/2011/12/Weber-Politics-as-a-Vocation.pdf.

West, Bing. 1972. *The Village*. New York: Pocket Books.

Wilkinson, Tracy. 2011. "Shadowy Group Says It Targets Cartel; Some in Veracruz Are Glad." *LA Times*, October 19. http://articles.latimes.com
/2011/oct/19/world/la-fg-mexico-veracruz-killings-20111020.

Wilson, Christopher, and Eugenio Weigend. 2014. "Plan Tamaulipas: A New Security Strategy for a Troubled State." *Mexico Institute*, Working Paper, October. Washington, DC: Wilson Center.

Wood, Duncan, Thomas Tunstall, Javier Oyakawa, Alejandra Bueno, Pilar Rodríguez, Joana Chapa, Manuel Acuña, and Oscar Lugo. 2015. *Economic Impact and Legal Analysis of the Shale Oil and Gas Activities in Mexico*. Washington, DC: University of Texas at San Antonio (UTSA), Association of Mexican Entrepreneurs (AEM), Autonomous University of Nuevo León (UANL), and Wilson Center.

Young, Angelo. 2013. "And the Winner for the Most Iraq War Contracts Is . . . KBR, with $39.5 Billion in a Decade." *International Business Times*, March 19. http://www.ibtimes.com/winner-most-iraq-war-contracts-kbr
-395-billion-decade-1135905.

Young, Shannon. 2013. "US-Supported Surveillance and Mexico's Energy Sector." *South Notes* (blog), July 10. http://southnotes.org/2013/07/10/us
-supported-surveillance-and-mexicos-energy-sector.

———. 2014. "American Media Misses the Story on Mexican Oil Reform." *Texas Observer*, February 10. http://www.texasobserver.org/american
-media-misses-story-mexican-oil-reform.

Zhu, Wenqian. 2013. "El petróleo de EU contiene a la OPEP." *CNN Expansión*, June 19. http://www.cnnexpansion.com/economia/2013/06/19
/petroleo-de-eu-tiene-a-raya-a-la-opep.

Zócalo Saltillo (staff). 2013. "Logra AHMSA récord en producción y Embarque." *Zócalo Saltillo*, November 12. http://www.zocalo.com.mx/seccion
/articulo/logra-ahmsa-record-en-produccion-y-embarque-1384237167.

Index

Page numbers followed by *f* indicate figures; those followed by *m* indicate maps; those followed by *t* indicate tables.

Calderón, Felipe (*continued*)
violence, 173; and military operations, 1; on oil discoveries in
the Gulf of Mexico, 181; and organized crime, 293n2; and security strategy, 104–105, 302n6;
and transnational interests, 253;
and US arms manufacturers,
228; and US energy policy, 306–
307n7; and war on drugs, 98,
128, 214, 215; and Zeta members
arrested, 298n11
Cali Cartel, 19–20, 267
California, 28, 42, 310n17
Camacho Cepeda, Virgilio, 178
Camargo, Tamaulipas, 26, 39, 198,
199, 270, 274
Camorra, 138
Campeche: and criminal paramilitary groups, 218; and disappearances, 224–225t; and expropriation, 223; and oil discoveries,
181; Zetas' control of, 49; Zetas'
expansion to, 41, 260
Campeche Basin, 160m
Campeche Sound, 218
Campos, Obed, 115
Canada, 233, 251, 302–303n16,
307n18, 308n13
Canales, Rodrigo, 67, 71
capitalism, 141, 213, 226, 230,
294n6
car bombs: and cartel wars, 38; and
social media, 32; in Tamaulipas,
189, 271, 276, 277; as terror tactic, 1, 37, 98; and Zetas' War, 42
Cárdenas, Antonio Ezequiel (aka
Tony Tormenta), 272, 278
Cárdenas, Enrique, 19
Cárdenas, Homero, 279
Cárdenas, Mario, 272, 278
Cárdenas, Osiel: arrest of, 27, 261,
269; extradition of, 32, 33; and
family connections, 62, 272, 278,
279; and Federal Judicial Police,
295–296n8; and Arturo Guzmán
Decena, 267; and Nuevo Laredo,

23, 24; and political connec-
tions, 25; and running the Com-
pany from prison, 28; sentence of,
270; as Zetas' founder, 50; as Ze-
tas' leader, 295n7; and Zetas' op-
erations, 268; and Zetas' origins,
21–22, 260; and Zetas' recruitment, 296n13
Cárdenas Batel, Lázaro, 98
Cárdenas-Vela, Rafael, 62
Caribbean, 19, 41, 302–303n16
Carrillo Fuentes organization, 71,
297n22
Carrizalillo, Guerrero, 184–185
Cartel del Golfo (CDG). *See* Gulf
Cartel
cartel formation, 9
Cartel of the Amezcua-Contreras
Family, 27, 260
Cartel of the Valencia Brothers: and
Juan José Farías, 122; and La
Empresa, 47; and La Familia Mi-
choacana, 261; and La Federa-
ción, 27, 260; and Tijuana Cartel,
46. *See also* Milenio Cartel
cartel wars, 10, 28, 159, 216, 221.
See also arms race
Casillas Escobar, Juan César, 26
Casino Royale, 43, 262
Castillo, Alfredo, 119, 122
Castillo, Blas, 278
Cavazos Lerma, Manuel, 25, 275
CDG (Cartel del Golfo). *See* Gulf
Cartel
cells: and Gulf Cartel internal con-
flict, 278; and kingpin arrest
strategy, 49–50; and Matamoros
explosions, 277; and Mata-Zetas,
43; and Sinaloa Cartel, 29; and
Zetas' criminal model, 66, 242;
and Zetas' growth, 41–42; and
Zetas' organization, 53, 56, 57,
60–61, 63–64
censorship, 147–148, 208
Center for Research and Advanced
Studies in Social Anthropology
(CIESAS), 75

kidnapping (*continued*)
    on drugs, 134; and Zetas' criminal model, 240; and Zetas' marketing, 68; and Zetas' rebranding, 250; and Zetas' subsidiaries, 56; as Zetas' subsidiary, 79; and Zetas' War, 271

killing industry (*sicariato*), 36–37, 64, 71, 76, 242, 300n17

Kinder Morgan Energy Partners, 306–307n7

kingpin strategy: and Calderón's war on drugs, 105; and DEA, 295n17; and fragmentation of criminal groups, 112; limitations of, 302n9; and Mexican government, 10; and roots of modern civil war, 127–128; and Zetas, 239–240

Kuwait, 312n30, 312–313n10

La Barbie. *See* Valdez Villarreal, Édgar (aka La Barbie)

La Compañía (the Company): and Carrillo Fuentes family, 297n22; collaborators with, 25–26, 297n21; and corruption, 247; and defeat of La Federación in Nuevo Laredo, 27; dissolution of, 33, 35; and divisions in La Federación, 32; and federal authorities, 300n25; as merger of Gulf Cartel and Zetas, 250; and Michoacán expansion, 46–47; and Michoacán violence, 48; and neoliberal reforms, 24; and Project Reckoning, 299n15; and stolen natural gas condensate, 244; and strategic alliances, 251; and Zetas' 2013 money-laundering case, 76

La Empresa (the Enterprise), 47, 298n6

La Familia Michoacana (the Michoacán Family): and ArcelorMittal, 178; and Coahuila Zetas' War, 44; and control of natural resources, 155;

and corruption, 247; as criminal paramilitary, 113; disappearance of, 265, 280; and diversification, 77; and iron ore, 172–173; and Knights Templar, 262; and La Federación, 29; and methamphetamine trade, 171; and Michoacán self-defense paramilitaries, 123; origins of, 37, 261; as TCO enforcer wing, 37; and terror tactics, 31; and transnational interests, 212; and Zetas' criminal model, 2, 46–48, 59, 117

La Fé del Golfo, Tamaulipas, 189

La Federación: and cartel wars, 28–29, 297n21; divisions within, 32–33; formation of, 26–27; and media war, 68; and narco-videos, 30–31; origins of, 268; as reaction to Zetas, 260; and strategic alliances, 251. *See also specific member cartels*

La guerra de los Zetas (Osorno 2012), 4

Laguna Madre, Tamaulipas, 187

La Huacana, Michoacán, 118–119

La Jornada newspaper, 30

La Libertad, Guatemala, 45

La Línea, 37, 221

land disputes, 18

landowners: and elite-financed paramilitaries, 110; and forced displacements by TCOs, 206–207; and hydrocarbon theft, 199; and Mexico's modern civil war, 213; and paramilitaries in Colombia, 140; and self-defense paramilitaries, 117–118; and Ternium, 177; and violence in resource-rich areas, 168–169, 171, 172, 185

land ownership, 207, 208m, 220, 222–223, 309n18, 309–310n9. See also *ejido* lands

land redistribution groups, 111

La Nueva Federación (the New Federation), 38–39

La Palma prison, 28

vestment, 230; government's fight against, 293n4; homicides related to, 100t; and hydrocarbon theft, 199–201, 217–219; and iron ore, 172–173; and lack of effect on ArcelorMittal, 178; and Los Zetas, 3; and Mexican government, 88; and Mexico's modern civil war, 137, 138; and Michoacán violence, 174; as military power, 89; and modern civil war, 126–127, 128–129; and natural gas condensate trafficking, 309n5; and natural resources trade with transnational companies, 184; and paramilitarization, 91–92, 121; and pattern of violence in extraction zones, 166; and Pemex's pipeline system, 243–244; and political control, 94; and retribution against anti-TCO reports, 294n12; and self-defense paramilitaries, 117, 124–125; in Tamaulipas, 193; and Tamaulipas government, 20; and Tamaulipas militarization, 208; and Tamaulipas oil resources, 196–197; and Ternium's operations, 177; and transnational interests, 226, 230; and US arms manufacturers, 228; and Valor por Tamaulipas, 147, 150–151; and war on drugs, 215; Zetas' transformation of, 66
Osborne, James, 236
Oseguera, Arquímides, 247
Osorio Chong, Miguel Ángel, 119, 191
Osorno, Diego, 4, 53, 54, 59, 141–142, 168

Padilla, Tamaulipas, 207
Paley, Dawn: on broken civil society, 193; on Colombia as pattern for war, 165; on Colombia's paramilitarization, 111–112; on conflict-driven economic opportunities, 131, 157–158; *Drug War*

Capitalism (2014), 294n6; on forced displacements, 206–207, 220; on media's role in Mexico's modern civil war, 152; on Mexico's modern civil war, 137, 138–139, 141, 213; on mining and capitalist expansion, 183; on reforms benefitting private investment, 229–230; on San Fernando Massacre, 94–95; on transnational corporate sector, 229–230, 252; on wars against people, 216
Palomo Rincones, Román Ricardo (aka El Coyote), 50
PAN (National Action Party), 88, 97–98, 253, 260, 271
Paperstorm (leaflet campaign), 149
Parachute Rifle Brigade (BFP), 296n9
Parácuaro, Michoacán, 119
paramilitaries: in Colombia, 110; and Colombian conflict, 140; and looting, 133–134; in Mexico versus Colombia, 111; and the state, 293–294n5; and violence in hydrocarbon-rich areas, 169; and violence in resource-rich areas, 183. *See also* criminal paramilitaries; elite-financed paramilitaries; self-defense paramilitaries
paramilitarism: and capitalism, 213; in Colombia, 111–112; of criminals and governments, 11–12; and cyberspace, 148–150; and elite funding, 115; and government-paramilitary ties, 121–122; as government response to TCO violence, 108–109; and land depreciation, 231; and Mérida Initiative, 230; and Mexican government security strategy, 113; in Mexican history, 108; and Mexican security strategy, 106; and Michoacán violence, 174; and modern civil war, 126–127; as reaction to Zetas, 85; and state sponsorship,

vigilante gangs, 113
vigilante groups, 92, 113, 115,
118–123. *See also* self-defense
paramilitaries
Villalobos, Joaquín, 62, 127, 128–
129, 131
Villanueva, Mónica, 142–143
Villarreal, Miguel (aka El Gringo),
279
violence: and ArcelorMittal, 178;
and beneficiaries of new civil war,
227; and Calderón's administration, 101; and Calderón's war on
drugs, 105; and civil war characteristics, 132, 132t; in Coahuila,
167m, 171; and criminal insurgency, 139; and energy industry, 168–169; and expropriation,
223; and extortion of local businesses, 80; and fear generation as
a goal, 61; and hydrocarbon-rich
areas, 155, 165; and hydrocarbon
theft, 218; in Juárez Valley, 221;
and land depreciation, 271; and
Los Filos gold mine, 185; as marketing tactic, 67–68; and Mexican government reforms, 89; and
Mexico's modern civil war, 138;
in Michoacán, 174, 175–176m;
and militarization of Mexican security strategy, 87; and modern
civil war, 139–141; monopoly on,
96–99; and plaza control, 53; and
resource exploitation during civil
war, 158–159; and resource extraction, 239; as sensationalized
by writers, 59; and silence zones,
165; as social control, 93; and social media reporting, 144; as state
right, 95–96; and symmetric nonconventional warfare, 135; in
Tamaulipas, 194, 208–210; and
third-generation gangs, 298n9;
and transnational interests, 212,
222, 226, 256; and war on drugs,
215, 283–288; and Zetas' criminal model, 54–55; and Zetas' de-

cline, 50–51; and Zetas' diversification, 79; and Zetas–Gulf
Cartel conflict, 187–191; and Zetas in Coahuila, 166; in Zetas'
model, 91

Waha-Presidio pipeline, 221
Waha–San Elizario pipeline, 221
war on drugs: beneficiaries of, 211–
212, 215–216, 284; and civilian
casualties, 141–142; and counterinsurgency, 138; as counter-
revolution, 213; as cover for repression, 214; and cyberspace,
143–153; and disappearances,
223; and dual function of paramilitary violence, 140; and esca-
lating violence, 38; as excuse for
militarization, 213–214; failure
of, 110; and increased violence,
98, 101, 103–104; and looting, 133–134; and Mexican government, 2–3; and modern civil
war, 126–127, 128; and money
laundering, 310n19; and paramilitarization, 113; and TCO diversification, 99; and unconventional security strategies, 111;
and US profits, 227–228; victims
of, 216–217
water, 167–168, 168m, 182–183,
206, 213, 216–217
Weatherford International Ltd., 190,
198, 254, 313n15
Weber, Max, 95
West Africa, 301n30
West Rail Bypass Bridge, 202, 204
West Rock Energy, 76
WhatsApp, 144
wikis, 7
Wilkinson, Tracy, 113–115
Wilson Center, 194, 204
wind energy, 168m, 169

Xe Services, 245, 255. *See also*
Blackwater
Xtreme Energy Group, 76